What Should Philosophy Do?

What Should Philosophy Do?
— *A Theory* —

Steven Yates

WIPF & STOCK · Eugene, Oregon

WHAT SHOULD PHILOSOPHY DO?
A Theory

Copyright © 2021 Steven Yates. All rights reserved. Except for brief quotations in critical publications or reviews, no part of this book may be reproduced in any manner without prior written permission from the publisher. Write: Permissions, Wipf and Stock Publishers, 199 W. 8th Ave., Suite 3, Eugene, OR 97401.

Wipf & Stock
An Imprint of Wipf and Stock Publishers
199 W. 8th Ave., Suite 3
Eugene, OR 97401

www.wipfandstock.com

PAPERBACK ISBN: 978-1-7252-6375-8
HARDCOVER ISBN: 978-1-7252-6367-3
EBOOK ISBN: 978-1-7252-6370-3

07/09/21

To the memory of my mother, Alice Mae Belles Yates
(November 14, 1923—April 14, 2011).

[W]hat is the use of studying philosophy if all that it does for you is to enable you to talk with some plausibility about some abstruse questions of logic, etc., & if it does not improve your thinking about the important questions of everyday life, if it does not make you more conscientious than any . . . journalist in the use of the DANGEROUS phrases such people use for their own ends. You see, I know that it's difficult to think well about "certainty," "probability," "perception," etc. But it is, if possible, still more difficult to think, or try to think, really honestly about your life & other peoples' lives. And the trouble is that thinking about these things is not thrilling, but often downright nasty. And when it's nasty then it's most important.

—Ludwig Wittgenstein

Contents

Preface | ix
Acknowledgments | xv

Introduction | 1

Chapter 1: What Is This Thing Called Philosophy? | 43

Chapter 2: Causes and Consequences of the "Retreat" of Philosophy | 80

Chapter 3: Worldviews and Philosophy | 124

Chapter 4: Worldview Evaluation and Philosophy I: Materialism and Secular Moralism | 173

Chapter 5: Worldview Evaluation and Philosophy II: Materialism and Science 209

Chapter 6: Philosophy's Present and Civilization's Future: Two Proposals | 253

Conclusion | 289

Bibliography 295

Preface

The first premise of this work is that professionalized, academic philosophy fell on hard times quite some time ago.

Those inside that profession will beg to differ, of course. They will point out what, to them, is obvious: that there has never been a time with more philosophical activity occurring than there is now. There are more books published, more professional journals; there are blogs and discussion forums, and generally more venues for philosophical discussion online and offline than ever before. Even during economic tough times, philosophy departments flourish and continue to draw in undergraduate majors and graduate students who pursue and obtain doctorates.

What they will also note, perhaps begrudgingly, is that quantity is not quality, and that much of what we see has little effect on the world outside any number of intellectual echo chambers. They might note, also begrudgingly, how many new PhDs find themselves adjunct-zoned, as opposed to obtaining gainful academic employment that pays livable wages. Many such people commute between two or even three campuses and have neither time nor the resources to pursue scholarly endeavors.

Things look different out here, outside The Profession. The author is an outsider, mostly (not entirely) by choice, and will discuss that in due course. Of more interest is that scientists and science presenters of repute such as Stephen Hawking and Neil deGrasse Tyson have declared philosophy dead. To them, science answers the questions philosophers struggled with and failed to answer. Perhaps they are just uninformed about professional philosophy, yes? But people listen to them.

The irony here is that we both can, and will, point to individual philosophers and philosophies of the fairly recent past that have exercised great influence over twentieth- and twenty-first-century politics, economy, and culture—quite apart from science. Very often this influence has *not* been beneficial. But if the belief that philosophy is dead should prevail, this influence will not be seen for what it is and evaluated for what it has done.

Negatives about philosophy are not new, of course. They go back well over 150 years. *Academic* philosophy, moreover, was declared "dead" more than once in jeremiads going back at least to the 1950s, a time during which the subject was arguably flourishing far better in terms of quality, and in a far healthier environment, than exists in academia at present. Many of American philosophy's most significant twentieth-century voices rose to prominence during that period.

There are indeed reasons aplenty for shunning not just philosophy but liberal arts generally in the present environment. First, as already implied, the job market for graduates with advanced degrees in the subject is horrid and likely to get worse. But more importantly, over the past thirty years, philosophy and other liberal arts subjects have been increasingly politicized, hijacked to further the agendas of specific groups, developing finally into what has become known as the culture of "wokeness" or "cancel culture" (identity politics on steroids, one might call it). For these folks, it will be a sufficient argument against nearly all the "Western intellectual tradition" that it is too white, too male, and too straight. I don't think they claim it is "too Christian," at least not with a straight face, but they might claim it serves up too much "objective truth" through its connections with logicality and the alliance of its mainstream with modern science.

Very few philosophers have attempted detailed responds to such allegations. The reasons why should be self-evident. Today, going up against the forces of identity politics can be career-ending and ultimately futile.

So despite the activity, philosophy as an academic discipline is in trouble—trouble made still worse over the past year, with a global pandemic that has shuttered a lot of universities and driven courses into the digital realm, further hobbling departments already in danger of being closed down (though there were instances of philosophy departments being terminated, victims of budget cuts, well before Captain COVID came to call).

This inquiry asks: can the subject be resuscitated, perhaps on new terms?

After all, philosophy has reimagined and repurposed itself several times during its two-and-a-half-millennia-plus historical journey. The idea that the time is ripe for its doing so again therefore surely merits a listen.

Thus in this book, I argue that, *Yes*, philosophy both can and should repurpose itself. Repeated like refrains through the pages to follow will be the following: philosophy is not an idle pastime to be conducted exclusively in academic cubicles, or by hobbyists. *It has a job to do in civilization.*

That job, I will argue, is to identify, clarify as much as possible, and critically evaluate *worldviews*—as they emerge and function (or fail to function) in civilization, how they condition public conversations about ethical issues and morality generally, and how they formulate and solve the problems they set for themselves. Worldviews can be found wanting, and philosophy, more than any other discipline, can recommend they be scrapped and replaced by more promising ones. Some of the latter may come from the past, perhaps reimagined for the present, or they may be something new, in need only of sufficient cultural breathing space.

We will develop in detail (Chapter 3) what a worldview is, to the extent the concept can be made precise: how its parts fit together, and what functions it serves. This will come on the heels of extensive discussion (Chapters 1 and 2) of how philosophy has conceived of itself in the past, and how it got into its present predicament—how it came to its present status as little more than an academic decoration, despite the civilization-shaping influence of a *handful* of its practitioners during the past century.

Academic philosophers will resent my description of their discipline as a *decoration* I get it. Understandably they see it as "essential" to the life of the mind, although the institutions in which they house themselves (with rare exceptions) mostly forgot about the *life of the mind* long ago. Answering how this happened will take us into a discussion of the Stages of civilization (Chapter 2), calling upon sociology's founder Auguste Comte whose Law of Three Stages provides an excellent if incomplete framework for approaching the problem. If we take Comte's framework seriously and can extend it, then given the multiple crises we face and our preference for avoidance, we can ask what Stage Western civilization is in now? What are its, i.e., *our* prospects for moving forward into a livable (or survivable) future?

This work, when all is said and done, will set about to accomplish three goals. There is the one above, and there are two others. We will want to provide a concrete example of what a systematic and detailed evaluation of a worldview looks like. The worldview I've chosen to evaluate in this work is what I hold is the prevailing one in Western intellectual, governmental, and commercial centers: *materialism*, whether *recognized* as such and *called* that or not. Materialism manifests itself in multiple ways, from its views on the cultural and possibly evolutionary basis of morality, of the origin of life and the nature of consciousness, to whether *persons* are more than cogs in the gig economy's neoliberal machinery (or bits of flesh to be thrown away under the abortionist's instruments if inconvenient).

Our evaluation will be negative, and we will recommend that loyalty to what we will come to call the Grandiose Assumption (that modern science leads to materialism and that materialism necessarily underwrites modern science) be abandoned. We can't compel this, of course, and we shall not try. What we will see is how important thinkers, having failed to show how materialism can answer philosophical quandaries about morality on the one hand, and consciousness and origins on the other, stop short of realizing that their first premise about what kind of world this is, not their evidence, analytic tools, or other factors, is at fault. Far from bringing about a world based on morality and freedom, it is now threatening a dystopian future in which we are thrust into the hands of a very few, a tiny, technocratic elite, who, without knowing it, are honoring Dostoevsky's adage that "if God is dead, then everything is permitted."

We will argue, following these realizations, that in order to complete the reimagining and repurposing of philosophy, philosophers need to think *very hard* about their allegiances, including how and where they are going to deliver their product. And what worldview they should embrace. Should it be an updated Christian ethos, or something more global or universal, encompassing religious sensibilities generally and leaving the specifics to particular cultures? Should it encompass the idea that not just persons but the *planet itself*—all life and all of Creation (if I may use that term with the capital letter)— have intrinsic value? Shouldn't a form of pluralism follow from this embrace, as we respect the rights of those in communities to organize in ways that meet their needs, satisfy their values, and bring stability and happiness into their lives however different they may be from our own? What light might such a perspective shed on, say, what we do about climate change—the effects of which all of us can see if we trouble to open our eyes?

Philosophers need to consider becoming *thought leaders*, that is, for what will amount to the next Stage of civilization, one Comte, with his nineteenth-century categories, could not have begun to imagine, and which has only become possible for us to imagine over the past few decades. To the extent, that is, that the Third Stage of civilization equated to modernity, and the Fourth Stage to postmodernity, we need to begin thinking about civilization's Fifth Stage.

Present-day academic institutions will not be sympathetic to this sort of thing. This work is an attempt to *disrupt the status quo*, and holds that this is *a good thing*, that *disruption is what is needed right now*, and *should not be shunned* by those who wish to become the philosophers of the future—if Western civilization, or the human race generally, is to have a future.

For what seemed alarmist and perhaps even hysterical until relatively recently is now obvious. We are at a precipice. What we as a civilization do in just the next few years may determine not just the fate of the West but the fate of the human species itself. Whatever frenetic philosophical activity is to be found in the departments, the journals, online discussion forums, etc., the echo-chamber effect has left us with a culture and civilization trying to function almost *without a philosophy—without consciousness of its own philosophical premises*. This is comparable, I will argue, to a blindfolded man trying to find his way across a busy street or highway with fast-moving traffic without any guidance whatsoever. His making it is not impossible, but not likely. The sensible thing to do would be to remove the blindfold and look around!

The same is true for Western civilization, broadly conceived. It is time to diagnose the problems of philosophy—structural and institutional as well as intellectual—and constructively suggest a new option. This will mean getting rid of the idea that philosophy owes special fealty to any present-day scientific consensus relevant to the Grandiose Assumption, and that it either is, or ought to be, under present circumstances, an exclusively academic endeavor.

Let us begin.

Acknowledgments

This book was written in a foreign country in near-isolation, away from the influence of other scholars. So there is no one I can thank for their advice or encouragement along the way. This book is the product of my own self-motivation from start to finish. Nor can I thank the Foundation of this-or-that for financial support. It is obvious, therefore, that whatever omissions or errors it contains are my own, and not of any former teachers, mentors, past colleagues, or organizations.

But since *nothing* is written in *total* isolation, I *would* like to acknowledge four people without whom I would probably never have written this, especially given my present circumstances (a "solopreneur" who *could* be using the time to *market his monetizable services*).

The first is my mother (see dedication) who gave me my first book on science at age five (it was a book about the planets), and who consistently encouraged me to read and learn. Just eighteen months or so later came the assassination of President John F. Kennedy. She was the first person I knew of to express skepticism towards the official account of what happened that day, and which was made concrete in the Warren Commission Report. She wasn't just being recalcitrant. As one who closely followed current events with a critical eye, she knew there were solid reasons for doubting Oswald was the shooter. My long-term takeaway was the realization that while we ought to listen to official voices (not that we usually have a choice), we shouldn't necessarily take their conclusions as gospel, nor as having the final word on a subject. As I was growing up, my father was known to say from time to time that "an *expert* is a man with a briefcase five miles from home." While obviously there are many areas where we would be remiss if we did not defer to demonstrated expertise, there are others where if we are honest about it, we have no idea who "the experts" even are or what qualifies them besides a combination of immense hubris and institutional power to control the narrative.

The second and third are more visible, even if in these cases I('ve) neither met nor interacted with either.

Paul Feyerabend's controversial *Against Method: Outline of an Anarchistic Theory of Knowledge* (1975) came to my attention when I was an undergraduate, an ex-science major who realized he was more interested in the metaphysical and conceptual underpinnings of science than in any particular science. Feyerabend's free-spirited questioning of assumptions others took for granted set me ablaze, and I had no trouble becoming convinced that his was one of the most significant contributions to the critical debate over the status of scientific knowledge and methodology, and of scientific institutions and intellectual centers, in the last century—conceivably greater than even Kuhn's, though Kuhn's modesty ensured that *Structure* would remain better known and more accepted. Although my MA thesis tried to *answer* Feyerabend based on what *formal* models of rationality and method can be said to have survived his critique, part of me, even then, was alert to the possibility that a larger sense of rationality, despite his "farewell to Reason" (1986), made Feyerabend's the most rational as well as compelling approach to knowledge and method that twentieth-century philosophy produced.

The next influence came from a different place in my life altogether. During my student days as a maniac collector of vinyl records (my primary hobby during those years) I'd encountered the work of British experimental musician, composer, visual artist, and producer Brian Eno. There is far more to him than music, however. During interviews, he sometimes laid out patterns of thought that *also* set me ablaze and prompted long walks afterwards. As a teenager Eno had been asked by someone he respected why someone as bright as he obviously was wanted to "waste his time" at an art school. He later said, this event "set a question going in my mind that has always stayed with me and motivated a lot of what I've done: what does art do for people, why do people do it, why don't we only do rational things, like design better engines? And because it came from someone I very much respected, that was the foundation of my intellectual life."[1]

Art for art's sake? Nonsense! Art has a job to do in society!

What struck me was that *this same line of questioning could be asked about philosophy*. Why are some of us drawn to philosophy? What does it do for us and why do we pursue it, instead of just doing "practical" and eye-to-business things? Why, moreover, when societies reach a certain level of development such as that of the ancient Greeks at the time of Thales of Miletus, did philosophers seem to appear? Since *qua* philosopher these folks are

---

1. Recorded in David Sheppard's remarkable biography *On Some Faraway Beach*, 45.

not scientists, *nor* political figures, *nor* businessmen, *nor* inventors (though they might contribute in all these areas, as Thales seems to have done), what does philosophy *qua* philosophy actually do, i.e., what does it accomplish in civilization, and for us in our lives?

Philosophers have answered this question in *numerous* ways, of course. It has done *many* things in modern civilization, as we shall see, not all of them *good*. Presently it is in trouble. I explain why in this book, and why it therefore behooves us to ask and answer the question, *What Should Philosophy Do?* This book tries to provide as good an answer as its author is able, ever mindful of our present path into an uncertain and possibly turbulent future.

The final acknowledgment is to a fellow whose first name is Richard and who made the remark that actually prompted me to stop *thinking* about a work like this and get busy *writing* it. I will leave his last name off, as I've no wish to "shame" him publicly. What he said to my face, back in 2013 (I think it was), was that he thought philosophy was a waste of time, that it did *nothing* of importance in society compared to science or engineering (he was a professor of mechanical engineering).

Not exactly the way to win friends and influence people. I was irate and defensive at first, but then I realized that Richard's comment was the kick in the *derrière* I needed to begin the work of setting out the answers I had been thinking about what philosophy did, or should do, in civilization. You hold the result in your hands.

Introduction

Scientists Reject Philosophy.

Is Western philosophy dead?

The late Stephen Hawking, the most renowned physicist and cosmologist of our time, said as much.

This is what he asserted at the beginning of his *The Grand Design* (2010):

> [H]umans are a curious species. We wonder, we seek answers. Living in this world that is by turns kind and cruel, and gazing at the immense heavens above, people have always asked a multitude of questions: How can we understand the world in which we find ourselves? How does the universe behave? What is the nature of reality? Where did all this come from? Did the universe need a creator? Most of us do not spend most of our time worrying about these questions, but almost all of us worry about them some of the time.
>
> Traditionally these are questions for philosophy, but philosophy is dead. Philosophy has not kept up with modern developments in science, particularly physics. Scientists have become the bearers of the torch of discovery in our quest for knowledge.[1]

The problem as he sees it seems clear. Knowledge in physics has grown by leaps and bounds. Philosophy has been unable to keep up.

Physics, as Hawking saw it, has wrestled *fruitfully* with questions philosophers once *thought* they could answer: questions about the origin of the universe, the nature of reality, and whether or not the world had a Creator.

Note the emphasis on *fruitfully*. Physics has been *fruitful*: productive of a steady stream of gamechanging ideas and new knowledge. Philosophy

---

1. Hawking, *Grand Design*, 5.

has not. Physics, especially physical cosmology, so Hawking's argument goes, has gotten us somewhere. Philosophy hasn't.

Hawking took some heat from professional philosophers. They charged that his contributions to physics, important as they are, don't confer expertise on philosophy. He stood accused of not understanding what philosophers do these days.

For example, Tim Crane at the University of Cambridge contended that Hawking's contention was itself philosophical, but "bad philosophy, because he is unaware of it as a discipline and a practice with a history." Greg Radick, of the University of Leeds, observed that major scientific voices of the modern and recent past—he cited Charles Darwin, Albert Einstein, and Noam Chomsky—were/are philosophically literate. They took the subject seriously. Rebecca Goldstein Newberger of Harvard and New College of the Humanities, stated that "if you're pro-reason . . . you need all the resources you can get." She called Hawking's remark "ill-informed, incoherent, and irresponsible—faced with today's extremes of irrationality."[2]

These responses, which were typical, seem to me rather weak and defensive. What makes them more than a kind of intellectual territorialism, a defense of something that really is obsolete? Hawking's views may offend many philosophers' sensibilities, but this does not mean he is wrong.

After all, for centuries now physical scientists *seem* to have gotten better and better at proposing and gradually improving their answers to questions about which philosophers have never agreed: of what is this world made up? How and why do physical laws work the way they do? How do the apparent components of physical reality relate to one another, and to our senses and scientific instruments? What are the best methods for finding these things out?

Some of our most interesting answers occur in a background filled with questions like, *Are there any reasons for thinking the universe had a Creator?* Hawking took this question seriously and engaged it. He ultimately decided in the negative. So the worst we can clearly accuse him of is inconsistency: denying the usefulness of philosophy while drawing a philosophical conclusion from his science. The point, though: a scientist used his science to reach the conclusion. A philosopher did not.

We are a part of nature, scientists say. So consider this query: is it possible to explain everything we observe around us—not just physical objects and the atomic particles making them up, but ourselves, our mores, cultures,

---

2. Reitz, "Is Philosophy Dead?," para. 6. These examples may be taken as representative.

our civilizations—exclusively in terms of this material world, in terms of what we can see, hear, and touch, using our brains, senses, and instruments?

In other words, without departing from materialism as a metaphysics, or from a naturalist methodology (we will call it)?

Philosophers appear to have been "scooped" on this as well. At first blush, scientists seem to have gotten lightyears ahead of us. Perchance because science has made genuine progress while philosophy has not?

Stephen Hawking is not alone in his negative assessment of the value of philosophy. Others in science share his views. One example should do, as he is fairly representative. Neil deGrasse Tyson, well-known science communicator and director of the Hayden Planetarium in New York City, opined during the question-and-answer session of a public talk with Richard Dawkins that while philosophy once had something to contribute to our understanding of physical reality, today it does not. Again, science has the best answers to such questions. At best, he adds, philosophy can wrestle with ethical conundrums.

His statement, unedited:

> Up until early 20th century philosophers had material contributions to make to the physical sciences. Pretty much after quantum mechanics, remember, the philosopher is the would-be scientist but without a laboratory, right? And so what happens is, the 1920s come in, we learn about the expanding universe in the same decade as we learn about quantum physics, each of which falls so far out of what you can deduce from your armchair, that the whole community of philosophers that previously had added materially to the thinking of the physical scientists was rendered essentially obsolete, at that point, and I have yet to see a contribution—this will get me in trouble with all manner of philosophers—but call me later and correct me if you think I've missed somebody here. But philosophy has basically parted ways from the frontier of the physical sciences, when there was a day when they were one and the same. Isaac Newton was a natural philosopher, the word *physicist* didn't even exist in any important way back then. So, I'm disappointed because there is a lot of brainpower there, that might have otherwise contributed mightily, but today simply does not. It's not that there can't be other philosophical subjects, there is religious philosophy, and ethical philosophy, and political philosophy, plenty of stuff for the philosopher to do, but the frontier of the physical sciences does not appear to be among them.[3]

---

3. "Poetry of Science," 1:03:12—04:46.

DeGrasse Tyson may seem more a media celebrity than a practicing scientist, but as with Hawking, people listen to him. As a trained astronomer his voice carries some weight. DeGrasse Tyson leaves subject matter for philosophers. They can sound off about ethics if they want. Or politics. Or religion.

All realms of mere *opinion*, presumably. Or perhaps *feelings*.

But they neither can nor should offer claims of *knowledge*, claims of factual *truth*. This would place them in competition with science, and that can no longer be allowed.

Many scientists probably take the obviousness of this for granted.

There are, of course, many philosophical topics that are only marginally if at all connected with science. The old chestnuts quickly appear if we allow them.

Theoretical physics cannot tell me how to live a good life, for example, or what the good society is like, and whether I am obligated to help my fellow man, or how.

Can science provide a basis for praising me if I treat my wife with respect or condemning me if I abuse her? The scientist would retort that this isn't his job, and he's right.

Does science also render the best advice on how to organize our lives and societies? This is a conundrum philosophers have wrestled with as far back as Plato. Some have thought so, and developed practical and practicing sides of the social sciences (sociology, social psychology, psychiatry and counseling, etc.) in specific directions around the idea. Whether their efforts have done good, harm, or a mixture of both, is a conversation worth having, or so I would hope.

But is that conversation a social-science one or a philosophical one, and if the latter, is it really just a matter of feelings?

Most economists try to draw reliable general conclusions from statistical aggregates, along with a few first premises about how supply and demand work and how we respond to incentives. But real, live human actors are not mere statistics. Nor are their motives exclusively (or even largely, except perhaps by duress) for mere economic gain. Can economics tell us what our motives *should* be, once we've grown conscious of them and able to take charge of them, at least in part? Many economists would also retort that this isn't their job.

Can scientists tell us how to determine what is—or should be—of *value* either in our personal lives today, in our communities, or in society at large? Can they tell us how we should prepare for an uncertain future?

Yes, many say unequivocally! Everyone following climate change discussions knows this!

For the most part, though, social scientists have consciously eschewed "value" judgments in favor of data collection, hypothesis testing, and attempted causal explanations of social phenomena. They try to identify best practices (for utilitarian purposes, i.e., establishing that if we wish to achieve optimal outcome x, our best bet is to do A consistently). Some of the results are useful; some not, as we would expect, as even our best methods invariably involve some trial and error.

The idea, though, that we answer to a Creator elicits indifference at best, and sometimes open scorn, from most of these folks. They regard it not only as delusional—given the results of science, especially on topics such as general relativity and evolution—but positively harmful. It is thus off the table. The New Atheism has now been around for a while, expressed forcefully by such authors as Dawkins and Sam Harris among scientists, Daniel Dennett and Philip Kitcher among philosophers, and the late Christopher Hitchens among journalists or public intellectuals.[4] A few media personalities have joined in over the years: Bill Maher comes to mind, as does the late George Carlin, some of whose routines as a stand-up comic ridiculed belief in the Christian God.

What these folks are saying isn't new, either. Well before Darwin published his *On the Origin of Species* (1859) we saw a rising intellectual-cultural *ambience* of skepticism about the idea of transcendent (nonnatural or supernatural) realities, led by Enlightenment philosophers (Diderot, D'Holbach, etc.). These men held that science was making religion a source of comfort at best, and an obstruction to social progress at worst. After Darwin, this tendency accelerated, eventually dividing theologians into "liberals" who accepted the claims of science as the new reality to which Christian theology had to conform or die, and "conservatives" (or "fundamentalists") who refused and continue to refuse.[5]

Twentieth-century theology, and many pastors and churchgoers, have straddled this divide ever since.

Hardly helping matters is how religion has become a lucrative source of income for "televangelists," a few of whom (such as the late Billy Graham) are doubtless sincere, while others can be seen as preying (not just praying!) on the emotions of easily-swayed followers possibly desperate for meaning in their lives. I don't think I need to list such folks. More than one stand-up comic has lampooned them with "Praise the Lord and pass the offertory plate!"

---

4. Dawkins, *God Delusion*; Harris, *End of Faith*; Dennett, *Breaking the Spell*; Kitcher, *Living with Darwin*; Hitchens, *God Is Not Great*.

5. See, e.g., Machen, *Christianity and Liberalism*.

The point is, religious institutions are hardly dead! There are theologians of various stripes; there are pastors; there are movements such as church growth, the Purpose-Driven Life movement, i.e., the so-called prosperity gospel (God wants you to be rich), and more.[6]

Religious-leaning publishers are doing well enough, putting out dozens of volumes every year. Christian print magazines and newsletters do very well. Christian websites get millions of hits per year.

Moreover, in almost all Southern towns stand a multitude of churches, sometimes on practically every other street corner.

All this said: surely no one in his right mind would claim that religion has much influence in intellectual centers—major universities and nongovernmental "think tanks." Its influence on major media is practically zero.

So does religious faith matter to the public? Yes, but church attendance has been dropping in the United States. It began to drop long ago in Europe.

More millennials than in any previous generation respond to polls, surveys, and questionnaire questions about religious affiliation with "None." According to a recent General Social Survey, over the past three decades the number of Americans claiming "no religion" has increased by 266 percent.[7]

Many if not most of those Southern churches, moreover, are quite old—sometimes well over a hundred years old. The majority of their attendees are the elderly, with some baby boomers at or near retirement age, with each succeeding generation's representation growing smaller.

What do those with "no religion" believe, philosophically?

It's hard to say, because professional philosophy's cultural influence is less than that of religion.

Scientists such as Hawking, and the New Atheists, imply that they know why. Large numbers of their colleagues would concur. What they claim to know might go something like this:

Truth (by which we need not have in mind a philosophical "theory" of truth) has been found in the sciences. It was not found in philosophy any more than it was found in religion. Scientific method does not commit to beliefs held dogmatically, based on religion, tradition, or emotion, instead of logic and evidence. What matters are hypotheses specific enough to yield testable predictions that when confirmed, become theories to be pursued further, replicated, and when further confirmed, added to the general body of accepted knowledge. They have successfully drawn general conclusions about how nature works, consistent with previous discoveries. Science continues trying to improve its generalizations, harmonizing theory with

---

6. Warren, *Purpose-Driven Life*.
7. Bauman, "Is America Becoming Godless?," para. 1.

continued observation and experiment. Science, unlike religion (or philosophy), is thus self-correcting. All its theories are subject to review and revision, and can be overthrown in the face of contrary evidence if a better theory explains that evidence. While often highly technical and demanding years of study, the sciences are ultimately very down-to-Earth. They don't postulate entities (e.g., a God or gods) that fail to lead to testable consequences, and so can't be said to *explain* anything in terms of causation. Nor do they try to deduce "theories of reality" (or some part of it) from first principles taken as proven or known *a priori* for certain, and able to generate a nonempirical, metaphysical system.

Hence the *epistemic authority of science* in modern intellectual centers, and in the adult world generally. Christianity, still a prevailing body of belief outside of science in much of the West, has lost most of its epistemic authority. This has resulted in a long-term exodus from churches, especially by the well-educated and the young who have grown up without it, and who have down-to-Earth problems to solve in *this* world for which prayers to a God seem to be useless.

Philosophers Ask Questions *About* Science.

And yet (beginning with a few mild and somewhat dusty skeptical queries about the above):

Have scientists' educations, and the educations of those who have fallen away from religious faith in favor of science (or, perhaps, some "fuzzy," un-thought-about version of it), prepared them to ask what the best trained philosophers have long wanted to understand about science?

For example: do the sciences bring any pre-scientific or nonscientific premises to their investigations? Do any such unstated assumptions shape their conclusions? Is the demarcation between scientific and nonscientific forms of life as sharp as is implied by the above narrative?

These are questions *about* science. As a youth, I wondered about them. My wonderings and wanderings as a university undergraduate brought me to the philosophy of science—to writers ranging from Alfred Jules (A. J.) Ayer, the British evangelist for Vienna Circle logical positivism, to historicists such as Thomas S. Kuhn,[8] and the more radical Paul Feyerabend who rejected the entire empiricist narrative about science as illusory.[9]

---

8. Kuhn, *Structure of Scientific Revolutions*.
9. Feyerabend, *Against Method*.

Other writers of various stripes soon came into my purview: Rudolf Carnap[10] and Carl Hempel[11] of the logical empiricists whose views corrected those of logical positivists; Sir Karl Popper the critical rationalist/falsificationist,[12] for a time the dominant thinker in British philosophy of science; other historicists such as Stephen Toulmin,[13] Norwood Russell Hanson,[14] Imre Lakatos[15] (the first two were very strongly influenced by Ludwig Wittgenstein's later philosophy, as were Kuhn and Feyerabend); Nicholas Maxwell's aim-oriented empiricism[16] (his term, influenced by Popper, as was Lakatos). There were others—Harold I. Brown provided the best book-length summary and critical discussion.[17]

What are "paradigms," and are they nonempirical controlling factors on the thought and activity of those doing "normal science" (Kuhn)? Is science then more a matter of "conjectures and refutations" instead of confirmations (the issue raised by Popper and pursued further by Lakatos)? Is observation "theory-laden" (Hanson and Kuhn)? Does unearthing the observations that might serve to refute a theory require a different and sufficiently developed but *incompatible* theory (Feyerabend)?

Does physical science presuppose, *a priori*, that the universe we wish to explore and explain is both (1) law-governed or ordered and not random or chaotic; and (2) that its ordered patterns or causal regularities are intelligible, i.e., explicable, to the human mind? Can we speak of, e.g., (3) the *aims of science* being to produce systematically better articulations of the specifics of this intelligible order in the various scientific domains (Maxwell's key contribution to this conversation)? And (4) do more recent theories *subsume* and *explain* older ones, or is there a systemic *replacement* when a new and presumably better theory replaces an older one (logical empiricism versus historicism: Kuhn, Feyerabend, Brown)? (5) Can there be any such thing as a *true* and *complete* scientific description of reality, as understood by the sciences in aggregate (Kuhn, Feyerabend, others)?

Is it conceivable that the most important scientific advances never proceeded according to an identifiable "rational" method at all, but rather on a mixture of various other factors, some operative in some cases but

10. Carnap, "Testability and Meaning, 419-71.
11. E.g., Hempel, *Aspects of Scientific Explanation*.
12. Popper, *Logic of Scientific Discovery*; Popper, *Conjectures and Refutations*.
13. Toulmin, *Philosophy of Science*; Toulmin, *Foresight and Understanding*.
14. Hanson, *Patterns of Discovery*.
15. Lakatos, "Falsification and the Methodology," 91–196.
16. Maxwell, "Rationality of Scientific Discovery," 123–53, 247–95.
17. Brown, *Perception, Theory, and Commitment*.

not others: recognition and reasoning about unanswered questions, careful observations and experiments where possible, historical happenstance, persuasion and propaganda techniques, political interference with a dominant narrative, and sometimes just plain luck of the draw (Feyerabend)?

None of these are *scientific* questions. They are *philosophical*. They may not be new, but what is worth emphasizing, over and over again if necessary, is that no specific science is able to answer them without circular reasoning, a fallacious pattern of thought a philosopher is uniquely qualified to spot.

Suppose reality is *not* ordered in the way we have come to think it is. Or that what we believe is its intrinsic order is a product of our structures or "categories" of consciousness (Kant), habits of thought (Hume) inculcated by a certain brand of education, or of the grammatical structure of our language (Chomsky), or our psychological need for order—or even "gendered" as a result of the majority of scientists having been men ("third wave" feminism)?![18]

This last in particular may seem silly or unintelligible to scientists of the Hawking and deGrasse Tyson mode, but following a generation of inquiry by those who self-identify as feminist philosophers the question is whether in this day and age we can rule it out *a priori*?

Suppose that the institution-bound authority of influential individual scientists has carried sufficient weight that theories continue to be held despite a lack of actual evidence for them, or worse yet, in the face of contrary evidence that has been ignored or suppressed.

Let's look at a brief example. For years, leading Czech-American archeologist Ales Hrdlicka insisted that human beings had been on the North American continent for well under ten thousand years (since the end of the last Ice Age). Operating from his home base at the United States National Museum (which would become the Smithsonian) and apparently a man with an authoritarian personality, his clout in the developing discipline of pre-Columbian archeology was such that others were prevented from considering the increasing physical evidence of settlements that were much older, e.g., those who became known as Folsom Man. Progress on the topic was delayed for several years. Not helping was the fact that the primary discoverer of Folsom and other remains was not a professional scientist but a former slave, one George McJunkin, a black ranch foreman who went west after the War Between the States. More than just an outsider, in other words.[19]

---

18. See, e.g., Harding, *Science Question in Feminism*.

19. Wilmsen, "Outline of Early Man Studies in the United States," 172–92; Adovasio and Page, "Searching for the First Americans," 15–29.

If one does a sufficient number of deep dives into the history of science, one soon realizes that such cases are not the exception. They are the rule. New ideas and sometimes even empirical findings often meet with resistance; anomalous data (violations of expectation) "are often not seen at all," as Kuhn put it in *Structure*.[20] Science journalist Stephen Brush once penned an article commenting on the situation and gave it the wry title, "Should the History of Science Be Rated X?"[21] At first glance, this seems reasonable. New ideas must prove their mettle. The inclination among scientists is that new discoveries must be integrated into an existing body of knowledge. If they seem to overturn what was previously accepted as true, the presumption is against their validity.

But if one takes the long view, the capacity of many sciences to deliver stable and truly validated results has been increasingly thrown into doubt over the past sixty years or so. Study after study is retracted, often in fields like medicine where lives are at risk if the practitioners fail to get things right. Are members of those communities alone positioned to diagnose the problems, or are they too close to them? Does the adage about the forest and the trees apply?

Reasons for this were brought to our attention by philosophers of science—those of that historicist school which included Kuhn, Feyerabend, and others figures named above. In a broad sense, the doubters also include major Continental figures such as the French poststructuralist Michel Foucault, among the first to take seriously the idea that—keeping this basic for now—how power operates across knowledge-disseminating institutions *can* throw off our best evaluations of what is true.[22]

Thus, even if one sees it as beyond rational or sane dispute that sciences such as physics or chemistry have delivered genuine, reliable knowledge, does it follow that their postulates about what is ultimately most real apply universally?

And finally, from whatever successes specific sciences have enjoyed, does it follow that religious or theological ideas are necessarily false or irrelevant or meaningless, much less harmful?

---

20. Kuhn, *Structure*, 24.
21. Brush, "Should the History of Science Be Rated X," 1164–72.
22. Foucault, *Archeology of Knowledge*.

Philosophy Is *Not* Irrelevant:
A Parade of Illustrations.

Wait a minute! some might be bursting to interrupt. *As you yourself have stated a couple of times now, there's nothing new about any of this!*

Moreover, the retort might continue, *in this day and age, why should anyone care? Go back to Hawking and Tyson,* and read *them this time!*

Or, perhaps, a more modest query, only slightly:

Does any of this really show that a world based on science, technology, and global commerce needs philosophy? What on Earth for? The subject is irrelevant, frivolous, the academic equivalent of games played by adolescents? Grow up already! Let's move on, when people have real *problems to solve?*

Here is the reason we shouldn't simply "move on": **philosophy isn't irrelevant!**

Is that too blunt and dogmatic? Let's look at it.

These dusty and arcane problems involving scientific knowledge barely even scratch the surface. Major political, educational, cultural, and yes, scientific tendencies in any society have philosophical moorings. If we are unconscious of them, we won't *think* about them, much less think *critically* about them.

They will still *be* there. They *will* affect our lives even if we refuse to look at them. When different peoples' beliefs, e.g., about their supposed *rights*, come into conflict, as they often have over the past seventy years, we'll see impasses and confrontations. We'll see increasingly extreme points of view thanks in part to technology. I think here of social media platforms which allow users to self-silo into online "safe spaces," echo chambers where their opinions aren't challenged. When challenges do appear, as they inevitably will, they won't even seem legitimate to those inside the echo chambers. Reason-based discussion will prove less and less feasible, civility will deteriorate, and the fringes of these movements will grow violence-prone when they don't get their way.

Is this sounding familiar?

This problem we *now* face is easy to illustrate. Note how many people casually throw around pejoratives like *snowflake, communist, libtard, racist, fascist, neo-Nazi, white supremacist, white nationalist, hate speech, homophobic, transphobic, feminazi, misogynist, toxic masculinity, white privilege—*

Did I miss any?

How many folks are using such words as weaponized rhetoric, without attending to their exact meanings if they have them?

And before going any further, it might be worth noting the distinction linguistic philosophers have long drawn between *use* and *mention*. If I say,

"So-and-so is a racist" or "She is a feminazi" in a context where the intent to label, shame, and then cancel is clear, those are *uses*. But if I were to observe that pejoratives like *racist* and *feminazi* are poor substitutes for criticism and almost certainly an obstruction to any real, constructive dialogue that might still be possible, those are *mentions*.

There are any number of somewhat broader terms, some of which have been around for a while, about which it might be good to have clarity at some point: *fundamentalist* (invoked briefly above, or its short form "*fundie*"), versus *secular humanist*. Or a more recent phrase: *false equivalence*. Or, perhaps, *conspiracy theorist*, if used for anyone who questions a dominant account or narrative of some dramatic event, and the motivations behind it. All, to varying degrees, wear negative connotations on their sleeves, and so, absent the sort of clarity philosophers can and should provide, are easily weaponized. *Weaponized* here means: used as the linguistic equivalent of a raised club to intimidate or bully people into silence, beat them into submission if necessary, or just lead them by their noses. *Virtue signaling* is now the term indicating that one has the "right" opinions on any of a variety of topics, and manifests this by exhibiting the right behaviors.

The later Ludwig Wittgenstein, to my mind far and away the past century's most important secular philosopher, defined philosophy as "a battle against the bewitchment of our intelligence by means of language."[23] His earlier philosophical incarnation observed that "in philosophy the question, 'What do we actually use this word or this proposition for?' repeatedly leads to valuable insights."[24] He had the language of philosophical problems in mind. But clearly, razor-sharp questions about meaning and use of far more common terms and adjectives have a role to play if philosophers choose to use them to examine the language of other endeavors: the sciences—or political economy.

For most if not all of the above terms and adjectives are associated with a political option. Critical thinking about political options places demands on philosophy as a core component of liberal arts learning. It should provide antidotes to weaponized language, intimidation and bullying, and being led by our noses into mindless virtue signaling (or worse).

Pulling examples from our list above, think of the ways one can use the term *liberal*—including simply as an insult. Or the term *conservative*. Or *neocon*. At one time, the first two had relatively clear meanings: more than one, in fact, inviting ambiguity and confusion among the unwary.

---

23. Wittgenstein, *Philosophical Investigations*, 47e.
24. Wittgenstein, *Tractatus Logico-Philosophicus*, 6.211.

Neocon is short for *neoconservative*. Some trace *neoconservatism* to a specific political philosopher, Leo Strauss. In truth, a particular neocon in the second Bush administration, Paul Wolfowitz, took a couple of courses under Strauss at the University of Chicago. Others see this movement which began to take over the Republican Party during the Reagan years as having started with disaffected Trotskyites—former leftists who had given up Trotskyite Marxism but remained committed to the more fundamental idea of a strong, centralized state and a strong military able to exact the will of a political-economic hegemony around the world.

Thus some terms "piggyback" on earlier ones. Consider *neoliberal*, in the sense of neoliberal political economy (referred to once in the foreword), which has little to do with *liberal* in either of the latter's fairly precise meanings, the classical one or its more recent meaning associated with expanding government programs led by the Democratic Party. Absent analysis, it is hardly clear what neoliberalism is or who its exponents today are, although University of Chicago economist Milton Friedman seems to have been the movement's first linchpin figure who actually used the term.

Or finally, since we just used it, consider the phrase *political economy* as opposed to *political science* and *economics*. The latter phrases imply intellectual-cognitive separation—and, of course, the disciplinary separation we see in the modern university system. The former implies no separation. It was once a standard phrase. It occurs in the subtitle of Adam Smith's classic work. Looking into how—and why—the two got separated is an interesting intellectual adventure in its own right.

Philosophy's Influence: Personalities and Movements.

If a philosopher has acquired a following outside academic philosophy *per se*, ignoring this is a mistake!

We mentioned Leo Strauss. It is impossible to understand recent US foreign policy, especially since the 9/11 attacks, without at least some knowledge of Strauss. Sometimes portrayed as a defender of liberal democracy and "American Exceptionalism," his actual views were anything but!

Strauss admired Plato and Nietzsche above all the other giants of the history of philosophy—finding continuity where others saw opposition. The continuity: Strauss, as both Plato and Nietzsche did, believed in the existence of an *elite* whose members are most fit to rule, because they instinctively understand deep and often unpleasant truths about the world the unwashed masses are not intellectually capable of comprehending, or emotionally able to accept and appreciate. Among these is the *inherent inequality* of human beings. However we cash the matter out, some people are simply *smarter* than others. Other things being equal, the smarter and cleverer automatically rise to positions of dominance. Because Strauss and his devotees were surrounded by academic believers in moral imperatives guided by an assumption of egalitarianism, they tended to operate by concealment. Strauss, in fact, believed that secrecy was an important tool of politics. It was important because otherwise, those who understood these sorts of truths would face not just ostracism but persecution.

For example, Strauss also saw *liberal democracy* as a mirage. It always has been. It and *equality* are two "noble lies" political intellectuals made up for consumption by the masses. "Noble lies" use language to bewitch their intelligence, to the extent they have any. Contrary to the American founders there are no *natural rights*, e.g., to life, liberty, and the pursuit of happiness. Contrary also to someone such as Rousseau, we are not "born free" any more than we are born equal. Our natural states are inequality, a struggle for existence, and the subordination of the inferior by the superior. When Strauss wrote a book with the title *Natural Right and History* (1953, note the singular instead of the plural), he was referring obliquely to the one "right" he saw as real: the *de facto* "right" of the superior to rule the inferior, and how history manifests this as a constant in stable civilizations whatever stories they tell themselves about *rights* (natural or otherwise), *liberal democracy*, *Divine Providence*, or what-have-you.

To Straussians, liberal democracy went wrong at the start with its inherent assumptions of the innate goodness of the masses and their capacity for responsibility. Strauss would have us look around at commercial society which has unleashed their passions, moved as they are primarily by fear and greed, and whose main preoccupations otherwise when not slaving to help their superiors are entertainment and fornication. A Straussian believes that the wise elite should rule because the masses need to be led.

Hence the Straussian philosophical influence on the neoconservative movement which emerged in the 1990s following the collapse of the Soviet Union as a force to be reckoned with, and then was swept into even greater influence in the Bush administration with the 9/11 attacks. Straussians were never influential in academia for obvious reasons, especially not in academic philosophy. Strauss's own home base was in the University of Chicago's *political science* program, not its *philosophy* department. Strauss's influence reached from there to think tanks and then into the US federal government, especially foreign policy, where the Straussian goal was to promote US military prowess for global domination—not because there is really anything truly "exceptional" about America (that's another of those "noble lies" using a word to bewitch our intelligence) but again, because those who understand the important truth that the strong should dominate the weak *ought* to carry forth such an agenda. And that those who would attack America—the present-day elites' seat of power—*need to be taught lessons they won't soon forget!*[25]

This one example indicates the delusional nature of the idea that a philosopher cannot wield influence in the body politic, an influence extending to matters of life and death, and that philosophy is therefore irrelevant! It is far from the only example!

Consider Herbert Marcuse, whose influence in the academy parallels, somewhat, Strauss's influence outside of it, operating from the opposite end of the ideological spectrum. Marcuse is more widely known, because his ideas found a lasting home in both academia and the larger culture. Originally of the Frankfurt School originating in Frankfurt, Germany where it created first the School of Social Research and then, in the United States, the New School of Social Research, Marcuse became a hero to early New Left students due to his drawing Freud into a Marxian aegis in *Eros and Civilization* (1955). Marcuse appealed to those who wanted to express themselves sexually—tendencies the Alfred C. Kinsey studies had unleashed with their implication that "traditional" sexual behaviors (e.g., monogamy, heterosexuality) were just one set of options among many which *ethically neutral science* showed were not as universal as had been thought and had nothing special to recommend them.[26]

In other words, unlike Strauss and his followers who looked down their noses on a prurient fascination with sex, Marcuse and his followers celebrated something they saw as natural, and which capitalism systemically repressed.

Then came Marcuse's full-on critique of capitalist civilization in *One-Dimensional Man* (1964), which appealed to those who resented capitalism's encirclements.

A keen observer of current events which included the rising unrest of ethnic minorities, Marcuse saw enormous potential in their gathering demands for justice and equality. He knew exactly what to do. In 1965, what actually became his most influential essay, the landmark "Repressive Tolerance," was published.[27]

In this essay Marcuse argued the provocative thesis that untrammeled free speech in the sense of the First Amendment continues the repression

---

25. Cf. Drury, *Leo Strauss and the American Right*.

26. Kinsey et al., *Sexual Behavior in the Human Male*; Kinsey et al., *Sexual Behavior in the Human Female*.

27. Marcuse, "Repressive Tolerance," 81–123.

of black Americans despite the previous year's Civil Rights Act. The problem is the systemic advantage of the white majority. It would ensure that their speech would be heard, not the speech of repressed groups. This was one form the "shackled runner" argument could take. President Lyndon Johnson had made this reference the year before as part of his defense of signing the Civil Rights Act of 1964.

Actual speech, Marcuse held, is not made *free* by an abstract Constitutional clause. Whether or not, and the degree to which, you are *free* depends on your position in racial and socioeconomic systems and hierarchies. The abstract right defended by Constitutional conservatives privileged traditional hierarchies and power systems, intentionally or not. These needed to be dismantled. The abstraction needed to be debunked, because speech by different groups could not be considered equivalent in social force.

Marcuse thus became the first to defend differential treatment as necessary to correct past wrongs. He wrote that "[l]iberating tolerance . . . mean[s] intolerance against movements from the Right and toleration of movements from the Left." This "would include the withdrawal of toleration of speech and assembly from groups and movements which promote aggressive policies, armament, chauvinism, discrimination on the grounds of race and religion, or which oppose the extension of public services, social security, medical care, etc."[28]

Marcuse thus saw "free speech" in the abstract as an *impediment* to progress. Taken literally and supported institutionally, it would permit white men to criticize and possibly neuter efforts to combat discrimination against minorities and women, serving the purposes of hidden *systemic* discrimination. (Eventually religious and sexual minorities would be brought under the latter umbrella.)

This is the philosophical origin of systemic racism claims that are everywhere today! They originated with a professional philosopher! They were continued, and further developed, by philosophers and those in cognate areas (literature, for example) who came in Marcuse's wake. They continue to be developed and used by today's movements (Black Lives Matter being the obvious one).

Unlike Straussians, *Marcusans* (we may call them) were welcomed in academia! They believed in equality, and saw systemic bias where equality was absent. They grew in influence in the groves of ivy in the 1980s, where there were huge publishing opportunities in academic fields where excitement and novelty were ends in themselves. In the long run, one cannot understand today's acrimonious debates over free speech on campuses,

---

28. Marcuse, "Repressive Tolerance," 109, 100.

claims of systemic racism, or the controlling influence on the national conversation identity politics now exerts (i.e., the politics of "woke"), unless one recognizes how it got started with Marcuse's "Repressive Tolerance" and the power that essay's ideas exercised on the original New Left, the ancestor of the present academic and cultural left.

Neither Strauss nor Marcuse wrote in an intellectual vacuum, obviously. It should be clear, they share some common premises. Both have ideas rooted ultimately in Plato's image of the perfect city (*The Republic*) guided by a wise elite, filtered through Hegel's dichotomy of the worldly experience of the Master (*Herrschaft*) versus that of the slave (*Knechtschaft*). Strauss saw the latter through the lens of Nietzsche, and Marcuse, through that of Marx. While Nietzsche saw the Master-slave dichotomy as part of the natural order of things, Marx believed historical forces would transcend and cancel it. Marx recast the Hegelian dichotomy in materialist terms as that between the world as experienced by the bourgeois owners of the means of production (capital) versus that of the proletariat (labor). He claimed to foresee the clash between the two that would destroy capitalism and free the proletariat, or its leadership, to establish socialism which would evolve into Communism (as Marx actually used this term, the historically perfected global city at the "end of history").

This Hegelian dichotomy, of *de facto* Masters wielding power over *de facto* slaves, has survived into the twenty-first century as that supposed grand divide between the dominant group in contemporary American life (white heterosexual Christian men) and repressed groups (African-Americans, Hispanics, women, homosexuals, transsexuals, non-Christians, etc.) with overlap between groups generating *intersectionality*. The antidote for systemic dominance is a systemic reversal of dominance until the earlier economic and cultural forces are "canceled," making genuine (universal) tolerance viable. Universal tolerance, that is, requires a period of *in*tolerance during which that which had been systemically dominant is repressed. Or as the cliché goes, you can't make an omelet without breaking eggs.

It took a number of years for Marcusans to march through the institutions, sometimes into academic departments and sometimes from law schools into the legal system, others going into media corporations, state and federal agencies, especially those overseeing public education, and eventually even into technology leviathans such as Google and Facebook.

By the 1980s—usually portrayed as an era of resurgent conservatism under Ronald Reagan—we began to see the slow and subtle introduction of controls over speech and thought about such subjects as race and affirmative action. The vigorous discussions seen in the 1970s in major academic journals began to disappear. And by the early 1990s we would begin to hear allegations of intimidation and even the bullying of students and professors deemed *conservative* or *right wing*—terms left undefined as weaponized words and phrases usually are, cast in a growing body of academic discourse as synonymous with past racist repression and thus, by definition, evil.

What was labeled *political correctness* by its detractors had been born, with Richard Bernstein possibly the first journalist to use the term in its present context and intent.[29] Critics of the usage wasted no time.[30]

This term, which some accuse the right of weaponizing, had been used decades earlier by Leninists for those who towed the party line too closely. The surging cultural left denied there was any such thing. What was different was the presence of voices in a position to demand respect, inclusion, and equal access to speech (as Marcuse had understood it). To these latter, white men railed against a changing culture out of the fear-based realization that they were losing the privileges to which they were accustomed. Racist, sexist, and homophobic speech and behavior were no longer tolerated.

The "culture wars" raged through the 1990s and on into the 2000s and beyond. One side cheered this rising tide of diverse voices: African-American studies, critical race theory, "third wave" feminism including feminisms of color and eco-feminism, queer theory, and so on. Many writers in the new movements appealed to the same European trends that paralleled the historicists: structuralism, poststructuralism, and deconstruction emanating from France in the hands of Foucault and Jacques Derrida, among others. Others went back to Simone de Beauvoir and sometimes to Freud and Marx.

Beauvoir, who had been Jean-Paul Sartre's significant other and an existentialist writer in her own right, was the first to argue for a distinction between *sex* as a biological category and *gender* as a sociological construction, the product of presumably changeable arrangements of the subordination of women by men resulting from differences in upbringing, education, standard vocational options, and so on.[31] Her work was studied by those who pioneered "third wave" academic feminism such as Judith Butler who did the most to popularize the idea of gender as a social or cultural "construct" subject to change through political activity.[32] The sex/gender dichotomy quickly caught on in an academia primed for deeper "waves" of Hegelianism, and has since become part of the sacred writ of identity politics, as Butler's writings also opened the door to sexual

---

29. Bernstein, "Rising Hegemony of the Politically Correct"; Berman, *Debating P.C.*
30. See, e.g., Wilson, *Myth of Political Correctness.*
31. Beauvoir, *Second Sex.*
32. Butler, *Gender Trouble.*

minorities. Another prominent "third wave" feminist, Catharine MacKinnon (whose field was legal theory, not philosophy), wrote articles with passages strongly suggesting that because of systemic male dominance in society generally and hence in all relationships, the distinction between voluntary sexual intercourse and rape was blurry at best.[33]

A few women scholars rebelled against such extremes, rejecting the suggestion that women were helpless victims of a "patriarchy." The most visible in philosophy was Christina Hoff Sommers.[34] Susan Haack also criticized "third wave" forays into epistemology, arguing cogently that the problems with "feminist epistemology" were not political but epistemological.[35] Other scholars of a more traditional bent saw the necessity for a strategy of opposition to these new tendencies which seemed to throw out accepted rules of what counted as a contribution to scholarship and why the literary "canon" still mattered.

Organizations such as the National Association of Scholars had formed, decrying what they saw as an academy rapidly abandoning quality control, politicizing hiring and promotions processes as well as academic publishing, in a bureaucratic ethos intent on serving ethnic and cultural diversity as ends in themselves. Their quarterly journal *Academic Questions* provided numerous instances of how classrooms had been transformed into launching pads for political activity posing as scholarship, with white men increasingly compelled to walk on eggshells around the growing number of female colleagues steeped in the latest "third wave" feminist doctrines (the number of black professors, in philosophy at least, all but refused to budge). By 1990 conservative authors had begun to warn of the consequences of an entire generation of students coming of age within this ambiance.[36] Millennials, indeed, were more accepting of it than any of their predecessors—perhaps because they were the most diverse generation in history and also the first to grow up with technology having global reach. Much of Generation Z, meanwhile, appears to have embraced the contemporary climate of "woke" with religious fervor. One reason is that what little exposure to conservative ideas these two recent generations have had has been infrequent, almost invariably outside classrooms, and drowned in mass media distraction and official obstruction.

---

33. See MacKinnon, "Feminism, Marxism, Method, and the State," 646–47.

34. Sommers, *Who Stole Feminism?*

35. Haack, "Science 'from a Feminist Perspective,'" 5–13; Haack, "Epistemological Reflections of an Old Feminist," 31–43.

36. See, e.g., Kimball, *Tenured Radicals*; D'Souza, *Illiberal Education*

Unlike earlier developments either in or influencing philosophy, criticizing the latest "waves" of new scholarship openly could severely damage one's career, as some of us learned the hard way—especially during an era when good (i.e., tenurable) academic positions were scarce. What happened was that rigorous discussions of, e.g., affirmative action programs and their effects, were stifled—very much in accordance with Marcuse's recommendations as Marcusans now had tenure and had reshaped the conversation. My own effort to connect the new scholarship, in the United States at least, to defenses of affirmative action hiring and preferential student admissions, especially after the Supreme Court's disastrous *Griggs* decision (1971) which redefined discrimination from a systematic practice of bigoted individuals to a systemic phenomenon the product of societal structures themselves, fell on deaf ears. I predicted that the tendencies I and others had documented would spread from academia through journalism and the legal system to every institution in society if they could not be effectively opposed, their first premises exposed and debunked.[37]

By the 2000s, somewhat sullied phrases like *affirmative action* and *equal opportunity* had largely disappeared except on formal legal statements such as the standard one about institutions being "equal opportunity / affirmative action employers." They had been replaced by *diversity* and *inclusion* (or *inclusive*), the rationale that survived the Supreme Court's *Bakke* decision (1978). Be this as it may, by the end of the millennium it was no longer possible to have open and critical discussions of, e.g., topics related to race or sex/gender, e.g., if men and women have different biology-based cognitive inclinations, without firestorms of controversy erupting. We regularly heard complaints from conservatives that universities were venues where you saw a diversity of *faces* but no diversity of *ideas*.

By the 2010s it was clear, these tendencies had indeed spread to every corner of the West, including corporate America's increasingly powerful technology leviathans. Consider just the case of James Damore, the software engineer at Google who was fired for circulating a memo criticizing the assumptions made by the company's attempts to recruit more women engineers.[38] Damore contended that due to scientifically well-understood cognitive differences between the sexes, we should expect more male than female computer engineers. Google's inability to recruit, hire, and retain more women could not reasonably be attributed to gender bias in the corporation or the profession more broadly.

---

37. Yates, *Civil Wrongs*; Yates, *Four Cardinal Errors*.
38. Damore, "Google's Ideological Echo Chamber."

Damore found himself summarily fired. He filed suit, but later withdrew his suit to pursue private arbitration which was settled out of court. This is not the only case we can point to, and it was far from the first. It will probably not be the last.

One of the arguments was that Damore was fired not for his criticisms of Google but rather because his memo's statements "regarding biological differences between the sexes were so harmful, discriminatory, and disruptive" as to be unprotected.[39] In other words, such claims are now seen as so inflammatory as to be no more acceptable than that chestnut about shouting *fire* in a crowded theater. Again in accordance with the differential treatment traceable to Marcuse's 1965 essay, the weaponized category *hate speech* has grown to encompass more and more such cases where someone has spoken against one of the new dogmas on race or gender or sexuality. It is probable, there are people in academia and probably in mass media who will characterize the sort of effort undertaken *here* to describe what has happened to public discourse as *hate speech*!

The point I am making is not about any policy or about political correctness or responses to it or about whether someone such as Damore should or should not have been fired, but rather what such cases illustrate about the influence of philosophy—even if it turns out to be *bad* philosophy. We have, in front of our noses, a sweeping sea change in Western culture, ranging across education at all levels, across mass and social media, and now permeating corporate life—even affecting the military. This sea change is traceable to the writings of *philosophers* (Herbert Marcuse and perhaps Simone de Beauvoir) whose thought had a long history behind it leading ultimately to other *philosophers* (Marx, and the historically pivotal G. W. F. Hegel without whom there would have been no Marx or Beauvoir or Marcuse).

Philosophy is irrelevant? Students should avoid it?

Try again![40]

Ayn Rand, Libertarianism, Their Fellow-Travelers.

Again: my target here isn't a political stance as much as those who believe philosophy has been buried by science, and that we can all go home complacently from the funeral.

---

39. Eidelson, "Google's Firing of Engineer James Damore," para. 2.

40. Some readers might complain that this section neglects the most influential figure of all on the cultural left, Saul Alinsky. But Alinsky was neither a professional philosopher, nor did he self-identify as one, so I leave the discussion of him for others.

Nor are Straussians and Marcusans the only groups strongly influenced by philosophy. Take Libertarianism. Since the early 1970s—by any measure a very interesting period in recent history to study—there has been a Libertarian Party. A Libertarian mindset (in a looser sense of that word) infiltrated the Republican Party starting in the 1980s. Whereas conservatives believe in Constitutionally limited government, many Libertarians believe in almost *no* government. A "night-watchman state," Libertarian (at the time) *philosopher* Robert Nozick called it. His *Anarchy, State and Utopia* (1974, in many respects a direct response to his Harvard colleague John Rawls's views) did more than any other single work to get Libertarian thought on the academic radar.

Ayn Rand's philosophy, most completely expressed in her 1957 novel *Atlas Shrugged*, was one of Libertarianism's chief antecedents, even if Miss Rand rejected it. She called her philosophy Objectivism.[41] Her uncompromising defense of capitalism was moral, epistemological, and finally metaphysical: acknowledge the finality of reality as disclosed by the senses and reason, or it will automatically work against you, and against a society. Miss Rand's is very definitely a view that philosophy has immense and sometimes immediate practical consequences, and so is *very* relevant. Her view of the masses, moreover, was very different from that of Strauss or Marcuse. For Miss Rand there were no "masses" as such. There are only individuals. Only individuals can apprehend reality, integrating perceptions with reason and planning courses of action. Only individuals can write constitutions or create business enterprises. *Collectivism* was one of her primary philosophical villains, in whatever form it took. A "collective" cannot write or produce. All it can do is form mobs. Organizations can be formed and divide their labors, but the actions taken and the thoughts behind them are products of individual persons. There is no collective brain, Miss Rand tells us, and therefore no such thing as collective action. Hence the fallacies, failures, and ultimately disasters collectivism brings about: its inability to produce anything of value, its parasitical nature, and its eventually forming tyrannies as the tyrants at the top of its ladder force cooperation from people and eventually destroy all human value. Miss Rand described her Objectivism as a celebration of life on Earth, which is the celebration of *individual* life and its conditions, especially the exercise of individual reason. Doing sound philosophy meant acknowledging the supremacy of reason in all human affairs; *this*, and its fruits, are the good. All else follows deductively.

Miss Rand—love her or hate her—offered what we will come to call a *worldview*: comprehensive in scope, applicable in one way or another to

---

41. Cf. Rand, *Introduction to Objectivist Epistemology*.

every area of thought and human life, unquestionably philosophical, and unquestionably influential in the world.

Her own favorite philosopher was Aristotle, whom she saw as the pinnacle of Western thought. Not all Libertarians concurred. To their credit, they've always been conscious of their roots, which sometimes draw on philosophers like John Locke (for property rights) and sometimes John Stuart Mill ("On Liberty"). They've had their share of in-house disputes, such as whether liberty is best defended on economic grounds, as a means to prosperity, or on moral grounds as an end in itself. Tibor R. Machan was the most prolific defender of the latter.[42] Forebears of the former include Austrian School economists such as Ludwig von Mises, Friedrich A. Hayek, Murray N. Rothbard, Llewellyn H. Rockwell, Robert Higgs, Hans Herman Hoppe, and (with important variations that led to neoliberalism, not Libertarianism *per se*), Friedman.[43]

Most academic philosophers have always ignored Miss Rand, of course, but they cannot deny her influence. None other than Alan Greenspan, who became chair of the Federal Reserve in the late 1980s, once sat at her feet. He went on to orchestrate what was either the largest economic expansion in recent history or the largest and first truly destructive credit bubble (the first of several), depending on who you read. He became a primary architect of what we might call *hyper*-capitalism, which others might simply see as neoliberalism.

Libertarians reference the *non-aggression principle* (NAP)—embodying the idea that one should never initiate force or fraud against another, or endorse any policy that employs such. The primary agency of force in civilization is the state. It follows that believers in the NAP want, at the very most, Nozick's "night watchman state" (minarchists) or to eliminate "the state" altogether (anarchists). *Anarcho-capitalists* would eliminate the state as illegitimate in favor of universal free markets. The most widely read recent authors with such views are probably Hans-Herman Hoppe and Robert Higgs.[44] They argue that eliminating "the state" is not only consistent with the NAP but would eliminate the distortions of "crony capitalism," including the hyper-capitalism of Greenspan's Federal Reserve.

Where the economic left went wrong, according to these thinkers, was seeing *capitalism* as the problem. We didn't, and don't, need to *replace* it with some kind of democratic socialism (or social democracy, if one prefers),

---

42. See, e.g., Machan, *Individuals and Their Rights*.

43. Mises, *Human Action*; Hayek, *Road to Serfdom*; Friedman, *Capitalism and Freedom*; Rothbard, *Man, Economy and State*; Rothbard, *For a New Liberty*; Hoppe, *Democracy*; Higgs, *Against Leviathan*; Rockwell, *Against the State*.

44. Hoppe, *Democracy*; Higgs, *Against Leviathan*.

we need to *discover* it by practicing actual free market economics, instead of a system of *corporate welfare*, in which corporate actors use government to distort the marketplace and give themselves unearned advantages. (Miss Rand thought government was essential for encoding "man's rights" and punishing violators according to the *objective* rule of law. It does not dawn on Libertarians that there may be reasons why no other forms of capitalism exist other than the neoliberal hyper-capitalism we actually see, which will mean that the *economic* left has a point.)

Greenspan ceased to be even remotely a Randian or a Libertarian eons ago, once he realized the power of the Fed to direct the economy. Libertarian efforts within the Republican Party were most visibly represented by Dr. Ron Paul who went into politics following a successful medical career. Dr. Paul's views clashed with Strauss-inspired neoconservatives in foreign policy, and with those who thought his call to "abolish the Fed" was beyond the pale.[45] With the rise of the Tea Party and his candidacies for the Republican nomination in 2008 and 2012, his son the (significantly named) Rand Paul's election as US Senator in Kentucky, and with mainstream political figures growing less popular and seeming to have less substance to offer, Libertarians and those who lean Libertarian within the Republican Party commanded slightly more attention. This didn't last, of course, as we know. Far more powerful sentiments rose after the financial crisis of 2008, continuing on into the last decade. In the course of this essay we will see why, although again this is no more a defense of Libertarianism (or, perchance, Trumpism) than it is an attack on the academic-cultural left, but to reiterate that highly influential political movements cannot be understood and evaluated apart their roots in *philosophies*.

Neoliberalism is associated with Milton Friedman who used the term openly much earlier than is generally recognized.[46] It is not *classical* liberalism any more than *neo*conservatism is a form of conservatism. It celebrates economic freedom, privatization, and growth, but draws on philosophical ideas (e.g., Lockean property rights) only to the extent these are useful to big business. Quite unlike Libertarianism, it sees "the state" (i.e., government) as essential in establishing prime conditions for "free markets."

The idea was forged out of earlier forms of "late" classical liberalism in the late 1940s when Hayek, Popper, and others in that orbit founded the Mont Pèlerin Society with the support of a handful of wealthy foundations. The Mont Pèlerins knew they needed a Americanized *The Road to Serfdom*. Friedman became their American protégé, and ten years later, his *Capitalism*

---

45. Paul, *End the Fed*; Paul, *Foreign Policy of Freedom*.
46. See Friedman, "Neoliberalism and Its Prospects," 89–93.

and Freedom became the American treatise they wanted.[47] Friedman went on to pen an article entitled "The Social Responsibility of Business Is To Increase Its Profits" which repudiated 1960s concerns and set the course for the central business-ethics premises of the neoliberal, which is that the aim of a business enterprise is profit and shareholder maximization, that other considerations, especially those calling for government regulation but actually anything draining profit margins, amounted to "socialism."[48]

Neoliberals, like Straussians, were, and are not entirely honest. Ideologically, they eschew economic planning (in *Road*, Hayek had developed the strange thesis that central planning was what had led to the rise of the Nazis in Germany). They do not object to planning if globally expansive corporations undertake it. Neoliberalism thus gained enormous support in that orbit regardless of what it was called. The 1980s, of course, saw Reaganism in the United States and Thatcherism in the United Kingdom, with the latter's infamous TINA pronouncement ("There Is No Alternative").

That decade ended with the spectacular loss of Eastern Europe by Soviet Communism. The collapse quickly spread to the Soviet Union itself, which went out of business in 1991. The sky seemed the limit! Neoliberalism (which we can now see is equivalent to hyper-capitalism and "crony capitalism") because the dominant philosophy of global corporatization at that point, with all that we have seen since: the rise of "free trade" (epitomized by the North American Free Trade Agreement, or NAFTA), the ensuing hollowing out of the US manufacturing base, the importation of immigrants, legal or otherwise, for cheap labor driving down American wages, a rising cost in almost every area of American living from health care to higher education, and a rising tide of inequality that would reach a point where a group of people that would fit comfortably in a college auditorium controlled more wealth than the entire bottom half of the world's population.

Modernity would overwhelm indigenous populations elsewhere, as corporate activity sought to transform as much of the world as possible into a single global shopping mall of mass consumption and disposability—seemingly the antithesis of what the Straussians wanted—but it was as if the two reached a kind of truce. Straussians tended to focus on foreign policy while neoliberals promoted global hyper-capitalism controlled by corporations and high finance. War, they realized, could be very profitable! It opened doors for the latter via lucrative rebuilding contracts. (Ask Halliburton, rebuilder of Iraq following that humanely disastrous misadventure![49])

47. Friedman, *Capitalism and Freedom*.
48. Friedman, "Social Responsibility of Business."
49. See Klein, *Shock Doctrine*.

The party ended in 2008, and what ensued was the slowest "economic recovery" in history. Wealth continued to concentrate at the top. The cultural left consolidated its influence in academia and at the street level, helped by mass media misreporting of events such as the Trayvon Martin killing. Many of 'the masses' were no longer buying any of it. Mainstream narratives were collapsing apace. In 2015, Donald Trump stepped into the limelight, and according to one narrative, noisily opened the lid on the cesspool of delusion and dishonesty American political economy and foreign policy had become.

At the time of this writing (January 2018 through September 2020) with Trump in the White House, which philosophies have influence may seem up in the air.

Never mind that now.

The point is, we have not one but (at least) *three* exemplars of highly influential contemporary tendencies whose origins and impetus cannot be understood without *philosophy*, a subject prominent voices in the sciences have told us we should ignore, that it is dead.

Are There Any *Good* Philosophies? What Is At Stake?

At this point, the critic might concede: there is *some* value to knowing about philosophy—*as long as we acknowledge that the subject has probably done more harm than good! Shouldn't we therefore* still *consider discouraging pursuit of it?!*

Even *this* engages the issue of the role of philosophy in civilization seriously, and lays ground for responding that declarations of its death are uninformed, irresponsible, even reckless.

Countless other public debates—over abortion, physician-assisted suicide, gun control, legalization of marijuana and perhaps other presently-illegal recreational drugs, the treatment of animals, the role of religion in public life, potential global imperatives created by allegations of man-made climate change, and other effects economies of consumption and built-in obsolescence and disposability have had on the world—can be illuminated by philosophy as different sides and in-house disagreements of emphasis engage each other. Some have different motivations as well as different premises.

What this all comes down to: *we can compare a civilization trying to solve its problems and move forward without philosophy, i.e., without consciousness of how philosophical premises are operating in its institutions and in all its major public conversations, to a man trying to cross a busy street or highway with fast-moving traffic while blindfolded.*

There's a chance he might make it, a small one, but the odds of his getting injured or killed are much greater.

One of my convictions is that the West is in trouble because it is both morally and epistemically adrift. When I began writing this book as a person who has lived overseas and communicates regularly with people who are not US citizens, it might have not been clear to US citizens that their nation was in trouble; recent events have almost surely changed that. But the problem of what to do about it, how to go forward constructively, has never been more acute. The world outside the United States is watching closely, moreover.

Without the capacity to look at itself and its various public conversations philosophically, i.e., to look at its institutions and practices as if from outside, especially their embodying premises about the world, about human nature, about what is of value to different groups, and their uses of language, a civilization—ours or anyone else's—is ultimately just as blind and self-destructive as that guy trying to cross a busy street blindfolded.

This translates into a civilizational *need* (not a mere *desire* on the part of philosophers) for a few citizens trained in critical thinking, skilled at analyzing language use, able to spot fallacies, likely to recognize and evaluate fundamental premises built into institutional practice, and finally able to connect the dots as it were, so that they see a larger picture. In the end, such citizens might be able to produce critical evaluations of what they see embodied in dominant institutions, including scientific and technologically oriented ones.

We are not talking about a need for mere hobbyists, or even more philosophy professors, but for people sufficiently well-informed and positioned to be listened to in the public square.

We are talking about the need for philosophers as *thought-leaders*: *influencers* (to use a trendy term). Although not in Strauss's or Marcuse's sense.

Despite its technological accomplishments and its having achieved a level of material prosperity unparalleled in world history, the West is severely troubled and divided. The rise of a Donald Trump is a symptom, not the problem. One way or another, Trump will be gone in a few years. The problems that helped elect him will not merely still be around if unattended to, they will be magnitudes worse!

The idea of American decline is no longer a "fringe" opinion. Some reputable scholars express it openly, frame it historically, and draw attention to America's worsening political dysfunction as well as growing and potentially destabilizing economic inequality. See for example leading military historian Alfred McCoy's *In the Shadows of the American Century: The Rise and Decline of U.S. Global Power* (2017). McCoy envisions a shift in global political-economic power eastward—towards China. This shift, he thinks, has already begun and other things being equal, will accelerate over the next two decades.

Europe has produced equivalent analysts of despair, in such thinkers as Christopher Booker, Richard North, and Claire Berlinski. One of the upshots of the conversation their works tried to prompt is the singular question of whether the European Union was a vast mistake: whether the kind of political-economic consolidation towards which globalization seems invariably to lead, brings genuine prosperity—or just encourages reckless economic and financial policies, massive inequality, and political instability when the have-nots begin reacting (think of the Syriza Party in Greece, Brexit, the *jaunes gilets* in France, protests against "austerity" elsewhere, etc.).[50]

The point is, there is now a solid basis for taking seriously that Spenglerian phrase, *the decline of the West*, and for raising the question of whether this decline can still be circumvented. If so, how? If not, what now?

My position is that if Western civilization is to have a chance, philosophy must have a place at the table. Its contribution, moreover, cannot be standard academic micro-specialization. It must engage existing debates *where they are* and find ways to take them to a level that will be fundamental but still productive.

What we must do is revisit the *worldview* that has been guiding Western institutions, revisiting its answers about our place in the universe and in nature, whether or not there is are values that stand above culture and above the global marketplace, i.e., whether we have *intrinsic* value as persons (not the *extrinsic* value—or disvalue!—of our group identification or our marketplace purchasing power)—and what we are going to do about it.

This, I will argue, is necessary for a productive conversation on where we ought to go from here. I cannot promise results that will make people happy—advocates of a given political perspective, or one claiming the mantle of science (or rationality). Nor will my results necessarily please those in authority. Philosophy has never been popular among a civilization's elites. It has always been a threat to those who prefer lives of *genuine* privilege and complacency amidst opulence and power. Socrates *was* put to death, after all. He had become a perceived threat to complacency and privilege in his *polis*.

---

50. See Booker and North, *The Great Deception: Can the European Union Survive?*; Berlinski, *Menace in Europe*.

But his endeavor endured. Philosophy survived, first in academies such as those Plato and Aristotle founded, then in the schools founded by the Epicureans and the Stoics; later in monasteries which nurtured thinkers such as Aquinas; and finally in modern universities where despite philosophy's reduction in status, one can still find deep and profound thought if one looks around. Important work is still being done. What is not being done sufficiently is applying it in any large way to the problems of civilization.

In other words, philosophy is not mere idle speculation. *It has a job to do* which is not currently being done on any scale able to make a difference. Science and technology may be reaching for the stars (literally!). We may have more conveniences and creature comforts than ever before. Markets may span the globe. But these will not prevent us from fragmenting culturally, slowly failing crucial litmus tests of civilizational sustainability, destroying ourselves from within.

It is sometimes said that ours is a cynical age, an age of materialism and moral subjectivism, in which *greed is good*—"Gekkoism" if you will—and with increasing precarity for those outside the infamous one percent. We live in a money-before-everything world, in which even those fortunate enough to have stable employment are almost expected to have at least one "side hustle" or be training for their "next career." Terms like *post-truth* are among those thrown around in an age of conspiracies and agendas. Amidst it all, we are hammered incessantly with distractions, many of them meaningless, all competing for our attention and using fear of the latest calamities—real or fake. Objectively knowable truth threatens to vanish, as if into a puff of marijuana smoke.

We have gone from the era we baby boomers remember as kids, in which technology sent men to the moon and returned them safely, to an era in which we use technology to take selfies and a rising segment of the population thinks the moon landings were faked. Perhaps I should note that *the idea of the Earth being flat* seems to have made a comeback.

It's on the Internet.

The Russians didn't need to interfere in the 2016 election. We are self-destructing on our own. If we cannot get past our present stage of civilization, we *will* join the long list of failures that have long passed into the history books. Apocalyptic? Yes, but with major motivating narratives having collapsed and nothing emerging to replace them, does anyone really believe the present state of affairs can be sustained much longer?

Articulating Philosophy's Job: "The Shape of Things To Come."

In what follows, I hope to begin a new conversation about the role of philosophy in civilization by answering the question my title asks, "What Should Philosophy Do?"

In other words, this book is an unabashed defense of the idea that philosophy not only is not dead but has an essential role to play in civilization. We will see an example of that role. Philosophy is not an intellectual game. It has, as I put it above, a job to do.

The author is an outsider, with an outsider's perspective. To the extent this is relevant, I maintain that it is a good thing. The author believes he has seen the forest and not just the trees. He believes that if more people became outsiders with the sort of perspective being an outsider encourages, we might get better thought leadership and better quality concern for the future. The author cares about the future and philosophy's essential role in that future.

I don't maintain these ideas are brand new. Few ideas, in or out of philosophy, are truly *brand new*. I *do* maintain that they haven't been put forth with sufficient focus and urgency, or shown how they apply to human life and civilization.

No less a figure than Ludwig Wittgenstein articulated the thought that first moved me to begin thinking about a manuscript such as this eons ago, long before recent events that motivated me to write it and make Wittgenstein's wise query my lead quotation. Back in the late 1980s, fresh out of graduate school, having no *real* worldview orientation but ambitious to the point of recklessness, I found myself struggling in a job market that seemed interested mainly in micro-specialists and various forms of political favoritism. Sometime during the 1990s I ran across what Wittgenstein wrote to Norman Malcolm decades before:

> [W]hat is the use of studying philosophy if all that it does for you is to enable you to talk with some plausibility about some abstruse questions of logic, etc., & if it does not improve your thinking about the important questions of everyday life, if it does not make you more conscientious than any . . . journalist in the use of the DANGEROUS phrases such people use for their own ends. You see, I know that it's difficult to think *well* about "certainty," "probability," "perception," etc. But it is, if possible, still more difficult to think, or try to think, really honestly about your life & other peoples' lives. And the trouble is that thinking

about these things is *not thrilling*, but often downright nasty. And when it's nasty then it's *most* important.[51]

This brought me up short. It should do the same for others. It made me realize how easily academics rationalize their beliefs and their language to themselves. Let me issue a warning: parts of this book will *not* be thrilling! They *will* be seen as offensive and even *nasty* to some readers. This book will *not* be politically correct regarding identity politics and the current wave of "wokeness." Critics will bash certain areas of my argument as "pseudo-scientific" or use some other weaponized phrase. Others may even call my efforts *racist, racist, racist* (because I'm a white male citing mostly white males). This book *does* set out to barbecue sacred cows. I make *no* apologies for this. If you think only the "experts" (i.e., members of academia's tenured caste with actual privileges, or the latest academic showmen or show-women or glorified celebrities of whatever race/ethnicity) ought to write books—or, for that matter, if you've read this far and think that you're about to encounter just one more recycling of stale gripes about how bad things are on campuses—you might as well close this book now. You are not suited for the sort of conversation we need to have.

For what follows will challenge central premises of present-day civilization, its prevailing worldview and metaphysics (yes, Virginia, it has one), the kind of political economy (best understood using that phrase) this worldview has brought about, and the shape of real power (*no*, it does not reside collectively in white men, whatever this would amount to).

We will shine a spotlight on weaponized words and phrases as we encounter them, revealing them for what they are. Their premises will be exposed.

Light has always been the most effective disinfectant.

Chapter 1, "What Is This Thing Called Philosophy?" will lay the groundwork and set the stage. I will examine four major historical answers to that question as well as some of the combinations and variants on them that emerged after the institutionalization of philosophy in contemporary academia.

My discussion will converge on my answer to, *What Should Philosophy Do?* It is an answer that will be repeated often in the course of this book, under the idea that repetition adds persuasive force (I am not so naïve as to think arguments and evidence alone will suffice in the present climate).

My answer: *philosophy should identify, clarify, and provide informed evaluations of worldviews*—*especially worldviews that are dominant in major*

---

51. Malcolm, *Ludwig Wittgenstein*, 35.

intellectual centers and other institutions—in a culture or civilization, with controlling effects on the relevant language.

Philosophy is uniquely positioned to provide this service, because philosophers are uniquely trained in such skills as critical thinking, and in the ability to see through public pronouncements and mass movements. It can illuminate their first premises. In first premises you will find the often-tacit worldview commitments. Most of the time these first premises go unnoticed. It is time to notice them.

Philosophy both can and should distinguish claims based on actual evidence from claims reducible to belligerent assertions based on ruses of various sorts, and in the end, on little more than authoritarian institutional systems. It can and should explain how this confusion arises and what its dangers are.

Chapter 2 will focus on recent European-American intellectual history to show how most of philosophy got into its present predicament as little more than an academic decoration, out of which sprang a few voices, rarely criticized, although their overall influence on civilization has been more negative than positive. Hawking's and deGrasse Tyson's calls for a funeral for the subject are hardly new, moreover. The idea of philosophy being dead, replaced by science, goes back in one form or another almost two hundred years! Its current crisis combines this with its being too white and too male—an obsession resulting from our having entered a different state or level or *Stage* of civilization from that of Hawking and de Grasse Tyson fairly recently.

Stage? Why capitalized?

I will orient my account around the *Law of Three Stages* proposed by Auguste Comte in the early to mid-1800s. Comte is best known for having founded sociology as an identifiable science and beginning the positivist movement in philosophy. Comte is not the only figure with a "stages" view of civilization, of course, but his outline of the Stages of civilization is clear, concise, useful, and capable of further development in ways that illuminate our present situation.

Comte posits three Stages and describes the thinking behind each, as well as institutions and norms they give rise to. Our discussion will converge on the Third Stage, that of modernity, and its central achievement: a civilization based on advancing science, changing technology, expanding global commerce, public education, and a firm commitment to the belief that progress is real, inevitable, and a public good. Comte himself would not have endorsed this kind of civilization (he was a socialist, not a capitalist), but that will be neither here nor there.

Third Stage thinking was seeded by the Cartesian turn and the early Enlightenment, which also bequeathed to us the idea of autonomous reason, whether purely scientific or technological, and secular notions of universal human rights that became highly influential in building up modern political systems, especially governments which purported to be democratic and led by representative bodies. We will investigate the largest population center of the Third Stage of Civilization: the Secular City (a term I've borrowed from theologian Harvey Cox who wrote a book entitled *The Secular City* in the 1960s). We will also explore the Secular University as our generic term for the primary intellectual center of the Secular City, tasked with training the City's leaders, workers, and everyone in between, in mindset as well as skill set.

Comte is not a "hero" of mine, though, and history did not end with his Third Stage. We will posit a Fourth Stage: *postmodernity*, a term perhaps again trendy-sounding but the best one close at hand. Comte, a historical optimist, could not have conceived of postmodernity. We will argue that Third Stage thought has proven to be untenable intellectually and that Third Stage civilization is unsustainable morally, politically-economically, and culturally. Such claims, I am again more than aware, are not exactly new. What will set our discussion apart will be maintaining that the only way to diagnose the problems fully is to examine the *worldview change* (a phrase not quite analogous to *regime change*, but useful nonetheless) that guided the rise and trajectory of Third Stage thought, and its effects on civilization and culture

This will bring us to Chapter 3. With the historical background in place, we will consider worldviews in detail: what they are, what their components are. We will outline the two most influential worldviews in the rise of Western civilization and culture: Christianity and Christendom, versus materialism guided by a methodology of naturalism. There are, of course, numerous variations on each, but our primary interest will be what the variations share, not their in-house disputes.

We will argue that the replacement of the former with the latter, first in the Secular University and then in the Secular City at large, had the long-term unintended consequence of bringing about a transition to Fourth Stage thinking through the failure of their theories of morality. This was far more tacit than overt, since it was not necessarily the product of systematic thought and criticism. The transition began first in the *avant-garde*, in the arts and literature, eventually of course philosophy, and gradually spread to the rest of culture. It is now arguably the prevailing form of life in media culture and in the *technosphere* (adopting the term coined by Russian-born computer engineer and author Dmitry Orlov[52]). Third Stage thought and culture is by its nature rationalistic in a broad sense. It is optimistic about human nature, and trusts human possibilities severed from the Christian roots that preceded it. Fourth Stage thought and culture is inherently antirational in this same broad sense. It is deeply pessimistic, skeptical of truth claims where not openly cynical, and ultimately despairing. As opposed to the universal human rights proposed by Enlightenment humanists, moreover, it turns back to tribalism and divides us back up into groups warring over narratives and spoils.

Our central contention will be that we cannot understand our present predicament without going into the role played by the materialist worldview in its various forms in creating its conditions, and that if philosophy undertakes the job of identifying, clarifying, and critically evaluating worldviews, philosophy will be uniquely positioned to diagnose our predicament and propose solutions to it by criticizing materialism. Not, that is, criticizing this or that form of materialism and proposing a better form of materialism, but in *criticizing the materialist perspective as a whole and recommending that it be abandoned and replaced.*

Chapters 4 and 5 will thus exemplify *worldview criticism*. These chapters will set out to do the job of philosophy in civilization. In Chapter 4, we examine all the major attempts to sever morality and justice from Christian theism and place them on some secular foundation, explicitly materialist or otherwise—be it human rationality (Kant), pleasure versus pain (the utilitarians), invoking some thought device such as Rawls's veil of ignorance, the Libertarian NAP, or anything else—and argue that they all fail, in some cases miserably, sometimes leaving us with consequences that are abhorrent. Many writers (e.g., twentieth-century existentialists) figured this out in their own way, but in their focus on the individual person and on individual consciousness, they did not think deeply enough about the metaphysics at modernity's core or wonder if this metaphysics was merely one option among two, three, or more. Hence their turn from optimism and complete loss of hope.

We will examine abstract theories of morality in light of public issues such as abortion and identity politics. The former illustrates how Third Stage thinking, willingly or not, makes it *easy* to write entire populations that are demonstrably human out of the moral community. The Holocaust was hardly the only such effort, or even the worst! We will see how prescient Wittgenstein's invoking the adjective *nasty* may have been. Writing entire groups out of the moral community reveals not merely the ultimate fruits

---

52. Cf., e.g., Orlov, *Shrinking the Technosphere*.

of Marcusan thinking but the disintegration of the Enlightenment view of universal human reason, of the idea that moral rights and obligations apply equally to all persons, and its replacement by tribalism. The real tragedy here is that with the civil rights vision that emerged in the 1960s we were just learning how to apply such ideas as moral equality of persons consistently in American society, when identity politics appeared and squandered it all. Such a theory of morality turns out to have no foundation and no teeth, given the view of the universe presented by materialism and by the naturalistic methodology behind it; there is ultimately no reason for persons and groups to do essentially as they please if they can get away with it. Materialists and naturalists will not approve of this argument, but I will argue that it is the only reasonable one.

Chapter 4, though, will have only showed that materialism and naturalism have undesirable consequences. This is not good enough. Chapter 5 will therefore mount a more direct attack, arguing that when one attends to the actual *results*, especially those of nuts-and-bolts laboratory *science*, as opposed to *theory, speculation,* and *extrapolation*, the materialism-naturalism axis has failed to solve the most important intellectual problems it sets for itself, problems it must solve if it is to maintain long-term credibility with men and women of intellectual integrity.

A brief digression, before we venture further. This book will not regale readers with a let's-just-get-back-to-God message, although after reading about the failures of secular systems, such a message may seem both understandable and tempting, even welcome, to some readers. That is not my purpose here. But what should be clear is that human beings cannot simply exist. They must have some *purpose*, or believe they have a purpose, for doing so. This belief, moreover, must be grounded in something *outside themselves and their personal psyches*. It cannot simply be "made up." A sense of high-order purposelessness destroys us psychologically, sometimes slowly, and in times of horrific crises, quickly. Psychologist Victor Frankl, in his massively important and influential *Man's Search For Meaning* (orig. 1955), was able to show how Nazi concentration camp inmates either drew on a sense of purpose that was larger than themselves and enabled them to transcend their immediate sufferings—or they died, often within twenty-four hours of losing all hope.

What is seldom noted is that what applies to persons in the short term applies to civilizations in the long term. Societies in which there exists a consensus of purpose through a connection to a transcendent realm, recognized and sanctioned by their leading institutions, appear to have more stability and staying power. Their kinship relations tend to hold, and their values are communicated from generation to generation.

Change may come, but it will come slowly, in response to demonstrably real problems, and not undertaken frivolously. Should this community develop economic arrangements characterizable as capitalistic, its members will have sensible safety nets apart from legislation from a central government to mitigate a commercial system's tendencies toward indifference or harshness, and to arrest irrational prejudices of various sorts. If they find the physical and natural order around them meaningful, as the product of a creative agency, they will lean toward developing technologies that try to harmonize with that creation instead of interfering with it. They will not see natural resources as something to strip-mine for profit maximization alone. Advanced civilizations that lose this sense of connection to a transcendent realm of value, which over the past two hundred years has been all of them, seem to slowly lose their *raison d'être*. Civilizations grown too large and haughty self-destruct, taking populations with them while inflicting increased damage on their surroundings.

Returning to Chapter 5, one of the things we shall see is that there are arguments against materialism that have nothing to do with anyone's religion. Materialist-guided intellectual research has failed to illuminate how consciousness and conscious self-awareness, with many of its properties such as the apprehension of language, can be generated by physical organic systems, the human brain and central nervous system. That consciousness and conscious self-awareness is an emanation of a properly functioning brain *only* has become one of the central sacred cows of the "scientific philosophy" of our time—despite the "hard problem of consciousness" (articulated by David Chalmers) and the rise of the "new mysterianism" (Colin McGinn's phrase) which ought to be seen as red flags highlighting the manifest failure of materialist approaches in the area of professional philosophy known as the philosophy of mind. The "new mysterianism" amounts to Third Stage philosophers throwing up their hands in gestures of despair in the absence of a viable scientific explanation—while still insisting on a dogma!

Moreover, and even more controversially: in a subsequent section of Chapter 5, and despite the belligerent attacks on alternatives such as intelligent design, we will see that despite over a century of efforts, we have *no* substantial empirical evidence that life can originate from nonlife. We have no evidence, either statistical or laboratorial, that it *could* happen. This, in fact, is a far worse problem than anything to do with Darwinian evolution *per se*. If naturalist-premised investigations have turned up no viable explanation for how life got started in the first place, there is little point in pursuing a critique of Darwinism, for there is no viable explanation for the coming into existence of entities on which Darwinian natural selection can operate.

Finally, to close out this core chapter, we argue that in all likelihood, by attempting to "explain" all cognitive activity in terms of brain function, including the rational adjudication of claims about reality and about the possibilities of rational adjudication as a process, materialism and naturalism radically undermine themselves from within. They are destroyed by their own internal logic. If one begins with their premises, one reaches the result that there is no reason to believe our cognitive faculties to be reliable and trustworthy guides in discovering any truth about the world. We are left without reason to believe the premise that materialism and naturalism are reliable or trustworthy, resulting in a kind of Pyrrhonian paralysis. Our argument ends with a *reductio ad absurdum* of the materialist worldview.

All of this can be accomplished without *mentioning* anyone's God, or Christian theology, or a Christian worldview. This is important because (1) many critiques of materialism clearly *do* have religious motivations, and (2) it is easy to think, therefore, that such observations can be generalized to *any* criticism of materialism whatsoever.

I will argue that the shoe is actually on the other foot. Materialist views of science have become core portions of a secular faith—what we will come to call the Grandiose Assumption—that materialism equals science and reason, and that science and reason equal materialism. One thinks also of that rather adolescent movement of recent years: the New Atheism (Richard Dawkins, Sam Harris, Christopher Hitchens, et al.). I will recommend that this also be put aside, its first premise being an illusion steeped in the faith that the Grandiose Assumption is now the only place to begin our inquiries about the way the world is.

Philosophy and the Future: the Challenge of the Present.

With an exemplar of worldview criticism under our belts, Chapter 6 concludes this book by undertaking a discussion of how philosophy can rise to the occasion of becoming an identifier and critic of worldviews.

Here we face major challenges.

Can philosophy rise to the occasion? This will be the topic of this book's final chapter.

At first glance, with the vast majority of serious philosophy confined to academia, this seems unlikely. Perverse incentives and an array of other structural forces are arrayed against it. Some may already be thinking that the brand of intellectual independence called for here could be career-destroying and therefore unrealistic. One need only consider the plight of a work force over half of which now consists of adjunct faculty—*contingent* faculty, if one prefers, part-timers working for wages so low that many must turn eventually to other lines of work—and who are therefore hardly in a position to undertake any of the recommendations put forth here. Such people dare not rock any intellectual boats even if they are so inclined if they want to survive in academia, and even then there are no guarantees.

Suffice it to say, the present state of affairs is not good for this or any other philosophical investigation aspiring to reassure anyone that philosophy is not dead. We could approach the situation in academic philosophy just by asking, *Where are the present generation's Russells, its Wittgensteins, its Ayers, its Quines, its Rawlses, its Nozicks, its Davidsons, its Searles, its Kripkes—or even its Kuhns or Feyerabends or Rortys?*

Whether through agreement or disagreement in varying degrees, their ideas and writings demanded—and received—engagement. Nearly all are gone. Most are no longer living. There are very few visible figures of that caliber under the age of seventy (Saul Kripke, possibly the youngest logician and metaphysician of any stature, is in his mid-seventies as of this writing), especially in the United States. David Chalmers is in his fifties, but he's Australian. The United Kingdom has produced a handful of thinkers under seventy, such as Tim Williamson and Nick Bostrom. Such figures stand out because they are rare. There are a few notable European figures still living who might be comparable outside the analytic school, such as the French founder of "*Nouveau Philosophes*" Bernard-Henri Levi (entering his seventies), or the Slovenian philosopher Slavoj Žižek (roughly the same age). Thus even in Europe, traditionally a hotbed of adventurous thinking, younger generations able to carry the torch have been rendered invisible if they exist at all.

The appearance: there are few trained philosophers whose output approximates even the *least* of the accomplishments of those listed above. There is a great deal of *paper* out there. There are probably more philosophy journals than ever before, the online environment simplifying their production. Most are filled with borderline-unreadable exercises in micro-specialization. Speaking as an ex-academic, I can certify: most of it isn't worth the attempt. There are thousands of blogs devoted to philosophy, some to this or that branch of the subject or this or that philosophical problem. A handful are worth following, but most are little more than exercises in narcissism and self-indulgence. There are probably a few philosophical gems out there, buried in the digital clutter and unnoticed. There are, of course, many talented philosophy *teachers*. I am talking about the discipline's intellectual *leadership*, or major *practitioners*. Philosophy *teachers* will not be able to do much about the issues to be discussed here if either they are off the tenure line or even if they have tenure but are in departments threatened with elimination due to budget cuts. There are already cases of philosophy departments succumbing to the budgetary axe.

How can philosophy resuscitate itself in this kind of environment?!

The answer begins by acknowledging that philosophy must change its methods and some of its allegiances, or it will be unable to survive either inside or outside the Secular University in our rapidly changing environment. In such cases, the Stephen Hawkings and Neil deGrasse Tysons of the world will be vindicated, but not for the reasons they cite!

Philosophers of the future, if there are to be such, must therefore get outside their comfort zones. They must get out of academic bubbles. They must adopt bolder agendas. In Chapter 6, I offer two proposals on how to go about this.

First, they must *take matters into their own hands*, write proactively, and not wait for or expect approval from within academia. They must become marketers of ideas writing clearly about real problems for real audiences and suggest solutions. They must become *thought leaders*. I provide a few examples, such as the revival of interest in Stoicism.

Second, philosophers must offer a *compelling vision*.

We will have walked through four (not three) Stages of civilization, finding ourselves presently in an unstable amalgam of the Third and Fourth Stages. The Third consists of a few who cling to Enlightenment thought, the New Atheists, and the multitude of micro-specialists. The Fourth has devolved from postmodernism through identity politics to the present cult of "woke" which seeks, irrationally and destructively, to "cancel" every element of the past that might hurt someone's feelings

Philosophers must get past all this and offer the way to what I will call a Fifth Stage of civilization. This will mean (among other things):

Ceasing to be intellectually handmaidens to the sciences.

Ceasing to "virtue signal" to the purveyors of identity politics as if this truly gained them respect (it does not).

Refusing, that is, to kowtow to the cult of "woke."

And then learning to market themselves and a body of ideas that really will matter to audiences across a world in crisis seeking answers.

This will not be easy or comfortable—it has not been easy or comfortable for *me*—but it will be necessary if philosophy is to remain alive and transform itself into an effective force for good in the world.

A Fifth Stage of civilization would be the first to be built consciously, and cautiously, from fragmentary thoughts that have been laying around disconnected from one another as if seeking consolidation. While taking care not to offer one more unworkable Utopia, philosophers could draw on many materials available even if their authors do not self-identify as philosophers. In Chapter 6 we will delve into some of these. Due to space limits, we won't get into all of them.

We mentioned Stoicism, the starting point of which is an all-important distinction between what we can control and what we can't, with the admonition to focus on the former, leaving the latter aside. Stoicism thus offers an excellent entry-point into any discussion of how *philosophy* can be made relevant to *life*, from daily living to planning for the future to the larger issues of our time beginning with *taking a stand for truth*.

Then there is *systems theory*, which offers a gold mine of insights on areas ranging from theories of reality to doing what is best for the planet to keeping families together to reducing one's stress, and therefore again connects with the problems of life. Systems automatically try to maintain stability both within themselves and with their environment, but face a variety of sources of potential disruption. Nassim Nicholas Taleb has produced works of immense value; his concepts of "black swan events" and, to a slightly lesser extent, "anti-fragility," have crept into popular discourse.[53] The above-mentioned Dmitry Orlov is a nonacademic essayist who deserves to be read for his useful insights into what is presently disrupting America and the world.[54] These writers sometimes (*often*, in Orlov's case) add an element philosophers often omit, thinking it unimportant: *humor*, without which we are *truly* lost!

For the larger picture of neoliberal capitalism, those seeking to focus on how global political economy actually works, with insights into real colonialism, might turn to a work such as John Perkins's *Confessions of an Economic Hit Man* (2004) and its follow-up (2016). Ask: are there philosophical insights to be gleaned about where we are, in our materialist world, from the willingness of those with immense amounts of money to throw around to exploit and destroy the lives and cultures of the moneyless and therefore powerless?

To find out if there might be alternatives to a growth-centered money economy and to GDP as a measure of economic health, one might examine Helena Norberg-Hodge's *Ancient Futures: Lessons From Ladakh for a Globalizing World* (1991, 2009). Ask if there are philosophical insights to be found in the destructive effects market capitalism had on this people, and whether this system, whatever its presumed strengths in the West, is the right system for all peoples everywhere.

If you have a taste for science fiction and you want insight into how the combination of government, corporate media, and academia work together

---

53. Taleb, *Black Swan*; Taleb, *Anti-Fragile*.
54. Cf. Orlov, *Five Stages of Collapse*.

to create a kind of artificial reality, the goal of which is control over mostly captive masses driven by the so-called "free market" to obey and consume, watch *The Matrix* (1999) or a predecessor with essentially the same message (but with plot holes and a much weaker ending), *They Live* (1988). For what a certain fraction of work has become during our Third and Fourth Stage amalgamation, track down *Bullshit Jobs: A Theory* (2018) by British anthropologist David Graeber.

In a real sense, we are encircled by an empire. In an empire, there is little that ordinary people can control. The most they can do is become as informed as possible and learn from others and from experience what kinds of mindsets, thoughts, and actions will expand what they can control in their personal spaces.

Such states of affairs are not new. Stoicism was founded in ancient Greece but drew its largest following in the Roman Empire, its major expositors ranging across the spectrum from a freed slave (Epictetus) to an emperor (Marcus Aurelius) and in between (Seneca). Stoicism provides carefully thought-out suggestions for how to live in an encircling and repressive societal order in which the individual person actually controls very little. In an empire in long-term decline, drawing their strength from coercion and violence, Stoicism might hold appeal. It shouldn't be surprising that it has made a comeback in the hands of competent writers such as Ryan Holiday, whose bestselling books have titles like *The Obstacle Is the Way* (2014) and *Stillness Is the Key* (2019). We shall be revisiting the Stoics in Chapter Six when we consider what philosophers can do to broaden their appeal today, in preparation for tomorrow.

Philosophers can absorb all these insights, integrate them, build on them, and set their sights on a new goal: transcending this unstable amalgamation in thinking about a Fifth Stage of civilization—hopefully before we all pay the costs of not doing so. We who self-identify as philosophers ought to draw on them nevertheless, for we should accept valid insights where we can find them. We should use what we find to begin building a better "professional philosophy," one that matters because it connects with the world outside the academy and provides a platform (not necessarily in the technological, Web-based sense) venue where peoples, philosophers or not, can discuss what is important to them, of value to them, and what will make their lives and the world as a whole better. Including where they differ about such matters, and why.

This could be the key to a better future. There may, of course, be little that can be done to stop the major anti-intellectual and destructive trends at this point. It sounds apocalyptic, but Third Stage civilization has doomed itself, and the Fourth Stage is not capable of changing course. I will sketch the outlines of a prospective Fifth Stage of civilization at the end of this work. We can position ourselves to guide its development, via the reconstruction and development of sustainable communities based on a sound worldview, one which recognizes the intrinsic value of all human persons and the need for a connection to the transcendent. The idea for sustainable communities to be proposed here will differ from what is being proposed now under that term, as will the results, should such communities actually be built.

A Fifth Stage of civilization will set about to end the sense of encirclement (by technology, by government, by the kind of political economy where money is the end-all, be-all, and gets the last word). Systems thinker and pioneering futurist R. Buckminster Fuller observed back in the early 1970s that we had the technology then to feed every man, woman, and child on the planet. So why aren't we doing it? The answer is that we have presumed scarcity, rather than trying to work toward a world of actual abundance. We can develop science and technology in ways that yield abundance, instead of preserving and maintain systems based on a presumption of eternal scarcity, for profit maximization. Instead, too, of the encirclements, distractions, and screen-addictions, the most visible fruits of the present-day technosphere.

But with this, we are ahead of ourselves. If you're still reading, your next action step is to turn the page and begin Chapter 1: how philosophy has conceived of itself in both past and present, and then, how it—and we—got ourselves into our present predicament. For my premise is that understanding where we've been is key to understanding where we want to go and how we might strategize on how to get there.

1

What Is This Thing Called *Philosophy*?

Getting Started

What should philosophy do? is, or should be, a perennial question for those who self-identify as philosophers. Unlike sciences such as physics or biology whose domain of inquiry is reasonably clear, philosophy's first problem is itself: its subject matter, its aims or goals, and its methods.

Thus before we can answer the question of what philosophy should do, we need a working answer to at least one prior question: what is this thing called *philosophy*? What is its proper subject matter or domain? What are its aims or goals? What methods should it embrace? What (if anything) should it shun?

A thorough discussion of the subject in its present state is likely to elicit additional questions, not all of them comfortable as we have already seen. Why should philosophy exist at all? What does it contribute to a world driven by science, technology, and commerce (except trouble)? What does it truly contribute to the lives of those of us who find it endlessly fascinating but nevertheless befuddling to the majority of nonphilosophers

Some of the latter doubtless see philosophers as wasting precious time and resources on pointless questions with no answers, or problems with no decisive solutions? What right do we have to prattle on about "philosophical problems" when there are *real* problems crying out for *real* solutions?

Heck, there are real problems right on university campuses, e.g., skyrocketing tuition costs and the student loan debt crisis, which affect far more people than the more highly publicized controversies over free speech on campus. And then there is the adjunct crisis, driven by a variety of factors starting with the overproduction of PhDs in a multinational professional environment in which there are far more PhD-granting departments, not just in philosophy but across the humanities, than are necessary.

These have all occurred right under professional philosophy's collective nose.

We'll tackle the first few of these questions in this chapter. Hopefully, before we are done we will be in a better position to know what we are looking for even if we don't have working answers to all of them. So let's get started.

Everyone who has taught philosophy at the university level has probably introduced it etymologically: the word derives from the two Greek words *philo* ("love of") and *sophia* ("wisdom") which, when put together, mean *love of wisdom*. While this is a place to start, it never gets us very far. It elicits the further question, *What is wisdom?* which without a lot of preparation takes us off into the weeds. Better to ask what philosophy is by looking at what philosophers have done, historically, and see what this implies about their best answers to what the discipline is and should do.

Historically, we can identify *four* clear if sometimes overlapping answers to the question of what philosophy is, with implications for what it should do, what methods it should use, and what its place in the world should be. These are, respectively: (1) philosophy as *grand theory*, the attempt to articulate a systematic and comprehensive view of the world and everything in it; (2) philosophy as the *analysis of language* and the elimination of linguistic-originated mental confusions that made us believe there were philosophical problems when really there are not; (3) philosophy as the *attempt to describe the human condition*, honestly and with authenticity, smashing all the fundamentally inauthentic systems that came before; (4) philosophy as *inherently revolutionary*, because the point is not simply to describe or even just to explain the human condition but to change it.

Contemporary academic philosophy gives us a few more.

Philosophy As Grand Theory

Philosophy as grand theory seeks a *theory of everything*, a comprehensive and consistent theory of reality as a whole, including our place in it and how we should live our lives and order our societies. We also see this tradition also variously called *speculative philosophy* or *theoretical philosophy* or *systematic philosophy*.

Philosophers as grand theorists start with a seeming constant in human experience or what seemed to be a necessary first premise in all our reasoning. Thales of Miletus, the earliest Greek philosopher of record, did the former when he stated (roughly) that *Water is the first principle of all things*. The very ubiquity of water—its presence all around us, its being necessary for life, its role in central activities of society such as agriculture—seemed to qualify it as first principle if there could be said to be such a thing.

Aristotle's *principle of noncontradiction* provides a case of the second, as the foundation of Aristotelian logic and cosmology. All contradictory judgments are necessarily false, Aristotle reasoned, and the principle needn't be proven both because *the very idea of a proof presupposes it*: without it our words or signs can mean anything. Language becomes nonsensical and useless. Rational discourse becomes impossible.

Thus the emergence of *foundationalism* at the core of grand theory: philosophy sought *foundations* or *starting points* or *first premises* (metaphysical, logical, eventually epistemological) and built edifices of reasoning on them.

Pivotal medieval philosopher and theologian Saint Thomas Aquinas's ambitious attempt to merge Aristotelian cosmology into Christianity, recorded in his *Summas*, offered a grand theory. The Christian God's existence as *Logos* and as Necessary First Cause as Aristotle had argued, and as the Old and New Testaments had had asserted ("In the beginning God created the heaven and the earth" [Gen 1:1]; "In the beginning was the Word, and the Word was with God, and the Word was God" [John 1:1]), became the grounding first premise not just of Christian theology and the larger culture of Christendom, but of all of philosophy and early science as well. Philosophy, Aquinas reasoned, could best be understood as "handmaiden" to theology. We seek to understand, that our faith might be strengthened.

Or consider the *cogito* of the next major pivotal philosopher, French rationalist René Descartes. Faced with the diverse cultures being discovered during the Age of Exploration, and with the skepticism put forth by his fellow French author, diplomat Michel de Montaigne, Descartes sought to revisit the whole enterprise of philosophy and provide a base or foundation of transcultural certitude that would ground all subsequent inquiry, from the sciences to Christian theology, applying universally to all peoples everywhere. This, arguably, was the initiator of Enlightenment thought, in the very assumption that it was possible for the individual human mind to raze all its premises and conclusions to the ground and start over.

As everyone knows, Descartes did this, famously invoking an *evil deceiver* instead of the *morally perfect Christian God* to justify even the razing of mathematics and geometry. He'd set out to discover *one thing* that seemed immune to doubt regardless of whether he was sleeping or awake, and which would be invulnerable even to the evil deceiver. Then we could rebuild our intellectual achievements to date on this starting point.

Cartesian method took him to the infamous *cogito*, whereas *I think, I exist, is necessarily true every time I pronounce it* (in his *Meditations on First*

Philosophy which many introductory philosophy students are assigned to read). Thus he exists, as an autonomous *thinking thing*: a mental entity (comprised of mental or incorporeal *substance*) with ideas, including the idea of a God whose existence proves to be rationally necessary and who by nature is not a deceiver (the Cartesian ontological argument).

What ensues is an account of the general trustworthiness of the senses and our ability to correct what errors we make with our reason, in a universe with a God at its helm. Descartes believed he'd solidly grounded the emerging studies of the heavens on necessities of thought: the mark of a rationalist in the newly self-conscious branch of philosophy that came to be known as epistemology.

What might be worth noting is how, in Descartes's writings, even more than in those of Anselm of Canterbury and Aquinas, the rational human intellect is *epistemically prior to Christianity's God*. This changed everything— a point we will discuss at the appropriate time.

Grand theory, in whatever direction a theoretical philosopher took it, was *integrative*. It did not, in the end, separate logic, metaphysics, epistemology, theology, ethics, and eventually political philosophy. All were part of the single grand system. Conclusions supplied by one philosophical domain had logical implications for those of others, so that (for example) a Christian philosophical foundation had implications for society's institutions and overall ordering. More exemplars of this kind of philosophy include Hobbes, Locke, Kant, Hegel, the Whitehead of *Process and Reality*, and possibly a contemporary figure such as Hungarian émigré Ervin Laszlo when he was writing *The Systems View of the World* (1972).

There have been almost as many such grand theories as there have been grand theoreticians in philosophy, however. This is a reason philosophy as grand theory began, very slowly, to lose ground during the 1700s as Enlightenment thought developed and its allegiances began to shift from rationalist grand theory towards empirical natural science—or *natural philosophy* as Newton and Hume called it (to distinguish it from *moral* philosophy).

For during the Newtonian 1700s, physical science was not just gaining traction by offering seemingly viable answers to longstanding questions about the nature of physical reality while philosophers spun their wheels, it was starting to have myriad applications (energy generation, propulsion, and more).

Hence the growing sense among philosophers themselves that grand theorizing as a method for philosophy was inadequate. Natural science had worked out methods for testing its ideas against experience and experiment, whereas philosophers tended to work from pure reasoning, as Descartes had done, and sometimes seemingly from little more than imagination. Science thus more and more began to nudge philosophy aside, a process that spanned the 1800s and was all but complete in major intellectual centers by 1900.

What was philosophy to do?

Philosophy As Analysis

A *second* view gained steady ground in the 1800s and became dominant in the English-speaking world in the 1900s. This was the view that *philosophy is the logical analysis of language*, leaving grand theory behind in order to undertake the painstaking effort to sort out the many confusions based on misuses of language implicit in much grand theory.

Thus *analytic philosophy*, or *philosophical analysis*, whose defenders held that philosophy *could not be more than this*.

Implicit here is the idea that many "traditional problems of philosophy," e.g., about the fundamental nature of reality, or about "free will," or even about the existence of a God, are unanswerable on their own terms. Neither science nor philosophy could tackle them effectively, because they were fundamentally confused. They involved unclear or mistaken uses of language. In the future, empirical science would *solve what was solvable*. Philosophy as analysis would *dis*solve the rest, having revealed their linguistic confusion and explained how we got confused.

By the mid-1900s, charting the logical properties of language, e.g., its semantics, the study of how language "hooks onto" the objects of experience, had become an end in itself rather than an attempt at dissolving the pseudo-problems of the past. Some analytic philosophers worked on such projects as a completed *formal semantics of natural language*.[1] Focus on—interest in—the "traditional problems of philosophy" had faded into the academic woodwork except as logical exercises taught to students. "Ordinary language" philosophy drew finer and finer distinctions within the linguistic "geography" of common speech: the many forms it takes, the many purposes it serves (asking questions, giving commands, telling stories, expressing feelings, offering speculations, ridiculing those who speculate differently, and sometimes issuing threats, none of which are true or false as such), and the many applications including to traditional areas of philosophy such as ethics.

The analytic tradition initially drew on the mathematical logic of Peano, DeMorgan, and Frege, the leading mathematicians and logicians of the 1800s. Frege in particular had drawn attention to logical and semantic "puzzles"

---

1. See, e.g., Nute, *Essential Formal Semantics*.

within natural language, often in light of scientific discovery, such as the seeming paradox of the empirical discovery of what, for philosophers, was a statement of a logical identity, that the *morning star* is the same as the *evening star*, as these two phrases refer to the same object, the planet Venus. That they do so was a discovery of modern astronomy, not of philosophical deduction. So is the statement of their identity *analytic* or *synthetic*?

Kant had bequeathed to philosophy the infamous cleavage between analytic and synthetic judgments, which sharpened Leibniz's earlier one between truths of logic and truths of fact, and Hume's division of meaningful statements into relations of ideas and matters of fact. The former were true structurally, by logic or by stipulated definition, and did not add to our *knowledge* of the world. The latter were empirical, and when true, manifestly *did* add to our knowledge. What puzzled Frege was how empirical science could deliver an analytic truth into our hands. His effort to resolve the quandary for all practical purposes began the analytic tradition in philosophy, with his conclusion that descriptive terms had the same *referent* but different *senses*. His famous article "On Sense and Nominatum" (sometimes translated from the German as "Of Sense and Reference") is essential reading for anyone seeking to understand the origins of twentieth century analytic philosophy.[2]

Thus began the positioning of philosophy on new ground, and with new aims. The analytic school made its way into the hands of luminaries such as Bertrand Russell and G. E. Moore, the former doing logic, linguistic analysis, and epistemology, while the latter began studying the *language* of ethics (thus inventing *meta*-ethics).

Philosophical analysis was not new, of course. The Socrates of Plato's dialogues had often turned his attention to analyzing words such as *virtue* and *piety* (*Meno* and *Euthyphro* respectively) after all, and questions of what such terms referred to were very much in evidence. The *Theaetetus* contains detailed analyses. It would be wrong to say that the philosophers of grand theory *ignored* the role of language and its logical structure in their endeavors. It was not their central focus, however. It was a means to grander ends. In the hands of Frege, Russell, Moore, and their proteges, this changed. By the 1920s such matters had become the central focus in professionalized *academic* philosophy in Great Britain, and had begun making incursions in American academic philosophy. Logical analysis of language became a powerful tool developed by Russell and Whitehead (in their *Principia Mathematica*), Moore in his *Principia*, and then Russell's genius student Wittgenstein in the *Tractatus Logico-Philosophicus*.

2. In Martinich and Sosa, *Analytic Philosophy*, 7–18.

Flourishing in the background was the *positivism* of Auguste Comte and Ernst Mach, building on Hume's empiricist criticism of metaphysics and the sense of a coming changeover in physical science prompted by, e.g., the Michelson-Morley experiment of 1887. In aggregate, these seemed to demolish grand theory in philosophy. Mach criticized the metaphysical components of Newtonian theoretical physics and sought their elimination. Some philosophers (Paul Feyerabend is an example whose thought we will also take up later) argued that this kicked open the door to the replacement of Newtonian physics and its absolutist notions of space, place, mass, etc., by Einsteinian special and general relativity theories and its very different (incommensurable) concepts. Comte's focus was broader. He sought the groundwork for an endeavor that would use the empirical science he'd founded, sociology, to apply scientific method to every area of society. Academic philosophers, who were increasingly the *only* philosophers to be seen or heard from, eagerly engaged new scientific ideas as their discipline became, increasingly, a "handmaiden" to science. The philosophy of science was born.

Integrating logical-linguistic analysis with the idea of philosophy as "handmaiden" to science was inevitable, and gave rise to the logical positivism of the developing Vienna Circle in the first two decades of the 1900s. Alfred Jules (A. J.) Ayer brought Viennese positivism to England and became its chief evangelist, especially when his key tract *Language, Truth and Logic* came out in the mid-1930s. Being mostly Jewish, other logical positivists were fleeing the Nazis and coming to the Unite States. Despite their thick German accents and residual anti-Semitism on our side of the Atlantic, they took English-speaking academia by storm, soon controlling the major departments and academic journals (founding a few more of their own). Major American universities from Harvard to Pittsburgh became their homes.

Analytic philosophy has remained dominant in the English-speaking world, though not without challenge as we'll see. Like grand theory did, it changed over time, often in response to its own results. Its *formal* or *ideal language* variant saw philosophy as bringing formal logic to the analysis of justification in science as well as to those "traditional problems of philosophy." As Wittgenstein put it near the conclusion of the *Tractatus*, the proper method of philosophy would be: "Whenever someone . . . wanted to say something metaphysical, to demonstrate to him that he had failed to give a meaning to certain signs in his propositions."[3]

Although Wittgenstein was no positivist, the movement swung such notions like wrecking balls against the cognitive meaningfulness of such

3. Wittgenstein, *Tractatus*, 6.53.

questions as whether God exists, whether religion is necessary for morality, whether "free will" conflicts with "determinism," whether "the mind" is something other than the brain, and so on. Key was Ayer's verification principle: the correct starting point was to divide all cognitively meaningful propositions into analytic and empirical. Propositions not fitting into either were cognitively meaningless. They were, at best, emotive. Thus Ayer's "ethical emotivism" and later variants on noncognitivist meta-ethics starting from the view that ethical ascriptions did not refer to real properties of things or states of affairs; they expressed something about *us*, be it our emotional responses, our desires, our prescriptions, our preferences, etc. What they were *not* is true or false, as with empirical statements in the sciences.

We've already seen that this ideal language approach fell out of favor, especially in the hands of the later Wittgenstein. It soon fell out of favor for analysts of science. The story is too long to do more than scratch the surface here, and in any event has been told compellingly elsewhere.[4] Ideal language analytic philosophy had proved too truncated. By the 1940s and 1950s it had generated curiosities such as Carl Hempel's "paradox of the ravens" and Nelson Goodman's aberrant predicates "grue" and "bleen," also called the "new riddle of induction."[5]

With the former, logical equivalences such as the contraposition of universal affirmatives, alongside the realization that an observation statement confirming a given universal affirmative also confirmed its contrapositive, seemed to permit the seeming confirmation of any conditional proposition by any observation statement whatsoever. I.e., *my printer is red* being a non-raven and a non-black thing, it confirms, *All non-black things are non-ravens*, the contrapositive of *All ravens are black*. So an observation statement about my printer confirms that all ravens are black. Intuition alone should tell us something is wrong, because this is silly. With the "new riddle of induction," absent an *a priori* (and hence nonempirical) principle of simplicity, observation statements that confirm *All emeralds are green* also confirm *All emeralds are grue*. The aberrant predicate *grue* (x is green before time t in the future but blue after t) seemed logically ineliminable even if scientific practice never formulated much less tested such theories.

The empiricism of "scientific philosophy" was in trouble. Its own tools of analysis—perhaps it was "analysis paralysis"—were undermining it from within.

4. See, e.g., Brown, *Perception, Theory, and Commitment*.

5. Hempel, "Studies in the Logic of Confirmation," 1–20; Hempel, "Studies in the Logic of Confirmation II," 97–121. See Goodman, *Fact, Fiction and Forecast*.

Wittgenstein's influence was waiting in the wings. Wittgenstein, who had left academia philosophy after publishing the *Tractatus* only to return with a fresh batch of ideas, was one of the very few philosophers to produce two entirely different philosophical approaches, the second of which was an incisive criticism and rejection of the first. There was continuity between the "two Wittgensteins." The later Wittgenstein set forth the view that "philosophy is a battle against the bewitchment of our intelligence by means of language."[6] But he remained silent about those things of which the earlier Wittgenstein had averred "we must be silent."[7]

Wittgenstein, unlike most of his colleagues and protégés, had read and absorbed writers from Kierkegaard and Rilke to Tolstoy into his overall outlook. This gave him an earnestness not seen elsewhere, and not understood by those who embraced what they thought of as his devotion to "ordinary language." *Natural language philosophy*, we might call it, started with his lectures in the 1940s and continued to develop in the hands of philosophers such as Peter F. Strawson, Gilbert Ryle, J. L. Austin, William Alston, John Searle, and others.

These men, alongside those of a more "scientific" bent such as J. C. C. Smart, would pioneer the *philosophy of mind* which began by asking, are there any distinctive *marks of the mental* compelled by any clear and sensible understanding of the words and phrases we used to talk about consciousness, sensations, sense data as "units" of experience, perception, knowledge, and so on? Were there any good reasons for thinking our cherished beliefs about a putative difference between *mind* and *brain* came down to more than matters of *vocabulary*, perhaps akin to our saying colloquially that *the sun is rising* when we know from modern astronomy that it isn't doing anything of the sort. Were there any reasons for thinking a materialist account of cognition would prove inadequate, even if mid-twentieth-century knowledge of brain functions was only promissory? Science had advanced by leaps and bounds in physics and biology and in the social sciences. Why would our understanding of our own cognitive faculties be different?

Philosophy's theoretical pretenses had been all but abandoned to the sciences whose instruments, conceptual and physical, seemed better equipped to explore even the domains of human thought. Some might argue that Saul Kripke reinstated a version of grand theory beginning in the 1970s with his possible worlds semantics,[8] but grand theory in this sense—if that's even the right phrase at this point—is very much a product of analysis

---

6. Wittgenstein, *Philosophical Investigations*, 109.
7. Wittgenstein, *Tractatus*, 7.
8. Cf. Kripke, *Naming and Necessity*.

and constrained by it: *analytic metaphysics* was a phrase bandied about back in the day as a sign that the subject had broken free of the logical positivist-empiricist straitjacket. Most Anglophone philosophers continued to focus on the language used to talk about knowledge, mind, etc., although more and more were drawing excitedly on a range of findings in modern linguistics, cognitive psychology, biology, and brain research. A unified science of cognition seemed on the horizon, and a number of philosophers saw their discipline as ideally merging with it. Stephen Stich, and Paul and Patricia Smith Churchland, are exemplars.[9]

Summarizing: the natural language school saw philosophy's past departures from our natural or "ordinary" ways of using terms such as *knowledge, certainty, perception,* and so on as causing confusion. Back in the *Tractatus* Wittgenstein had observed that "In philosophy the question, 'What do we actually use this word or this proposition for?' repeatedly leads to valuable insights."[10] The working assumption was that distinctively *philosophical* problems arose from logical or semantic error or "language going on holiday," another Wittgensteinian phrase, this time from *Philosophical Investigations*.[11] Or just the possibility that the developing cognitive sciences hadn't advanced far enough. The "problems" promised to vanish when the linguistic confusions are sorted out *and* when cognitive science was brought to bear on them.

This approach to philosophy seemed unnaturally limited, however, even as it continued to spread in American institutions. Some observers were acutely uncomfortable with it, and it occasioned articles with titles like, "American Philosophy Is Dead."[12] Recall, from the Introduction, what Wittgenstein himself had written to Norman Malcolm. While the analytic tradition surely offered some powerful techniques, something seemed missing!

Where, in any of this, were "the problems of everyday life"?

The history of philosophical ideas in a broad sense discloses at least one tradition that focused primarily on the everyday experience of the individual person in a world he found himself "thrown into, not having been asked." The results were not always pretty.

---

9. Cf. Stich, *From Folk Psychology to Cognitive Science*; Churchland, *Scientific Realism and the Plasticity of Mind*; Churchland, *Neurophilosophy*.
10. Wittgenstein, *Tractatus*, 6.211.
11. Wittgenstein, *Philosophical Investigations*, 1.38.
12. Feuer, "American Philosophy Is Dead," 31.

Existentialism and Modern Civilization

This third approach was being pursued across the English Channel, and it probably became more widespread in spirit than is generally recognized. Unlike speculative grand theory and painstaking linguistic analysis, existentialism spread into both "highbrow" and popular cultures. By the 1940s the term was regularly bandied about in trendy French cafés and even in some American ones by scruffy-appearing men who wore dark clothing, rarely smiled, and smoked too many cigarettes (some as we'll see were heavy drinkers as well).

Existentialism de-emphasizes grand theory and analysis in favor of *attempts to describe the human condition.* Existentialist writers portrayed human beings, sometimes themselves and sometimes characters in fiction, as "trapped" in the world itself, like flies on flypaper, or in some cases, "trapped" within structures of civilization experienced as inauthentic (dishonest, including within themselves).

The list of exemplars of existentialism usually begins with Søren Kierkegaard's unique post-Kantian and anti-Hegelian Christianity of the early 1800s. The individual believer stands in his smallness, finiteness, and isolation before an infinite and incomprehensible God whose existence he cannot prove; and also against corrupt and worldly institutions such as the Church of Denmark which have all but forgotten this God. Such institutions merit only denunciation, and Kierkegaard's wars of words with the Church of Denmark became legendary in their time. One also finds significant strands of existentialist thought in Russian writers such as Fyodor Dostoevsky, when one of the characters in *The Brothers Karamazov* ponders whether "if God is dead then everything is permitted" (not an exact wording but the basic idea). Friedrich Nietzsche, whose pivotal ideas we will explore, openly pondered the consequences of the sentence *God is dead* for modern man.

Although one can find twentieth-century theologians classifiable as existentialist in a broad sense (e.g., Karl Jaspers, Karl Barth, Gabriel Marcel, and Martin Buber among others), by and large existentialist philosophers tended to be atheists—choosing to believe in a supernatural god accomplished nothing for the human predicament, which was choice in a world experienced as chaotic and absurd. Consider the atheist *Weltschmerz* of Jean-Paul Sartre or the absurdism of Albert Camus. Influential American literary figures of the early twentieth century wrote fiction and plays with what I would argue are definite existentialist overtones: F. Scott Fitzgerald, Ernest Hemingway, Samuel Beckett. Absurdism clearly reared its head in modern art before it appeared in literature. Think of Dadaism, that product of the devastating effects of the Great War (World War I) on the *Zeitgeist* of the late 1910s and 1920s which, during a period of rising prosperity and the sense of hedonism prosperity always seems to give rise to, would set the stage for Fitzgerald's and Hemingway's novels and short stories. Both lived unhappy lives. Fitzgerald considered himself a failure as a writer, reduced to writing "popular" pieces for Hollywood consumption to survive financially. He died in his late forties of a heart attack, but arguably had already severely damaged his health with alcohol. Hemingway, meanwhile, was almost surely the greatest stylist the United States will ever produce. Clearly, however, he experienced lifelong restlessness, poured out in his writing when not adventuring. He drank heavily as he turned out masterful short stories and novels depicting our fundamental lostness, and our need to stand defiantly against an indifferent and sometimes hostile universe. Finally, suffering from deteriorating health and worsening eye problems, he committed suicide in 1961.

What do we mean, *absurdism*? We mean that we humans seek a God, want immortality, or at least a sense of importance in the scheme of things, a sense that *our lives matter*, in a world that *metaphysically denies us each of these!* Life begins violently as we are thrust into the world at birth; it ends in death, violent and bloody if in war, and otherwise sometimes just lingering and painful, leaving loved ones in sorrow. In between there is often much suffering and frustration of our most meaningful aspirations. And after death, what? Nothing? This was the conclusion suggested by modern science. Summation: life seemed destined to involve the living in a horror show at worst and a battle against chronic boredom at best, interrupted by periodic pleasantries such as drunkenness and fornication, and perhaps mitigated by artistic or literary works for those able to create them.

Existentialists occasionally penned massive treatises such as Heidegger's *Being and Time* or Sartre's *Being and Nothingness*. Interest in the former remained mostly confined to academia because he wrote no fiction. The latter expressed his dark vision far more accessibly in novels such as *La Nausée* or plays such as *No Exit*. Camus's *L'Etranger* depicted Meursault, the Absurd Man, shooting an Arab man on a beach repeatedly for no discernable reason. Arrested, tried, and sentenced to death for his crime, at the end he lays open his indifferent heart which reflects the "the benign indifference of the universe."

Camus also penned the nonfiction essay "The Myth of Sisyphus" which pondered whether the most fundamental problem of philosophy was suicide, i.e., whether or not life was worth living. He did not conclude that we should take our own lives, of course. What he counseled was to reconcile life's basic absurdity—rejection of which amounts to living *inauthentically*—with finding within the absurdity spectacles to enjoy, love for another, and finding within ourselves the desire to minimize suffering in the world. Whatever else, we must make choices, and those choices become our essence. When we choose, Sartre would say, we define for ourselves what it means to be human ("*existence precedes essence*"), and we choose "in anguish" because when we choose for one we choose for *all*—we are saying that this is what it *means* to be human: an ethic glancing back, almost wistfully, at Kant's imperative.

The question seldom taken up by professional academics of any discipline: *To what extent did significant fractions of ensuing generations become "native" existentialists or absurdists?* While characters in the novels and plays of a few writers, e.g., the UK's Angry Young Men (e.g., playwright John Osborne, or novelists John Braine, John Wain, and Alan Sillitoe) would assert themselves in futile defiance of the world, the Beat Generation of the 1950s and the hippies of the late 1960s would take Camus up on his challenge. Their hedonistic appeals were just to enjoy life through enriching one's experiences living fully in the present.

This included using mind-altering (sometimes body-altering) recreational drugs. Aldous Huxley opened the door, so to speak, with his *The Doors of Perception* (1954) although drug experimentation had already begun apace. Think of Jack Kerouac and William S. Burroughs; or, by the start of the following decade, Timothy Leary's experiments with LSD and William Alport's forays into Eastern religions, renaming himself Ram Dass and advocating a philosophy of *Be Here Now* (1971), his main tract under the latter name. Hippie culture would embrace LSD ("acid") and incorporate its visions into their music, which they called "acid rock" (famous bands such as Pink Floyd, Jefferson Airplane, and The Doors who took their name from Huxley's book; or shorter-lived acts with bizarre names like The 13th Floor Elevators, Red Crayola, Strawberry Alarm Clock, Bubble Puppy, and so on).

By 1970, things were ending badly. Some rock musicians had "burned out" from brain damage, e.g., Syd Barrett, the original Pink Floyd singer. Others had died from drug-related mishaps. Elvis Presley had been the first highly visible figure to die courtesy of the rock 'n' roll lifestyle; in the early 1970s he was joined by Jimi Hendrix, Janis Joplin (of Jefferson Airplane), Jim Morrison (The Doors' lead singer), Gram Parsons, and others less known. The total number of rock musicians who have overdosed or sometimes committed suicide, as did Kurt Cobain in the 1990s, is surprisingly large. Public rock music shows, moreover, started out proclaiming peace but began to display a penchant for deadly violence, as with the infamous Altamont show on December 6, 1969, a free concert with the Rolling Stones headlining, patrolled by Hell's Angels, the motorcycle gang—bad judgment on a par with putting the Mafia in charge of bank deposits. Campus protests against the unpopular war in Vietnam turned horrifically violent with the Kent State killings on May 7, 1970, in which National Guard troops panicked, opened fire on a crowd of students, and killed four innocent bystanders, causing campuses to erupt nationwide.

The above three paragraphs may seem digressions but they are not. For one of my key assumptions, following Wittgenstein's remark to Malcolm, is that *we cannot neglect the effects of philosophical first premises on lives and on cultures or subcultures*—formulated explicitly or not. These interpenetrate one another, and have effects we can document. Or to put the matter in parallel to Wittgenstein's remark above: *What is the use of philosophy if it does not improve our thinking about culture/subcultures, about civilization, about its trajectories as disclosed by modern and recent history, and about what the future might bring if these trajectories hold? What is its use if it does not expose the ways our so-called leaders have sometimes used language to mislead, and if it does not expose the ways, whether through inattention or purposeful deception and self-deception, we've allowed ourselves to be misled, and sometimes misled one another?*

As a civilization, are we, or are we not, badly off course? is a question we will raise repeatedly in this essay in various contexts, as we explore the interplay between philosophical tendencies and the larger culture, between ideas and their consequences. The above events did not reflect what *everyone* was doing, obviously, just what the media of the day played up—because it was trendy and exciting (and because this made money for media corporations).

The trends of the 1960s, even the handful of beneficial ones, had no staying power. All were soon overtaken by other priorities, especially when Watergate came to light. The 1970s marched on. What had been a strong economy the decade before weakened substantially. Economic policy changed to accommodate changed conditions. Some of these changes made matters worse. Reagan came in 1980, and it was "morning in America." Arguably—a point we shall return to—by the 1980s the Western world had abandoned the idealism of the 1960s and became suffused with materialism. The corporate world embraced the neoliberal philosophy of Milton Friedman and his proteges: business is about profit maximization exclusively. For a while, this seemed to work and be worth promoting on a global scale, especially after the collapse of the Soviet Union. But the giddiness over "economic expansion" and wealth accumulation as ends in themselves, continuing into the 1990s and beyond into the 2000s, in itself masked growing despair, reflected in rising rates of mental illness and suicide, especially among the young and among those less susceptible to giddiness of chronic change that left them unable to control their economic destinies.

"System-Smashers"

An actual digression might be in order at this point. We might also divide historically major philosophers into two broad camps: *system-builders* and *system-smashers*. The architects of grand theory were system-builders. So were many analysts. They found the equivalent of grand theory in natural science instead of philosophy, and built their analytic systems using the tools of formal logic and the close study of language.

The system-smashers overlap with existentialists in spirit, agreeing in their attempts at *ruthless honesty* or *authenticity*. They did all they could to throw cold water on the idea of any kind of abstract approach to the world or human life. They are far more the antithesis of grand theory than is the analyst. While very aware of how language is used, system-smashers have little patience with philosophical analysis. Life is inherently *messy*, they seem to shout. Human institutions are messy, because human life isn't all that predictable. Even science—once they turned their attention to the philosophy of science—is far messier than any of its philosophical images. Are we going to accept and embrace messiness as a given, as a path to a richer existence, or continuing with self-deceptive theorizing?

The system-smasher posed a *de facto* dilemma, that is. Live in a mental prison of abstractions that negate life as it really is, or throw away the abstractions and embrace life's complexity and unpredictability as part of our commitment to an authentic existence. Abstractions supply anchors of various sorts. But life in the modern world had come to seem increasingly rudderless. A rudderless existence seems hazardous and even frightening at first glance. But in fact, it is pregnant with possibilities and opportunities.

Hence the system-smasher, taken on his own terms, was usually less pessimistic than the existentialist. On occasion he even seemed joyous!

Who were these system-smashers?

The earliest we know of were Plato's and Aristotle's nemeses the Sophists. Consider Thrasymachus who appeared in *The Republic* and opined that "justice is the will of the stronger party," because (once we've done the minimal analysis) the stronger party gets to define what *justice* means. Or Protagoras, the history of philosophy's first out-and-out relativist ("Man is the measure of all things"), because "human" experience differs vastly from person to person based on a multitude of factors.

Michel de Montaigne, mentioned briefly above, doubted the prevailing conclusions of his era. He was the system-smasher who pondered the implications of discoveries made during the early Age of Exploration, and wondered whether the ideas and beliefs of Europeans had anything special to recommend them. His writings worried Descartes and did much to motivate the latter's search for a bedrock of epistemological certainty and a full restoration of a metaphysics appropriate to a Christian civilization coming into scientific consciousness. The philosophical problematic shifted from metaphysics to epistemology, however, and what ensued is too well-known to recount here in any detail. Suffice it to say: the trajectory led straight to Hume's skeptical reasonings about causal reasoning as more than habits of thought, to Kant's system-building reiteration and then to Hegel's additional system-building incorporating historical change as a progression of dialectical developments that pulled in persons as pawns of these vast forces. Kierkegaard's system-smashing revolted against this notion and again situated the individual person and his subjectivity front and center, and we came almost full-circle.

Nietzsche is surely a modern system-smasher *extraordinaire*. He recognized that the "death of God" at the hands of Enlightenment philosophers and modern science meant the death of all those things to which God's existence had given meaning, including not just Christian but secular moralities that sought, without honestly acknowledging it, to place fundamentally Christian messages (e.g., equality, founded on the notion that all are equal before God; natural rights, etc.) on nontheistic foundations. Nietzsche's deconstructions were scathing and devastating. I am unconvinced that any of his interpreters, at least those I've encountered, fully appreciate *how* scathing and *how* devastating. Nietzsche sought to be liberating, to open the door for a fully new morality for *this* world, this "revaluation of all values" we've mentioned, an *actual* secular morality suited for life in an exclusively material world. Such a morality, he realized, would inevitably be based on the supremacy of those who had mastered the complexities of *this* world, leading invariably to the idea of the moral excellence of aristocracy and strength (not mere survival), and of vivacity and cunning—up to and including the masculine prowess of the warrior! These elements in Nietzsche are not the ones talked about by the professionals, of course. They prefer to emphasize Nietzsche's anti-Christian tendencies, or how he influenced Heidegger and later, Foucault, or how he prefigures postmodernist views of science with statements like, "it is just beginning to dawn on us that physics, too, is just an interpretation of the world."

The later Wittgenstein had definite if far more refined system-smashing tendencies, although they were mostly directed at the ideal language analytic philosophy to which he'd been a key contributor. A more powerful (and more public) linguistic system smasher was, of course, George Orwell with his ironic deconstructions of how language is used by totalitarians to manipulate and control. If one reads *1984*, one does not forget how his Ministry of Truth operates! By and large, academic philosophers have not wanted to take their analyses of natural language in directions that would challenge the dominant political economy and, by extension, their role in this political economy by virtue of their inhabiting a certain kind of institution and living a certain kind of life, all wrapped in specialized jargon. Euphemisms offer a potential goldmine of analytic exercises, all but unexplored by the unadventurous. Aldous Huxley's works also smash the Enlightenment-derived notions of the application of scientific technique to ourselves and our institutions as anything more than authoritarian instruments of population and mind control.

One might think of Kuhn's dissection of the positivist and empiricist images of science that still largely prevailed in the 1950s as a form of system-smashing in the doubts they raised about whether the enterprise is taking us closer and closer to something called "the truth" (understood as a complete and consistent description of reality as it is in itself, apart from any consensus or set of beliefs about it). Kuhn was joined, as we saw earlier, by other figures such as Toulmin, Hanson, and others who found positivism inadequate; one might also mention chemist-turned-philosopher Michael Polanyi, who stressed the personal commitment of the scientist to the premises embedded in his work.[13]

An even better roster of twentieth-century system-smashers would have to include Kuhn's one-time colleague from his days at UC-Berkeley, the iconoclastic Paul K. Feyerabend. Feyerabend's incisive critique of the very idea of an abstract method characteristic of all "good" (i.e., methodologically correct) science began making the rounds in the early 1960s, and even more so in the 1970s.[14] Feyerabend has often been characterized as "anti-science." This misgrasps his project, and the nature of system-smashing generally among those who take seriously the history of ideas. Feyerabend's work proposes the same choice: misleading and unhelpful abstractions, or the real world of particularity in all its messiness? Real science, he argues forcefully, does not and could not have followed the abstract methodologies proposed for it by twentieth-century philosophers of science, especially positivists and logical empiricists (but also Popperians and Kuhnians). Had thinkers such as Copernicus and Galileo been bound by rules requiring them to submit their basic ideas to empirical testability, or falsifiability, or consensus, or "peer review" (their "peers" being all Aristotelians and Church loyalists), they wouldn't have gotten anywhere! The Scientific Revolution itself wouldn't have been allowed to happen! A world about which we know less than we think, Feyerabend argues, calls for a

---

13. Polanyi, *Personal Knowledge.*
14. Feyerabend, *Against Method.*

proliferation of competing and sometimes mutually contradictory theories and methods for exploring it. We take an honest (authentic) look at the history, and we see more methodological opportunism than we thought was there if we weren't looking for it!

What helped inspire science in the past could improve it today, Feyerabend continues, through competing theories in, say, quantum mechanics or even competitors with Darwinian evolution in biology. What is arrogant and short-sighted—inauthentic—is to pretend that our present-day standpoint is somehow special, in lengthy and constantly changing sequences of historically embedded narratives toward which the past somehow pointed.

Behind Feyerabend's critique is still more. What really matters in life, and in society? Abstraction-dominated conceptions of "knowledge," or actual improvements in the flesh-and-blood human condition that might be made possible with a proliferation of ideas, theories, methods, and "forms of life" (a Wittgensteinian phrase—the later Wittgenstein's brand of system-smashing having been a key influence on Feyerabend's thought)? Feyerabend's views drew at least part of their impetus from larger tendencies current at the time, including civil rights and democratization more broadly, the struggle against an imperialist war, to the rising fascination with "alternative" ideas, whether associated with science or not. Critiques of modernity had arisen both outside and within philosophy. For again, looming like a colossus over all our thought—analytic, continental, existentialist, system-smashing, or otherwise—were the imposing structures of industrial civilization itself, especially its tendencies toward microspecialization, centralization, and hierarchy, guided by capitalist political economy as it had matured during the post-war years, with the very real encirclements around human life and limitations on freedom these involved whether faced honestly or not, and which prompted elements of the Marcusan rebellion (other rebellions as well).

These limitations have always given rise to restlessness of varying degrees and kinds. Even Max Weber's optimistic attempt to integrate Christian convictions with the "spirit of enterprise" of modern capitalist civilization ended with ominous references to its building, around the person born into its circumstances, an "iron cage."[15] For power systems suffuse it, their efficacy financial instead of political. This is their prime directive, for most ordinary people: integrate into hierarchies and cooperate with those controlling them from the top, or be without a job. And then you cannot pay for goods (e.g., food) and services (e.g., electricity). These are the encirclements we mentioned, surrounding every inhabitant of industrial civilization (even

---

15. Weber, *Protestant Ethic*.

those holding the financial levers). These systems *must* reach into the natural world since industrialism is inevitably extractive and confrontational in its approach to natural resource systems outside it (e.g., oil). And what cannot be made profitable is not pursued for long—except perhaps on the margins, by hobbyists.

Feyerabend understood these things. Others had gotten there long before him.

Marxism and (Often Versus) Its Step-Children

A *fourth* answer to the question, *What who*u*ld philosophy do?* was provided by *classical Marxism*. Karl Marx put it thus: "philosophers have hitherto only *interpreted* the world in various ways; the point is to change it" (*Theses on Feuerbach*).[16]

Classical Marxism—expressed in Marx's multi-volume life's work *Das Kapital*, both praised and denounced, and which he did not live to complete—viewed a society's philosophy and intellectual activity generally, and its political or governmental institutions, as emanating from its "superstructure," a result of its relations of production, invariably protecting and furthering them. The dominant political economy of Western civilization was, and remains, capitalism: based on accumulations of capital by private economic actors. Key to capitalism was ownership of the means of production (private property) by the bourgeois class, while the proletariat class owned only its capacity for labor (job skills of various sorts). These processes and relations—extraction of natural resources, capital accumulation, capital versus labor—have remained.

Marx's challenge to philosophers: recognize that class struggle, not ideas, is the driver of history and historical change, and that the state, academia, and other institutions protect the class that dominates through ownership of the relations of production. Turn attention from pointless disputation over the "traditional" philosophical problems to those who control capitalist relations and hence hold the reins of power. This would include gaining consciousness of how relations of production generate class consciousness, and thus make room for intellectual disputation among the privileged class.

Das Kapital was Marx's attempt at a detailed analysis of exactly how capitalist machinery works and how it affects its participants at every level. Marx never denied that capitalism was the greatest engine of production

---

16. Original German: "*Die Philosophen haben die Welt nur verschieden interpretirt; es kommt aber darauf an, sie zu verändern.*" Marx and Engels, *Karl Marx Friedrich Engels*, 5:20.

and growth ever seen. Where his thought went after this, remains controversial and contentious. Capitalism could produce wealth but not distribute it in any fair or equitable way, but the supposed *injustices* of capitalism weren't Marx's central focus. Rather, he considered capitalism *irrational*, wasteful of resources both human and natural: overproducing in some areas while neglecting crucial others if they were unprofitable. The inflictions it placed on the proletariat would eventually prompt organized rebellion and violent overthrow.

Elaborating: capitalism must grow, Marx contended, or fall into crisis. This is reflected in capitalist economists' obsession with *economic growth* as a measure of health. Capitalist endeavors had to profit to survive, and they profited more if they kept wages down. But if wages were lowered, absent sufficient growth workers had less money to spend on what capitalists produced. Capitalism's capacity to reinvent itself, e.g., with mechanisms such as credit spending, might have amazed (or dismayed) Marx. But as capitalism grew to global scale—a crucial point, as we will see—the divisions it would aggravate between a shrinking minority of haves (bourgeois elites) and the multitudes of have-nots (proletarian masses) would invite *world revolutionary consciousness*. This in turn would lead the have-nots to rise up against the haves. Capitalism would then be replaced by socialism, instituted as the *dictatorship of the proletariat* which would continue until capitalist relations of production and the institutions to which they gave rise had been eliminated. There would be nothing left for social classes to struggle over. The state had existed primarily to protect existing relations of production. With these eliminated and class distinctions vanished, the state would "wither away" and socialism would evolve into Communism: the actual "end of history."

With the collapse of the Soviet Union, Marxism became an object of ridicule outside academia and handfuls of enclaves in university towns. For Communism was dead, was it not? Had it not been one of the twentieth century's most spectacular flops? The "end of history" could be reconceived as the end of the ideological conflict that had given rise to the Cold War.[17]

Not so fast. More recently, and especially since the 2008 financial meltdown, interest in Marx's analysis of capitalism has returned. *What went wrong with Marxism?* is surely a valid question for philosophical as well as historical attention.

For Marx, too, had postulated specific stages historical development must go through. Marx had studied Hegelian dialectic, which must be understood in order to grasp what he was up to. Each stage or state

---

17. Cf. Fukuyama, *End of History*.

of affairs history goes through tends to generate opposites to dominant tendencies. For Marx: dominant institutions tended to generate opposing class interests. These inevitably clash. Out of that clash comes the next stage. In this way, agrarian feudalism gave rise to industrial capitalism as the rising bourgeoisie freed themselves from the chains of the feudal lords and landowners by producing their own wealth. Soon the bourgeoisie become a force to be reckoned with, and then the dominant force as the feudal lords were overthrown. The creation of bourgeoisie-dominated civilization would set the stage for the next clash, which would begin as the bourgeoisie increasingly impoverished the proletariat its machinery had generated. Resolving this clash would give rise to socialism as the proletariat freed themselves from the chains of their capitalist money titans and also become a force to be reckoned with.

In other words, *a capitalist stage is essential for socialism*. If the historical process is interrupted by some group of actors *trying to artificially hasten the building of socialism, this would disrupt what must occur*. According to Marxist analysis of the Soviet Union, the Leninists tried to do just this: go directly into socialism from agrarian feudalism without permitting a capitalist phase to develop and generate wealth to be distributed. *The capitalist phase was needed*. Without it, Leninists, and later Stalinists, doomed themselves to poverty, and to a failed model not really deserving to be called *socialist* (some have called it *state-capitalism*, a deformation of capitalism).

Many who professed Marxism seemed to forget what was going on in classical Marx. Or they never learned.

The Frankfurt School, assembled in Frankfurt, Germany, and which eventually produced Marcuse and his Marcusan acolytes, is an example. They concluded that a case for Marxism based exclusively on claims about relations of production, i.e., economic relations, had failed. An honest look at the Soviet economy revealed something barely functional. Its species of central planning was manifestly a disastrous failure. It precipitated mass starvation hastened by Communist policy when peoples in, say, Ukraine, resisted collective farming.

The Frankfurt School looked at the European proletariat, moreover, and saw no spirit of revolution. They saw instead Weber's spirit of enterprise! The proletariat did not oppose the bourgeoisie, they wanted to *join* the bourgeoisie. Some were planning, working hard, and doing just that! Capitalism was proving tremendously resilient. By the early 1940s it was surviving its worst crisis to date: the American Great Depression. It had evolved, modified itself, softened its rough edges with "socialist" elements such as the American New Deal (labor protections, a minimum wage, Social Security, and so on).

Antonio Gramsci, the Italian Marxist, had reached very similar conclusions independently. He argued that if capitalism was ever to be overthrown, Marxists would have to capture and destroy "capitalist culture" from within, especially its Christian elements (he appears to have been conscious of the effects of worldviews on populations). Marcuse came out of the Frankfurt School. He'd studied Freud as we saw, and knew how to exploit growing Kinseyite calls for liberating human sexuality from Christian-based constraints. He probably studied Gramsci as well, going on to exploit minority interests. Many of those I've labeled Marcusans read Gramsci as well as they began their "long march through the institutions" to transform them from within. Hence cultural Marxism intended to replace Weberian capitalist culture. It is not a "conspiracy theory" but a fact of twentieth-century intellectual and cultural history.

What the cultural Marxists overlooked is classical Marxism's implication that capitalism had to become a global phenomenon before it would give rise to full revolutionary consciousness within a global proletariat. It must adopt what Leninists would call imperialist measures, provoking wars where necessary, in order to grow (the Leninists had that much right). There must be no viable escape from the "iron cages" of capitalist relations. Capitalist culture would commodify everything and encircle everyone. It would gave rise to a multiplicity of products, services, and forms of life of various sorts—many of them quite enjoyable to their participants, but meeting very few actual human needs, just the need for employment and for money to be constantly changing hands. Meanwhile, a subtler human need, for meaningful work, would go begging. The fundamentally "unheroic" nature of work within the capitalist machinery was something Schumpeter noticed, which he thought would contribute to undermining support for capitalism.[18] Schumpeter was not a Marxist. He was one of the great scholars of the complicated forces at work in capitalism he thought would doom it as its masses eventually voted themselves into socialism. Marxists, that is, were hardly alone in noticing that the bulk of the work capitalism makes available consists of drudgery which its participants must keep telling themselves is necessary to keep its systems running, earns them an "honest living," etc., and then thanking God it's Friday! They rationalize away David Graeber's "bullshit jobs," characteristic of "late capitalism," which produce nothing essential, accomplish nothing worthwhile, and are entirely unnecessary as in the final analysis they contribute nothing useful to society.[19]

---

18. Schumpeter, *Capitalism, Socialism, and Democracy*.
19. Graeber, *Bullshit Jobs: A Theory*.

Neither Gramsci nor the Frankfurt School appear to have understood this. So they looked to culture instead of economics. They looked to sexuality, and to disenfranchised groups such as African-Americans, women, and eventually homosexuals, while fiercely opposing Christian influence coming from the Weberian "Protestant ethic," and the nuclear family. They founded schools such as the School for Social Research which, when it moved onto US soil, became the New School for Social Research. The idea was to infiltrate education at all levels and begin the job of fomenting unrest and division, driving groups into opposed camps if that is what worked. Frankfurt School Marxists indeed sought to change the culture, hoping to undermine capitalism from within until its cultural support systems collapsed. They've largely succeeded at this in our time. But their success has not built anything resembling a viable socialism.

Marcuse and his followers' emphasis on power and supposed relations of domination based on ethnicity and gender gave rise to identity politics, as we saw. Unfortunately, the Marcusans ignored most of what was valuable in Marx—the analysis of capitalism based on the idea that the fundamental cleavage in industrial civilization is *class*: the dichotomy between those who own the means of production and those who do not. Identity politics, in its attack on heterosexual white men, set Marxism aside. How so? Because obviously there are too many heterosexual white men who are poor and therefore marginalized in terms of class, especially after almost five decades of stagnant wages, including the outsourcing of manufacturing to third-world nations, and the rising replacement of jobs by technology (automation)—all given the resilience of our specific Anglo-American capitalism as it moved towards globalism in the hands of the real power players. Some have figured out that this system is not a democracy despite votes taken every two or four years.[20] One of the ironic results of identity politics is that we could maintain our present rule by a capitalist oligarchy of plutocrats—not of the 1 percent but the .0001 percent—if that .0001 percent was 13 percent black, (roughly) 52 percent female, and perhaps 4 percent homosexual, and consistent cultural Marxism would have say that "social justice" had been delivered![21]

What was the reality? That following the collapse of the Soviet Union, industrial and information-age capitalism *achieved* near-global dominance: *globalization*, driven by growth, technological advances, and the continued lure of profitability. Sometimes the ideology behind it is called *globalism* (a term I used above) which promotes not just outsourcing but free trade

20. See Gilens and Page, "Testing Theories of American Politics," 564–81.
21. Cf. Fraser, *Fortunes of Feminism*; Gutting and Fraser, "Feminism."

(i.e., trade deals enabling the largest corporations to do as they please), open immigration and a dissolving of national borders, and networks of international "non-governmental" organizations (NGOs) to manage it all. Two prominent examples of such organizations are the World Trade Organization and the World Economic Forum. China embraced significant elements of capitalism while controlling them, and lifted tens of millions of people out of crushing poverty even as they work long hours for impossibly low (by Western standards) wages. There are very few places left that have not been pulled into the globalization octopus, into a money economy, and into a consumer-focused lifestyle. Urbanization, it is often said, is the wave of the future. Those that resisted this tide and kicked out global corporations have paid a steep price. Look at Venezuela.

It's all begun to destabilize in ways that go outside the scope of this discussion. But an array of events and circumstances, allegations of man-made climate change, the financial meltdown of 2008, Brexit, the Trump election, the fact that many on the left supported their own "populist" Bernie Sanders, all ought to make us wonder if a globalized system based on endless growth on a finite planet with finite resources, much of it fueled by debt, and which certainly *appears* to funnel wealth and power into the hands of a small, cosmopolitan financial elite or billionaire class, is sustainable. Indeed, the "red insurgency" of populism and economic nationalism that began to appear after 2008 crisis and culminated with Brexit and the Trump election in 2016 would suggest that a largescale *spirit* of rebellion against globalism is very much in evidence—even as the organized *cultural* left (and a few who are elsewhere on the political spectrum) rejects this rebellion as "fascist," "white supremacist," etc.

Unfortunately for the few leftists who are intellectually serious, there is almost no evidence of sufficient organizational capabilities or resources by the proletariat. The latter, much as Marx predicted, are indeed an increasingly impoverished *precariat*—adjuncts in higher education being just one increasingly visible example—unlikely to organize a revolution against the financial and other corporate elites.[22] The latter, whose numbers have shrunk in size to a number who would fit inside a large classroom with room to spare, are increasingly rooted in financial institutions built up through investing ("passive income" or "money making money") rather than producing ("active income" making money by actually *making things*, producing something). Despite the reaction to "Trumpism" which turned increasingly violent in 2020, this kind of system seems destined to experience more crises and worsening waves of unrest. It could destabilize on a

---

22. Cf. Standing, *Precariat*.

large scale. But the elites are more than able to protect themselves within securely gated and carefully guarded enclaves.

The multidisciplinary question of whether capitalism as a system of political economy is the best we can do remains alive. Unquestionably, another meltdown is coming. The only disagreement is over when (and the global pandemic of 2020 may well have precipitated it by the time this reaches print).

Philosophers today seem to have little useful to say regarding this fourth historical answer to, *What should philosophy do?* Surely the retribalization offered by identity politics will not suffice. Let's attempt a summary of this complex section. Philosophers who see merit in what we've observed above can surely ask a few pointed questions Can global capitalism survive its repeated crises? These include economic-financial ones (1970s, 1987, 2000–2001, 2008–9, 2020). They include ongoing debt spirals (national, corporate, personal, student loan, etc.). They include worsening inequality and potentially destabilizing conditions of the precariat versus the dramatic concentrations of wealth. Finally, they include allegations that industrial civilization has disrupted natural climate cycles (man-made climate change again) as well as led to dramatic and worsening pollution not just of water tables, rivers, and streams but of the oceans—nonbiodegradable plastic waste, other products of a political economy dependent on endless mass consumption and growth and which must go *somewhere*. The contamination of water tables by chemicals of various sorts—pharmaceuticals, bovine growth hormones used in factory farms, preservatives and other food additives, etc.—threatens not just other living things but our own long-term health on large scale. There is much more to ecology and environment than concern about climate change.[23]

This kind of inquiry, whether it is possible to transcend the capitalism we have now, has enormous potential for a serious left, but this is conditional on the willingness of serious leftists to take the courageous leap of putting identity politics aside as a horrendously wrong turn, originating more with Marcuse and de Beauvoir than with Marx, sapping their energy and destroying their credibility Sadly, it may not be possible to do that in present-day academia, at least not openly, and keep one's career intact. "Wokism" may still be on the ascendent, both in academia and in the larger culture, as when the National Football League "takes a knee" or when academics design programs for dissemination in corporate America drawing strength

---

23. Cf. Fitzgerald, *Hundred-Year Lie.*

from their ability to "shame" white people.[24] This is a matter we will take up in Chapter 6 and in our Conclusion.

Philosophy as Mental Hygiene

We've outlined four major historical answers to our title question, *What Should Philosophy Do?* The academization of the discipline has delivered a few lesser ones, especially if philosophers self-identify not just as scholars but as *teachers*. The teaching of philosophy suggests an important role for the discipline as a kind of mental or intellectual "hygiene" for students, a clearing away of unsatisfactory mental activity and resulting debris for those who engage it.

Philosophy so understood involves promoting critical thinking skills: the philosophy professor, using examples from history or current events, outlines the logical machinery for understanding what sound reasoning is, why it is important, what can go wrong, and how not to be led down false rabbit trails (like the idea that logic is, in some sense, a "white male social construct," whatever this is supposed to mean). Good arguments, whether in or outside of philosophy, have specific structures, because logical thought is governed by normative rules. From given premises, a given conclusion follows, either necessarily (deductive logic) or probabilistically (inductive logic). That conclusion can then be used as a premise in subsequent reasoning.

Courses in logic and critical thinking can also help students discern when a crucial premise is missing or unstated and what this might imply, and in general how to distinguish cogent from fallacious reasoning. There is room, in such courses, for detailed discussion of language, categories, and concepts, how they all fit together, and in general the structure of our conversations about our surroundings. When I taught such courses, my students sometimes reported back how valuable the experience was, how it helped them understand conceptual systems that applied to other subject matters, as well as help them determine when misleading language was being used to sell them bills of goods in other walks of life.

Philosophy courses also have the potential to investigate the *limits* of intellectual reason, although this may be a tougher row to hoe. Several major and sometimes pivotal figures in the history of philosophy saw reason as inherently limited. For Hume, it was the slave of the passions. This basic idea surely has applications and illustrations in today's world! Kant saw reason as structured by categories of the understanding brought to experience *a priori*, actively shaping it instead of passively reflecting it. The mind, that is, is not a

---

24. Cf. DiAngelo, *White Fragility*.

"blank slate" on which experience writes, a neutral receiver of "impressions" (Hume) or "sense data" (logical positivists). It is an active agency. Reason being *human* reason, we experience the world in a human way, one shaped at least by language and culture. Experience by its very nature is not neutral but reflects human minds, human needs, human interests.

This pivotal realization conditioned much subsequent philosophy. We are still wrestling with the consequences. As we noted above, for Hegel the slave brought a fundamentally different perspective to experience than the master, and once combined with the materialism of Feuerbach, this gave rise to the Marxian tradition. As we saw in the Introduction, recent players on the academic scene modified this Hegelian dichotomy to favor specific groups. Philosophers can look at identity politics and see its roots clearly— also seeing (if they try) how the so-called alt-right has employed *these same roots* on behalf of straight white men. Shining light on how each group is using language to grab for political advantage is surely something philosophers can do: a potentially invaluable service!

What might such philosophers conclude? That as often happens, a fundamentally sound idea is picked up by advocates who lose all perspective and run with it off the nearest cliff. If formulated in a dichotomized, deterministic fashion, it indeed becomes impossible for members of one group ever to truly understand the experiences of another group, which must therefore be expressed only by their own: the political landmine into which many have inadvertently stepped. But such premises guarantee the inevitability of communication breakdowns.

In our present environment of media saturation and technological hyper-connectedness (with more than a little addictive behavior to such), all of us now have quantities of information at our fingertips previous generations could not have begun to imagine. This has come with its share of problems and dilemmas. There are countless narratives out there, many of them inconsistent with one another, and few of them lending themselves to easy validation or evaluation. This invites confusion and paralysis. The issues are formidable. Should we trust "alternative media"? Why or why not? The tendencies of forums, social media, etc., to allow users to silo themselves into echo chambers or online "safe spaces" where their premises won't be challenged is now well-documented. This has doubtless contributed to the present polarization of discourse in the larger society. Is "legacy" corporate media as trustworthy as we are "supposed" to assume? Why or why not? "Legacy" media have always reflected governmental-corporate interests which are hardly neutral. Arguably, as Edward Hermon and Noam Chomsky claimed as far back as the 1980s, traditional corporate media serve the interests of those in power.[25] "Alternative media" was, at least in part, an intended corrective to this, however imperfect. Now, according to one narrative, with the "fake news" meme and Google's use of AI to adjust its algorithms, powerful interests are fighting to recover the loss of "alternative" influence that unquestionably contributed to Donald Trump's winning the White House in 2016.

We have never lived in a time when there were so many points of view with free reign all across a media-saturated landscape, and conceivably many exemplars of bad reasoning or uses of language to manipulate or to gain (or regain) territory. Some public issues are notorious for strongly held, polarizing beliefs, and given these effects of social media technology, implications that if you disagree with someone's opinion, to that someone you are not merely wrong but illegitimate—*evil*, in some cases. This is a product of the "safe space" effect.

We need not pretend there were no echo chambers before, of course, or that these problems emerged only with present-day technology. But technology has enhanced and sharpened them—sometimes just in response to how consumers have chosen to spend their money, or have been lured into investing their time.

Philosophers are in a position to draw attention to and examine all this, and draw the implications. Thus philosophy as mental hygiene, which could easily translate into social and cultural hygiene in the hands of the right philosophers.

Applied Ethics / Contemporary Moral Issues

And speaking of public issues, since around 1970, we had already seen a shift of emphasis in academic ethics towards applied ethics as opposed to theory and analytic moral philosophy.

Discrimination and affirmative action; abortion; euthanasia and physician-assisted suicide; health care and whether in advanced civilizations it is, in some sense, a right; sexuality in its various manifestations; our impact on the natural environment; inequality, poverty, and the global distribution of wealth; corporations, whistleblowing, and business ethics generally; ethics and advertising: recreational drugs and decriminalization; capital punishment and the treatment of prisoners more broadly (the privatization of prisons surely belongs in here somewhere); the treatment of animals and whether they have moral properties because they can feel pain and experience pleasure; personal privacy, again in this age of hyper-connectedness;

---

25. See Herman and Chomsky, *Manufacturing Consent*.

war, terrorism, and security in the post-9/11 world freedom of speech, on college campuses or on social media platforms or in general.

These and possibly others cried out for philosophers' attention, and they received it. Books and articles in applied ethics began pouring out of academic and even a few mainstream presses starting in the early 1970s. New journals appeared. This was a healthy response to the demand that philosophy be relevant to moral issues debated in contemporary society, trying to bring philosophical reason to bear on the decision-making necessary today. Some of these problems have arisen during the course of cultural changes welcomed by some but not others. Some were created by our own technological advances, whether in lengthening the human life span or extending the communications grid across the globe. There is a sense in which we've become victims of our own successes Change may be for the better or not, but one thing is for certain: it always comes with a price.

Thus an additional view of what philosophy is and what it should do: *apply its analytic tools to the framing of the public moral issues of our time, evaluating and making recommendations for, moral decision-making.* The majority of moral philosophers of the past century have been utilitarians in one or another sense of that term. Others have followed John Rawls or some variation on the deontological perspective in his *A Theory of Justice*, or the libertarians who saw value in, say, Nozick's work (which Nozick himself, interestingly, drifted from as his career moved on).

One applied ethicist has become notorious outside professional philosophy: Peter Singer, who calls himself a "preference" utilitarian. Over a period now approaching fifty years he's produced a steady stream of often-provocative articles and books on topics ranging from our moral responsibility to animals to world poverty to abortion and euthanasia to the ethics of war and peace in the age of the so-called war on terror. Some of Singer's views have provoked outrage. He's been one of the few to bite the bullet and admit that most of the arguments in defense of a right to an abortion can be used to justify infanticide, and concluded not that abortion is wrong but that infanticide may indeed be justifiable in specific circumstances such as a birth with severe deformity or mental retardation. This (understandably) brought upon him the wrath of productive citizens who happen to be handicapped. Singer appears not to have noticed that one of the premises he uses to justify that animals have moral properties, that they experience pleasure and avoid pain, can be used to argue that fetuses have rights. Direct observation has shown that fetuses have sufficient awareness that they will try to avoid an abortionist's instrument and can make facial expressions indicative of experiencing momentary intense suffering before their lives are snuffed out.

My view is that all such issues can be made sharper and placed in perspective through the approach to philosophy advanced in this work, as well as sufficient attention to the historical development of our present state of affairs. One of the things that has made moral conversation difficult if not intractable has been the lingering influence of twentieth century positivism which did not see moral judgments as cognitively meaningful, ethical statements as capable of truth or falsity. This has encouraged either ethical relativism which sees morality as a cultural artifact or a subjectivism which sees it as little more than personal choice, as in consumer culture. Such conclusions would seem to make moral disputation pointless. But there has been no stable consensus on how moral judgments are cognitively meaningful. How we got into this predicament is one of the matters we will deal with at length.

Worldviews in Civilization: The Background and a First Look

In the early-1800s we were not in a position to discern that the West was undergoing a slow *worldview* shift—not a *paradigm* shift in Kuhn's sense, but something slower and more seismic. This shift (greatly helped along by theories such as Darwin's and Freud's) would be largely complete in the major intellectual centers by around 1900: prestigious universities primarily, but also in centers of economic gravity where monetary gain was becoming the core priority as an end in itself.

One of the aims of this work will be to explain in detail what worldviews are, how they function in civilization, what occurs throughout a civilization when one worldview replaces another, how this change in *philosophical* orientation gradually brings about seismic cultural changes over generations, and how to evaluate the results by bringing the philosopher's analytic tools to the identification and evaluation of worldviews. This includes how language can be used to express worldview commitments, or hide them.

Now that we are in the twenty-first century, with an abundance of twenty-twenty hindsight, the time for an illumination of what this shift amounted to and an assessment of the results has never been better! For *first* it delivered to us the *Zeitgeist* of modernity, of which global consumer capitalism is a central feature. But there is more to this *Zeitgeist* than global consumer capitalism. Where is the locus of power? Is it with those who own and control the guns, what we might call *the power of the sword*, or with those who bankroll those who control the guns, what we might call *the power of the purse*? Marxists targeted capitalism as the enemy, more in its irrationality than in its ugliness and indifference to personal aspirations that cannot be monetized. They saw it as doomed to be replaced by a socialism about which Marx himself said very little. Nowhere has this happened on any permanent basis. Even the "social democracies" of Europe have a capitalist base. Nowhere has private ownership of the means of production been abolished, although there are places where much of it (not all!) is highly regulated, taxed and controlled. Financialization is the key here. It unleashed capital in the latter third of the twentieth century, surrounded by the neoliberal variation that saw profit maximization and capital accrual as the only purpose of business. As we saw above, after the Soviet Union collapsed, capitalism became the global reality, so that even the Chinese Communists, so called, embraced their own variation of it.

Second, however, this shift provoked an undercurrent of unease actually going back to nineteenth-century writers such as Dostoevsky, and in the twentieth with existentialists. While those movements have passed for everyone except historians, perhaps, the unease remained. Whatever "magic" global capitalism seemed to work, the unease has broken out into a massive global unrest. Some comes from the right, the Trump phenomenon being merely one exemplar. Sometimes it comes from the left, as with the Syrizas in Greece a couple of years before, and with Bernie Sanders' supporters in the U.S. It manifests itself in different ways in different places. But much of it appears to be directed against elites, products of financialized capitalism, absurdly wealthy not really having produced anything except "passive income," perceived as hopelessly out of touch with the mindsets of the peoples of the various nations, and also—rightly or wrongly—perceived as wanting global power (a so-called "new world order"). The elites clearly exist, unless the World Economic Forum and surrounding "Davos culture" are to be dismissed as "conspiracy theories." Arguably they began to push back in 2016. They produced their own "conspiracy theory" of Russian collusion in a futile effort to delegitimize the Trump election. More recently, the COVID-19 pandemic erupted as a global problem with more than one narrative behind it, and be that as it may, "global problems call for global solutions." However one sees these events, we seem to be at a crossroads, one at least as large as previous pivotal moments which ignited revolutions and sometimes world wars. Indeed, the fate of Western civilization itself seems to hang in the balance!

Now suppose we peel off an additional layer of the conceptual onion, and view the problem not through the tempting lens of political-economic categories, or even simply as competing conspiracy claims. Suppose we recognize that that *all the major, earth-moving ideologies of the past seventy years, be they of the right or of the left, as well as developments such as growing technocracy that have ascended knowing no specific ideology, all share common premises because they share the prevailing worldview that dominated once the seismic worldview shift was complete in the early 1900s.*

Suppose, moreover, we discover reasons to believe *this worldview is the problem*, *that it has run its course, that it is now doing more harm than good.*

Would it not be reasonable to conclude that this worldview, if we can identify it clearly, ought to be repudiated and replaced before we can expect to make any further sustainable progress in creating a better human world?

The past century saw some of humanity's greatest technological achievements, results unimaginable during the century before. But it also saw some of the most horrific acts of mass violence ever witnessed—wars as well as genocides—resulting in the deaths of millions of innocent people. Mass violence wasn't invented yesterday, of course. But never before were there weapons able to lay waste to entire continents. Did the shift of worldviews that actually began in the 1700s, increased apace in the late 1800s, and culminated in the 1900s, made us better people? Or was there something terrible that had been there all along, made stronger and more dangerous by the technical prowess modernity unleashed?

We are told by pundits that violence in the world has diminished over the past century, while prosperity has risen. As generalizations these are almost certainly true. But as *more* than generalizations, they are also useless. We do not live in a world of generalizations, we live in a world of specifics, of situations, of *particulars*. The major cities of America have never been as violent as they are right now, and abstract global statistics ring hollow to the dozens if not hundreds of those losing loved ones. Claims of globally rising prosperity, too, are economic abstractions. The numbers may show a great rise. But it is common knowledge that wages have been stagnant for five decades now as millions of people in advanced nations like the United States have seen everything rise except their salaries, watched their standard of living begin to decline especially over the past thirty years or so, and have concluded that dominant narratives about the benefits of globalization are false and to be rejected. Hence again Donald Trump. Similar conflicts are playing out elsewhere: in the United Kingdom, Europe, India, Brazil, Chile, and elsewhere.

Major challenges thus stand before us as a civilization. Some have to do with the consolidation of wealth and power in the hands of this tiny, global superelite. Others we have mentioned, such as claims of damage to the planetary ecosphere and to our own mental and physical health. These claims have their challengers. But are the claims themselves crazy or outrageous?

Philosophers can speak from a variety of perspectives to reasons why we should be concerned about the environment and our planetary future.

Sadly, the idea of truth itself has fallen on hard times, amidst the multitude of clashing narratives. We've seen a seismic shift of a different sort, that of the Stages of civilization we have mentioned, and not just its dominant worldview. Among the consequences has been the retribalization of identity politics and the destructive effects of the cult of "woke."

Where do we go from here?

The challenges seem overwhelming—surely too much for philosophers!

Indeed, bringing them under one umbrella may seem quixotic. Yet I believe our concept of a prevailing worldview that has run its course can help, even if it cannot solve every problem. Let's come full circle back to: *what is this thing called philosophy?*

Philosophy in Academia, In Our Present Moment: A Frank Look At a Disaster

Today, the philosopher is usually (not always!) a professor, instructor, or doctoral candidate. Sometimes he or she works in a "think tank." What can such folks do?

What is also needed is *a frank discussion of the political economy of academia, and what this political economy has done to philosophy. And what philosophy has thereby done to itself.*

I don't refer here to positivism and analysis. Consider "adjunctification," which is happening to the professoriate generally, and which has provoked substantial unrest among younger aspiring scholars and talk of the precariat. Some are forming unions and getting outside political support, much to the chagrin of administrators, motivated by perverse incentives of their own.

Arguably, philosophy began to fall on hard times after the academic job market collapsed in the 1970s. Bold scholarship able to issue challenges to dogmas and had the potential to undertake the challenges outlined above was muted. This was noticed by none other than Harvard's Hilary Putnam, who commented on it in the late 1980s, wondering where all the younger voices were, in an interview that appeared, in all places, in *U.S. News & World Report*.[26] Paraphrasing: younger generations should be saying things his generation found horrible. But they weren't. The younger voices of the profession were largely silent. Putnam's privileged tenure-class status was betrayed by his befuddlement at why my generation (those of us who came of age during the 1970s and 1980s) was so quiet.

We were too busy trying to survive!

26. Sanoff, "Bringing Philosophy Back to Life," 56.

Although there were highly visible exceptions (we'll be engaging several), scholarship overall was deteriorating for those who *did* survive. Why? Because the priorities within all the liberal arts disciplines were changing, along with the personalities. First, in the United States at least, the generation that bequeathed to us the major accomplishments of twentieth-century philosophy aged, retired, and began to pass away one by one. Most of its youngest members are now in their eighties (a small handful, such as Saul Kripke, are in their seventies). They have not been replaced by equally visible scholars of comparable merit. Incisive philosophical writings comparable to Wittgenstein's *Philosophical Investigations* or Quine's "Two Dogmas of Empiricism"; or Rawls's *A Theory of Justice*; or even Thomas Nagel's brilliant "What Is It Like to Be a Bat?" and John Searle's equally brilliant "Minds, Brains, and Programs" are now very rare.[27]

What is to be found is a proliferation of micro-specialized books and articles guaranteed to gather proverbial dust on library shelves, because truth be known, and it sounds blunt, but almost no one cares.

The Marcusans survived. They are everywhere, in every variety, in every color of the rainbow. We have "African-American philosophy," feminists of every variety, "queer theory," the even more recent transgenders, and possibly more *outré* forms of academic life that might appear before this has time to reach print, indicative of the new tribalism. These people are not a numerical majority by any means, but their aggressiveness is such that one must suspect: the rest of the profession is afraid of them. This fear is largely justified. The campus environment has been so poisoned that a single verbal misstep, or an allegation of sexual misconduct from a student or colleague (real or imagined!), can destroy a male professor's career in one fell swoop. Ask either Peter Ludlow, formerly of Northwestern University, relieved of his position after an ill-advised date with a student turned into a hostile he-said she-said that disrupted his classes and forced cancelations. Or Colin McGinn, who resigned from the University of Miami at Coral Gables following complaints of unwise advances towards a graduate student.

The situation is even worse. Making claims that would have been common sense fifty years ago (e.g., that sex is determined biologically, and is not subject to change) can lead to loud allegations of "transphobia," the latest in a string of *fake phobias*, one might call them. One is attacked offline and online by emotionally outraged mobs.

---

27. Wittgenstein, *Philosophical Investigations*; Quine, "Two Dogmas of Empiricism," in Quine, *From a Logical Point of View*, 20–46; Nagel, "What Is It Like To Be a Bat?," 435–50; Searle, "Minds, Brains, and Programs," 417–57.

One consequence is that only an outsider such as myself, operating apart from the groves of academia, is in a position *even to assert these realities frankly*. I cannot be fired from an academic position I do not have!

Suffice it to say, the present poisonous environment is hardly conducive to serious discourse able to address what philosophy is or what it should do.

Now obviously: trenchant work of philosophical interest is being produced, but often by nonphilosophers in the professional sense. Stephen Hawking is the example we cited at the outset; so are the books by someone such as Nassim Nicholas Taleb which range across problems such as induction, risk, and how to make the systems on which we base our lives more resilient (his curious term for this last is *anti-fragility*). Love him or not, much of Jordan Peterson's work and activities are relevant to philosophy, in their bringing forth, visibly, devastating criticisms of the various forms of the new tribalism. There are others, but something is missing.

What is missing is the job philosophy is uniquely for. If the professionals do not do it, or if what they do just serves a political agenda or is just irrelevant, others will step in. One way or another, the job will get done—but not as effectively as if trained philosophers were doing it.

Philosophy is not a game, or hobby, or armchair activity. It should not conceive of itself as a handmaiden to science, or religion, or some agenda of "woke." The best thing would be for this work to entice a few of the professionals out of their academic boxes. All this may strike some readers as not just politically incorrect, but harsh and unempathetic. I would rather this *not* be the case, and would implore such readers to hear me out.

The way we will proceed will open doors to new possibilities. Is a world of greater fairness and empathy possible? If so, it will be because we will have achieved a world of greater abundance (but less emphasis on "wealth building"), less centralization, less surveillance, and therefore more genuine freedom and cooperation on common problems. *Genuine* freedom, after all, is not simply the freedom to participate in markets and consume; it includes the choice to *not* participate in them, if one wishes to *make* that choice. Is a world possible in which those whose superpower talents are enormous but unsellable to the masses can nevertheless thrive?

Genuine freedom is also the freedom to disagree with those who have cultural power (whether they think so or not) because they can shout the loudest in an online (or physical) mob. Is a world possible in which civil discourse has been restored?

Can we start to build the sort of world in which most threats of war have been eliminated, because we are no longer fighting over scarce resources (the obvious scarce resource being oil)? We can't say at this point, but criticizing the prevailing worldview might hold an important key to opening all these doors.

My conviction, given our present state of affairs, is that we have little to lose by trying.

Civilization has gone through stages. We will survey them. We are presently caught between two stages, one which is slowly collapsing, with a replacement that is equally unsustainable.

A new stage of civilization may be possible, if we can build it.

At least, this is what I shall argue in the material to follow, one stage at a time. Chapters 2 through 5 will lead the way, and in Chapter 6 and the Conclusion I will make the proposal more explicit, along with suggestions on how to go about carrying it out.

All of this will be philosophy *doing its job*. And what is this job? To formulate as explicitly as possible: what I will argue is that *philosophers ought to identify, investigate, clarify, and then critically assess or evaluate worldviews—understood not as mere products of grand theory (although they may have partial roots in one or another grand theory of philosophy's past) but as somewhat organic systems of thought, integrated seamlessly into the larger culture and civilization of which they are a part: into its institutions and into the warp and woof of the lives of millions of people. And therefore not always formulated clearly and explicitly.*

People's lives—including the lives of those who self-identify as philosophers—are shaped by forces they are usually in little position to see clearly, much less understand, much less control. This is due primarily to the shaping of their educations by these systemic forces. These latter are conditioning them to accept the "bullshit jobs" a highly centralized civilization provides, while insisting to them that they live in a "democracy" and are (neoliberal economic hero Milton Friedman's phrase) "free to choose."[28] The book of this title which Friedman and his wife wrote together laid out, for public consumption, the basic principles of neoliberalism.

Philosophers need to claim a larger vision which possesses them and gives them a standpoint outside these forces. The job of identifying and attending to supervening worldviews, diagnosing their effects and suggesting remedies, should rightly fall to philosophers. Hence the vision for philosophy I will attempt here. I will urge other philosophers to cease being either handmaidens of science or kowtowing to those whose only interest is their political agendas.

If you believe you are *not* "free to choose," determine why not, and if you are so inclined, do something about it.

---

28. See Friedman and Friedman, *Free to Choose*.

If you believe you *are* "free to choose," then *own* it, and *act* on it! Let us now proceed with an account of how we got here.

2

Causes and Consequences of the "Retreat" of Philosophy

If you got the impression from Chapter 1 that academic philosophy is in something of a mess, you would not be wrong. The problem is not just its infection by movements such as identity politics, which are symptoms, not causes (just like Trump is a symptom and not a cause). For decades the discipline has been mostly unmoored from sustained consideration of first principles, despite worthwhile accomplishments and notable exceptions to such judgments. It has been constrained by the political economy of academia and accepted this fate with little comment, even seen it as a badge of maturity. Academic philosophy has been buffeted by fads, of which identity politics is just the latest and noisiest. Sadly, loud as its voices are, they are no threat to the real loci of power in the world. If anything, they are being *used* by those with real power.

It might be of interest to explore how we got here. What factors caused, or led to, the "retreat" of philosophy as we call it. What were the consequences, both for philosophy itself and for the larger culture? We've encountered some already. Does postmodernism enter this picture at some point? More than an artistic and academic fad, does it reflect a specific breakdown whereby a science-based philosophy issued challenges both to society and to itself which it failed to meet? Dare I ask: has Western civilization suffered due to a widespread *neglect* of philosophy while its academic permutation assumed that all was well?

In answering these, the last two of which will recur throughout this work, we will see why a new vision for philosophy which places worldviews and their evaluation at the center of attention is necessary, and ought to be undertaken as quickly as possible.

The Law of Three Stages

Retreat in the title of this chapter (and our opening paragraphs above and elsewhere in the chapter) is in scare quotes because it should be clear: philosophy's "retreat" was a retreat from visibility, not influence. A civilization's *de facto* choice is not *whether to sustain a philosophy*, but *what kind of philosophy it will sustain*, and whether this will result from conscious decision-making, a product of deliberate and purposeful national and international conversation, or if the matter will be left to chance—as with that fellow we mentioned trying to make his way across that busy street blindfolded.

Philosophy today has very little visibility, despite more people self-identifying as philosophers than ever before. "Applied ethics" has done little to affect the national conversation for the better. Most scientists who take philosophy seriously, finally, are their own philosophers (like Hawking). This is the "retreat" of philosophy. *For as a conscious endeavor, philosophy did retreat into an academic cubicle, from which it seldom emerged.* It exercises no real *thought leadership* in the world. By today's standards, it is too demanding, offering little sexiness and excitement. The *philosophical* direction of today (as opposed to its political-economic direction) has indeed been left mostly to chance—to the winds of fashion and whims of the marketplace. Not to mention what suits the interests of the moneyed and the powerful.

Diagnosing the reasons for this will better position us to answer our central questions: *what, in this civilization, should philosophy do?* What responsibility should it assume for shaping the future? And *how* and *from where* should philosophers seeking to undertake this task operate? Will they be able to continue to operate from academic cubicle-land?

The history of philosophy, as we saw above, discloses pivotal figures—whose work shaped or reshaped the discipline by reconfiguring existing problems and setting the stage for new ones. Plato and Aristotle are such figures, basically founding the Western tradition, greatly influencing major Christian theologians from Augustine to Aquinas.

The latter became the pivotal figure of the late medieval era with his effort to merge Aristotelian and Christian thought into a single system. His system gave rise to the broad tradition of natural law. God left two "books": the Holy Scriptures, and Nature herself. The order and bounty of the latter manifested the hand of the Creator, as well as implicit guidelines for how we should live, paralleling commands in the Old and New Testaments: natural law ethics (in which *sexual activity*, for example, ideally expresses love within Christian boundaries but is primarily for procreation).

Descartes's *Meditations* redefined philosophy again with his *cogito*, his contentious claim to certainty based on the reasoning of an autonomous intellect. This shifted the philosophical conversation from metaphysics and theology to epistemology. The ensuing trajectory through so-called continental rationalism and British empiricism led to the *cul-de-sac* of Humean epistemic skepticism and sensualism: about our knowledge of causality in the world, personal identity in ourselves, and morality.

Kant became the next pivotal figure. His *Critique of Pure Reason* and other major works set Western philosophy in new directions. Kant sought both to answer Hume's skeptical arguments (the end-result of the Cartesian inward turn), and place morality on what he saw as its only possible solid footing in the face of an increasingly assertive scientific determinism. The noumenal, transcendental will acts morally if it acts for the sake of duty against inclination, a species of experienced causality in the world of phenomena.

After Kant, philosophy fragmented, because subsequent philosophers had widely different interpretations of (or uses of) Kant's works: Hegel, Fichte, Schleiermacher, Schelling, Schopenhauer, and so on. Philosophy was more and more hitting an implicit barrier, however: science seemed to be doing a better job answering questions about the world and our place in it. So in an age of rising science in rising industrial civilization, the question was obvious: *is this the best way to do philosophy?*

I believe the next pivotal thinker we should consider is Auguste Comte, because he had a definite answer to this. His answer was a straightforward *No, it is not. Philosophy can no longer compete with science, and it shouldn't try.*

Comte is known for two concrete achievements: founding sociology as a special science with its own identity, and establishing positivism which embodied the above sentiment. The former set out to apply the latter, advocating adapting and applying methods of empirical science and technique to the study and improvement of society (the origins of technocracy).

Comte developed a conceptual vehicle for understanding Western civilization's long-term intellectual development: the *Law of Three Stages*, developed in his "*Cours de Philosophie Positive.*"[1] He didn't invent the idea that we can isolate "states" or "conditions" or "stages" through which a civilization passes—earlier versions of this idea can be found in Vico and Condorcet. But Comte gave the idea its clearest and most concise expression. It is important to note something not entirely clear in Comte's own writings: his stages are *not* historical epochs with distinct beginnings and endings. They exist side by side: uneasily at best, sometimes in conflict. It will not be hard to see why.

---

1. Lenzer, *Auguste Comte and Positivism*, 71–86.

The first Stage or state—First Stage thinking, we will call it—is the "theological or fictitious." In Comte's words:

> the human mind, seeking the essential nature of beings, the first and final causes (the origin and purpose) of all effects—in short, absolute knowledge—supposes all phenomena to be produced by the immediate action of supernatural beings. . . . The theological system arrived at the highest perfection of which it is capable when it substituted the providential action of a single Being for the varied operations of the numerous divinities that had been before imagined.[2]

First Stage thinking could be called the state of Basic Faith, or perhaps Unquestioning Faith. It looks to inscrutable, supernatural agencies as first causes: spirits, demons, etc. As it advances it consolidates these into a single, specific Supreme Being (the Christian God; or for Muslims, Allah), opposed by another singular agency, the devil or Satan. The political expression of First Stage thinking tends to be theocratic and authoritarian, with power centered in a king or other ruler whose power is divinely ordained, usually alongside a priesthood or some equivalent. The two control the public mind whether through a promise of eternal reward in an afterlife alongside the Supreme Being or fear of everlasting hellfire and damnation, sometimes, for any doubters and skeptics, hastening the process with execution by some spectacularly nasty and painful means.

First Stage thought, however, cannot survive the influence of intellectually curious souls who don't accept the authority of a monarchy or priesthood on their word that they alone speak for God. Historically, philosophers tended to cast cold water on such notions as the "divine right of kings," a prevalent notion in First Stage cultures. Thus begins the advance to Second Stage thought.

Comte's next stage is "metaphysical and abstract":

> In the metaphysical stage, which is only a modification of the first, the mind supposes, instead of supernatural beings, abstract forces, veritable entities (that is, personified abstractions) inherent in all beings, and capable of producing all phenomena. What is called the explanation of phenomena is, in this stage, a mere reference of each to its proper entity. . . . In the same way, in the last stage of the metaphysical system, men substitute one great entity (Nature) as the cause of all phenomena, instead of the multitude of entities at first supposed.[3]

2. Lenzer, *Auguste Comte and Positivism*, 72.
3. Lenzer, *Auguste Comte and Positivism*, 72.

Second Stage philosophy began (as far as we can determine) with Thales of Miletus and saw its first full expression in the philosophies of Plato and Aristotle. It was exemplified in grand theory or speculative philosophy. Its more recent variations could be called the stage of Pure Reason, given its expression in the philosophies of Descartes, Kant, and Hegel: grand theory in all its diversity, products of an abstract intellect able to grasp reality in its essentials.

Second Stage thinkers may conclude on the basis of very detailed reasoning that God exists, or that he doesn't, or that his existence lies beyond proof or disproof. Descartes believed the first. Julien de la Mettrie and Baron D'Holbach concluded the second. Immanuel Kant, the third. In its moral and political expression, Second Stage thought in the Anglo-American and Austrian worlds saw the individual as fundamental. This is a clear implication of Cartesian method, in which the individual philosopher can raze all his former beliefs to the ground and reconstruct a systematic philosophy from scratch. John Locke's *tabula rasa* on which experience writes is a direct descendent of the Cartesian intellect. Lockean Second Stage moral and political philosophy implies individual rights are grounded in the special relationship human beings as both intellectual and moral agents bear to Nature: *natural rights*, recognizing conditions for human flourishing that exist independently of legal structures, reflecting that in this world Nature is the arbiter of the conditions of life, to which societies either conform or perish.

Second Stage philosophers are very different from one another. Hume's brand of empiricism reached far different conclusions about the possibility of justifying our claims to knowledge; and he rooted morality not in a relationship we supposedly bear to the world but in sentiment and social utility. Believing he'd corrected Locke's epistemological errors, he famously rejected metaphysical reasoning at the end of his *Enquiry Concerning Human Understanding*:

> If we take in our hand any volume; of divinity or school metaphysics, for instance; let us ask, Does it contain any abstract reasoning concerning quantity or number? No. Does it contain any experimental reasoning concerning matter of fact and existence? No. Commit it then to the flames: for it can contain nothing but sophistry and illusion.[4]

This powerfully anticipated the rise of Third Stage thought. Comte again:

---

4. Hume, *Inquiry Concerning Human Understanding*, 173.

> In the final, the positive state, the mind has given over the vain search after absolute notions, the origin and destination of the universe, and the causes of phenomena, and applies itself to the study of their laws—that is, their invariable relations of succession and resemblance. Reasoning and observation, duly combined, are the means of this knowledge. What is now understood when we speak of an explanation of facts is simply the establishment of a connection between single phenomena and some general facts, the number of which continually diminishes with the progress of science. . . . In the same way, again, the ultimate perfection of the positive system would be (if such perfection could be hoped for) to represent all phenomena as particular aspects of a single general fact—such as gravitation, for instance.[5]

With this, we are on the way towards the view of philosophy as, at best, a handmaiden to science, and destined for academic cubicle-land. The Third Stage or condition of civilization could be called the stage or condition of Science and Utility. Third Stage intellectuals looked to science for explanations. They operated within a Third Stage ordering of disciplines, with physics its ideal. Philosophy's epistemic authority declined.

One might think of Comte's Law of Three Stages like this: *First Stage thought* reflects a community in its *childhood*, in which its people, elites and commoners alike, look to gods or other supernatural agencies and finally to one God for explanations and security, analogous to children who see a parent or parents or adults generally as godlike beings whose powers they cannot comprehend. Ideally, they love their God and are loved by him.

Second Stage thought suggests *adolescence*: its intellectuals reject First Stage authority, but their reach inevitably exceeds their grasp. They articulate systems of thought they have no shared criteria for testing; hence everyone is different and ultimately there is no sense of progress being made. Some might explain the seeming ordering of the world through an analogy to a watch, its parts adjusted one to the others, its purpose to display the time; and since the watch required a maker the vastly more complex universe required a Maker. Others will throw cold water on such arguments by claiming to find significant disanalogies. *A priori* methods aren't adequate to the task of scientific explanation, any more than are the actions of most adolescents adequate to life, with their new drives, sensations, and ambitions, taking chances, breaking rules whose purposes they don't understand, which they vaguely (or openly) resent and will circumvent if they can. The

---

5. Lenzer, *Auguste Comte and Positivism*, 72.

apriorist wants epistemic certainty, just as the adolescent mind impatiently "wants it all, and wants it right now."[6]

Third Stage thought, in this case, signals that a civilization's intellectuals have outgrown childish fantasies and adolescent extravagances. Entering *adulthood*, they embrace adult realities and adult responsibilities. The intellectual centers of Third Stage civilization relinquish supernaturalism in all forms, be they First Stage faith or Second Stage apriorism and "divine watchmaker" reasoning. Third Stage thinkers repudiate earlier philosophers' quest for certainty as futile. They accept, based on what they see of its rise, that science is the natural heir to philosophy, that it delivers the kinds of answers philosophers sought, but does so in a scientific way, in empirically verifiable and improvable ways.

Among the adult realities science revealed well before Comte's time was that our planet seems to occupy no special place in the universe. Copernicus had "decentered" Earth from its privileged place in Aristotle's cosmology and which Christianity had assumed. Galileo used that new instrument, the telescope, to offer empirical evidence that Venus orbited the sun, not the Earth, that Jupiter had four moons, and that there were mountains on the moon. The heavens, that is, did not display Christian-Aristotelean quintessential perfection.

Kepler followed up by rejecting the "perfect circles" of the celestial quintessence. Newton showed, finally, that the principles governing physical reality as a whole could be understood without a division between terrestrial and celestial realms. Universal gravitation, expressed mathematically, explained both the motions of moons and planets in the sky and falling objects and projectiles near the ground.

Thus came an unprecedented revolution in human thought, which proved unstoppable when it began to bear technological and commercial fruit.

Darwin appeared to "decenter" *us* from *our* privileged place at the center of the biological world. The human race, according to the theory of evolution by natural selection, may be the most complex species in existence, but we are still just one of many species in the tree of life, having emerged over a long period of time as a result of a continuous natural process that had *no* goals, much less the production of beings like ourselves. The point is, there was (and is) no need to posit anything other than natural processes to explain ourselves. We have no need to posit a Creator to account for our existence. The removal of morality from the realm of revelation was

---

6. For the sake of argument I am setting aside research suggesting that the phase of life casually called *adolescence* is itself a product of industrial civilization.

inevitable. Morality was neither handed down by a supernatural agency nor did it originate in a transcendent Platonist realm nor with a Kantian rational will that science could not observe. Hume, looking across that bridge toward civilization's Third Stage, opened the door to what ensued with his idea that ethics was based on the sensitive rather than the cognitive side of our nature, and was fundamentally grounded in an agreement in sentiments about what was useful in society.

For Third Stage thinkers, that is, our capacity to behave morally is just one of many traits with survival value. As a source of cooperation it benefitted social groups of various sizes as far back as hunter-gatherer days, and brought benefits to settled societies later.[7] Human gatherings were not sustainable if their members couldn't trust one another. Hence truth-telling, promise-keeping, injunctions against harming one's own, etc., became moral imperatives in most cultures. Perhaps our moral agency rested on little more than such down-to-earth realizations that our actions affect others whether for better or for worse, that cooperation improves our chances of survival, that happiness spread to others is more beneficial and productive than unhappiness (or happiness just for oneself), and that alleviating suffering is better for any society than causing or allowing it.

Those who pioneered these advances found them exciting and forward-looking. What came before seemed backward and benighted. Founders of early Christian churches and denominations were bound to First Stage dogmatism, unchanging and incapable of being criticized. Pivotal philosophers up through Kant and his successors were Second Stage thinkers. They, too, began by seeking propositions immune to critical evaluation. Figures from Comte and Darwin up to Stephen Hawking were Third Stage thinkers standing at the culmination of this trajectory, as were founding fathers of analytic philosophy such as Bertrand Russell whom we will encounter below. Ideas were held because the best evidence we had supported them, and as more evidence was accumulated, if it forced us to revise our ideas we did so—or so was the image of science promulgated by early (and later) positivists.

Third Stage thinking takes another step with *meliorism*, the idea that we can improve ourselves not just technologically but *morally*—actually *becoming better people*, through our own efforts, in Third Stage civilization. This, too, ran counter to our Christian inheritance. According to Christianity, we are born in sin, in rebellion against the morally perfect God. Such dogmas will invariably hold us back, reasoned Third Stage thinkers. All they had to do was observe that science doesn't point to God as really existing,

---

7. Cf. Axelrod, *Evolution of Cooperation*.

and with science and technology starting to make the world better, something neither religion nor philosophy could do, Comte and his followers were optimistic—in a word, *positive*—about our potential.

The price tag would be setting aside beliefs in God as a transcendent authority imposing limiting beliefs such as "sinfulness."

Positive science was thus hopeful about our capacity to discover more and greater truths, and to make use of scientific discoveries for societal as well as technological improvements. Years of careful study in subject domains (astronomy, physics, chemistry, biology, and now in sociology and perhaps soon psychology) gave scientific experts the final say in providing a *consensus* on what was true or credible in their domains.

Thus the state of affairs as the twentieth century dawned. One reason philosophy "retreated" was that philosophers reached their own consensus. In matters epistemic (and metaphysical and eventually ethical), science had, and ought to have, the final say.

Settled Science, one might call it. Theories such as Darwinian evolution exemplified Settled Science at the start of the new century.

Settled Science would shift its conceptual frameworks or paradigms from time to time. This was not really a problem, since as noted science was always making new discoveries. Openness to progressive change was a sign of health, not a crisis. For again, Third Stage inquiry was not about obtaining epistemic perfection but improving our knowledge piecemeal, then applying it to improving the material conditions of life. It seemed to be succeeding brilliantly. As humanity marched further into *modernity*, into a civilization based on science, technology, commerce, education, and progress, new inventions appeared one after another: automobiles, refrigerators, freezers, washing machines; aircraft; radio and television; microwave ovens; the transistor; fiber-optics; eventually, with miniaturization, the desktop computer and finally as the end of the century approached, the Internet. Afterwards: smartphones, apps, and far more.

Defenders of Third Stage thinking would conclude—still do—that its era of dominance has seen greater knowledge accumulation and more improvements in the human condition than ever before.

If you were some kind of anguished existentialist concerned about "living authentically," or a Beat who saw it all as "absurd," realistically what did you have to complain about? Really? Relax! Or as Generation Xers would say: *chill!*

Get some perspective!

For the most accomplished civilization in human history sent men to the moon seven times (six landings) and returned them safely—an achievement that would have been deemed impossible by our ancestors!

The most accomplished civilization in human history came to span the globe with its technology and markets! Diseases were being eradicated, poverty was indeed being reduced, the human life span was being extended. Life was better wherever modernity took hold.

Things were, and still are, getting better and better![8]

The Secular City, the Secular University.

Thus the question, *Does Third Stage civilization even need philosophy?* Small wonder philosophers have a tough time earning a living in our Secular City, and that the Stephen Hawkings of the latter are declaring the subject dead.

Okay, but what do we mean, *Secular City*?

Theologian Harvey Cox wrote an influential book with this title back in the 1960s. "The forces of secularization," he observed at its outset,

> have no serious interest in persecuting religion. Secularization simply bypasses and undercuts religion and goes on to other things. It has relativized religious worldviews and thus rendered them innocuous. Religion has been privatized. It has been accepted as the peculiar prerogative of a particular person or group.... The gods of traditional religions live on as private fetishes or the patrons of congenial groups, but they play no significant role in the public life of the secular metropolis....
>
> This is the age of the secular city. Through supersonic travel and instantaneous communication its ethos is spreading into every corner of the globe. The world looks less and less to religious rules and rituals for its morality or its meaning ... For fewer and fewer does it provide an inclusive and commanding system of personal and cosmic values and explanations.[9]

Clearly, such remarks apply to *philosophy* even more than to *religion*. Churches, synagogues, other houses of worship, are still a visible part of the landscape in every city and town, after all. Philosophy, on the other hand, has no "houses of worship," nor has it ever sought to build any. The only place philosophy found a home in the Secular City is in academia: what we will come to call the *Secular University*.

Once, long ago, philosophy was central to learning. It was the "queen of the sciences" all of which branched off from it. Newton and his progeny, as we noted, called themselves natural philosophers. In its "retreat" from the big questions, philosophy lost most of its visibility. Much of this can be

---

8. Cf. Ridley, *Rational Optimist*; Pinker, *Enlightenment Now*.
9. Cox, *Secular City*, 2–3.

attributed to the successes of science and technology—as Hawking and de Grasse Tyson among others would point out.

More recently, philosophy's role in the Secular University has been diminished even more. This is largely an effect of the mounting expense of higher education which has driven many students from majors deemed "not marketable." Philosophy may now be *more* private than any religious denomination. What this means: there are exacting discussions in refereed journals of academic philosophy over such matters as mind and consciousness, over the interpretation of the words of historical figures and the implications of contemporary moral concerns, and much more. But almost no one believes philosophy has much impact outside academic circles. There are exceptions, as we have seen. But truly fundamental discussion, when it occurs at all, is inconsequential in the Secular City, which responds to the pretenses of philosophers with a collective yawn.

Nor does the Secular University look to philosophy for wisdom or guidance, any more than it looks to theology.

Thus while there might be some, in and out of academia, who find the subject interesting, by and large philosophy is little more than a curiosity to most people, including most university students. Even those who respect the image of the philosopher as someone "wise" may deem it beyond their grasp. They may be wrong, but have neither the time nor the motivation (nor the money!) to find out. Education in the Secular University, followed by life in the Secular City first trains them and then keeps them too *busy, busy, busy.*

I am using *Secular City* and *Secular University* in a somewhat different way than Cox used the first, hopefully without doing the phrase injustice. *Secular City* is a handy phrase for the aggregate achievements of modernity: scientific, technological, commercial, governmental, educational—a worldly environment with divisions of labor and a need for trained specialists, demanding a practical, down-to-earth, eye-to-business focus for those who wish to do well and prosper. The most visible embodiment of modernity is *the big city*: urban and suburban skylines of steel and glass (replacing the smoke-belching factory towers of yesteryear); highways, streets, parking garages, pavement generally; landscapes of green here and there in between street, glass, and metal structures. Apartment complexes and tall towers for high-density living and working. Rows of subdivisions interspersed with big-box stores and shopping malls and restaurants for every palate from fast food to fine dining. Vehicles of all kinds filling (sometimes choking) those streets, roads, and superhighways. Abundant foot traffic. The sound and perhaps sight of an ascending or descending airplane. Constant motion; an omnipresent sense of activity (even at night). A marketplace, with a few government regulations seen by most as sensible, delivering the satisfaction of every human need and want for the prices it sets, determined by supply, demand, and what consumers are able and willing to spend.

The Secular University trains the Secular City's future professionals and employees to fit available slots in its various forms of organizational machinery (known as *jobs*). It became an appendage of the Secular City and its values long ago. Thus whatever its stated pretenses, its largest embodiments (e.g. "flagship" state universities) have done less and less over time to nurture the "life of the mind." For the majority of Secular City denizens, the Secular University means athletic contests. Secular University athletic departments are sources of diversionary entertainment (and revenue!). While obviously needing input from intelligent people, the Secular City professes little need for intellectuals, and so warehouses them in Secular University cubicles in buildings sometimes existing (literally) in the shadows of the football stadium.

Some business professionals sense the need for ethicists, especially when an Enron or a Bernie Madoff make headlines. The political class ignores philosophy, except for occasional (and often negative) references to Ayn Rand. Did anyone hear much in the way of philosophical ideas in any recent presidential debates (the most recent, as of this writing, being those of 2016)? There are hot-button issues aplenty: race, inequality, health care, sexual misconduct, abortion, guns, climate change. But what I recall most from 2016, aside from observing directly how easy it is for politicians and pundits to lead people by their noses with phrases and memes, I recall personal attacks aplenty, and at least one unprecedented attempt by a major candidate for the highest office in the land to delegitimize an entire group of voters ("baskets of deplorables").

Might the absence from our media-saturated public consciousness of the kinds of logical and moral constraints philosophy might supply be contributing to the polarization of the country and the diminishing quality of civic discourse?

Open charges that one has committing an informal fallacy (e.g., *ad hominem*), however, sound strangely quaint in this brave new world. We chuckle uncomfortably.

Almost as if, in exchanges between adults in the real world, such things are out of place.

Even before this, during my own career as an academic philosopher, I had more than one student tell me, with the assurance of the college sophomore, "Everybody has a philosophy."

With this one remark, philosophy is privatized.

Naturally, everybody's "philosophy" is different. None are "true" or "right" in any objective sense; nor are they "wrong." To say that these days is to be *insensitive*. What's "true" is what's "true for you," based on your feelings. We never want to hurt anybody's feelings with critical analysis. The implications of this subjectivism have not been pondered enough. Nor has the paradox of advocating *tolerance* as an island of absoluteness amidst the vast sea of subjectivism on our "woke" campuses. For in this vast sea is public shaming aplenty for this or that perceived infraction, with other denizens of the Secular University doing the expected public virtue-signaling. *Public* here includes social media, obviously, through which words and images are shared everywhere almost instantaneously on multiple platforms.

Do we see how philosophy's "retreat" has had not just isolable historical *causes* but specific *consequences*: not just an inability to recognize the influence the philosophers and movements we surveyed above have had, but that it has become harder and harder for people with different philosophies to talk to one another. Mere disagreement with a "woke" point of view is heard by its true believer as a signal of hate, not merely to be scorned but treated as *evil* and to be *canceled*.

Sadly, for decades the Secular City cultivated indifference to matters philosophical, and hence indifference to those values able to sustain civil discourse. The philosophies that have been influential have indeed made things worse. "Wokism" is an existential threat to civil discourse, and to civilization itself of whatever Stage.

What initial takeaways do we have here?

First, Secular City preoccupations and values, oriented around commerce and enabling technology, created a civilizational environment in which conscientious philosophers concerned with truth or a moral outlook on the world as ends in themselves are unlikely to be noticed. Few philosophers do what is necessary for visibility in the Secular City. They don't have business or marketing skills, or interest in such. Most are bashful introverts, and not assertive. In a fast-paced world, the philosopher's preference for patient reflection goes against the grain. The soft voice of the careful and responsible thinker is inaudible against the cacophonic background of advertising campaigns, talk-radio shouters, political debates, sexy reality TV escapades featuring the latest celebrities, Hollywood productions, and rapid-fire Twitter feeds. The occasional philosopher who speaks up is akin to a whisperer amidst cheering throngs in a sports arena.

Second, Secular City institutions are by nature hierarchical and bureaucratic. Without lines of authority and obedience to superiors, they can't function. What penchant philosophers have for questioning authority goes against this grain and is therefore unwelcome. The Secular City mindset emphasizes conformity and rules to be accepted and followed, not flouted. It emphasizes practicality over ponderances unless the latter are tied to economic projections or investments or other activities suggesting profitability to business or usefulness in government. This pushes aside all of what the philosophical whisperer wants to encourage.

None of this began yesterday. As far back as the 1850s, a low-key cold war was brewing between scholars and professional educators who favored liberal arts learning versus a rising tide of vocationalism. Education was already dividing into what seemed to favor landed and moneyed elites versus that of the laboring masses. The land grant system (created by the Morrill Act which Abraham Lincoln signed into law as a wartime measure) sought a compromise. It led to "A&M" (for *agricultural and mechanical*) public universities with an eye to serving the needs and wants of big business as it rose in stature, while ensuring places for liberal arts learning in its cubicles.

And although private liberal arts colleges remained to serve the children of the elites, what should be clear is that overall, vocationalism won this cold war. Thus began the public Secular University, growing into modernity alongside, and inside, the Secular City, as its servile educational appendage. The only vocation for philosophers in this environment is teaching, and what is taught is decorative rather than practical—an ode to the past, perhaps, but not intended to contribute much of utility to the present.

Thus philosophy's marginalization. Philosophers were less and less heard from, except for the occasional Bertrand Russell who was jailed more than once for his antiwar activities, or were doing something the big business elites believed they could use (e.g., John Dewey and progressive education). Otherwise, unless there was some kind of celebrity angle or momentary spectacle, philosophy all but disappeared unless it involved excitement or outrage.

An example was Peter Singer creating a storm of public controversy suggesting the moral acceptability of "after-birth abortions," stating that doctors should be free to euthanize infants born severely deformed on the spot, a claim that had members of the disabled community gasping in disbelief. His claim was not about disabilities *per se*. It was that self-awareness is part of personhood, that newborn infants are not self-aware, and hence have no inherent right to life.[10] Actually, Singer—as a defender of the moral right to an abortion—had gone further than that. He had rejected the idea that *birth* is a crucial divider between personhood and nonpersonhood. Philosophers could have observed that in the absence of any theistically grounded conception of the sanctity of human life, a topic

---

10. Singer, *Practical Ethics*, 142.

of limited interest in the Secular City and therefore in the Secular University, lines of reasoning such as Singer's (and he was hardly alone) would be very hard to refute. Singer's worldview, we might add, was Darwinian like that of all "scientific philosophers" in a Secular University where philosophy was a handmaiden to science.

We can count such cases on our fingers, however.

Generally, in the Secular City and even in the Secular University, the philosopher is at best a harmless eccentric and at worst a troublemaker (as Marcuse was sometimes viewed). He or she may try to elicit thoughtful responses from students in the classroom and sometimes even succeed, but overall the philosopher flourishes by furthering or at least not trying to undermine Secular University policies. Although a handful of philosophers have gotten their fifteen minutes of fame here and there, in an environment of total media saturation and ever-shortening attention spans amidst the many distractions and constant noise, few in the Secular City or even the Secular University will encounter their names. Few will associate anything they see and hear with a philosophical perspective or worldview. What they will see and hear are buzzwords, phrases, and memes designed for influence but not to be thought about.

A few years ago, they heard about a *war on terror*, but again with rare exceptions, no one afforded them the tools to ask questions like, *Who is a terrorist and who is not, and why?*

Or to evaluate for themselves the commitment by their leaders who have declared war on a *tactic* and not named any actual *foe* other than some easily-demonized agency such as an Osama bin Laden.

Present-day "woke" targets such as "systemic racism," I would argue, are no different.

But again, despite the noise and conflict, shouldn't we just relax? The Trump years will pass, after all, and we will again see leaders in all areas of science, technology, geopolitics, etc., who are *wise* in some sense of this term. We will elect them, will we not? Is America not still the Exceptional Nation among Western democracies?

And as things in the Secular City get better and better, what is really more important than public health and safety, new technology-based conveniences, and money changing hands?

Third Stage Civilization: Nietzsche's Warning and the Emergence of Unease.

So is the philosopher simply an oddball or misfit? A doddering old fool stuck in the past, and not much worthy of being taken seriously?

No one doubts or denies the achievements of Third Stage civilization in every area of science, technology, and commerce. We have skylines our ancestors could never have imagined. Technologies that would have seemed to them products of magic. We can transport ourselves safely from continent to continent in a matter of hours, while our progenitors had to spend weeks crossing an ocean such as the Atlantic, many not surviving the voyage. Our communications grid spans the globe. Using devices we can hold in one hand we can talk in real time to someone on the other side of the world.

Third Stage "scientific philosophy" simply accepts that science alone discovers truth about the world. Technology works because its operating principles reflect physical realities uncovered by science. Third Stage (i.e., mature) philosophers may concern themselves with justification in the sciences. Or ponder the mystery of how conscious self-awareness or "mind" fits into the scientific picture of the world. Or they may work for a more "diverse" Secular University. They may reason from moral premises taken as givens: more equality is better than more inequality; rights ought to be respected; (for Libertarians) one should never initiate physical force against another. Philosophers' reasonings in all these areas and others besides fill bookshelves in university libraries. Philosophy, one might say, found its place in the cubicles and classrooms and libraries of the Secular University.

Nothing like Third Stage civilization had ever (that we know of) been attempted before. It assertively challenged all earlier premises about what kind of world this is, who we were, and what we were capable of. It posed added challenges for itself. And it soon confronted profound *unease*—a mood impossible to dispel by means of pithy questions of the sort we used to open this section, or suggestions that we just *relax*. We may have gained much in this civilization. But have we lost a few things in the process? The acute unease many people will likely experience with positions such as Singer's surely suggest that we've lost *something*! Especially with medical technology growing by leaps and bounds, able to sustain life by artificial means—or to *shut it off* if it becomes inconvenient or expensive! Was a philosophical enterprise reduced to academic decoration positioned to meet the challenges Secular City advances were posing?

From the start, there were writers who believed that our actual freedoms and capacities as persons for a fullness of life were being diminished, not enhanced, by modernity. A few nineteenth-century writers rejected the very grounding of Third Stage philosophy from the outset. Søren Kierkegaard, for whom this world is in not the last analysis rationally comprehensible, would *never* have been tempted by it. He was repelled by rising commerciality in his native Copenhagen, and by the superficiality of the Church of Denmark in accommodating it.

Fyodor Dostoevsky, who obviously never heard of Kierkegaard, developed fictional characters who would wrestle in their own ways with the fate of a moral view of the world in the developing Secular City. He would have found Comte's Law of Three Stages horrifying (not to mention Singer!). He saw Christian belief withering before the onslaught of modernity and its encirclements. His *Notes from Underground* (1864) portrayed the mindset of the faceless clerk, cursed as it were by an ability to think and a sense of his identity as *more*, but trapped in and enraged by the machine bureaucracy encircling him (and one should consider that in Dostoevsky's day, such systems were in their infancy). And what of the implications of the scientific view of the universe for a moral view of the human world? Dostoevsky's final work, *The Brothers Karamazov* (1879–80), is known for the line often attributed (incorrectly) to central character Ivan Karamazov: "If God doesn't exist, then everything is permitted."

One could call this the *first* challenge to Third Stage thinking within the Secular City. It was based mainly on unease with where Third Stage ideas seemed to take us. Why are we not permitted to treat God's removal from the scene as an instrument for total liberation: political, commercial, sexual? Why not sweep aside all that had gone before and instead rest society's foundation on Scientific Reason? (The Jacobins of France had, of course, looked at the matter in just that way.)

Nietzsche merits being identified as the next pivotal figure. He saw more clearly than anyone before what the end of Christendom portended. The loss of Christianity's God indeed meant the loss of every idea and value belief in this God sustained. Interestingly, Nietzsche directed as much rebellion against the secular moral philosophies which had appeared or were appearing as he did Christianity. He believed they dishonestly tried to retain an essentially Christian morality without the supernatural, and so were doomed to fail.

Within the *ethos* of Christianity, moral commands have force because moral agents—persons—are created by and servile before God, their intrinsic value and moral accountability originating with God. Absent God's mercy and grace through Christ's saving power, disobedience to God's commands calls down eternal punishment on sinners: all of us.

With God dethroned, as it were, replaced by, e.g., Kant's categorical imperative, we have the servile mindset of the moralist without the substance.

For absent God, there is neither reward for turning to him nor any threat of punishment for sin. Hence there is no justification for the servile mindset other than the psychologically-imbedded morality of the slave—the same notion we saw above gleaned from Hegel. Nietzsche proposed a "revaluation of all values": a revolution in our thinking about moral*ities*: slave or master? A morality for the slaves of an extinct God (and his presumed Earthly servants)? Or one suited for the indifferent universe of the advancing Third Stage conception of the world in which we become our own masters?

To frame Nietzsche's realization more starkly: *there is nothing in the physical structure of the universe disclosed by natural science suggestive of morality as* philosophers *had conceived it, much less religionists.*

Nietzsche could thus speak of the "genealogy" of morals. He could begin studying moralities with the presumed detachment of the scientist. What sort of morality, he asked, might be suitable for human life in a universe indifferent to life—perhaps even *hostile* to it? His answer: a morality which identifies as *good* all those things life can do to increase its capacity to survive, grow, strengthen itself, and *thrive*, doing what it has to do to *dominate its environment.*

Thus Nietzsche called for getting rid of Christian categories altogether (e.g., *good* vs *evil*). The morality of the future in a world without God would be a morality of strength, health, courage—even the prowess of the warrior—standing up and *defying* the indifference of the universe, as its adherents *mastered* their surroundings. What enhanced the capacity of the strong and dominant was *good*. What interfered with this capacity or its exercise was not *evil* (what did *that* mean, anyway?) but simply *bad*.

What was holding modernity back, in that case? Christian moral categories, whether they appeared in Christian encyclicals or secular moral philosophers' treatises. Hence Nietzsche's scathing broadsides.

To *not* create this new morality *now*, moreover, would be dangerous. Not doing so would leave a moral *vacuum* when Christianity's collapse was complete, leaving *nothing*. Not creating a morality shorn of Christian foundations threatened the world with an "advent of nihilism" (from *nihil*, Latin for *nothing*). Nietzsche saw this as the greatest danger facing humanity in what we are calling Third Stage civilization. To be sure we understand Nietzsche was *not* a nihilist. As a system-smasher in our sense above, he was tearing down what he saw as dated and hopeless. He was exposing elements in secular moral theories (especially Kant's) that were no longer tenable for the same reasons an out-of-date worldview was untenable. And he wanted to warn the world of the nihilism to come as these theories lost their legitimacy alongside Christianity if *nothing* appropriate for Third Stage civilization replaced them.

It was a tall order few understood. Did Nietzsche himself believe it would happen? His "last men" were those masses who couldn't rise to the occasion and who would become the slaves of the aristocracy of Masters, assuming such Masters actually appeared. Nietzsche's writings grew more anxious and extreme in the 1880s. Insanity finally struck him, leaving him unable to care for himself. His challenge to post-Christian Third Stage thought stood, however. Would an aristocracy of Masters appear? Such Masters would carry forward optimistically, with strength and courage! But where were they?

What ensued in the decades to follow was an existential choice for philosophers and literary figures: *cosmic optimism* or *cosmic pessimism*? Cosmic optimism may be broadly seen as the idea that however it occurs, all that happens in the world will work itself out so that persons can be hopeful for the future. Cosmic pessimism is the opposite view that, in the end, perhaps because life ends with death and because the human race itself is doomed to eventual extinction, all is futile and hopeless.

Christendom as a civilization had been optimistic by default: God existed, was supreme over the world; this meant that Providence held, and believers were assured of their place in heaven and in a final resolution for all historical conflict. Third Stage "scientific philosophy" set out to sustain optimism, but on an entirely different footing, one based on human possibilities instead of divine providence.

Cosmic optimism was clearly "built into" Third Stage civilization, given its assumptions about the possibilities of science, technology, commerce, and education. Belief in the inevitability of progress is by definition optimistic. But if Third Stage civilization failed to meet Nietzsche's challenges, it would be unmasked as self-deceptive. Third Stage thought would then be brought into question in various ways. It would start to break down, first at the margins, and then closer to its center. Its breakdown would herald something Comte nowhere imagined: a Fourth Stage incorporating a cosmic pessimism in which hope was lost: not merely hope for a new morality but hope for meaningful human life, for truth itself, and possibly even reasons why the human race should survive.

Bertrand Russell's Brand of Hope.

Bertrand Russell became the first major analytic philosopher focusing on language and science. Our focus here will not be on works such as his (and Whitehead's) *Principia*, however, but on a short "popular" essay he penned: an essay entitled "A Free Man's Worship." It was not widely read by his fellow analysts. This was a sign of the times. Third Stage philosophers were already growing unconcerned with writing for an audience of nonspecialists. Russell was an exception. He was able to write for both specialists and nonspecialists.

"A Free Man's Worship" is Third Stage through and through. Russell appears to have suffered none of the anxieties that drove Kierkegaard, Dostoevsky, or Nietzsche, moreover. Unlike them he was "at home in the universe," one might say. His essay calmly poses essentially the same challenge as Nietzsche did, however: ground morality on human-created values and aspirations alone, in the universe science seemed to disclose. Russell's was not a morality of strength and prowess. It was a follow-up to earlier secular moralizing dating back to Hume, that of social utility adding quests for peace and justice—to be held despite the seeming emptiness of the universe.

Russell opened his essay dramatically (this is worth quoting at length):

> To Dr. Faustus in his study Mephistopheles told the history of the Creation saying:
>
> "The endless praises of the choirs of angels had begun to grow wearisome; for, after all, did he not deserve their praise? Had he not given them endless joy? Would it not be more amusing to obtain undeserved praise, to be worshipped by beings whom he tortured? He smiled inwardly, and resolved that the great drama should be performed.
>
> "For countless ages the hot nebula whirled aimlessly through space. At length it began to take shape, the central mass threw off planets, the planets cooled, boiling seas and burning mountains heaved and tossed, from masses of cloud not sheets of rain deluged the barely solid crust. And now the first germ of life grew in the depths of the ocean, and developed rapidly in the fructifying warmth into vast forest trees, huge germ springing from the damp mould, sea monsters breeding, fighting, devouring, and passing away. And from the monsters, as the play unfolded itself, Man was born, with the power of thought, the knowledge of good and evil, and the cruel thirst for worship. And Man saw that all is passing in this mad, monstrous world, that all is struggling to snatch, at any cost, a few brief moments of life before Death's inexorable decree. And Man said: 'There is a hidden purpose, could we but fathom it, and the purpose is good; for we must reverence something, and in this visible world there is nothing worthy of reverence.' And man stood aside from the struggle, resolving that God intended harmony to come out of chaos by human efforts. And when he followed

the instincts which God had transmitted to him from his ancestry of beasts of prey, he called it Sin, and asked God to forgive him. But he doubted whether he could be justly forgiven, until he invented a divine Plan by which God's wrath was to have been appeased. And seeing the present was bad, he made it yet worse, that thereby the future might be better. And he gave God thanks for the strength that enabled him to forgo even the joys that were possible. And God smiled; and when he saw that Man had become perfect in renunciation and worship, he sent another sun through the sky, which crashed into Man's sun; and all returned again to nebula.

"'Yes,' he murmured, 'it was a good play; I will have it performed again.'

"Such in outline, but even more purposeless, more void of meaning, is the world which Science presents for our belief. Amid such a world, if anywhere, our ideals henceforth must find a home. That man is the product of causes which had no prevision of the end they were achieving; that his origin, his growth, his hopes and fears, his loves and his beliefs, are but the outcome of accidental collocations of atoms; that no fire, no heroism, no intensity of thought and feeling, can preserve an individual life beyond the grave; that all the labours of the ages, all the devotion, all the inspiration, all the noonday brightness of human genius, are destined to extinction . . . all these things, if not quite beyond dispute, are yet so nearly certain, that no philosophy which rejects them can hope to stand. . . .

"Brief and powerless is Man's life; on him and all his race the slow, sure doom falls pitiless and dark. Blind to good and evil, reckless of destruction, omnipotent matter rolls on its relentless way; for man, condemned today to lose his dearest, tomorrow himself to pass through the gate of darkness, it remains only to cherish, ere yet the blow falls, the lofty thoughts that ennoble his little day."[11]

Thus the words of a philosopher who had placed Settled Science (note how he capitalized *Science*) on that positivist altar, expressing the conclusion that if the scientific view of the universe as then conceived was true, then again, in terms of morality we are on our own.

To this extent he agrees with Nietzsche.

We should instill in ourselves ideals which make our world better for all, however, or at least make life more tolerable for as many people as

11. Russell, "Free Man's Worship," 46–48, 56–57.

possible, ideals aligned with meliorism as noted above (and with the utilitarianism of his godfather, John Stuart Mill).

We find nothing in Russell about Masters, which implies the existence of slaves, figurative or actual.

Nietzsche would have seen this as just one more dishonest lapse back into Christianity-without-the-supernatural.

Thus the first tension within Third Stage moral philosophy that would start to tear it apart, and from which most philosophers "retreated." Equality, justice, and peace for all, or as much as is humanly possible, following someone such as Russell or some other humanist thinker who trusted in fundamental human goodness (an idea going back at least to Rousseau), or at least the idea that we are born morally neutral and hence can *become good*?

Or the rise of Masters who would rule as they saw fit because they *could*, and did not eschew war if it served their purposes (such notions go back to system-smashers such as Thrasymachus who see justice as the "will of the stronger party")? Strauss and his followers were sympathetic to this, and I would argue, an implicit and latent version of this idea is very much in evidence in present-day technological and especially financial power centers in the West, and possible elsewhere as well (mainland China?).

The former would uphold Enlightenment-derived ideals they saw as applicable to all—just as God had created all persons in his image. There's our Christianity-without-the-supernatural. Philosophers and other humanists would speak of *rights* of various sorts: negative rights, positive rights, or just universal human rights: moral claims others were obligated to respect even if just to leave the rights-claimants alone. These might include such rights as to a minimum wage, or a minimum standard of living. Secular Libertarians would speak of an absolute right to liberty, based on the NAP, which might conflict with the idea of positive rights (another tension to be considered below, in Chapter 4).

Those who believed Nietzsche's was the truer perspective would embrace such views as the existence of a natural aristocracy (Straussians included themselves in this aristocracy), a denial that there are any such things as "rights," and that rulership over the masses—or, under neoliberalism, rich rulership over the poor and middle-class—is the natural order of things. And for the neoliberal with a dark sense of humor, "he who dies with the most toys wins"!

In short, these various voices issued a challenge to Third Stage philosophy *and* Third Stage civilization. With Russell's brand of hope maintained in the face of Settled Science: if meliorism is true, then show this by creating and sustaining a morality for a world without a God in it based on peace, justice, and universal human rights—or, for those so include, on the NAP. Accept the adult responsibility that comes with Third Stage life.

Or, with Nietzsche, fail to do this and fall into nihilism. Eventually destroying ourselves with the worsening destructive power our own technology would unleash.

How did we do?

"Things Fall Apart; the Center Cannot Hold...."

War, exploding across Europe in 1914, rocked the hopes and ideals of Third Stage meliorists. During ensuing years and decades, new tyrannies arose, some indeed posing for themselves as aristocracies of Masters both willing and able to vanquish (not merely conquer) those deemed unfit for life in their world.

Only in the still somewhat Christianized United States did we see anything even remotely resembling Russell's brand of hope, and even there, only in part.

Elsewhere, the twentieth century visited upon us unprecedented levels of genocide that horrified moral consciences of all stripes. Nietzsche would surely have been horrified as well, as dictatorships actually having none of the traits he ascribed to the Masters he envisioned embraced *brutalism: might is right and can do as it pleases because who is going to stand in its way* (Mao: "Political power grows out of the barrel of a gun") *even if this includes murdering millions in cold blood while leaving millions more in abject misery.*

It was as if history itself was *mocking* our Third Stage meliorist pretenses.

Philosophy, having "retreated" to embrace its role as handmaiden to science, was no longer in much of a position to challenge the gathering Settled Science consensus within the social sciences, especially anthropology, about the nature of morality: it is a *cultural artifact*. It might sometimes give voice to our "ideals" about peace and justice, but morality changes from culture to culture, or from one historical epoch to the next within the same culture (as the nearly all cultures once embraced chattel slavery). Morality, according to Third Stage scientific thought, is not "anchored" in a transcendent realm outside human aspirations. It does not exist outside a sentient being's preference for survival over death, happiness over unhappiness, or pleasure over pain—or, perhaps, for reason and order over unreason and chaos—when indeed these preferences can actually be given force. Its specifics change from place to place, so that homosexuality could be rejected as immoral in Christian cultures but embraced as a higher type of love than heterosexuality in the

Greece of Plato's era. Anthropologists such as Franz Boas and especially his student Ruth Benedict would make all this explicit.[12]

In the latter, desirable behavior is inculcated through local upbringing and it becomes habitual; the moral *language* surrounding it reflecting its desirability to the culture. Those who do not develop socially approved habits are dealt with by what Mill called social sanction, sometimes harshly. There may be a moral "police force," even absent a priesthood. It may be a state institution with police powers, or just the local equivalent of neighborhood watch. It may be a (manufactured?) public consensus to provide a basis for social sanction, so that the result of breaking the rules is ostracism (or *canceling*). The difference is one of vocabulary, not substance. In Third Stage thinking, morality's authority comes down to the authority of those cultural "masters" able to speak for it and direct it. Nietzsche saw more clearly than Russell where such views ended—although also by the 1930s and even in the 1950s, Russell would embrace what he saw as the prospects of social engineering by a scientifically-informed elite of technocrats.[13]

But otherwise, *everything is arbitrary!*

Where were professional philosophers while all this was going on? In the English-speaking world, most had embraced logical positivism and their status as handmaiden to science. Some gave voice to this latter with a Humanist Manifesto, a slight update on the Russellian brand of hope adding new wrinkles such as democratic socialism (e.g. through John Dewey, although other philosophers signed it).[14]

Such efforts rang increasingly hollow when weighed against man's continuing inhumanity to his fellows when he got his hands on power.

The art world, reflected in art history, reflects its own response to latent Third Stage premises. In their own way, they did the job philosophers were ceasing to do, and they began to do it not long after Dostoevsky's characters began suggesting universal permissiveness if God did not exist. Why, artists began to ask, should art represent reality? Why, given the ideas gaining currency, should it depict human beings as having any specialness apart from the natural world order? The trend toward nonrepresentational art begun by the Impressionists of the late 1800s (examples: Claude Monet, Paul Cezanne).opened the door. Marcel Duchamp, one of the inventors of Cubism, walked through it. In Duchamp's best known painting, *Nude Descending a Staircase* (1912), the human figure blends so perfectly into the background as to be virtually invisible.

12. See Benedict, *Patterns of Culture*.
13. Cf. Russell, *Scientific Outlook*; Russell, *Impact of Science on Society*.
14. Dewey et al., *Humanist Manifesto*.

What better way to depict the very thing Dostoevsky had warned about, to wit, the disappearance of human agency in the naturalist's universe. In the Darwinian world in which we are just big-brained animals, we can speak, we can bathe, and we can build machines, but nothing else about us stands out. Beavers build dams, after all. Ideals of justice and peace? Ink on paper. And if we are made up *exclusively* of the same atoms and molecules as our surroundings, an original and talented artist can represent this by blending us seamlessly into them in a painting.

Absurdism then reared its ugly head—especially after the Great War. Human life could be depicted as absurd when it could be destroyed wantonly, without reason, almost randomly, via bombs dropped from those new machines, aircraft, without so much as a backward glance. The Dadaists, combining the Surrealism of Salvador Dali and the Cubism of Duchamp and Pablo Picasso, then tossing elements of Freud in for good measure, openly celebrated absurdity. They were consistent. The absurdity of all human life and activity meant the absurdity of art. Again, Duchamp portrayed this the best, as seen in his *Fountain* (sometimes incorrectly called *Urinal*)—it was indeed a urinal, a random object or "readymade" put on a pedestal for an exhibit back in 1917 and displayed as art.

In the post-Great War world, Ernest Hemingway's novels and short stories (e.g., *The Sun Also Rises* in 1926, and "Soldier's Home" in the previous year's *In Our Time* collection) depicted disillusioned expatriates and former soldiers who sensed being lost in a world that had demolished their (mankind's) ideals—able, perhaps, to stand defiant like a Nietzschean Master (e.g., like a bullfighter in *The Sun Also Rises* or, later, in *The Old Man and the Sea* in 1952) but compelled to concede the long-term futility of it all. Hemingway finally took his own life in 1961.

Other writers and artists pursued similar themes, often in increasingly extreme ways. F. Scott Fitzgerald's *The Great Gatsby* (1925) portrayed the restlessness and rootlessness of the generation coming of age in the Great War's aftermath, as well as the fruitlessness of materialism. At the end of the day, despite his parties Gatsby has no real friends. Nor are relationships real. All are deceptive. Narrator Nick Carroway leaves New York to return to his Midwestern home fully disillusioned. Author Fitzgerald turned to alcohol which eventually ruined his health. He died of a heart attack in 1940, aged forty-four.

Nonrepresentational art got more extreme with Abstract Expressionists such as Jackson Pollack, who laid canvasses on his studio floor, poured paint on them, allowed it to dry, then hung the results on walls as art. Pollack, too, was a heavy drinker and died in a one-vehicle alcohol-related traffic accident in 1956.

The rise of polytonality and atonality in music mirrored the conclusion that if all was arbitrary, so was the traditional musical scale. Austrian-born composer Arnold Schoenberg thus threw out the traditional scale and substituted the twelve-tone serialism for which he is best known. The resulting compositions bordered on unlistenable, sometimes trying the patience of audiences. But maybe the distinction between performer and audience was also arbitrary and optional. Schoenberg's American aesthetic descendent John Cage blurred this difference, and between music and random sound. In his infamous *4'33"* (1952), the "performer" sits before a closed piano for the duration of the piece. The audience hears only random sounds, which could range from someone in the audience coughing to traffic going by outside. In other words, not just tonality but the rules of composition themselves can be discarded at will, just as the idea that art should be representational had been discarded over a century before.

Aesthetic values—like moral values—were cultural artifacts only.

Among philosophers, the ideas in "A Free Man's Worship" and "Humanist Manifesto I" languished for a long time. In the late 1940s, Walter T. Stace revisited them in the title essay of his collection *Man Against Darkness* (orig. 1948; the title alone ought to indicate something unsettling was happening):

> So long as there was believed to be a God in the sky . . . men could regard him as the source of their moral ideals. The universe, created and governed by a fatherly God, was a friendly habitation for man. We could be sure that, however great the evil in the world, good in the end would triumph and the forces of evil would be routed. With the disappearance of God from the sky all this has changed. Since the world is not ruled by a spiritual being, but rather by blind forces, there cannot be any ideals, moral or otherwise, in the universe outside us. Our ideals, therefore, must proceed only from our own minds; they are our own inventions. The world which surrounds us is nothing but an immense spiritual emptiness. It is a dead universe. We do not live in a universe which is on the side of our values. It is completely indifferent to them.[15]

Neither Russell nor Stace questioned the metaphysical and methodological premises of Third Stage thought. They subscribed fully to its core tenet: in matters epistemic, Settled Science gets the last word. Settled Science has made it incredible that *anyone's* god exists. The world is physical or material, and contains no "numinous" or "spiritual" elements. Life is indeed brief, and ends with death which is the extinction of the individual personality. In terms of morality and purpose we are on our own.

The absurdist chooses to face this honestly and derive what fleeting pleasures and adventures this brief passage has to offer. Among these were the pleasures of swimming in pools and having sex with young girls that the character Meursault enjoyed in Albert Camus's *The Stranger*—prior to his shooting the Arab. And recall how, in the essay "The Myth of Sisyphus," Camus identifies the fundamental problem of present-day philosophy as suicide. Camus escaped by recommending seeking out the pleasures life has to offer, and to make the decision that we're all in this life together. Hemingway, who had lived a life of adventure, did not escape.

The Beats pursued lives devoted to immediate pleasures enhanced by the recreational drugs of the day. The hippies of the 1960s, many of them conveying idealistic messages of peace and love, continued with the more

---

15. Stace, "Man Against Darkness," in Stace, *Man Against Darkness and Other Essays*, 1-2.

extreme explorations of induced substitutes for the realities around them with, e.g., LSD, delivering "nonrepresentational" experiences.

In the 1970s that kind of scene seemed to calm down somewhat. Kids cut their hair and returned to conforming, a cynic might say. The culture itself shifted as the idealism of the recent past began to dissipate. Arguably, the Yuppies (1980s and beyond) very much fit the bill as Nietzsche's "last men" (and women). Eventually, too, we went from Martin Luther King Jr.'s stirring call to be judged "not according to the color of our skin but the content of our character" to the verbal violence of "gangsta rap" and eventually to the tribalism of identity politics and finally our present cultural nihilism: "wokism." Feminism, meanwhile, went from its second-wave calls for equal pay for equal work (1960s) to defenses of abortion (1970s) and its infamous third wave blurring of voluntary sex being akin to rape (1980s and beyond).[16] And of course, alcohol and recreational drugs continued to be a problem.

Not only were there fewer and fewer visible signs of Russellian ideals; not only were we no longer getting along; but arguably the world was getting more hostile as it grew more frenetic and fast-paced. Many of us traded technological visions of colonizing space to present-day addictions to screens as a mode of escape.

As for suicide: its rates have climbed, along with the psychological disturbances that give rise to thoughts of ending one's life. Victims included many who were judged highly successful by Secular City standards (one thinks of prominent singers / songwriters like Kurt Cobain and respected actors / entertainers like Robin Williams).

Russell maintained his views to the end of his life, professing peace and social justice in a world that was delivering neither. Stace developed an interest in mysticism and began to explore Eastern faiths. It was as if, as he got older, he found the worldview behind "Man Against Darkness" less and less satisfying and was casting about for something else, something no longer to be found in the West. Leo Strauss and his disciples would appear and further their agenda. As would Herbert Marcuse and his progeny. There would be no peace, and while poverty was mitigated somewhat, massive inequality remained. As neoliberalism started taking hold in the 1980s, gulfs between rich and poor would widen instead of lessen, along with a mindset holding that if you are poor it is exclusively the result of your own bad choices. Not the choices of those for whom gaming the financialized system was a fine science to use for self-benefit while furthering policies limiting options or actually causing harm to others.

16. See MacKinnon, *Feminism Unmodified*.

Third Stage political-economy had given rise to capitalist civilization and its living standards, giving rise to that befuddled, "What are these people complaining about?" But the fragmenting of the Third Stage intellect and culture on many levels and in multiple arenas—artistic, literary, and philosophical—was delivering more and more unintended consequences, many of them not as visible as technological change. Modernity as a way of thinking and living seemed to be inducing, in the asker of such befuddled questions, a myopia that was a condition of psychological survival in a world of encirclements and deceptions. This myopia was not for everybody. Those who rejected it as "inauthentic" immediately experienced the unease.

As William Butler Yeats had written in his most famous poem *The Second Coming* back in 1919, illustrating the shadow of unease falling over modernity even then,

> Things fall apart; the center cannot hold;
> Mere anarchy is loosed upon the world,
> the blood-dimmed tide is loosed, and everywhere
> the ceremony of innocence is drowned.
> The best lack all conviction, while the worst
> are full of passionate intensity.

Postmodernity, Narratives (Official and Otherwise), and the Emergence of Fourth Stage Civilization

By the final decades of the last century, we were hearing more and more about *postmodernism*, *postmodernity*, and the "postmodern condition." What was/is postmodernism? And what is this "condition" (Stage?) called postmodernity? The terms have never been easy to define, for they involve many things, all of them casting doubt on all that came before. For Jean-François Lyotard, the "*postmodern* [was] incredulity towards metanarratives."[17] What is a *metanarrative*? A second-order account of first-order narratives, i.e., guiding bodies of ideas presented as *stories* orienting us in the world, e.g., *progress* as understood by the historians of modernity, or a supposed *method* such as that found in the sciences told in exemplars such as Galileo and Newton, or those to come from positivists. Narratives are stories of all kinds told to make sense of the passing show and give legitimacy to our convictions about it, and about ourselves as truth-discoverers and truth-tellers. Truth itself becomes a kind of narrative. A

---

17. Lyotard, *Postmodern Condition*, xxiv.

CAUSES AND CONSEQUENCES OF THE "RETREAT" OF PHILOSOPHY

postmodernist would classify what we're doing *here* as a metanarrative, and express his incredulity (alas, it's already happened).

The results we just saw in our cursory survey of literary and artistic products of the Third Stage era are telling. But they are only the beginning. The idea that Third Stage thought and civilization were making unqualified *progress* was running up against objections in a number of arenas: philosophy of science and political economy among them. This became the case by the end of the 1960s. Three decades later, the Internet appeared and began its epistemic democratization of discourse. The results of that did far more to call the Third Stage consensus about the world into question.

First, analytic philosophy of science, via its precision, unintentionally undermined positivism's core tenets about how science operates (formulating hypotheses to explain phenomena of experience; experimenting, testing them step by step confirming them as theories for further refinement, extension, prediction; or possibly disconfirming them). Logical empiricists—the immediate descendants of logical positivists—discovered for themselves the weaknesses of formal logic as a tool. Their arcane but profound question: what justifies rational assent to the truth of a general proposition based on evidence? The question had seemed easy enough, but their tools turned up paradoxes.

For example, Carl Hempel formulated the paradox of the ravens.[18] Nelson Goodman uncovered the unusually named *grue* (or *grue/bleen*) paradox.[19]

The first noted that by a rule of propositional logic known as *contraposition*, "All ravens are black" is logically equivalent to "All non-black entities are non-ravens." Leaving technicalities aside, according to the rules of formal logic, every observation statement that confirms the former also confirms the latter. The result is that every observation of something that isn't black and isn't a raven confirms "All ravens are black" just as much as every observation of a black raven. Now since we could have used any universal affirmative not necessarily "All ravens are black," then *any particular statement whatever can be interpreted as confirming any universal statement whatever!*

This was absurd!

The *grue* or *grue/bleen* paradox noted that every observation statement that confirms the truth of "All emeralds are green" also confirms the truth of "All emeralds are *grue*," where *grue* is the property of emeralds being green before time *t* and blue after *t*. Since the number of times *t* is

---

18. Hempel, "Studies in the Logic of Confirmation," 1–26; Hempel, "Studies in the Logic of Confirmation II," 97–121.

19. See Goodman's "New Riddle of Induction," in *Fact, Fiction and Forecast*, 59–83.

potentially infinite, the observation statement "This S is P" confirms not just "All S is P" but an infinite number of predicates, variations on, "All S is observed to be P before time *t* or not observed but non-P after *t*." (*Bleen* just reverses the colors.)

This, too, was absurd.

Something was wrong. For *scientists* would obviously never even *formulate*, much less *test*, much less *confirm*, statements employing such predicates. This meant *philosophy* (not *science*) was off track.

Goodman called this *the new riddle of induction*. The original problem of induction, dating to Hume who never called it that (the word *induction* had yet to be coined) came down to: given the logical possibility that circumstances might change, how do we justify knowledge claims about the unobserved based on what we've observed? The Third Stage theorist of science could retort that such demands for certainty were wrongheaded and anachronistic, but *logical* justification seemed to call for more than mere consensus.

Historicists, Stephen Toulmin being the first, called out the formal logic of the logical empiricists as truncated and simplistic.[20] Such tools should be abandoned if our goal was to understand how science really works. It was necessary to look at history, at actual scientific communities, and how they reached conclusions. When we did, we saw a far different enterprise. The cause was quickly taken up by others such as Norwood Russell Hanson and those we have already met, Thomas S. Kuhn and Paul Feyerabend.[21] All these writers had studied the writings of the later Wittgenstein, the system smasher of ideal language philosophy. Wittgenstein had realized that its tools, the formal logic of the positivists/empiricists, was unsuited to the complexities and usages of natural language.[22] Apparently it was unsuited to natural science as well.

Hanson famously contended that observation in science is "theory-laden"; we do not, that is, approach facts, events, or experimental results neutrally but rather through the lens of a theoretical perspective. This perspective is epistemically *prior* to observation and conditions what the scientist sees. Kuhn's follow-up thoughts stressed the role of paradigms in science, and how major scientific changes always involve the replacement of one comprehensive paradigm by a sometimes incommensurable new one: the culmination of *revolutionary science*. The result was that the experienced

---

20. See Toulmin, *Philosophy of Science*.

21. See Hanson, *Patterns of Discovery*; Kuhn, *Structure*; Feyerabend, *Against Method*.

22. Wittgenstein, *Philosophical Investigations*.

"world" of the scientific community is changed at a fundamental level: different entities existed; or older ones fell into new relationships with one another. *Normal science*, a puzzle-solving endeavor, begins anew, defining the fundamental *truths* of the discipline anew by redefining what counts as the solution to a problem. (Feyerabend supported revolutionary science as *a permanent feature* of healthy, i.e., nondogmatic, science—something very different from *Settled Science*!)

What Kuhn's fellow philosophers found disturbing was his suggestion of the difficulty of clarifying what it meant to say that paradigm changes brought a science closer and closer to something called Truth, if Truth were construed as a complete, paradigm-independent description of the world. Descriptions are invariably dependent on language, sets of interdefined scientific terms (e.g., for physics, *space, place, mass, force, weight, motion, velocity*, and so on.), the meanings of which were paradigm-bound. When one set was replaced by another such set one had change, but there did not seem to be any higher-order, stable standard against which to measure both before and after, to ensure that change was *progressive*. To say just that the more recent theory captured more of what physical reality was like—*really*—involved circular reasoning if each theory defined physical reality (Truth) in its own way.

Feyerabend's brand of system smashing, as we've seen, was more radical. In his view, the very idea of a unique *scientific method* able to explain past progress and provide always-reliable advice on how to proceed in the present fails the test of history. *Method*, not just truth, is historically embedded. What this means: *Settled* Science is a myth akin to the myths of religionists and ideologues. History, Feyerabend believed, clearly showed that scientists have used different methods at different times. They've proceeded opportunistically, not "rationally" (whatever that means). If a given rule or method seemed to solve a pressing problem, the "good" scientist had no qualms about using it—even if it came from outside science (e.g., Kepler's and Newton's occasional invocations of astrology, the actual source of action-from-a-distance metaphysics that formed the basis of the theory of universal gravitation). One might also cite Christianity as a source for the very presumption of a world capable of rational explanation because it had been created by a God who was a rational Agent—in Greek terms, a *Logos*—not a whimsical "evil deceiver" (Descartes), a presumption that had appeared in Greek and Roman philosophy but reached its fullest articulation once the world of ideas was Christianized.

What was especially upsetting were Feyerabend's suggestions that nonscientific and "pseudo-scientific" practices, theories, traditions, and worldviews could improve the quest for knowledge *today*—or at the very least, we had no solid basis for *ruling them out*. He thus defended astrology from what he considered incompetent criticism, and came out in defense of other unorthodoxies and heresies ranging from acupuncture and herbal medicine to Biblical creationism, all as having rights, in principle, to a place at the table.[23]

Feyerabend's heresy comes down to the idea that when all is said and done, *there is no such thing as Settled Science!* There is consensus, agreement, dogma, but little to confirm that any of this is more than authority's demand for conformity, the larger scientific community's comfort with stability, and the willingness of all to expel annoying dissidents. The kind of justification Settled Science had arrogated for itself was an epistemic mirage. Nowhere to be found was a distinctive "method" definitive of science. This turns out to be a tenet of an intellectual ideology, or dogma.

Thus the partial collapse of the Third Stage image of science into the rising Fourth Stage.

Postmodernism had arrived at a similar place from a different (but overlapping) route. In France, Michel Foucault was exploring a range of ideas converging on the complex relationship between institutional structures based on power and claims to knowledge deriving from that sense of epistemic authority.[24] What they did was blur knowledge claims into power systems of various sorts so that the two became indistinguishable. Foucault became associated with the movement known as *structuralism*, although he would distance himself from that label, the result being "post-structuralism." Instead of paradigms we have *epistemes*: community-bound tacit conditions for what is to count as a possible contribution to a discourse, scientific or otherwise. Foucault, like Feyerabend, stressed that science did not exist in a special realm apart from the larger culture. In our terms: much of science done in the Secular University is not separate from local states of affairs in the Secular City—especially its funding mechanisms. This is just part and parcel with the Secular University being an appendage of the Secular City, including its military divisions, otherwise known as the defense industry, often the source of lucrative contracts funding scientific research. Could the conclusions of such research be deemed *neutral*?

Did such tendencies go overboard? Arguably as we'll see presently, maybe they didn't go far *enough*, or in the right direction. Language, scientific or otherwise, serves a variety of human interests, some of them not truth-*seeking* but truth-*concealing*. George Orwell expressed this better than any analytic philosopher in *Nineteen Eighty-Four*, with its coinage of terms like

---

23. Feyerabend, *Science in a Free Society*.
24. See Foucault, *Order of Things*; Foucault, *Archeology of Knowledge*.

newspeak and *memory hole*. Language is human, all-too-human, and it both can and is used to "bewitch our intelligence" (Wittgenstein).

Fourth Stage philosophy thus added its distinctive voice to Fourth Stage art, literature, and music, expressing its own unease and further undermining confidence in Third Stage thought. From the emerging perspective, given the ubiquity of language and its potential for deception, class, race/ethnicity, gender, etc., all of which became core preoccupations in the hands of the Marcusans, what sense was to be made of the idea of *universal* truth, *neutral* rationality and justification, or of *pure* and *uncontaminated* observation?

None, it seemed!

With Fourth Stage philosophy we were trending towards something more radical than just identity politics. Fourth Stage thought revels in paradox, disruption, discontinuity, incongruity, and a sense of intellectual infinite gamesmanship in which the purpose of thought is not some final state such as Truth but just to continue the play.[25]

The thing is, this was not all fun and games.

We've observed that identity politics (for example) poses no real challenge to the loci of power in the Western world. If anything, it is an academic distraction, sometimes more absurd than Dadaism (as when it proclaims, in all seriousness, that you can choose any "gender identity" you like) but most often simply irrelevant. Which begs us to ask: what are the real-world consequences of *a philosophical vacuum*—of having philosophies some with considerable influence but which are intellectually unserious, in a cultural and political-economic ethos absent *conscious* philosophical conversation occurring at any level of *fundamentals* or *first premises*?

What emerges is a kind of nihilism—combined with the brutalism of those who do as they please because they *can*: in a political economy that works to their advantage. Think yet again of the cult of "woke" and its erasure of historical monuments, evidence of history tainted or not, over the past year.

What occurred first was the transition from a Third Stage culture of optimism of the sort that used technology to send men to the moon and gave us inspiring television shows like *Star Trek* to Fourth Stage pessimism in which technology turns inward, addicts people to screens, produces selfies and films such as *The Hunger Games*. (Popular music went from the smooth harmonies of doo-wop to the violence of "gansta" rap; even celebrity sex appeal went from the elegance of Marilyn Monroe to the onstage porn of Miley Cyrus.)

---

25. Cf. Carse, *Finite and Infinite Games*.

Hope, in other words, is canceled along with history; the United Federation of Planets is replaced by Dystopia. The flaming out of optimistic meliorism went from art and literature to popular culture, in which one does not have to be a conservative (I hope!) to see as crude, decadent, and uncivil in comparison to past decades. The *general* idea of progress has been thrown into doubt even if we see progress in a few specific scientific areas like physics and astronomy (think of exoplanets), and in ever more efficient technologies (e.g., ever-faster instant messaging systems empowered by G5).

Political economy reveals a similar trajectory, especially over the past thirty years. As the 1990s began the Soviet Union collapsed and what Francis Fukuyama then called "the end of history" began.[26] Consumer capitalism had won the Cold War hands down! Or so went the narrative. Preceding years had seen the rise of neoliberalism in the Anglo-American worlds (Reagan in the United States; Thatcher in the United Kingdom). The 1990s saw unprecedented technological change and the beginnings of wealth consolidation based primarily on IPOs and financial instruments, in which growth was punctured by relatively sudden (but not unpredictable) financial crises such as 2008 and now 2020. Concentrations of wealth, which meant consolidations of power to dictate terms to governments via money flows, had begun to worry observers years before, it was clear, rising prosperity was not being shared by all, for previously prosperous sectors of populations (e.g., the American middle class) were losing ground. We saw the emergence of younger commentators such as Thomas Piketty.[27]

Arguably, the United States squandered its opportunity to assume genuine world leadership. Even before 2000, we saw evidence that the end of the Soviet Union wasn't the end of history (Fukuyama, to his credit, repudiated the idea). On September 11, 2001, the United States was attacked by terrorists directed from abroad. Or so we were told that was what happened that morning (there are "alternative" narratives, but hold that thought). In any event, it was an opportunity for Americans and their leaders to reflect on where they stood in the eyes of the rest of the world. Instead, six weeks later, the United States invaded a sovereign foreign nation, Afghanistan, beginning a war that is still continuing as of this writing, while passing draconian domestic legislation (the USA Patriot Act), eventually militarizing police forces and setting the stage for today's clashes over police brutality. While I question the narrative that white police are singling out unarmed black men in a "systemically racist" country, no serious person doubts that twenty-first-century police are more violent than their predecessors.

26. See Fukuyama, *End of History*.
27. See Piketty, *Capital in the 21st Century*.

The political class set the country up for the present mess, because voters were scared of another attack, and because it *could*.

But no longer were there many secrets! The Internet saw to that!

The Internet has been our era's Gutenberg Press, uniting most of the globe into one network and bringing quantities of information to our fingertips that our ancestors never dreamed of. Much of what we know of the above states of affairs, after all, we know because of the Internet. No longer is it necessary to traipse to Secular University libraries to do research. One can access multiple websites and research any topic one likes from the comfort of one's home study (or bedroom, for that matter).

Surely, if we are assessing the idea of progress, this counts for something!

Yes, but the Internet, too, has been a mixed blessing. It has democratized information because of open access—and because anyone with minimal skills can put up a blog and present information from any point of view he/she thinks is defensible, posing as an "expert."

The democratization of information has had its healthy side. It has exposed lies, genuine conspiracies, chicaneries of all sorts, originating in media and intellectual centers we once turned to expecting to receive the truth, or at least the best ideas available, without purposeful distortion. Methodological pluralists like Feyerabend (who, sadly, passed away in 1994 from an inoperable brain tumor, and so did not live to see the Internet's fruits) would have reveled in seeing the websites and e-newsletters of organizations such as the Discovery Institute, presenting issues like Darwinian evolution and abiogenesis from the point of view of intelligent design, able to compete directly on the level field of cyberspace with the Darwinists in the Secular University.

Sometimes the democratization of information has posed a threat to political-economic power. It exposed the idea that globalization was making everyone better off (or that given sufficient time will do so) as very questionable, when by the start of the new millennium it was clear this was not happening. Instead, Western populations were caught in what one author called a "race to the bottom."[28] Economists' dogmas that free trade and open immigration policies make societies better off were thrown into doubt. Plain, "Main Street" experience made things look otherwise, especially once the stock market starts scaring simultaneously with a portion of the middle class pinwheeling over the economic cliff. Inequality has grown ever since, of course, from this and from other causes.

---

28. Tonelson, *Race to the Bottom*.

A democratization of information allows one to find out, almost instantly, what is occurring on the other side of the world, be they events associated with American-led wars and mass migrations and their effects on cultures, or natural phenomena such as earthquakes, typhoons, etc. It enables anyone online to locate and talk to boots-on-the-ground sources, and thus to debunk what a mainstream source (who was usually not there) is saying. Independent investigations threw cold water on official narratives. We saw alternatives, for example, to the official conspiracy theory of 9/11 as directed by a man in a cave somewhere in the Middle East, conducted by a group of nineteen people whose names failed to show up on official passenger manifests.[29] This, of course, is just one highly visible example, and again, is not the sort of thing that began yesterday.

Note my usage of *official narrative*. The phrase, when used (and with the right tone of voice), is intended to take its referent down a peg or two. During the past two decades we have seen a decline in the epistemic authority of official narratives offered by governments, by corporations if the lure of profit seems a source of bias, and by designated "experts" in areas ranging from science and history to political economy. It seems clear, the collapse of official narratives about globalization and immigration as well as the growing influence of identity politics on the culture outside the Secular University empowered the rise of Donald Trump (no, it wasn't the "racism" of the majority white middle class declining in stature after over three decades of economic and cultural assault, although the growing resentment of white middle class against what was being done to it from multiple forces might have had something to do with it).

A parallel collapse of official narratives fueled the Brexit victory in Great Britain a few months before Trump won in the United States. Collapses in prevailing thinking in the EU about immigration and economy had already empowered "populist" leaders such as Viktor Orbán in Hungary who immediately instituted EU-defying anti-immigration policies. Other "populist" leaders won major elections, such as India's Narendra Modi who rose to prominence on a pro-Hindu platform, and Brazil's Jaro Bolsanaro who survived an assassination attempt before winning his election in 2018. *Populism* is not an ideology as such. It is reactive. It is the visceral response of political-economic self-identified outsiders against those designated as arrogant, out-of-touch, elites wielding power by financial means—such as the EU's European Central Bank or the Wall Street leviathans in the United States.

An *epistemic populism* would be the quasi-Feyerabendian idea that numerous theories, conspiracy claims, etc., have been illicitly excluded

---

29. See Griffin, *New Pearl Harbor*; Fetzer, *9/11 Conspiracy*.

from the intellectual conversation because they threaten the institutional dominance of intellectual elites and their favored narratives, and have the right to a place at the table.[30] Such ideas have proliferated on the Internet in ways that would have jolted even Feyerabend. We have seen the rise of influencers who very much scare the dickens out of those who would appeal to what remains of Third Stage expertise. Thus we have seen pushback.[31] The unresolved ambiguity—we are not in a position to resolve it here—is whether a mostly unrestrained pluralism is more likely to uncover truth, especially truths that were being suppressed—or whether it serves the postmodernist abandonment of the idea of objective truth and neutral, disinterested inquiry. The former suggests the possibility of a newfound optimism; the latter accords with the pessimist's loss of hope and applies it to epistemology and methodology.

Internet proliferation has its dark and problematic side. *No one* has the time or resources to personally validate all the information that can be had online from often conflicting websites. Consequently there really is "fake news" online. There are bogus quotes from the Founding Fathers; there is misleading and therefore potentially dangerous health information; there are nonsensical inferences from valid doubts about official narratives of 9/11 (e.g., that the Twin Towers weren't struck by planes at all!). The World Wide Web is where you will find claims that we never went to the moon and that the Earth really is flat. The Web is mostly unregulated, even with the tightening of search algorithms by Google (whose search engine is the most widely used) to ratchet down access to sites deemed questionable. This was a two-edged sword, as it made no distinction between clearly false information and viable challenges to official narratives. But anyone believing and wanting to read about a given Internet theory can find it—"alternative" sites aren't censored as such. Hence in the last analysis no one has a means of keeping out *all* false or unreliable information.

In today's era of multiple competing narratives, online self-siloing, and breakdowns in civility, *never has critical thinking been more necessary.* But the subject historically entrusted to teach it has "retreated." This is one reason many cannot now distinguish legitimate disagreement from so-called hate speech. The evidence is overwhelming that the Secular University is no longer doing its job in teaching the subjects that would lead to such discernment.[32]

---

30. See DeHaven-Smith, *Conspiracy Theory in America.*
31. See Nichols, *Death of Expertise*; Andersen, *Fantasyland.*
32. Cf. Arum and Roksa, *Academically Adrift.*

What are professional philosophers doing about this? Again, not very much. As we noted, the voices that drove the subject during the twentieth century passed away long ago and have not been replaced by equivalent voices able to break out of the swamp of information overload and the "attention" economy. Those few who are passionate about "relevant" issues seem unable to hold a candle to figures of the past. Meanwhile, the things dividing us bray ever louder.

Fourth Stage thinking repudiates Third Stage ideals, such as the objectivity or neutrality of inquiry, even in the sciences—just as Third Stage thinking had repudiated the quest for certainty. It casts a cynical eye on appeals to rationality, then sets about to deconstruct them by exposing hidden biases or interests of one sort or another. Fourth Stage thinking celebrates quips like, *It is impossible to convince Peter of* p *when Peter's paycheck depends on his believing* not-p.

Encouraged by the system-smashers of history, the Fourth Stage mind celebrates not inspiration but transgression, not unity but fragmentation, not morality and justice for all but tribalism. Identity politics has done its share of this, but identity politics is a product of Fourth Stage academic culture, not its cause. Again, like Trump, it is a symptom and not the problem. The Fourth Stage replaces epistemic and cultural optimism which saw a bright future for humanity with epistemic and cultural pessimism in which hope is lost—and in which there are philosophers who go as far as to think we and the planet would be better off if we "voluntarily" went extinct.[33]

To extend an analogy we developed near the start of this chapter, to the Fourth Stage thinker, it seems that our civilizational adulthood, our standing on our own feet historically, epistemically, and culturally, has ended up in the infirmity and senility of old age. We lost our sense of direction and began to drift, probably by the 1970s when references to postmodernism in art first surfaced.

Since then, compulsive growth has overwhelmed and destroyed indigenous populations in the name of transforming as much of the world as possible into a single global shopping mall, technology has turned inward, wages have stagnated relative to the income of those at the top, our health has been systematically undermined as chronic conditions are managed for profit (leaving us vulnerable to a nasty bug like the current coronavirus), and finally, we've had to contend with claims that our civilization is disrupting the planet's climate systems and ecosphere. Some now argue that industrial civilization is finished.[34]

---

33. See MacCormack, *A-Human Manifesto*.
34. Clugston, *BLIP*.

The American political system is bordering on dysfunctional. This should be evident when an outsider who had never held political office was able to demolish his opponents in debates without much more than a few very well chosen phrases ("make America great again," "drain the swamp"), a solid command of how to use both traditional and social media, and an uncanny ability to connect meaningfully with an angry and resentful base, some of whom were genuinely suffering in the so-called new economy. Many Republican voters didn't especially like Trump, but for them (and for evangelical Christians) he became the only game in town.

The dysfunction is not limited to Republicans. Progressives, knowing of Hillary Clinton's elitism and her checkered past which included the destruction of entire nations like Libya and Honduras when she was Obama's Secretary of State, turned to a self-identified socialist, Bernie Sanders. They could argue (if they wanted to) that the DNC stole the nomination for Clinton using "superdelegates" from the one candidate who might have defeated Trump.

A question philosophers could address at this level is, "Is the United States really a Constitutional republican democracy?" We raised this above and cited the widely-circulated article that seemed to answer this question: Martin Gilens and Benjamin I. Page, "Testing Theories of American Politics: Elites, Interest Groups, and Average Citizens."

Political philosopher Sheldon Wolin had written a few years before of what he called *inverted totalitarianism*: a totalitarianism not of kings or emperors or dictators or even presidents but systemic in nature, making it hard to recognize as such.[35] Both political parties are now perceived as more alike than different in serving corporate interests and sustaining dangerous foreign wars. Is there any wonder we have "populist" movements here and abroad? Entire populations are alienated from institutions they once trusted. This is no more a phenomenon of the "right" alone than it is of the "left" alone. It is a phenomenon of Fourth Stage civilization.

In other words, there are issues aplenty: we could extend this discussion almost indefinitely. Summing this section: our Secular City presently stands within an uneasy mix of Third and Fourth Stage thinking (with some elements of First and Second). Third Stage thinking, which valued truth and considered it obtainable by experts, has lost much of the credibility it once possessed. Much of this is its own doing. Akin to its accusations against Second Stage system building, its reach exceeded its grasp. There are problems of life and human organization which science and technique cannot solve. It is unclear that problems created by technology will be

---

35. Wolin, *Democracy, Inc.*

solved by more technology. Third Stage thinking seems unable to answer the challenge that it has confused, on a large scale, reliable knowledge with institutional authority, and that if our goal really is to find truth (and is it?) then our institutions now stand in the way.

Hence the rise of Fourth Stage civilization, in which belief in and commitment to objective and neutral truth is lost, leaving us with a babble of conflicting voices. In this era of omnipresent social media and its competing, clashing narratives which few of its users are in a position to validate, truth seems to have dissolved before our eyes. What replaces it? The postmodernist sense that as popular Australian blogger Caitlin Johnstone put it in a Medium column a year or so ago, society is made of narratives. It's competing, clashing narratives "all the way down." The quest to get past narratives seems futile! Truth has disappeared![36]

Amidst Plagues of Brutalism, the "Retreat" of Philosophy Must End

The "retreat" of philosophy has had relatively few causes but many consequences. This chapter may seem like overkill. But perhaps only overkill will draw attention to the magnitude of the problems of a civilization which, *de facto*, has no conscious and disciplined philosophy, in which philosophy is regarded as a decoration, a leisure activity—philosophers having retreated into cubicles in an equally troubled academia, while the actual philosophies, products of opportunism and chance, are wreaking havoc.

We need a novel program for philosophy. The program to be developed in this book will draw on ideas of the past, but reformulate them for the present. For all the above issues cry out for fair-minded philosophical analysis in light of first premises. The program I will propose places worldviews front and center. Not political economy, not race or ethnicity or gender. Not even class. Worldviews. It will propose that the problems with these stem primarily from a certain worldview having been in place, confused with Settled Science, and not much questioned even as Settled Science has come into question.

We will propose that philosophy should identify and evaluate worldviews. Philosophers should not be afraid to recommend scrapping a worldview if it manifestly gives bad advice, or cannot solve the problems it creates for itself, or if it is proving to be destructive rather than constructive. Its destructiveness may well be a sign that its theory of reality, or of humanity,

---

36. Johnstone, "Society Is Made Of Narrative."

is *false*. False ideas, generally speaking, may by chance solve a few limited problems for a time but ultimately go down blind and harmful alleyways.

The program to be developed here will try to force philosophy professors out of their comfort zones.

They have it in their power to ignore all this, of course. Who am I to call professional philosophers as a group onto the carpet and tell them they have a job to do besides teach their classes as inoffensively as possible and write books and articles almost no one will read?

But what are they to say in the face of the problems and issues sketched above, and which actually barely even scratches the surface!

Most philosophers, as "good men and women of the left," will say they *care* about, e.g., massive and growing inequality. A few (Harry Frankfurt is an example, with his *On Inequality*[37]) have addressed the topic. Most have little to say beyond the usual bromides that end with an appeal to vote for Democrats, which tells us all we need to know of their knowledge how the American political system really works.

Of course they care, but present policies and practices, including most of what is published as philosophy, are going nowhere. They seem like products of Nietzsche's "last men" following the "advent of nihilism" he warned about—and "last women," if they believe a loss of their "reproductive rights" is really a large-looming problem.

Speaking of supposed "reproductive rights"—and to really take us out of our comfort zones—could we not envision a future civilization that values life in itself, that sees the past near-seventy years of legal abortion as a silent holocaust worse than anything the Nazis perpetuated, directed not against a demonized minority but those unborn and therefore utterly defenseless? Abortion stands as a glaring exemplar of the general loss of respect for human life, sanctioned in law since 1973, defended on the basis of euphemisms such as the one above, or the bromide about women's right to "control their own bodies"?

Sorry, honey, but it isn't *your* body but the body of another living being *period!* A being that is more vulnerable than any other human population on the planet *period!*

What was that about judging the morality of a civilization by the way it treats its most vulnerable populations, those least able to organize and fight back against repression—or, in this case, worse!

The humanness of unborn babies is a fact of biology, not philosophy. (Small wonder Third Wave feminists passionately hate the subject.) That abortion is an insidious form of brutalism has never, to my knowledge, been argued by an academic philosopher. Sadly, in today's academic environment, few would dare.

---

37. Frankfurt, *On Inequality*.

I am more than aware that some will label these remarks as "misogynist," etc., *ad nauseam*, and see them as beyond the pale. They will raise specters of a certain Margaret Atwood dystopia. Their resort to verbal epithets ("bewitching our intelligence by means of language") and scare tactics instead of real analysis speaks volumes!

For abortion is just an extreme form of brutalist disdain for lives regarded as expendable because they are inconvenient, or to be dispensed with because one *can*. Brutalism has other manifestations, and obviously not all of them come from the left. Consider the high incarceration rate in the United States, especially of African-American men, often resulting from their inability to afford decent legal counsel. Neoliberalism is the culprit here, encouraging privatization of everything, including prisons to be run for profit. Private prisons invite a mare's nest of perverse incentives: fill them, because more prisoners mean more money for the owners; and it means feeding them largely inedible food because edible food costs more and lowers profits. Progressives are *right* to criticize this brutalist abomination.

Lesser degrees of quiet brutalism have emerged in our postmodern Fourth Stage Secular City. This is the sort of brutalism that criminalizes feeding the homeless. It is evident in the let-them-eat-cake attitude those with wealth sometimes exhibit towards the less fortunate, who may have been thrown out of work via the hollowing out of the country's manufacturing base or by automation. Brutalism is manifest when employers pay workers as little as they can get away with legally, and without a minimum wage, would pay even less. It is manifest when they fire human workers and install machines when the minimum wage is raised.

Brutalism is evident in academia in the form of the adjunct crisis—hiring instructors as part-timers paid as little as possible while the university president and football coach are paid six figures. The response of the Libertarian who reminds adjuncts about supply and demand as if these were not manipulated, and recommends that if they do not like the labor situation in academia they can "go to work for Geico," is also brutalist. (One such person actually does this; to save him embarrassment I will leave him unnamed.)

This all calls for philosophy that can and will challenge injustices and brutalisms of various sorts across the ideological spectrum, including those not on its doorstep but in its front room. Such a philosophy will have an intellectual foundation to operate from (issues about "foundationalism" notwithstanding). Its practitioners will have examined the prevailing worldview that cuts across modernity and postmodernity and found it wanting. They will have traced the sources of brutalism and dehumanization in whatever form to unconscious worldview-based premises operant in their institutions: unconscious because the "retreat" of philosophy left the matter to chance.

If there are reasons for thinking philosophy is *not* dead, they will be found in a program that turns a culture's attention to *worldviews*: identifying them, clarifying them, making clear the connections between worldviews and philosophy and between worldviews and civilization, then providing incisive evaluations based on their capacity to solve their own problems, their overall self-coherence, and their overall effects on civilization. Worldviews are not the sorts of things that can be tested "scientifically." They *can* be judged inadequate and deserving of being rejected, however, if they create more problems than they solve.

The "retreat" of philosophy must end. There is no more room for the mere analyst of language, or historian of philosophy, or reconstructor of science, or any other sort of intellectual navel-gazing. *That* sort of philosophy *needs* to die, and good riddance! There is, however, the danger that given how the Secular University works, philosophers who seek to be influencers on the scale necessary to be effective at carrying out what is proposed here will face real difficulties. This is a topic we take up in the final chapter. Universities are unaccustomed to anyone issuing *real* challenges to power.

Nevertheless, philosophy must change or continue, at best, to wither on the vines of ivy—victimized, in the end by "budget cuts." That could happen anyway, of course; and so there is nothing to lose! Philosophy must address not just the Secular University but the larger Secular City. It will have to be denunciatory at times. If *my* words are harsh, it's because I care! And I figured out long ago that most institutionally secure people need fires built under them before they get up off their duffs and do something! My hope is that we can get past mere harsh words, and that this work will be an instrument for change, through its program for what philosophers should do. To the specifics of this we now turn.

3

Worldviews and Philosophy

While there are sterling exceptions, for the majority of college and university undergraduates, philosophy is little more than a curiosity that has nothing to do with their majors.

I once taught introductory-level courses in philosophy on a regular basis. Sometimes I would ask, as a final exam question (from a choice of several options), what the student believed he or she had gotten from the course. I once received this response:

> Well in this class I learned a lot of stuff that is truley [sic] unnecessary. Philosophy is very interesting but to me it is an excuse for the smart people to use big words. I did not come to this class because I did not understand. Now I am suffering the consequence of maybe failing and not being elegeble [sic] for baseball in the spring.

What a revealing comment, on many levels! Leaving aside the abysmal writing and spelling, it speaks volumes about the overall mindset of many university students. It speaks to those teaching students in whom intellectual curiosity is dead, and who came to a university primarily to get a credential and/or participate in sports.

And whose primary motive may be understandable: upon graduation they want a job that pays enough so they can dig their way out from under an avalanche of student loan debt. They do not see liberal arts learning as useful to this end, not in a job market that is hostile outside technology, engineering, and perhaps business, despite all the crowing about how great the economy is doing and how low the unemployment rate is.

Philosophy: *unnecessary . . . very interesting but . . . the smart people use big words.*

It isn't obvious to students in the Secular University, itself in business to train future employees and nurture mass consumption in the Secular City, that philosophy supplies any value at all. In its present form, as a decoration in institutions where revenue-producing athletics and business schools are a far higher priority, it won't be.

Whatever we might say in criticism of the Secular University's priorities (of which we could say plenty!), academic philosophy has done little to help its cause.

For as we've seen, most of it is irrelevant to the problems of life, and of civilization. Where it turns out to have been influential, its influence has done more harm than good!

How can professional philosophers change their own best practices? is therefore a question that should be of importance to them, especially in an era of Secular University budget cutting. Philosophers were central to building Third Stage civilization. Philosophy's decomposition (among that of other disciplines) helped bring about Fourth Stage civilization, which is proving to be a slow-motion train wreck. Can philosophy position itself to once again contribute to what Richard Rorty (a Fourth Stage philosopher *extraordinaire* in his own quiet system smashing) called the *conversation of the West*?[1]

I think so, but doing so will require reinventing itself, with a new vision of its purpose.

The vision I am proposing formally: *identifying, clarifying, and critically evaluating* worldviews. Specifically: *philosophy, at its ideal best, will become the enterprise which seeks to identify, clarify, and evaluate worldviews in institutions such as education, culture, or civilization as a whole. In the end, philosophy is indeed the quest for a comprehensive worldview that is self-consistent, adequate to known facts, and existentially complete in the sense that it leaves us "at home" in the universe and able to live fulfilled, happy, and peaceful lives.*

A worldview that does not accomplish this last will hardly enable a civilization's long-term sustainability. Whether a worldview meets the above criteria of excellence or not can be determined from outside, by properly schooled, future-focused philosophers of integrity and earnestness. An excellent worldview, we might call it, is excellent because it excels at helping us all, philosopher or not, identify, address, and work out humane solutions to real human problems, small and large.

We now prepare by addressing the obvious questions: *what are worldviews?* What are some examples of worldviews? What is their role in civilization? Is there a prevailing worldview that cuts across both our present-day amalgamation of Third and Fourth Stages? How is the philosopher

---

1. Rorty, *Philosophy and the Mirror of Nature*.

supposed to proceed in evaluating a worldview and providing concrete advice on what to do?

What Are Worldviews?

The term *worldview* is used loosely in popular discourse. Let us make it a bit more precise. Doing so will have limits, since to a great extent, a functional worldview in civilization is bound to be more organic than formal, implicit rather than explicitly stated, shaping experience rather than being shaped by it, and tacit in Michael Polanyi's sense unless something about it begins attracting attention.[2]

Think of that colorful story of the two young fish swimming past one of their elders who asks them, "How's the water today, boys?" After a while one of the younger fish turns to the other, a perplexed look on his face (assume we can imagine a fish looking perplexed) and asks, "What in the world is *water*?"

This may be the best account of what it means to be immersed in a worldview. Those unreflectively immersed in it will have trouble even seeing and understanding, much less being able to evaluate, its first premise(s).

To the extent they can, they will see its first premise(s) as *true* and probably *obvious*. They may question the intelligence, sanity, seriousness, or motivations of someone who challenges their first premises.

Part of our job as philosophers is to question the obviousness of first premises.

John Kekes developed a useful model of worldviews.[3] Kekes (eighty-four years old as of this writing, in accordance with my contention that almost all significant academic philosophers are well over retirement age) is a rare exception to the rule that philosophers have had little to say on such topics. His writings stand out as addressing "big" concerns the majority of his colleagues tend to dismiss, and from perspectives they disdain. After characterizing *perennial* arguments within philosophy—"arguments about morality, logical consistency, religiosity, education, aesthetic sensibility, rationality, culture, democracy, scientific or historical understanding, and knowledge,"[4] he turns to the idea of what a worldview is, and develops its components.

What he means, initially and roughly, by a *worldview* is "a set of common values that give meaning and purpose to . . . life, that can be

---

2. See Polanyi, *Tacit Dimension*.

3. Kekes, *Nature of Philosophy*. Cf. Maxwell, "Science, Reason, Knowledge, and Wisdom," 19–81.

4. Kekes, *Nature of Philosophy*, 17.

symbolically expressed, that fit with the situation of the time, as well as being linked to the historical past, and that do not outrage men's reason and at the same time appeal to their emotion."[5] It is revealing that Kekes does not cite a philosopher here but rather a cultural anthropologist, one of the more prominent names of the last century in that field, Clyde Kluckhohn.[6] In their hands together, the idea takes further shape.

> I shall say that something qualifies as a worldview only if it has the following five components: a theory of the nature of reality or a *metaphysics*; an account of the human significance of the nature of reality or an *anthropology*; a system of ideals or a *culture*; an explanation of the discrepancy between the ideal and the actual state of affairs or a *diagnosis*; and a program for overcoming or minimizing the discrepancy or a *policy*.[7]

We'll have some terminological quibbles, but note the comprehensiveness. This goes against Third (and Fourth) Stage thinking. The question, though, is whether we find poorly articulated worldviews in this sense in Third (and Fourth) Stage civilization. The answer is that of course we do! We find them in all societies, even in so-called "primitive" (i.e., First Stage) ones. Are we able to discuss them effectively? Where do we get the tools to do so? From philosophy: for each of the schools of thought encountered in Chapter 1 has something to contribute.

Let's get clearer what we are talking about. According to Kekes's taxonomy, a worldview has five essential components, a *metaphysics*, an *anthropology*, an axiology or *culture* with ideals, a *diagnosis*, and a *policy* or *prescription*.

A *metaphysics* is a theory of reality. What exists? What is most real? Is there just *one* fundamental constituent to reality (monism)? Or are there *two*, neither of which is reducible to the other, as Descartes concluded (dualism)? Or are there *many* different kinds of irreducibles (pluralism)? What relationship holds between them, and between us as perceivers, thinkers, and actors in the world?

These are the kinds of questions philosophers need to raise in determining just what is believed by purveyors of a worldview, and how clear the beliefs are. The vast majority of philosophers of mind, despite many variations and disagreements over specifics, appear to support a materialist monism in which the *mind* is just the *brain*—or, perhaps, the brain and central nervous

---

5. Kekes, *Nature of Philosophy*, 58–59.
6. Kluckhohn, "Culture and Behavior," 297–98.
7. Kekes, *Nature of Philosophy*, 59.

system perhaps including our sense organs. This may be why they have a "hard problem" of consciousness (among other, older quandaries).[8]

Third Stage philosophy emerged out of frustration with Second Stage apriorism and speculation. It turned to empirical science to tell us what was real and irreducible, because its methods of inquiry purport to be evidence-based and self-correcting.

The whole problem with metaphysics, "scientific philosophers" insisted, is that the first premises of a metaphysical system can't be tested empirically. But they insist we can nevertheless make the right inferences about what exists at the most basic level. When we look at the brain, what we see is an immensely complex but fundamentally *material* system which we can study and gather data about, piecemeal. Hence what we will come to call the Grandiose Assumption: that science requires (or leads to) materialism.

But what do we *do* with the data of conscious, focused experience, the existence of which seems presupposed by our ability to *study* anything? Much less when we speak of the sense of privileged access we all have to our own experiential manifold, or of the intentionality of the process of focusing, selecting, and gathering data? None of this seems akin to the material causality evident in, e.g., physical objects when they fall or collide, or even the more complex causality of biological systems when they grow and change? And what of the evaluative component of our results: the fact that we judge some ideas *superior* to others on various grounds, including conduct to which we apply the categories of morality.

The idea that the manifold of consciousness and its intentionality has *no explanation whatsoever* within the parameters supplied by materialism is, at present, a philosophical and scientific heresy, despite the *oddness* of these phenomena, i.e., their vast *differences* from processes we have no trouble describing in material cause-and-effect terms (falling bodies, combustion, the growth of plants, and so on).

Even odder, on the face of it, is *abiogenesis*, the idea that life can come from nonlife by unplanned and undirected material-causal processes alone. This has been an obsession with one strain of science for over a hundred years now. But hadn't the idea of *spontaneous generation* not been empirically refuted? Why did twentieth-century science resurrect the same basic idea in a new guise? Is life somehow different from nonlife in ways that create problems for *any* abiogenetic theory? *Heresy!* says the scientist and the "scientific philosopher." They don't use that word, of course.

Such quandaries indicate the role metaphysical components of worldviews play even in the so-called empirical sciences, how worldviews

---

8. See Chalmers, *Conscious Mind*. For extended discussion see Chapter 5.

condition scientists' handling of putative empirical issues, and how alternative tacit worldview commitments intrude.

They can't see the metaphysical "water" they are immersed in.

The term *anthropology*—Kekes's *second* component of a worldview—is typically used for the social science, which divides into physical anthropology, cultural anthropology, anthropological linguistics, and so on. We are using the term differently, more akin to how Catholic social thinkers use the phrase *philosophical anthropology*. Kekes is using his term to speak of the "human significance of the interpretation provided by metaphysics . . . warranted [as a separate concern] by the existence of a uniquely human perspective."[9]

In this perspective, some states of affairs are *important* to us, and this guides our motivation to address them. If the metaphysical component of a worldview attempts to identify and describe what is real, then the anthropological component develops a scale of *importances*, especially given the prevalence of problems to solve and the fact that we have to choose what to pursue.

So how do we arrange such a scale? *Survival* is a primary problem for any community to solve: obtaining or growing and distributing sufficient food, finding uncontaminated water, building stable shelter, caring for and raising children, and so on.

But human beings *qua* persons have never been content with mere survival, especially not once they developed civilizations able to satisfy the basic needs of most of their members. Human beings have always needed some larger purpose for their being here, some reason *why* they exist that transcends the immediacies of their lives and societies, including survival. Some find that purpose in a Higher Power, such as the Christian God. Others invoke a set of principles to be internalized in their conduct for living an ideal life, such as those found in Buddhism. Either could give rise to philosophy, in which we seek integrated answers to questions like, Given that reality is such-and-such, where do we fit in? How (and why) did we come to be? How should we live our lives, and what should we establish as long term goals for our societies, such as realizing ideals such as justice and peace?

The fact that some members of our pluralistic Western world believe our highest goals should be to serve a Higher Power, while others have concluded that in the universe disclosed by empirical science we are on our own, is indicative that different Stages of civilization will sustain different worldviews.

---

9. Kekes, *Nature of Philosophy*, 60.

The possible answers to such questions take us to Kekes's *third* component of worldviews. I prefer the term *axiology* to *culture* (a term most writers again use with a far different reference class). *Axiology* has to do with the study of *value* in the broadest sense of the term, going beyond importances necessary to ensure survival.

There are at least four isolable senses of the word *value*.

(1) There is *moral* value in the sense of right and wrong, just and unjust, good versus evil, presupposing standards of moral conduct or of rightness and justice and goodness. *Ethics* is the theory of morality—its nature, foundations, etc. In First Stage thought, morality issues from commands handed down by that Higher Power. Second Stage thought *can* sever the connection between morality and a Higher Power. Influenced by the Enlightenment, major Second Stage philosophers thus proposed specific ethical theories, e.g., Kant's deontology and Mill's utilitarianism. Such thinkers still see a universal morality as possible and plausible based on features about *us* (Kant: our capacity for reason; Mill: our preference for happiness over unhappiness).

Within Third Stage thought, the idea of universal morality starts to collapse, as we saw above. Morality becomes an artifact of culture as the anthropologist uses that term. Cultures are different from one another, arising in different environments and hence having different problems to solve. Hence they end up with somewhat different moralities (note the plural).

(2) There is *aesthetic* value in the sense of questions like, What is beauty (in art, in music, in sculpture, in architecture, in the natural world itself)? Are there boundaries, moreover, to art and music and sculpture? Are aesthetic tastes personal, or are they, at best, cultural artifacts, too, so that again there is indeed better versus worse, but "better versus worse" is always culture-bound? Third Stage thought seems to leave room for both, opening doors as it does to a multitude of forms of life ranging from Michelangelo to Marcel Duchamp.

(3) There is *economic* value, or *exchange* value, the worth of various produced goods in a marketplace. We speak of the *labor* theory of value built into Marxism (although Marx did not invent it), versus the *subjective* theory of the Austrian school in which the value of a good is measured only by what a consumer is willing to pay for it—the locus of value is in the *mind* of the consumer, in his/her *private* scale of importances. This being unknowable by any central authority, the Austrian school rejects any and all forms of central economic planning and price controls. Prices, wages, and so on, must be fixed by the market process itself. Economic logic alone necessitates this. The debate between different schools of exchange value in economics could

be understood as a debate between Second Stage (apriorist) and Third Stage (empiricist) models of inquiry.

And finally (4) there is *epistemic* value, the value placed on knowing *truths* or *facts*, on having knowledge generally of 'the way things are,' and acquiring more of such. Most of us, I think, believe truth is more valuable than falsehood whatever philosophical conundrums exist about the nature of truth, and even if some maintain that the masses in civilization must hold to some ideas about itself that are probably not true but are part of its cultural cement, as it were, believed by the masses but not the elite who "know better" (Strauss). Third Stage thinking sees empirical science as the sole reliable means of learning "the way things are." Fourth Stage thinking throws cold water on the idea that our discourses ever bring us closer and closer to "the way things are," if by this we mean something more than giving the ideas we approve pats on the back. But then there is the disturbing thought that some of our institutions and their authority structures are actually *hindering* the discovery and communication of what is true, "the way things are," if these seem to threaten ideas held very strongly, because the authorities identify with them.

Are values in all or some of these senses *discoveries*, even if they are in *us*, as part of our nature? Or are they *inventions*, just in case there is nothing axiological to be discovered in the universe at all? Different answers to this question are indicative of differences of worldview.

Understanding Kekes's *fourth* component invites us to imagine a world that has nothing fundamentally wrong with it: our highest ideal again, whether in Russell's or some other sense. A state of affairs in which the problems that confront civilization are solved or did not arise to begin with: then we can *diagnose* why the ideal has not been realized. Plato was the first philosopher we know of to attempt this, and the detailed description Socrates drew in *The Republic* continues to resonate over two millennia later. The plan there was to sketch an ideal society, one in which all is in harmony, with conflicts between classes or other divisions between citizens simply not arising, and explaining why not.

A Utopia, in other words.

A recent Utopia is that of Edward Bellamy, in *Looking Backward: 2000–1887*, published in 1886, envisioning a communal world of peace and harmony where private property had been nationalized (Bellamy avoided the word *socialism*): a system having resolved all major human conflicts and able to meet the needs of all.

Such visions are dangerous, as all thoughtful students of the problem know. What if a given philosopher's Utopia ignores, or conflicts with, relevant facts of human nature? All of them, in fact, do. The response always goes something like: *human nature is malleable*, a product of its time, institutions; or, that the phrase *human nature* doesn't refer to anything substantial at all.

Biology suggests otherwise, and so does history. The world's most brutal dictatorships resulted from efforts to force-fit all-too-human populations into an abstract image which left no actual room for real, flesh-and-blood human beings. The Utopian thinks it *should* work, and under rightly designed, socially engineered conditions, it *will*, dammit! Philosophers have gotten a bad rap due to their role as "founding fathers" of such efforts even if it be unfair to hold them personally accountable for all the ill uses to which their ideas have been put (Marx being the obvious example).

Be this as it may, we usually have a regulative ideal of some kind in mind when criticizing the actual, even if our ideal is that of piecemeal improvement instead of a comprehensive plan. For Libertarian minarchists, for example, the ideal is of a civilization whose government is very small (like Nozick's "night watchman") and has strictly limited powers defined by a founding document such as the US Constitution. For theoretical anarchists, even this allows too much state power, because its minions both can and will eventually reinterpret its founding document, increase their power in steps until it is all-encompassing, it will all be legal, and in a couple of generations we'll be back where we started.

The point is not to try to resolve that dispute here but to articulate the reality that (1) it is a meaningful dispute for those who wish to live lives free of authoritarian interference, with practical consequences, and (2) philosophers are best suited to grapple with it publicly because the history of the discipline provides both the raw material, proposals for political systems of varying degrees of completeness (or criticisms of such), and techniques for reasoning effectively about their various successes and failures.

Thus according to Kekes the *fifth* component is *prescription* or *policy*: how do we begin to bring the actual in alignment with our ideals?

That, of course, assumes we *can* or *should* attempt to do so.

Philosophers should demand clarity of political-economic ideals and subject them to critical evaluation in light of history. If an ideal has proven not realizable, as with Communism, then it is rational to jettison that ideal and try something more promising. Discussions of ideals should incorporate such questions as whether societies or civilizations *can* be centrally planned, as if we really had a complex readymade system in our minds (the Platonist "republic" or Bellamy's Utopia), or whether "planning" should be loose, open-ended, and guided by heuristics (e.g., other things being equal, allow individuals maximum freedom to choose their own paths to the greatest extent compatible with social stability). Third Stage civilization jettisoned philosophical Utopias of the Platonist sort, but nevertheless grew highly centralized *as if it were planned*—and to a great extent, where the corporate and financial centers had the reach and the resources, we saw piecemeal social engineering, i.e., *planning*.

John Kekes is not the only contemporary philosopher to have grappled with the worldview concept. We might find it useful to consult the United Kingdom's Nicholas Maxwell. Although Maxwell does not use the term *worldview* his call for a revolution in the aims of science, of rational inquiry itself as exemplified by science, is surely relevant to a discussion such as this. Beginning in the 1970s he called for an *aim-oriented empiricism*. This began by identifying the broadest conceivable aims of science, to render the world or some part of it intelligible. This *a priori* premise, not empirical considerations alone, decides between theories or broader paradigms.[10] This is a reason why actual science does not suffer from any "grue/bleen" paradoxes, for instance. What Maxwell calls *standard empiricism* fundamentally misrepresents the aims of science.

Maxwell observed that in actual science, scientists both do and should choose the *simplest theory* compatible with known facts or observations. While many philosophers would concur with this much, Maxwell goes further by insisting that this *commits them to the metaphysical idea that the world itself (or the part of it being explored) is simple* in the specific way the theory requires. We've never used complex, inelegant, cumbersome theories except when we were off course, as was Ptolemaic astronomy and phlogiston chemistry, and we would never formulate much less test a theory invoking a property such as *grue* or *bleen*. Why not? Because we never assume that's how the world is. Nature's laws and properties of entities do not abruptly and inexplicably change. If we encounter discontinuities and incongruities, we incorporate them into theories seeking some higher-order explanation that preserves the commitment to simplicity: as Ockham's Razer asserts, *we never multiply explanatory hypotheses or principles beyond necessity*.

Contrary to the very baseline assumption of Third Stage positivism, that is, *science both is and must be an inherently metaphysical enterprise, guided by metaphysical assumptions at the core of every theory scientists entertain*. This is why the best and most revolutionary scientists, from Newton down through Einstein to Hawking were also philosophers even if, like the latter, they ultimately disdained philosophy as an autonomous enterprise. Maybe Hawking disdained professional philosophy because in the end, he'd had to do his own philosophizing.

10. Cf. Maxwell, "Rationality of Scientific Discovery," 123–53, 247–95 ; Maxwell, "Induction, Simplicity, and Scientific Progress," 629–53; Maxwell, *From Knowledge to Wisdom*.

Maxwell's proposal for academic inquiry tries to integrate best practices for the sciences with the improvement of human life in society in ways somewhat amenable to our aims here, as he urged the application of the aim-orientation that worked so well in science even when unnoticed to educational and broader social policy.[11]

Maxwell's views have depth and earnestness, and they merit more study than they have received in the Secular University. Our view here goes even deeper, or tries to do so. What are the most fundamental premises guiding not just science but our entire Third Stage view of the way the world is, how we fit in? What does history actually disclose about the rising and falling of civilizations? What is (or should be) of value in life? Are there general answers to such questions? We've looked at such ideals as Russell's, which were shared by many thinkers of his and subsequent generations. How do we explain the discrepancy between such ideals and the world we actually inhabit—which seems consistently to thwart our highest aspirations?

Is there really a dynamic, or "law of history" written within the astounding rise and now the conceivable fall of our technologically advanced civilizations? It is hard to say, as we have only this one example of such a civilization to work from.

The clarity and ease of using Comte's conception of *Stages* suggests something of this sort, however, especially if we can spot systemic causes of phenomena within it such as outbreaks of war, the rise of consumerism and debt, the emergence of destabilizing levels of inequality, or dangers to public health.

Are there factors that start to work almost automatically against advanced civilizations if they get too large and complex? For example, does the necessity for growth manifested in capitalism eventually run up against surrounding systems (e.g., ecological ones) and begin to destabilize those? Does the need for growth call for policies that eventually destabilize them from within (e.g., the perceived need to borrow against the future and go into debt to keep consumers spending and the economy growing)?

Philosophers, again, are best suited to formulating and grappling with these kinds of questions. Economists, who differ from economic historians, they might observe, are simply too close to the situations. They are caught up in technicalities, so that they, too, miss the forest for the trees. Are mathematical models the best tools to use when investigating the real economy? Should they simply assume that we're all instances of an abstraction, *homo economicus*? Where did this abstraction come from?

---

11. See Maxwell, *How Universities Can Help*.

It isn't that what we're talking about is not being done. It is. Consider the context for Stephen Hawking's "philosophy is dead" remark. One of the problems is that philosophy dropped the ball. As a result, the job of understanding the nature of reality was taken over by specialized theoretical physicists, many of whom concluded, not entirely unreasonably, that understanding the origin and nature of physical reality can be accomplished without philosophy. Hawking's conclusion, which was that theoretical physics can explain origins without ever resorting to any creative act by a supreme Creator, is surely of great interest to philosophers! It should interest all educated people who might look to philosophers for guidance on such matters! Science, when it makes such pronouncements, ceases to be empirical and becomes philosophical.

Is the question of the existence of a Supreme Being of value to us, both as persons and as members of communities? Is the world fundamentally different somehow, if one answers this question in the negative, as opposed to in the positive? There are myriad other matters having to do with axiology: our responses to totalitarianism and violence, our thought about the nature and future of civilization generally, that should interest philosophers. Major works exist on each of these areas, often written by nonphilosophers. For if philosophers do not do the job for which philosophy is ideally suited, others will do it for them.

One way or another, the job will get done. The situation is no more complicated than that.

A civilization will have a worldview. It may be, as I said above, tacit and organic: integrated seamlessly into institutions and practices, especially political economy and education, but ultimately in the way most people live their lives. It will define what is expected versus what isn't, or is rejected. For much of the history of the West, our worldview was tied to Christianity. Christendom rejected homosexuality, for example, on biblical grounds. Modernity has tied its worldview to science, technology and commerce: the Secular City, with public education and the Secular University designed to pass the values of the Secular City to future generations and ensure their compliance and furtherance of Secular City's values and goals. These have no particular quarrel with homosexuality as such, and hence none with gay marriage as such. Hence the conflict. The point is, wide discussion of philosophical fundamentals has been less and less on the table. The overall results have caused the foot dragging by those who still derive morality from their faith, and plenty of unease as we have seen even among those who do not, whatever their embrace of sexual diversity

I will argue below that Western civilization has been the scene of an ongoing clash between two worldviews, that of Christianity and its variants, versus materialism or materialistic naturalism which has also had variants ranging from Marxian dialectical materialism to the materialism of those who claim to draw their impetus from modern physical and biological science.

Philosophers today have trouble saying such things. The topic is uncomfortable. This is because a latent positivism of sorts still exercises great influence among professional philosophers. Thus they still avoid open discussion of metaphysics from this perspective while offering comfort and privilege to a specific metaphysics (or one of its variants). The privileged metaphysics is materialism and materialistic naturalism, flowing from writers ranging from Darwin to Freud to Russell, guiding the philosophies of science and mind, and now directing the New Atheism of someone such as Dawkins. Simultaneously, philosophers have refrained from discussing metaphysics as it pertains to real world issues, even if it is easy for others to see how a multitude of cultural clashes of our time result from clashes of values with deeper roots in first premises: a clash between worldviews, in other words. Fourth Stage thinking, in its repudiation of the idea of transcultural truth altogether, has been even less helpful.

So what do worldviews look like, when clearly articulated? Let's find out.

The Worldview of Christianity/Christendom

Christianity, or embodied in culture as Christendom, provides an archetypical worldview as well as a body of religious belief, in that its metaphysics is clear as glass.

The Christian worldview's primary propositions:

1. *Metaphysics*: the Christian God exists, is the sovereign Creator of all things ("In the beginning God . . ." Gen 1:1), and is the most fundamental Being in all reality. God is eternal and uncreated; He "always was and is" (Heb 13:8; 1:8; Mal 3:6) because his existence is not spatiotemporal, as is ours. The child's (or athiest's) question, "If God made the world then who made God?" is therefore senseless and uninformed. The world we observe, observed by us and studied by the sciences which are strictly limited to space and time, is his creation which reveals his handiwork in a multitude of ways as well as work prepared for us to do (Ps 19:1; Eph 2:10). It depends for its existence on him, and he can alter its characteristics at will. Trinitarians, moreover (who are the

majority of Christians) see God manifested in three distinct Persons: Father, Son (Jesus Christ), and Holy Spirit.

2. *Philosophical anthropology*: humanity was, is created in the image of God ("So God created man in His own image; in the image of God created He him; male and female created He them," Gen 1:27). Our finite rationality and capacities reflect God's infinite rationality and wisdom. Our capacity to comprehend the world around us is a product of our finite rationality grasping that which was created by a perfectly rational God. What sets us apart from the rest of spatio-temporal creation is our having been created in God's image. This is the "divine spark" in us, and the source of whatever can be found in us that is *good*.

3. *Axiology*: our having been created in God's image, universal moral agency is possible—because they have intrinsic value, *all* human lives *do* matter!—as does the Creation ("and God said that it was good. . . ." Gen 1:31). *This*, and not our capacity for reason, or to experience happiness or pleasure, or any other worldly trait, is the source of our moral agency and moral properties, which extend to the unborn ("Before I formed you in the womb I knew you; before you were born I sanctified you. . . ." Jer 1:5). God provided his moral code, or set of commands, in the Ten Commandments (Exod 20), in the Sermon on the Mount (Matt 5–7), in Paul's epistles, and elsewhere in Scripture.

4. *Diagnosis*: humanity fell into sin (Gen 3:1–24), as man preferred *his* autonomous choices to following *God's* specific commands: the common-denominator explanation of our social and moral failures and the failures of all civilizations including Third Stage modernity. We were not designed to live according to rules of our own making. ("For all have sinned and come short of the glory of God. . . ." Rom 3:23). While we can work and improve specific aspects of the material human condition because of our ability to grasp physical law and use it to our advantage, sooner or later it always goes off the rails. This happens because of sin, because we cannot *save* ourselves from the real world consequences of sin, which include conflict. And above all, we cannot absolve ourselves of sin. We cannot stand before a perfectly holy God who cannot tolerate sin in his midst ("For the wages of sin is death . . ." Rom 6:23, death here meaning eternal separation from him). We are unable, *in principle*, to

5. *Prescription* or *policy*: Jesus Christ as Savior—source of salvation—for all who sincerely repent of their sins and invite Christ into their lives (John 3:16), although God's perfect grace and eternal magnificence will only be revealed and fully realized in the next life (1 Cor 2:9). This world will remain fallen, will hate Christians and Christianity, who themselves will continue to sin whether they want to or not. For God's salvation is an unearned gift ("by grace ye are saved through faith, it is the gift of God through Jesus Christ our Lord . . ." Eph 2:8–9). We are advised to develop society and write policy according to what is prescribed in Scripture (Exod 20; Matt 5–7). This need not be a theocracy. But avoiding theocracy is possible only by building Christian communities from the bottom up. If the masses are educated into Christian principles from childhood, then later as adults they will impose these on themselves from within, and they need not be imposed from without by the state.

According to the Christian worldview, that is, the most fundamental entity in existence is God, whose independence of the Creation is given and whose sovereignty over it is absolute. God is, for the philosophically articulate Christian, *foundational* with respect to the created order. The latter is ontologically dependent on him. God's existence and actions transcend the finite spatiotemporal created order we inhabit, and to which our brains are limited. Since we are in sin in addition to our brains being limited, we have no actual grasp or understanding of God beyond what Scripture reveals: as truths to be accepted, not hypotheses to be debated even when we don't understand them. E.g., what does it really mean to say that God is omniscient? Does this mean he knows all things past, present, and future? If he knows the future, how does this leave room for human free will or even his capacity to take action? How can we *know* any of this as *we* are not omniscient?

Small wonder Pascal could call God "infinitely incomprehensible"!

The Christian worldview suggests guarantees that physical and biological realities are governed by regularities science has discovered, because its God is a God of order, not randomness or chaos. The nature of created kinds, including us, are such that certain practices work, moreover, i.e., achieve viable and beneficial results, while others do not ("natural law" according to some Christian writers). We are able to apprehend moral truth as emanating from God's perfectly holy nature even if it is not taught to us explicitly (Rom 1:20).

The Christian worldview's ideal is a life—and civilization—that aligns with God's will and commands. Philosophers and theologians should not expect to understand the mind and ways of God, although a vast literature records our attempts, as well as the attempts of the occasional Pascal and Kierkegaard to cast doubt on God's comprehensibility.

For the philosopher or theologian to understand God, he would have to *be* God!

Our mortal existence *limits* us, and is made worse by our being fallen beings in a fallen world that has, in a sense, turned hostile towards us so that much of the work we must do just to survive is by nature unpleasant (Gen 3:17–19).

With these remarks, we have a Christian *metaphysics* and a Christian *philosophical anthropology*.

Christian *axiology* or culture denies moral relativism. It denies that morality is a cultural artifact. It does not necessarily deny cultural *relativity*, which is just the empirical observation that cultures have gone their own way and developed their own ethical beliefs. What is typically the case is that morality applies *to one's own tribe*, and not to all of sentient humanity. God's morally perfect nature established him alone to establish a morality for humanity as a whole.

It might be said that these were communicated just to Moses, and he communicated them in turn just to the Israelites (who promptly broke every one of them—over and over). The point is, the world operates according to rules: moral as well as physical. Physical rules describe how physical entities in fact behave causally. Moral rules lay out how moral agents ought to behave normatively.

Thus, there are definite rights versus wrongs in every area of human life and conduct, from sex and marriage and family relationships, to the handling of money and finances, to the organizing of our societies; for the alleviation of poverty where possible; and for our interactions with the environment. But attempts to obey moral rules are not what wins favor with God. This is because as sinners we invariably fall short of the perfection God requires. The resolution is to turn to Jesus Christ who paid the price for human sin. God is both merciful and graceful. He is merciful in that he does not give us the punishment for sin we deserve. He is graceful in that he gives us what we do not deserve, which is salvation and eternal life with him.

This, by the way, is what sets the Christian worldview apart from all other worldviews, theistic or otherwise. *Christianity alone asserts that human beings cannot save themselves by their own efforts.* Other religious worldviews—Islam, Buddhism, Hinduism, etc.—try to provide means by which their followers can save themselves, at least in principle—or live "rightly," having ideal principles for life in this world. But one never knows one has done enough, or followed the rules closely enough. Christianity maintains that Jesus Christ is the only path to salvation, and at a personal level, and that the believer can have *assurance* of his/her salvation and eternal destiny. This hasn't been easy even for Christian philosophers and theologians to wrap their brains around. Some Christian sects have tended to lapse into a "legalism" holding that God grants special passes to those who follow the rituals of a given church or denomination. But this is not what Scripture says. "Legalism" therefore departs from the Christian worldview.

Thus the Christian worldview's *diagnosis* and *prescription*. Christianity's explanation of the discrepancy between the ideal and the real is *sin*—our ancestors chose, at the beginning, to disobey an explicit command from God. Christians disagree on how to read Genesis. Biblical literalists see Adam and Eve as physical humans like us, our first parents who turned away from God during that crucial temptation in the garden of Eden; others note that *Adam* is Hebrew for *man* and choose to read their story of disobedience to God as symbolic of the disobedience of us all. We need not resolve such points of exegesis here. The point is, we separated ourselves from God and have paid a steep price. Whether we read God's curse upon the world following the entry of disobedience to his commands into the world as literal or metaphorical, following its pronouncement nature turned indifferent and even hostile to humanity. Human beings had to labor to transform what they could find into edible food, protective clothing, workable shelters, etc. Labor hurts! Much work is bound to be dismal, dull, drudgery. Industrial civilization set about to make things better. But painful and often backbreaking labor was replaced by monotonous and often dismally boring labor, that of masses spending the bulk of their waking hours working for someone else to obtain money. For in an industrial system, money is the bottom line. A tacit worship of Mammon, the product of money's encirclements, becomes a core element of the culture, whether of the masses or their overseers (business owners, government, etc.). In the former, it may be an involuntary fealty. A "dismal science" enshrines it all. This "science" studies the processes, in a depersonalized, clinical fashion, of how human beings produce and distribute the means of their survival and advancement in what the Christian sees as a fallen world. It turns the results into reams of data expressed in its own hyperspecialized jargon. To accept all of this, tacitly or otherwise, is to be "well-adjusted" or simply "adjusted."[12]

No one can say the Secular City hasn't achieved anything. It is, nevertheless, bound to be a flawed product of beings trying to follow their own

---

12. See Putney and Putney, *Adjusted American*.

paths, or paths of their favored institutions or tribes, and herein we find our diagnosis of the problems we have had, all down through the ages—the empires, the wars, the mass slaughters of innocents, the economic depressions, etc.—and the problems with those who would seize and consolidate power, generally by controlling economies and flows of resources (and weapons and narratives).

One of the most interesting features of the Secular City, viewed from within a Christian worldview, is how it created surrogates for God. One sees these as serving purposes that religion once served, enabling the Secular City's denizens to carve out at least some meaning in some area of lives often filled with low-grade suffering (Thoreau: "living lives of quiet desperation"). We mentioned Mammon, god of corporate entities who wield it, and *de facto* tyrant encircling the lives of the masses who need it to live. Science and Reason are other obvious surrogates, flourishing within the Secular University. Technology is a surrogate in the minds of many technologists and especially technocrats. State Power is a god in the Secular pantheon, wielded by political classes, although political instruments tend to be mostly impotent without Mammon behind them, compelling the political class to look to Mammon to further their goals. Sexuality in its various manifestations is clearly a powerful surrogate for God, and was worshiped in cultures long before the modern Secular City came along and placed female Sexuality on a pedestal.

And finally, one of the most visible Secular gods outside those wielding these levers is Self—observed with absorption, pampered, modified (through fad diets and exercise regimens or surgical procedures), exalted, photographed, paraded, or striving for Self-Actualization. When made highly visible and combined with Mammon and often Sexuality, we have the worship of Celebrity, with which many lesser selves follow because they identify with Celebrity. They would *be* Celebrity if they could, but of course there is only room for a certain amount of Celebrity just as there is potential market saturation of anything in the Secular City This means that those who enter the game too late are simply out of luck.

Of course, all these surrogates for God fall short of the real thing. Which is why, in the end, they fail. They do not satisfy in the present, and as it is never made clear that they constitute blind alleys, Secular City denizens pursue more and more of them! False idols by their very nature fail to satiate. Rather like pornography, a corruption of the false god Sexuality, it becomes impossible to get enough!

As the Secular City became the most advanced collective achievement of a sinful species, money and power more and more tended to get the last word. The Secular City went in the direction of the wills and choices of those who amassed the most of both; the rest found themselves dependent whether they knew it or liked it or not. Having to trade time for money is a form of dependence, after all. And, if this is you, you and your children were more likely to be sent into coal mines to be worked until your lungs were destroyed, or shipped off to fight wars begun by those wanting access to resources (think: oil). Individual persons, that is, are expendable. Their value is extrinsic and tied directly to what they can contribute to the system in terms of labor or fighting ability or, if they are very fortunate, ideas with exchange value. Commercial men and women are interested in what sells, and, sadly, not whether or not it is healthy for persons, communities, or the planet itself over which humanity was given "dominion" (Gen 1:26). Biblical dominion did not mean a license to plunder. It meant responsible use of what was gifted to us by our Creator.

The path to salvation—the *only* path to salvation, for the Christian—is Jesus Christ, who sacrificed himself on the cross, took humanity's sins onto himself, so that we might be absolved and stand pure before a holy God. He did not come to condemn a Secular world, but instead that through him, that world might be saved (John 3:17). This is the Christian worldview's prescription, or policy (although *that* term seems a bit awkward in this context).

I do *not* claim this what *all* Christians either preach or practice, Christians themselves being sinners who happen to have turned to Christ. We have seen, across history, countless forms of corrupted Christianity, including some that try to merge Christianity with materialism in the economic sense (e.g., the so-called prosperity gospel: God wants us to be rich). There is nothing unexpected about this, given that building even the ideal Christian society is impossible for sinful men and women.

The Secular City was possible, but it was only going to go so far. Its self-destruction was inevitable, as all civilizations eventually self-destruct (or are conquered). We can speak here of nuclear and biochemical weapons, consolidations of wealth and power in the hands of the very few; we can speak of the avalanche of public and private debt, and the destruction of the value of currencies; or possibly of man-made climate change if it is real, and other forms of ecological disruption such as oceans filling up with discarded non-biodegradable plastic.

The Christian worldview is not pessimistic, though (except to materialists, whose views we will consider presently). Christians look to the future with ultimate hope—be it for their personal futures or the future of the human race as a whole: the saved portion, anyway. Those who invite Jesus Christ to come into their lives as personal savior will experience heaven in the afterlife. Those who do not, will experience hell. All we truly know of hell is that God is totally absent, and that those who go there will suffer punishment for unrecompensed sin eternally. Civilization will be transformed in the end only by God. The believer's destination will be the paradise of the Heavenly City as imagined by writers such as Augustine of Hippo, not our present-day Secular City. Most assuredly, though, those who became believers in this life will be tasked with things to be done there. They will not be the kinds of tasks we have to endure now.

Christianity has been, and remains, a major influence in the world. It is growing in the East, as its influence wanes in the West. The Secular University rejects its overt supernaturalism as backward, First Stage primitive faith believed without evidence. Second Stage Christians sought rational proofs for God's existence, but since these made rational proof logically prior to and epistemically more fundamental than God, they inevitably fell short. Second Stage Christianity thus opened the door to skepticism and eventually atheism. Third Stage thinkers picked up on such weaknesses, finding notions such as sin and salvation also backward, perhaps even repellent in light of the Third Stage meliorist hopes. The Secular City "bypassed" the Christian worldview as irrelevant. It doesn't help government or business except by becoming a participant (televangelists take in millions per year; megachurches are thriving; Christian rock is also a big ticket item).

In the world of science, technique, and utility, Christianity is an obstacle. Secular City leaders and its "well-adjusted" denizens prefer what they can see, hear, taste, touch, and smell. They are unconscious empiricists. They are attached to *this* life, in *this* world. They lose patience with what seems otherworldly and impractical. So what is their tacit if not explicit worldview? What is the explicit worldview of Secular City intellectual centers, which we've collectively called the Secular University? Let's find out.

The Worldview of Materialism

The terms *materialism*, *materialistic naturalism* (or *naturalist materialism*), and *naturalism* are often used almost interchangeably. Let's settle on *materialism* to designate the worldview, the primary alternative to Christianity in the West, prevailing in Secular University thought, and more tacitly in the Secular City. *Modern* materialism might be even better, to distinguish what we see today from past forms of materialism such as those of Democritus or Lucretius or Epicurus. *Naturalism*, then, is a broader metaphysical concept, incorporating a *methodological* prescription to avoid referring to anything outside this world, especially anything supernatural, as having explanatory force or significance.

What, then, does modern materialism assert, and what makes it a distinctive worldview?

Sticking with the Kekes's five categories:

1. *Metaphysics*: first off, what exists, exists in space and time. *Reality*, that is, is coextensive with (and just means) *spatio-temporal* reality. A "reality outside space and time" makes no sense. What exists in space and time are a relatively few kinds of entities and forces in various combinations discovered by physical science. It is easiest to designate them as physical or *material* entities. They are in no sense *mind-dependent*, that is. Their totality is the physical universe, self-existent, uncreated, and guided by *natural* processes to be uncovered by naturalist methodology, even if puzzles remain about many of the specifics such as its origin and the origin of life.

2. *Philosophical anthropology*: humanity came about through a continuous process, natural selection, without a designer or any such agency. Our differences from other species are differences in *complexity* and biological *configuration*, not differences in *kind*. Human consciousness, including conscious self-awareness, is ultimately a product of the human brain, senses, and central nervous system—as is the awareness any animal has of its surroundings. Certain wavelengths of radiation are visible to us as colored light, that is, because of the physiology of our eyes and the way the information they send to our brains via neural impulses is interpreted. Our only access to the world is through our five senses. Our experience is a "construction" only in the sense that the structure of our senses imposes biology-based limitations on what we apprehend, although language, culture, and personal habituation are also factors. We see what it is *important* to us to see, i.e., what has survival value and what we believe will help us.

3. *Axiology*: morality, in accordance with the conclusions of Third Stage thinkers such as Ruth Benedict, is partly evolutionary and partly cultural. It cannot be anything else. This need not exclude the possibility of establishing "our highest ideals" to pursue as we advance. For this does not render morality "arbitrary." Systems of moral beliefs, e.g., based on the benefits of kinship and cooperation, had survival value. This made them nonarbitrary. More specific practices, such as homosexuality (Benedict's favorite example), are indeed culturally relative. They will be rejected in some

cultures and embraced in others. That said, it is not wrong to say that as members of communities or of the human species as a whole, we are fully responsible for our moral lives, even if we may more fully realize moral lives in well-governed societies. But no god or other invisible entity will "punish" us if we fail to do so. We are, that is, "on our own" in a universe that is indifferent to our choices and ideals. We pursue them as ends in themselves, for our social and civilizational own purposes which range from acquiring knowledge, becoming happier, enjoying social peace, and other goals worthy of a sentient species.

4. *Diagnosis*: various civilizational immaturities including irrational superstitions, greed, and (perhaps) an obsession with *self*; flaws in how we educate and socialize children; poverty; colonialism, and wars fought to control resources or access to them; and a few related factors such as long-standing prejudice against "the other," i.e., racism or ethnic prejudice, sexism and misogyny, a sense of entitlement however based (white privilege, male privilege, national privilege, the privileges of wealth, etc.), all help explain our not seriously reaching for those "highest ideals" of freedom, equality, universal prosperity, sustainability, and peace. False values have been built into our institutions: educational, ecclesiastical, governmental. Little can be worse, however, than condemning humanity as being inherently evil ("born in sin") and redeemable only through a supernatural agency, proofs for the existence of which have failed all our best rational and empirical tests.

5. *Policies and prescriptions*: implied in the diagnosis. Better education, to transmit not just knowledge but acculturation; checks, balances, regulatory control over greed wherever found, an inculcation of responsibility, if not to bring about equality than at least to lessen poverty through responsible work. Eliminate racial prejudice; eliminate unearned privilege; end wars of choice. Oppose the use of force and violence as a means of accomplishing goals. In some versions of materialism as the basis for a quest for a life of responsible freedom, we see extensive efforts to discredit and eventually work to eliminate supervening authorities such as the state in favor of complete freedom of individuals to set the course of their own lives.

Such are the ideals, many of them inherent in Bertrand Russell's "A Free Man's Worship." They are inherent in numerous humanist tracts of the past century, despite multiple variations.

To reiterate: materialism contrasts with Christianity in maintaining that *reality* just means *physical* reality, which is not the product of a higher power. It came into being through processes partially unraveled by theoretical physicists such as Hawking, whose tools are mathematics, not invocation of a god or any other supervening agency.

The appearance of "design" is just that, *appearance*. All physical and biological phenomena are describable in terms of complex ordered systems governed by biochemical and behavioral constants—uniform "laws of nature" if you will—and it makes little sense to suggest that the world could be otherwise. Scientific communities have little patience with ideas that don't suggest testable consequences. The academic philosopher who chops logic, or ponders weird predicates like *grue* and *bleen*, is thus wasting time (and university resources).

The materialist's anthropology tells us, in accordance with the scientific discipline, that we (*Homo sapiens*) emerged through biological evolution from primate ancestors through natural selection probably a few tens of thousands of years ago (possibly more time was needed). While there are differences of opinion over the specifics, evolution is a natural process not guided by any higher intelligence. We have the explanation of how complex systems arose from simpler ones over eons of geologic time and gave us the world we see today.

The evolutionary perspective thus sees humanity as resulting from the continuous process of adaptation to changing conditions, such as the end of the most recent Ice Age. By presenting our species with immediate and serious problems to solve, the Ice Ages may have put us on course toward eventually founding the earliest relatively stable agricultural societies.

Species—and those members of a species—with natural advantages are those most likely to propagate. Nature favors the most adaptable: those best able to cope with changing conditions in their proximate environment. Species' coping mechanisms have always included influencing the environment as well as being influenced by it. Corals thus build reefs; beavers build dams; human beings invented agriculture and eventually built civilizations that learned to extract fossil fuels with waste products sufficient to threaten to disrupt global ecosystems.

While this last development may be unfortunate, nowhere does something called *sin* enter the picture. It's just that nature favors the more assertive—up to a point. In civilization, which changes a lot of basic conditions, a people can be creative at solving problems or conniving at temporarily evading them. Nature herself does not care, but will adjust accordingly. She may adjust us out of the picture, if the planet becomes progressively less habitable (i.e., because of limits of human physiology their societies cannot adapt indefinitely).

A materialist's best philosophy of persons and their hopes and ideals can rely only on what is unique—so far as we know—to human beings, this being our capacity to reason abstractly and communicate using signs. Our physiological needs include: oxygen from the air (abundant and so not a problem), water (cleanliness helps!), food with the right nutrients, shelter from the elements. As social beings, we need companionship, to have or be able to form kinship relations, and we suffer when these are either lost or not made. We seem to be unique in our formal and linguistic capabilities, the key to abstracting from immediate experience and learning from the experiences of others. While other species may have such capabilities in limited degrees, they do not build technologically advancing civilizations.

We can thus predict the future in light of the past, use the known to navigate our way into the unknown at least somewhat, and imagine states of affairs other than, and better than, present ones. In a sense, we are problem solvers, and when we solve problems we suffer less, making our imagined ideals worthy of pursuit.

Humanism, generally, holds that morality is uniquely *human*, not derived from an omniscient immaterial intelligence. This latter notion makes no sense to the materialist, as again, for him/her *intelligence* is just a systemic capacity, that of creatively imagining and reasoning one's way pursuing solutions to problems, be they scientific/intellectual or practical. A scientific genius such as Newton can show that the forces at work in the heavens are the same forces at work on projectiles or falling objects. Combustive force equals propulsion, and thus came steam engines and eventually railroads. In our time we have learned to at least simulate certain aspects of human intelligence ("weak" artificial intelligence or AI). We find few reasons for thinking that a properly programmed computer wouldn't have a "mind" in some sense of that term ("strong" AI). There is no need for the philosopher or theologian to appeal to anything nonphysical at any point along this progression. The materialist thinks that given the enormous successes of science and technology in the twenty-first century this shouldn't be controversial. We may even find ways of using AI to enhance our own cognitive capabilities ("transhumanism"), no less than we use artificial limbs to replace lost organic ones.

Some philosophers of mind have used the term *physicalism* to contend that "mental" phenomena must be neurological, i.e., physical brain events (or processes). In all investigations and analyses, say such philosophers, resist all temptations to invoke nonnatural or supernatural causes, be they a Christian deity or any *other* nonphysical causal agency (methodological naturalism). This would include so-called "paranormal" or psychic phenomena, e.g., Uri Geller's claims to be able to bend metal spoons with his mind. Such claims, studied under controlled conditions, do not appear to yield consistent or reliable results that can be replicated. Magicians can duplicate them and hence show them to be little more than parlor tricks, and for the materialist this is true of "paranormal" fads generally.[13]

Secular ethical theories for Secular University philosophers and their compatriots elsewhere have come down to a choice between three systems.

(1) There are rationalist systems such as Kant's deontology (from the Greek word *deontos*, meaning *duty*), which deduces duties and ways of arranging society through pure reasoning. Although Kant's original effort was fundamentally Second Stage, the twentieth century's John Rawls used the same basic idea, that we could reason our way to the principles of a just society.

(2) There is utilitarianism in its various forms, starting with Bentham and Mill, proceeding eventually to someone such as Singer. These take as their starting point the idea that most of us seek to maximize happiness or pleasure while minimizing pain and suffering, and that the good society is the society in which the happiness of the many is pursued as "the greatest amount of good for the greatest number of people." There are, of course, variations such as that between act and rule utilitarianism, or Singer's "preference" utilitarianism. We are not as interested in the difference as we are the similarities, and how a utilitarian ethos is to be applied. Societies must be arranged to increase the overall amount of happiness or pleasure, including acting in ways to raise the standard of living of peoples across the world if we can do so without diminishing our own beyond the ability to satisfy our basic needs. All remaining debates are over details.

(3) Finally, and far less popular among academics (but not to be dismissed on casual *ad populum* grounds) are egoistic theories such as those of Ayn Rand and Libertarian philosophers who have sought to provide free-market capitalism with a philosophical foundation (we have cited Robert Nozick and Tibor R. Machan; there are a number of others); and the not-unrelated economists derived from the Mises and Mont Pélerin Society groups organized in the 1940s which birthed contemporary neoliberalism. Worth noting is that not all who profess some kind of Libertarianism commit to materialism. Some openly profess Christianity.[14]

---

13. Cf. Gardner, *Fads and Fallacies in the Name of Science*.
14. See Cobin, *Christian Theology and Public Policy*.

Reconciling the two can be problematic. But matters of worldview are rarely a priority even among Christians.

What has been keeping us from realizing the ideal state of affairs, whether from the Kantian (or post-Kantian) perspective, the utilitarian one, or the egoist/libertarian/neoliberal one? Insufficient attention to the need to use reason instead of other human faculties, in the case of the first and the third; in addition, for the third, the continued desire of some to live at the expense of others, and to use the state as an instrument of power and wealth redistribution. Insufficient understanding of, and willingness to work toward, bringing about a happier world, a world with less suffering, in the case of the second. Advocates of the utilitarian perspective such as Singer (one thinks of his landmark "Famine, Affluence and Morality")[1] argue that among our moral failings is a lack of perspective. We Westerners see ourselves as at the center of the world, just as the ancients thought the Earth was at the center of the universe. We are wrong. The lives of others matter if they suffer. One of the triumphs of the Enlightenment was to realize that morality, however conceived, cannot apply just to one's own tribe. It must apply to all who are sentient, can experience pleasure, and will flee suffering if they can.[15] The *moral community*, that is, is the *entire human community*—and more, since higher animals can suffer. Thus for Singer, animal suffering through human mishandling of whatever sort is a moral wrong. An imagined world in which animals are not captive and made to suffer by human beings pursuing profit would be morally superior to our world.[16]

The materialist *prescription*: despite setbacks such as world wars, dictatorships, even acts of genocide, we must remain optimistic and continue to pursue Third Stage ideals. This means applying scientific learning and rational thought to more and more areas of human life, including understanding emotions and integrating them into this larger perspective. Sometimes we will disagree over the best ideals. Some see the good society as the more equitable society; others see it as the society that maximizes individual liberty, even if at the expense of equality. Civil dialogue over such disputes and compromise must continue. Failure to persist could doom us. We will fall on our faces a few times—possibly hard!—but we have and will continue to make progress.

One thing we should *not* do is demand instant solutions, any more than we demand epistemic certainty, that province of First Stage religious belief that never asks questions and Second Stage apriorism that establishes a first premise and then never questions it again. Our complex reality is

---

15. Singer, "Famine, Affluence, and Morality," 229–43.
16. Singer, *Animal Liberation*.

such that certainty does not exist and that piecemeal solutions are our best hope—our *only* hope. What we should not do is "cop out" by looking back at nonnatural or supernatural interventions.

It all comes down to education. Whether major industrialists who promoted public higher education were materialists in my sense may be questionable. My guess is, they didn't give the matter much thought. They were men of this world, of the world of the emerging Secular City, the workings of which their thinking gave priority. Thus John D. Rockefeller Sr. endowed the University of Chicago, while other industrialists endowed other significant intellectual centers. Large foundations were created and began to bankroll efforts to learn the best practices for educating and buying and selling and living in the Secular City as it matured and grew more complex.

This meant passing more and more controls into the hands of *experts*: technical specialists. There was far too much to be known for any one person to master. Yet the need for a leadership that could cut across disciplinary and institutional boundaries seemed a given. Surely we wanted populations who could be content, if not always happy, in this environment as it grew, changed, and in time, improved. Their pondering whether they were trapped in an "iron cage" was clearly undesirable. Technocratic controls would benignly manage such populations in ways that would discourage such sentiments. Technocracy works under the assumption that human nature, even if the product of millions of years of evolution, is sufficiently pliable for such purposes and can be managed by applying scientific principles. The first thinker to open this door, building on Comte's Third Stage view of applying science to society, was Frederick Taylor, in his *Principles of Scientific Management* (1911). As a school of thought technocracy was thus widely discussed in the 1930s and beyond, especially when former Trotskyite James Burnham published *The Managerial Revolution* (1941), which argued that capitalism was being replaced by what he called managerialism. Technocracy continues to be of great interest. Answers have always been sought as to what was wrong and how to fix it from the top down. The most visible philosopher to develop technocratic ideas was, again, Bertrand Russell, although others have chimed in, for or against.[17] It was clear: if the mixed-economy species of post-New Deal capitalism was to continue to work, it was necessary to keep it moving through constant exchange and innovation. The former would happen only if consumers opened their wallets and bought what capitalists

---

17. Russell, *Scientific Outlook*; Russell, *Impact of Science on Society*. See Hubbert et al., *Introduction to Technocracy*. See also Khanna, *Technocracy in America*. For a detailed history and critique of the very idea of technocracy see Wood, *Technocracy Rising*.

produced. The latter called for freedom within the ever-shifting bounds of what markets would support: Schumpeter's "creative destruction."[18]

I do not mean to imply that materialists agreed/agree on every detail we've set down, but they agreed/agree on the basic premises. Nor can I end this section without observing that stern and sometimes very specific warnings were issued as to where this brand of science applied to human beings was threatening to take us. Aldous Huxley's novel *Brave New World* (1931) and its nonfiction follow-up *Brave New World Revisited* (1958) are the obvious exemplars with their suggestion that materialist assumptions about human nature lead invariably to soft totalitarianism, we might call it: the use of behavior modification and conditioning instead of threats and guns as instruments of control—or in economists' terms, the use of incentives to obtain desirable forms of mass behavior.[19] One thinks also of Sheldon Wolin's inverted totalitarianism, a totalitarianism of systems rather than a visible dictator. There were, and are, many other warnings, many of them from modern and contemporary science fiction, and as we get further in this essay, we'll see the inconvenient quandaries showing how materialists' responses are unsatisfactory.

Worldviews in Collision I—
The Historical-Intellectual Backstory

These, then, are the two major worldviews that have shaped Western civilization (leaving aside for now variations on each, and others whose influence has been, overall, much smaller).

That the two are incompatible should be self-evident (the so-called prosperity gospel notwithstanding). Each asserts a metaphysics the other denies. The logical possibilities: one may be true and the other false, or they are both false.

It should already be clear how many public conflicts reflect, in one way or another, worldviews in collision. Decisions consistent with one automatically work against the other, even if the decision-makers are oblivious to philosophy and first premises.

This is a reason philosophy is necessary.

Let's go a little deeper into the "backstory" here.

We sometimes say that modern civilization has an essentially Christian foundation. The basic idea is true enough if oversimplified. The modern West rose scientifically, technologically, politically, and economically,

18. Schumpeter, *Capitalism, Socialism, and Democracy*.
19. Wolin, *Democracy, Inc.*

because for centuries its thought leaders took for granted a Providential God, Creator of the world and humanity.[20] The Creator, a rational agent himself, had made a world that was ordered and intelligible to finite rational agents, persons of intrinsic value as the culmination of Creation. Our ability to grasp how the world works was possible because we were created in God's image: rational agents coming to understand a rationally ordered universe created by a rational Creator/Designer.

Aristotelianism is arguably another main pillar of Western thought and shaper of what became best in the West. Aristotle's god was more of an abstraction than a person, a "Prime Mover" or "Uncaused First Cause." What orders the world are forms or universals, though not in Plato's sense as they are not apart from the world in an ideal realm but inherent in the world, and thus can be grasped through the study of particulars. The latter, objects of experience, are unities of form and substance. Aristotle went as far as was possible to go without Christianity's specific Creator God who is a Person and not an abstraction. Be this as it may he laid the groundwork for several sciences, the Christian element being added later.

Plato before Aristotle had his Demiurge as Creator in the *Timaeus*, shaper of the world from form and substance even if forms were grasped through insight into a prior existence. Thus the ancient Greeks who followed one or the other and so were not Christians could also see the world as intelligible, graspable through human reason. They articulated a Second Stage metaphysics of universals, eternal and serving as the metaphysical basis for the classification of the particulars we experience in the spatiotemporal world.

Saint Thomas Aquinas tried to unite Christian belief and Aristotelian cosmology into a single package. His most important Second Stage conclusion for our purposes was that we inhabit a moral world because moral guidelines are built into its innermost workings (*natural law*). Morality is thus *not* a product of evolution, *not* a cultural artifact, and *not* an invention. We can learn about God both through his Revealed Word and by observing his Creation. "Laws of nature" are part of God's Design. Morality is built into its structure. There are definite rights and wrongs not just in Scripture but in the fact that immoral conduct, forbidden in Scripture, often leads to suffering or bad consequences. We have meaningful obligations to one another in communities, not because we've evolved cooperatively but because moral principles accord with the way the universe actually works in all the relevant areas. (Take the Ten Commandments and negate them completely: "Thou *shalt* steal; thou *shalt* covet: thou *shalt*

---

20. Stark, *Victory of Reason*.

not honor thy father and thy mother," etc. Would any such ethical system work? Of course not, because nothing about it would fit the natural law built into the way the universe was designed.)

Western philosophy began to go off the rails step by step. Within First Stage forms of life worldview postulates are to be accepted as *givens*, not proven or argued for either *a priori* or based on experience. The brand of Second Stage philosophy and philosophical theology put in motion both by Aquinas (and Anselm of Canterbury before him) which sought to establish the necessity of God's existence as the result of a proof rather than accepted as a given raised the possibility that the proof, a product of a human mind rather than Scripture, might be wrong. By its nature a *proof*, based on logical argumentation, calls for evaluation and the evaluation might prove negative. Then what? Is *skepticism* about what was formerly *given* then warranted?

The situation would get worse. With the Age of Exploration, Westerners came into contact with other cultures with different bodies of belief—different gods, different habits, different moralities, or so it seemed at first glance. Doubts soon arose about Western Second Stage epistemic supremacy. Montaigne's system-smashing work gave them voice. Did *anyone's* conclusions about the world, about who we are, about what we ought to do, apply to *all* peoples, universally, as Christians and Aristotelians (and Catholics who embraced Aquinas) had thought?

René Descartes then broke with all previous philosophy by seeking an (not a metaphysical) foundation and validation for all human thought that would answer that question once and for all: with *absolute certainty*. His method was that of provisional, methodical doubt, stripping away all belief logically capable of being false, until he arrived at a proposition that seemed completely immune to doubt. In other words, Descartes become the first philosopher to work under the assumption (which none of the system smashers had made) that our autonomous, private intellects are capable of such a feat: that the individual human mind could use Pure Reason to divorce itself completely from experience, upbringing, cultural heritage or tradition including belief in God (what exists instead might be an Evil Deceiver!), razing every belief and cognitive achievement to the ground, even if only provisionally, and starting over from scratch.

Descartes's methodological maxim was: *if it be logically possible that* p *is false then set* p *aside* . . . He arrived at: *cogito, ergo sum* (even if his major works do not contain those exact words). He concluded that he must exist in order to doubt, or be deceived by an Evil Deceiver. What was he, then? A "thinking thing": a *mind*. He then attempted to build anew from this single, rationally-established, apodictically certain first premise—going through a proof that God exists, cannot be a Deceiver, or allow him as a scientist to be deceived beyond his ability to ascertain truth about the world. What was the world? Matter. Thus began modern, as opposed to medieval, Second Stage philosophy—and the start of Western liberalism in a broad sense of that term which based itself on a foundation of the possibility of rationally-grounded human autonomy, the essential purity of logical/rational methodology, and the epistemic irrelevance of the past.

Thus the Cartesian revolution in Western philosophy!

The Cartesian *cogito*, as we've noted in passing, was logically and epistemically prior to God (as was Aquinas's method deriving from Aristotle's *logos*). Descartes's ontological argument for the existence of God is rather *strange*: that he, René Descartes, has an *idea* in his autonomous intellect or mind of a perfect God; but since he is an imperfect being within a sea of human imperfection, this perfect God must exist in order to have given him the idea. That *perfect* could be nothing more than a misleading word in his *vocabulary* seems not to have occurred to him.

It bears emphasizing: God's existence is now no longer a given but the result of an argument. What was given had shifted to the autonomous human intellect and logical/rational method, which comprised the core of coming Enlightenment thought and classical liberalism. If the autonomous human intellect can formulate an argument, it can criticize one as well, because *no one had (has) ever discovered an argument that is completely impervious to all possible criticism*. Thus was the stage set for the downfall of Christian theism, when Cartesian and other arguments were criticized and failed to stand up to criticism. Thus was set the stage further for the downfall of Second Stage thinking generally, and for philosophy itself when it was compelled to "retreat" in the face of advancing science in the Secular City (and University). Third Stage liberalism would prove to be just as vulnerable. It would just take longer for it to fall.

Science began to follow notions laid out by Roger Bacon, a contemporary of Aquinas's, and became empiricist and pragmatic—the early seeds of Third Stage thought. The scientific revolution happened, causing the fall of the Second Stage Aristotelian edifice—eventually (and unfortunately) to include such elements as natural law which would be replaced by positive law (in a nutshell, law is of human origin exclusively—a product of a legal system—so that we have the rights those in power say we have, no more and no less). Newtonian natural philosophy culminated in Hume's empiricism, while the rising bourgeois culture championed aggressively by writers such as Voltaire (who participated in this culture and thus saw its power from the inside) exacted further changes. The economic side of liberalism challenged the then-dominant feudalism which was strongly tradition-bound and had existed mostly unchanged for centuries. Changes would accelerate, and along with them—especially in the hands of the Jacobins whom we will encounter in a minute—would come rising contempt for traditions seen as embodied in such notions as the divine right of kings, the increasingly despised landed aristocracies, and much more besides.

The Enlightenment further articulated the Cartesian idea that our intellects could sever all ties with religion, tradition, etc., and be *free*, i.e., autonomous. (The term *liberalism* derives from the Latin word *liber*, after all, meaning *free*.) Intellectual *maturity* would start with our autonomy and learn to extend and wisely use its newfound freedom. Immanuel Kant issued the classic challenge:

> Enlightenment is man's emergence from his self-incurred immaturity. Immaturity is the inability to use one's own understanding without the guidance of another. This immaturity is self-incurred if its cause is not lack of understanding, but lack of resolution and courage to use it without the guidance of another. The motto of enlightenment is therefore: Sapere aude! Have courage to use your own understanding!
>
> Laziness and cowardice are the reasons why such a large proportion of men, even when nature has long emancipated them from alien guidance (*naturaliter maiorennes*), nevertheless gladly remain immature for life. For the same reasons, it is all too easy for others to set themselves up as their guardians. It is so convenient to be immature! If I have a book to have understanding in place of me, a spiritual adviser to have a conscience for me, a doctor to judge my diet for me, and so on, I need not make any efforts at all. I need not think, so long as I can pay; others will soon enough take the tiresome job over for me. The guardians who have kindly taken upon themselves the work of supervision will soon see to it that by far the largest part of mankind (including the entire fair sex) should consider the step forward to maturity not only as difficult but also as highly dangerous. Having first infatuated their domesticated animals, and carefully prevented the docile creatures from daring to take a single step without the leading-strings to which they are tied, they next show them the danger which threatens them if they try to walk unaided. Now this danger is not in fact so very great, for they would certainly learn to walk eventually after a few falls. But an example of this kind is intimidating, and usually frightens them off from further attempts.
>
> Thus it is difficult for each separate individual to work his way out of the immaturity which has become almost second nature to him. He has even grown fond of it and is really incapable

> for the time being of using his own understanding, because he was never allowed to make the attempt. Dogmas and formulas, those mechanical instruments for rational use (or rather misuse) of his natural endowments, are the ball and chain of his permanent immaturity. And if anyone did throw them off, he would still be uncertain about jumping over even the narrowest of trenches, for he would be unaccustomed to free movement of this kind. Thus only a few, by cultivating their own minds, have succeeded in freeing themselves from immaturity and in continuing boldly on their way.[21]

Thus although Kant himself was a Second Stage thinker, his essay accelerated the train crossing the previously unseen intellectual bridge from the Second Stage autonomous individual intellect to the Third Stage underpinnings of the Secular City which encircled "autonomous" agents in the "iron cages" of the various professions and walks of life. One thinker had already envisioned what this Secular City might look like, complete with its Secular University. This was Francis Bacon, in his *The New Atlantis* in 1626. In the following century which saw the acceleration of this process, Jean-Jacques Rousseau proposed *El Contrat Sociel* (1762) which argued from the fundamental pristine goodness of a humanity abstracted from its corrupting education and other institutions (as well as from sin in the Christian sense). He substituted a "general will" that would emerge from the goodness of "private wills" freed from all sources of corruption and subordinating themselves to the whole. This turned out to be a dangerous turn.

For just a few decades later it inspired the Jacobins, led by Maximillien Robespierre (among others), a disciple of Rousseau. They applied this kind of notion to politics and swung it like a great club against those hated institutions, the monarchy and the aristocracy. Their Cartesian conclusion: every institution (e.g., the monarchy, or the church) or practice could be subjected to the spotlight of Reason and, if found wanting, razed to the ground, as we sought to build the Society of Reason. History shows how this turned into the bloodbath now known as the French Revolution. The Robespierre Jacobins had no qualms about guillotining thousands, even of those in a different Jacobin faction, the Girondins, as they established their Reign of Terror. It all led ultimately to the Napoleonic era which, for a time, would restore order and stability.

The train leading from Second to Third Stage thought and civilization continued to accelerate. Following Comte a few decades later, we could describe the "enlightened" portion of European (and by this time, American)

---

21. Kant, "What Is Enlightenment?"

humanity as trying to rise from the "adolescence" of speculative Reason of philosophers to the "adulthood" of full scientific Reason of scientists (that term being coined by William Whewell in the 1830s).

Worth noting is that the masses in Anglo-European culture had never sought "individual autonomy" nor relied on abstract reasoning able to establish "first premises." They still adhered to beliefs and traditions integrated into their daily lives, embodied in institutions from their churches to the governance they preferred. These had been in place as parts of organic wholes for as long as anyone could remember. Some ideas and practices, such as the belief in a Providential God, were assumed to have been vetted by time and longstanding practice as well as established by the authority of Scripture. If such practices were so long lasting, there must be a reason. Departures from them based on the doubts of intellectuals therefore seemed, if one actually thought it through, a bad idea!

Especially when they led to events such as the guillotining of anyone questioning the new order, eventually those who departed even a scintilla from what the newly ascended powers demanded! Was this what rationalists really wanted? Such quandaries stood at the root of what eventually became the modern conservative tradition, standing mostly alone outside the mainline of philosophical Cartesianism and political-economic liberalism, made most concrete in the thought of someone such as Edmund Burke, the most articulate respondent to the bloodbath Jacobinism had brought about in France, based on the idea that autonomous intellects can raze everything to the ground and start over.[22]

Worldviews in Collision II—The Rise of the Secular Mass: Autonomous or Controlled?

We see three lines of interrelated development here. The *first* is the long-term replacement of a traditional way of thinking, tied to Christendom. This way of thinking didn't obsess over "foundations" of knowledge because it considered those problems solved. What replaced it was the Cartesian-Lockean-Humean-Kantian axis which created new and unsolved versions of them. Instead of the Christian person with a soul we had the Cartesian autonomous intellect, the root of that abstract entity, "the individual": the Lockean *tabula rasa* who faces the world as a blank slate, and later, the Kantian rational will able to act from duty alone. This entity would survive into the Secular City as *homo economicus*, a curious creature as we will also soon see.

22. See Burke, *Reflections on the Revolution in France*.

The *second* line of development was the growth of this Third Stage mindset and the secular world to which it gave rise, out of the perceived weaknesses of Second Stage thought. The worst of these seemed to be its inability to establish any intellectually credible basis for believing that a Christian deity really exists. Or, that if he does, he has any viable role to play in the Secular City. This was the product of the failures of efforts to prove, using logic and/or evidence, that God must exist. Clearly, science and technique were making genuine progress. The world was comprehensible: the human world as well as the natural world. So why posit a metaphysical distinction between the two? Whatever could be said of "thinking things," "corporeal bodies" clearly existed.

The *third*, accordingly, would be the replacement in the intellectual centers of the Christian worldview by the materialist one, once this second line of development was far enough along. It was moved along first by materialists such as Étienne de la Mettrie and then by other Enlightenment luminaries such as Denis Diderot and Baron D'Holbach, who paved the way for the Auguste Comtes and Frederick Taylors and James Burnhams who came along later.

While rejecting aristocracy and monarchy alongside Second Stage (Christian-derived) thought, some who came in the Enlightenment's wake grew uneasy. When they put their Kant aside, they didn't see "autonomous individuals" with "rational wills" but undisciplined mobs. They saw how humans brought together in the public square of the expanding cities tended to aggregate into *crowds*. Crowds were far from rational—they were easily led by their emotions in the hands of clever con artists (of whom there were plenty even then). This was noted by writers such as Scottish journalist Charles Mackay in 1841 and again by social psychologist Gustave Le Bon in 1895.[23] One could then begin to wonder whether the Cartesian autonomous intellect was a figment of philosophers' imaginations—or, *at best*, a product of a certain kind of emotional temperament, education, and standoffish behavior, hardly spread across the general population in what we might call the *Secular Mass*: ripe for those "iron cages" to come.

For those who believed the emerging Secular Mass needed controls instead of autonomy could find plenty of ammunition just by observing, as Mackay and Le Bon had done. One could easily conclude that those purportedly wise enough to articulate "high ideals" would remain an intellectual elite of sorts, a Third Stage equivalent of the priesthoods and aristocrats of old—and potentially dangerous to rising powers that had other plans for the world.

---

23. Mackay, *Extraordinary Popular Delusions*; Le Bon, *Crowd: A Study*.

The problem, first, is that Secular City maturity in the sense we sketched in Chapter 2 is a *faux* maturity. The growing urban populations would not, because they *could* not, fill the shoes Enlightenment philosophers wanted them to wear. What the latter expected of the Secular Mass was unclear. Did they expect that, with the right kind of education and what a soon-to-develop school in psychology would call positive reinforcement, this Mass would become men and women of autonomous Enlightened thinking in Kant's sense? If that were to happen, then genuine Enlightenment as Voltaire and Kant envisioned it would be possible. If not, they would remain essentially a *mob* or *crowd*, the Enlightenment would remain fundamentally Utopian, and the philosophers would be seen as increasingly irrelevant in their necessary "retreat."

As for the crowds, they would not be merely *susceptible* to controls, they would *need* to be controlled, especially given the anonymity of the Secular City. Absence of control systems of various sorts would mean increasing disorder and chaos, as those within the Secular Mass sometimes fell into conflict with one another, and would not (because most could not) control their passions without external restraint.

Secular Mass passions could be directed by other means, it was soon discovered. By the end of the first quarter of the twentieth century, this was clear to those whose job it was to move them with, e.g., advertising, and/or public relations. Edward Louis Bernays, whom history credits as the Father of Public Relations, left us this revealing comment from the open section of his infamous tract *Propaganda* (orig. 1928):

> The conscious and intelligent manipulation of the organized habits and opinions of the masses is an important element in democratic society. Those who manipulate this unseen mechanism of society constitute an invisible government which is the true ruling power of our country.
>
> We are governed, our minds molded, our tastes formed, our ideas suggested, largely by men we have never heard of. This is a logical result of the way in which our democratic society is organized. Vast numbers of human beings must cooperate in this manner if they are to live together as a smoothly functioning society.[24]

In other words, Secular Mass behavior in the Secular City had to proceed down fairly specific paths, according to preplanned patterns, or the City could not function. The "iron cages" were ready for occupation! There would be some room for deviation—for entrepreneurship, for example, as

---

24. Bernays, *Propaganda*, 37.

well as among artists and other bohemians. Entrepreneurs would be accepted if their products were easily integrated into the larger economy. Not just anyone would be inclined to be an entrepreneur. But enough would that it would be necessary for the Secular City to "evolve" devices such as occupational licensure to restrict the number of entrants into any particular market, lest the result be overproduction and collapse when there weren't enough consumers for all that was likely to be produced. As for artists and other bohemians, they would find themselves restricted, usually happily, to the City's margins where they would be seen as harmless amusements and distractions if they kept out from underfoot, their rantings against "the system" (i.e., the "iron cages") limited to leaflets almost no one outside their own communities would ever see.

How does all this play into the rising clash between the two worldviews we outlined?

The Christian worldview sees us all as sinners in need of redemption, and warns that all attempts to build Utopia are doomed to fail. Societal improvements may be possible, but are apt to be limited, and to go off the rails if those limits are reached and then surpassed. The materialist worldview, at least as it manifested itself in the thinking of a Comte or a Russell, regards the concept of sin as meaningless and thus sees civilization as capable of indefinite improvement through the wise cooperative intersections of science, technique, commerce, and education. Beyond that, the implicit theory of *personhood* under materialism is a morass of ambiguity. Especially as the idea of the human being as a rational Cartesian-Kantian agent began to break down in the hands of the Le Bons of the world, and disappear entirely in the hands of their successors such as Bernays.

The classical economists of the Third Stage tacitly accepted that Cartesian-Kantian agent, whether he appeared as "the individual" or, later, as *homo economicus*, the "sovereign consumer"—or more precisely, producer *and* consumer motivated primarily by ethically neutral economic (material) considerations. Within classical liberalism there was no opposition *as such* to religious beliefs or artifacts, so long as they could be monetized, and the church like every other institution had to support itself monetarily. In the Austrian school of economic thought which we've encountered twice before, *homo economicus*'s only scale of values is in his head: *subjective valuation*, reflected by the choices he actually makes in the marketplace.

A consistent Christian worldview cannot, therefore, accept the Cartesian autonomous individual mind "severed" intellectually from the body, isolating its content, razing it all to the ground and starting over from scratch. Christians have been thrown by the idea that Descartes saw his philosophy as Christian, because of its role for the Christian God. But

God's role in Cartesianism is that of a cog in its deductive machinery, a bridge between the mind's inner stage and the external world. The Cartesian method was doubt, not faith; and the *cogito*, not God, was the starting point of its metaphysics and epistemology. Cartesian philosophy was therefore an implicit *foe* of Christendom, not its *friend*; and this could be said of every strand of philosophical thought Cartesianism precipitated, even those that *seemed* to be Christian, or at least *seemed* Christian-friendly (as some classical liberalism did).

In essence, Descartes invented "the individual" as a philosophical abstraction, something quite different from the flesh-and-blood person pondering the stars or laboring and buying in the marketplace; then standing humbly before God, a sinner begging for mercy and grace. The abstraction then showed up as Locke's *tabula rasa*. Hume's radical empiricist excursion into the mysteries of "personal identity" showed how vaporous this entity really was. But it reappeared again as Kant's autonomous "rational will" following the transcendental turn. Finally, the classical liberals found it useful as *homo economicus*, who became the "sovereign consumer" making "autonomous" choices in the marketplace. Today, Randians, Libertarians, and economists of that Austrian school invoke their version of the entity regularly as they make it their moral and/or economic center, ignoring the Le Bons and the Bernayses.

My view is that nineteenth-century writers basically deconstructed the Cartesian-Kantian abstraction. Mackay and Le Bon showed with examples how easily people are led or otherwise behave in crowds, which are natural aggregates (undergoing a "Cartesian quest for certainty" is not "natural" behavior, after all!). Bernays and a few others such as Walter Lippmann picked up where they left off, and other early architects of advertising and marketing clearly assumed that persons were fundamentally self-interested and emotion-driven (*not* autonomous), easily incentivized, and therefore easy to manipulate by those who learned how to appeal to their own drives and desires.[25]

Thus arrived a materialist equivalent of the Cartesian "individual." Materialism in its modern sense actually began with Second Stage philosophers such as de la Mettrie (author of the tract, *L'Homme Machine*) and d'Holbach (also a determinist, having inferred universal determinism from Newton's physics). As Comte and other early social theorists developed their ideas about human behavior along the lines of Third Stage empiricism which eschewed abstract calls for certainty in favor of the pragmatism and problem-solving of empirical science, materialism applied to human

---

25. See, e.g., Hopkins, *Scientific Advertising*.

beings appeared the natural route to follow. Christians—who had mostly accepted the Cartesian abstraction without realizing it—found themselves intellectually "outgunned" as it were in the Secular City whose thought leaders were more and more drawn to "managers" of "the public mind" or "public opinion."[26] Lippmann, it might be worth observing, was the first to introduce the notion of the "manufacture of consent" Noam Chomsky would make famous decades later.

For as should be clear by now, Secular Mass man was not intended to see the "iron cage" of encirclements falling into place all around him. By the twentieth century *work*, for instance, was tacitly understood as *employment*, work for others, an authority. *Authority* was to be obeyed without question *especially* in the workplace (almost as if the workplace was a tiny First Stage island which replaced God with the boss). This was very different from what Kant had envisioned! *Democracy* was the vehicle through which Secular Mass man (and, with universal suffrage, woman) was told he (she) had a voice through his (her) *vote*. Finally, expanding *mass media* was to be seen as a source of truthful information and practical guidance, and not as "manufactured consent." All this began with public education: children assembled in highly regimented classrooms, preparatory for adult lives of regimentation in "iron cages," reinforced by an increasingly integrated business-governmental support structure.[27]

The majority fell in line, as majorities inevitably do.

But that minority of uneasy and alienated voices refused to go away. For them, the Third Stage sensibility in which "reason" (or "science" or "scientific management") gets the last word, philosophically or sociologically, was crashing on the rocks of the historical events we've surveyed. Or failing as an account of their actual experience. Result: Third Stage thought and social engineering would eventually begin to lose credibility for a significant fraction of a generation (the early Baby Boomers). By this time (with a few exceptions such as the "Jesus freaks"), the Christian worldview no longer seemed a viable option. Hence the growth and spread of the Fourth Stage sensibility, already waiting in the arts and in literature.

The first incipient Fourth Stage thinkers were Kierkegaard, Dostoevsky, and especially Nietzsche. The first doubted (contrary to Second Stage philosophers) that God's existence could be proven but nevertheless should be respected and treated with reverence; hence Kierkegaard's personal war against the churchmen of his time whose worldly (Third

---

26. See Lippman, *Public Opinion*.

27. For a detailed account of what really happened with modern schooling see Gatto, *Underground History of American Education*.

Stage) "Christianity" was indistinguishable in practice from the incipient materialist worldview of unbelievers. The second, in the mouth of one of his characters, told us that "if God doesn't exist, then [in principle] everything is permitted." His novels dramatized how things looked once one accepted this in his personal life. The third warned that if Third Stage thinkers could not find a credible grounding for morality in a world without a Providential God at its helm, the specter of nihilism loomed, and if loosed upon the world, would wreak havoc in the century then just around the corner when "the center did not hold."

Materialism had a foothold in the intellectual centers by Nietzsche's time, especially in the English-speaking world. Outside the walls of ivy, the Christian worldview was still very much around. The former's hold on Western culture was still very tenuous, therefore, whatever Settled Science and its defenders said. Efforts at compromises not so much between the Christian worldview and materialism as a whole but with the economic side of each had appeared. Max Weber had brilliantly articulated one compromise to which I've all along been referring (recall: the "iron cage" was his metaphor) His was a version of (Second Stage) Protestant thought in which (Third Stage) industrial capitalism could feel at home.[28] The final pages of Weber's ambitious but honest effort should make *us* uneasy, however, with those references to the aggregation of subtle controls falling into place around the Secular Mass, hopefully hidden by "public opinion," advertising, and other Secular City noise. Since by using incentives instead of guns, the controls would usually be effective, attempts to reconcile Christian belief with "free market" principles would continue, and be very influential.

Materialism still faced staunch opposition of various stripes from alert adherents to a Christian worldview. The real "cold war" had begun. Sometimes this "war" would be fought in books; sometimes in courtrooms; sometimes in classrooms; sometimes in media caricatures. It would be fought especially in the courts, and in the Supreme Court of the United States. Academic philosophy, sadly, would sit mostly on the sidelines. We would not see the various battles laid out in terms of worldviews. It is time to do so now.

Worldviews in Collision III — The Real Cold War Commences

The "cold war" between Christianity and materialism was not recognized for what it was in large part because the dominant positivist narrative

---

28. See Weber, *Protestant Ethic*.

made it difficult to speak and write clearly about worldviews and first premises. But by the 1920s some theologians saw clearly what was happening. Presbyterianism's J. Gresham Machen, for example, wrote of the growing divide in his denomination between those adhering to an actual Christian worldview versus theological "liberals" or "modernists" who were trying to accommodate it to, e.g., Darwinist biology. What resulted from the latter was a subjectivized "Christianity" robbed of its substance (which necessarily included supernatural events and agencies).[29] Machen would found Westminster Theological Seminary and other important Presbyterian organizations that would slow if not prevent the marginalizing of the Christian worldview in the Secular City. His work, and the institutions he founded, would influence further Christian philosophers such as Francis A. Schaeffer, a lot of whose work would emphasize how the trajectory of Pure Reason through the revolutionary Second and optimistic Third Stage led to a pessimistic Fourth Stage.[30]

The first highly visible clash between the two worldviews came during this period (the Roaring Twenties) with the Scopes Trial. It was an era of freewheeling prosperity whose Secular Mass seemed eager to embrace an implicit materialism. State laws forbidding the teaching of the theory of evolution in public schools, however, illustrated the grip the Christian worldview still had. In Tennessee, where John T. Scopes taught biology, the anti-evolution law was called the Butler Act. The event itself was likely orchestrated from within the intellectual centers to begin the job of getting Darwinism (and, *a fortiori*, materialism) into schools, and encouraging "liberal" Christianity (as opposed to "fundamentalist" followers of Machen) with the idea that Christianity and Darwinism were compatible.

To make a test case, Scopes taught Darwinism openly, or so his students would testify. He was arrested and prosecuted under the Butler Act. Prosecutor and three-times presidential candidate William Jennings Bryan crossed verbal swords with famed defense attorney (and convinced materialist) Clarence Darrow. These were the two most skilled orators of their time, ensuring a public spectacle that would be reported by hard-boiled Darwinian (materialist) H. L. Mencken whose sarcasm was intended to skewer the prosecution on the sharp points of Settled Science. Mencken referred to the case as the "Monkey Trial," a phrase that caught on. Scopes was found guilty and fined $100, although the conviction was overturned on a technicality.

The case went down as a milestone, presented as a clash between the progressive and forward-looking versus ignorance and backward

---

29. Machen, *Christianity and Liberalism*.
30. See Schaeffer, *God Who Is There*; Schaeffer, *How Should We Then Live?*

superstition. Evolution was by this time, after all, basic Settled Science, applicable to planets and stars and galaxies no less than to the origins of species. To question an evolutionary account of all things was to step outside the boundaries of intellectual respectability.

For there now seemed little reason to invoke God's Providence or other holdovers from the previous two Stages. Occam's Razor, the methodological principle that had served science well in the past, suggested what Pierre LaPlace was reported to have said two centuries before, referring to God's existence: *I have no need of that hypothesis*. Besides, large swaths of theological communities were accommodating theories such as Darwin's, Machen and later Schaeffer notwithstanding. The "higher criticism" of Scripture had set out to remove its supernatural elements. From scholars' standpoint, it had succeeded. Events such as the resurrection, essential to any complete Christian worldview, were treated as allegorical at best. And at worst, not only did such events never happen, scholars were appearing who doubted that such a person as Jesus Christ ever lived.[31]

Here, then, is where Settled Science had brought us. The universe, as understood by twentieth-century cosmology, came into being somewhere in the neighborhood of fifteen billion years ago. Physicists, culminating in Stephen Hawking, have taken significant steps toward unraveling the "big bang" that created the universe, somehow configuring mathematically describable physical systems and law in the first few nanoseconds of existence. The Earth, along with the rest of the solar system, formed from prior existing interstellar debris around four and a half billion years ago. Life originated from nonlife perhaps one to two billion years ago, and began to proliferate in multiple forms between six hundred million and a billion years ago. Dinosaurs came to dominate the world of three hundred million or so years ago.

Humanity is a newcomer to the scene, as our immediate primate ancestors split off from other primates, and those from earlier, smaller mammals, a few million years ago, with *Homo sapiens sapiens* evolving on the African continent a few tens of thousands of years ago. The earliest civilizations, in the Middle East, date from around five thousand to fifty-five hundred years ago, when we ceased to be hunter-gatherers, invented agriculture, and began to build stable communities that developed into the first cities. Our growing quest to understand the world around us led first to religion, then to philosophy, and eventually with rising command over our surroundings, to physical and biological science. We used what we had learned to build the Secular City and the Secular University. Science and technology have transformed our lives, and if we can at last put chains on our darker tendencies ranging

---

31. See, e.g., Wells, *Did Jesus Exist?*

from the superstitions of the past to greed, nationalism, and war in the present, science and technology have the capacity to build paradise on Earth. They have already taken us into space. Someday, conceivably, they will take us to other solar systems where we might find other beings like ourselves and not have to be alone in a godless cosmos.

This timeline and its topics provided a silent backdrop for public controversies to come. Following Scopes, the next one of major significance for the "cold war" between worldviews was the conflict over sponsored prayer in public schools. The first significant case was *Everson v. Board of Education* (1947). The court applied the supremacy of the federal government over the states granted by the Fourteenth Amendment to deny that states or state-level institutions could sponsor religious practices because these violated First Amendment church-state separation. In other words, even though the Establishment Clause states that "*Congress* shall make no law," this doesn't apply just to Congress passing laws but to all legislative bodies at whatever level and branches and institutions thereof making policy. On this ground *Everson* voided state-sponsored prayer in public schools as unconstitutional. This set the stage for the next case, the better known *Engel v. Vitale* (1962), in which the court again held that state officials violated the Constitution by sponsoring a prayer invoking the name of "Almighty God" for recitation at the beginning of the school day, violating *Everson*'s redrawing of the Establishment Clause.

What does the full Clause state? What it says: "Congress shall make no law respecting an establishment of religion, or prohibiting the free exercise thereof." The first thing to note is that its spirit clearly predates the preoccupations of the Secular City. One precedent goes back at least to the English Bill of Rights of 1689 which secured the right of English citizens to be free from Roman Catholic dominance. Another precedent is in the Virginia Statute for Religious Freedom drafted by Thomas Jefferson in 1777 (getting through the Virginia General Assembly in 1786) which repudiated the Church of England in Virginia and proclaimed freedom of religious choice for everyone, including Catholics, Jews, and all the Protestant denominations. There was worry that the US federal government would establish a church along the lines of the Church of England, so the Establishment Clause was written to circumvent such plans. The idea of a "wall of separation between church and state" appears nowhere in any official government proclamation but in Jefferson's letter to the Danbury Baptist Association in 1802, even if the phrase has become shorthand for the Establishment Clause.

What Jefferson appears to have meant reveals his own Enlightenment roots: religion is a personal matter and not something government should involve itself in. Jefferson himself appears to have been a deist, one of those earlier intellectual compromises between Christian theism and extrapolation from the physics of Newton. Maybe, that is, God created an exclusively mechanistic reality he either can't or doesn't interfere with (e.g., to perform miracles such as raising his Son from the dead).

Now to be sure, the Court never said children and teenagers cannot pray in school; it said there can be no *official* or *sponsored* prayer. So to that extent, "free exercise" remains. Liberal secularists have had a field day with this, sneering that Christians who see themselves as marginalized or under subtle attack in the Secular City are delusional. But consider: in the Secular environment the "free exercise" or expression of one's faith becomes, as Machen observed in the 1920s and Cox in the 1960s, an exclusively privatized and personal exercise, based on subjective feelings rather than perceptions of the real (metaphysical, worldview-based) presence of a Supreme Being in the world and in one's life. It is thus quixotic and pointless if children and teenagers can pray privately but are otherwise completely encircled by the trappings of secularism.

A choice had been made. It spanned decades, for worldview change never happens overnight. It was the *de facto* choice of materialism over the Christian worldview in all public institutions. Even if one could pay lip service to the other, the two do not portray the world or human nature or personal conduct the same way. What one forbids, the other allows. They do not make the same educational or political or economic recommendations. It is extremely dubious that both can coexist in the same governmental or other organizational structure. If interpreted substantively instead of subjectively, a civilization will necessarily embrace one and hobble the other, with all the cultural consequences this entails.

Consider abortion, which was bound to arise when sexual liberation (given sanction by materialism) resulted in an upsurge of unplanned pregnancies. The debate over whether a woman has a right to end a pregnancy, ending the life of her unborn baby, raged both before and after *Roe v Wade* (1973). Claims on behalf of a right to an abortion *starkly* manifest the clash of worldviews in the Secular City. As we will see in more detail below, abortion is *not* a clash over who or what is *human*, or over *criteria for personhood*, or whether anyone has a "right to be born," or whether women have a right to control their own bodies.

In *one* worldview, every human being, understood as every entity with complete human DNA, is a creation and gift from God however we interpret this, and hence has both age-specific moral responsibilities and *moral sanctity*: a human being cannot be *killed wantonly*: "Thou shalt not murder" (Exod 20:13). This does not *derive* from culture but stands *above* it as a transcendent truth. Its source as an absolute command is outside physical, spatio-temporal reality.

In the *other* worldview, there are no transcendent truths or absolute commands, and hence no "moral sanctity" in that sense. We are, in the last analysis, big-brained animals: one species of primate among many, and as we've seen, our morality is part evolutionary development and part cultural artifact. Both can be retooled to fit a changing culture (adaptation).

Given this view of ourselves, we can struggle all we want over, e.g., criteria for deciding who is a person and should be protected. We are still going to have a hard time avoiding the slippery slope Peter Singer went down, leading to the conclusion that not just abortion but infanticide is morally justifiable under *some* circumstances. Indeed, if conscious self-awareness is your basic criterion for having moral properties, then many late-state Alzheimer's patients probably fail to qualify and can be euthanized morally, as can brain-damaged patients in permanent comas!

Or to cut to the chase, one worldview, *if cashed out properly and completely*, sees human life as having *transcendent-originated intrinsic value*, and therefore is to be protected whatever the cost. The other sees *all values as man-made and extrinsic, including that of human life*, which is therefore *always in principle expendable*—subject to the whims of positive law, political economy, and cultural trendiness.

Could this be one aspect of the nihilism Nietzsche warned of, that no substantive but only emotive meaning is to be assigned to phrases like *the sanctity of life*?

The *actual empirical science* is as clear as it can be. The unborn are *human* because they have human DNA/RNA. That is our sole, scientific criterion for determining what biological species a living entity belongs to.

But *empirical science alone* manifestly cannot derive anything *morally significant* from this. That is the job of the particular *worldview* in which science operates in a culture, and it is manifestly *the job of the philosophers in that culture to draw attention to this*. Muddling the matter further is the obfuscation surrounding the relationship between science—even if understood as a method, as opposed to concrete bodies of findings or results—and the worldview of materialism. Our term for this muddle is the Grandiose Assumption.

The Grandiose Assumption.

Consider the statement above, of where Settled Science has brought us? How much of it can we *honestly say we know is true*?

Settled Science by its nature cannot declare *certainty* at any point, because Third Stage scientific method repudiated the quest for epistemic certainty. And indeed, *Settled* has meant *temporary* more often than not in the history of science (example: Newtonian mechanics would have been considered Settled until late in the 1800s). Science itself doesn't have a problem with this, because information changes and our scientific explanations must change with it. New, advancing, and ever more precise and higher resolution scientific instruments have made possible the exploration of realms hitherto unknown. Thus we assume we know far more today in in a pragmatic sense of knowledge. And processes from *evolution* (including *biogenesis*) to the idea of *a universe approximately sixteen billion years old* are now taken as epistemic givens based on extrapolation. Certainties or not? Here those who speak of Settled Science may say no but with knowing smiles.

Settled Science assumes, that is, that all or nearly all of the above narrative is *true* and *established*, meaning: unlikely to be reversed or overturned by future discoveries, and that only "Biblical fundamentalists" or "pseudo-scientists" or "cranks" question it. This is the case, even though much of the narrative manifestly extends well outside what evidence-based empirical science can induce.

It is a given in the philosophy of science that empirical observation always *underdetermines* theory: that is, theory invariably goes beyond what can be seen or demonstrated in a laboratory (and wouldn't be very interesting if it didn't). Setting aside for now criticisms of the official narrative on "scientific method" such as those of Feyerabend, how is Settled Science to proceed?

Going back to those weird predicates *grue* and *bleen* for a moment, we observed that what makes them weird is that they would never be proposed, much less tested, much less confirmed, in science. Why not? Because again, no one *ever* assumes that the universe or any part of it might work that way! Although daily life sometimes suffers abrupt discontinuities (e.g., a personal health emergency, the effects of a sudden economic downturn, a political upheaval, the abrupt onset of a pandemic), science never assumes that some well-known constant is going to change abruptly, arbitrarily, and inexplicably.

It assumes this without empirical evidence—flying in the face of those emergencies and downturns and upheavals and pandemics which demonstrate clearly that *sometimes things do change, and with lightning speed!* If the human world can change (explicably for those "in the know," sometimes being changed by aggregate human actions or a singular action of someone with a great deal of power), then why *can't* the world of physical reality change (also explicably, if changed by an Agency we are in no position to see, hear, taste, touch, or smell unless He wills it)?

In other words, not only is it the case that empirical observation alone *cannot decide between scientific theories* without postulating some kind of nonempirical principle such as, "the universe is a place of uniformity and order, and not a place where laws change or are changed arbitrarily," there is at least some reason to suspect *the principle might actually be false!*

In which case, empiricism leads us not towards *truth* but ever-deeper into *error!*

If empirical observations alone cannot rationally decide between *theories in science*, then how can we ever think they could rationally decide between far less immediately visible but larger-scale *worldviews*?

Surely we shouldn't be tempted further by the idea that empirical findings somehow show that materialism is true, because *nature is uniform* or from any other intellectual mantra. If nature is uncreated, why should we believe in its uniformity?

Because, the naturalist will respond, empirical science doesn't disclose any nonuniformities.

It doesn't? If we think about it, the response is question-begging. Some believe they have uncovered evidence of vast nonuniformities in Earth history, which may or may not point to a literal Great Flood or some geologic cataclysm that would have been observed as a Great Flood.[32] It seems clear that asteroids, or large meteors, have impacted the Earth in the past, causing mass extinctions. One of these appears to have killed off the dinosaurs, and created space for the rise of mammals, and eventually us, given the evolutionary timeline.

Natural phenomena all, says the naturalist. But where do we draw the line in a non-question-begging fashion?

What we call the Grandiose Assumption comes down to the following: *science requires materialism* and *materialism grounds science*. Nothing else is scientific, or leads to science. Settled Science must assume materialism, so that there can be no room in rational inquiry or in fact-based or evidence-based results for anything else, for any other worldview-grounded premises or conclusions about what kind of world this is. Reality equals physical or *material* reality. Our sole source of knowledge is our five senses and their extensions in the form of scientific instruments, mathematical inferences, and similar extrapolations from observation, corrected by reason.

End of conversation.

I do not want this misunderstood. It should be clear:

Whether in doing science or planning our lives, we *do* in fact operate from the unstated premise that the scientific domain at stake (or the world itself) is lawful (ordered and not chaotic) and/or not apt to change abruptly and inexplicably. In life in communities and even in the Secular City, if we think major disruptive change is a possibility, we try to anticipate it by working out an account of what is happening (say, with

---

32. Cf. Hapgood, *Earth's Shifting Crust*.

the economy, or with political unrest) and *rationally plan for it based on regularities we know and enable us to predict the future in light of the past.* We do not assume that an economic downturn or an episode of unrest or the appearance of a new disease simply happens and presents us with an abrupt structural change in the way the world is working that has no discoverable cause. Events and their causes, including those of life and society, are taken as existing independently of the consciousnesses of observers and assumed to be intelligible to our minds. These might be the laws of projectile motion in physics or supply and demand in economics or the fact that human beings respond to incentives.

In that case, the crux of the issue:

There is nothing in this intelligibility itself enabling us to determine empirically or by deductive reason alone, whether it is the intelligibility of a self-existing and uncreated universe, or the intelligibility of a universe that had a Designer/Creator.

We might even find ourselves stopping, scratching our heads, and wondering why events in the naturalist's conception of the universe should be predictable at all. Maybe ultimately they aren't; maybe the "order" we think we perceive is just a brain construct or psychological façade created by our need to feel secure or safe in the world, and the existentialist or Dadaist is the person who has, in his own way, figured this out. (On the other hand, and in fairness, reconciling plagues and hurricanes and tsunamis with the will of a benign Providential God necessarily takes the thoughtful person deep into philosophical theology to look for reasons why that God allows such things if he is truly omnipotent and can stop or prevent them.)

The point is, *intelligibility* is *worldview-neutral*. There may be more than one explanation for why the world should be ordered and lawful, and not chaotic or subject to sudden and inexplicable change. Or why a tsunami might wipe out tens of thousands or a pandemic might kill millions before it runs its course.

Observed events' and scientific achievements' aggregate relationship to materialism is the same as their relationship to the Christian worldview: compatibility. Order and intelligibility does not prove or disprove, support or debunk, either one. There may be reasons for favoring one or the other on other grounds as we will see, but there is no reason to think this decisive.

This means that philosophers above all should not grant the necessity of the Grandiose Assumption.

On this point, the "retreat" of philosophy did us no favors. Beginning with Comte's positivism and proceeding through early analytic philosophy, it effectively precluded sustained discussion of worldviews on the grounds that metaphysical propositions were not verifiable, testable, etc. (which indeed they are not, at least not in laboratory-fashion), and thus cognitively unhelpful if not actually meaningless.

There is a sense, though, in which if philosophy "retreated," science did as well. Science's "retreat" was different. It "retreated" from philosophy *into* the Grandiose Assumption, into a materialism it could only grant a silent and uncritical nod of approval. For operationally, materialism seemed functional. It seemed to "work." Or perhaps it was the broader naturalism that seemed to "work"; it is hard to tell. In any event, the "God of the gaps" (the God who explained what materialist-grounded science had not yet explained) was dying. Genuine gaps in our knowledge were being filled, one by one.

What "worked," however, was not the Grandiose Assumption but the above premise, that the world is lawful and not chaotic or subject to arbitrary changes, and that its order is intelligible to the human mind. Science cannot proceed without these. But these do not require the Grandiose Assumption, which science can therefore jettison if good cause emerges (it will).

I submit that the Grandiose Assumption has thrown not just science but much public conversation off track. Many issues outside of science *per se* (abortion is an example) remain in muddles because worldview commitments stand unidentified as such.

Not just scientists but public commentators of all stripes have consistently conflated science as method and body of known observation with materialism as a worldview. The non-discussion of worldviews, a legacy of positivism and a product of the decline of educational standards and quality generally, has mostly hidden this conflation. It is past time for the matter to be discussed openly. *The outcome of many separate conversations could turn on what we do next. Do we continue to assume that materialism provides the best basis for understanding who we are as human persons as well as what kind of world this is? Does it set an unstated ground for what kinds of policies should carry us into the future? Or is it time to consider pursuing something else?*

We can't answer such questions without actually *practicing* the evaluation we are recommending for philosophy. We need to take a closer look at materialism as a worldview from various conceivable angles: its cultural consequences—especially in light of an evaluation of secular moral theories—and whether or not it really is consistent with known facts and evidence. We will find that on all such grounds, and others besides, materialism as a worldview falls short of the mark. Before we are done, we will indeed urge philosophers to abandon not just materialism but its broader naturalist parent as hopeless dead ends.

4

Worldview Evaluation and Philosophy I: Materialism and Secular Moralism

It was a dark and stormy night . . . at a secluded estate near Geneva, Switzerland, in the second decade of the 1800s.

A group of Romantic fiction authors and poets including Lord Byron and Percy Shelley had convened and were holding a contest among themselves.

Who could pen the *scariest story*?

Each person in attendance would submit an entry. As a group they would judge the winner.

Third Stage philosophy was still young but gaining ground courtesy of promoters from Voltaire to Kant. Comte's work was still in the future. The Romantics traced their intellectual lineage to Jean-Jacques Rousseau, who had written of innate human goodness but not found it in advancing science or technique or even in the arts. His celebrated essays evinced an even-earlier unease.

Among the writers in this select group was Percy Shelley's wife, the youthful (just eighteen at the time) and enormously talented Mary Shelley, daughter of philosophers William Godwin and Mary Wollstonecraft.

She came up with the idea of a laboratory scientist, a pioneer of Third Stage thought in our sense. We aren't told precisely how, but he's figured out how to create life in his lab: *an artificial man*! He's somehow learned, that is, how to "infuse a spark of being into the lifeless thing" he had stitched together, "infusing life into an inanimate body." The experiment of the century had worked: it's "watery eyes" opened; it rose and walked!

We now know Mary Shelley's scientist as Dr. Victor Frankenstein. His creation was human enough to desire companionship, but so ghastly in appearance as to drive townspeople away screaming in fright. The artificial man, first confused and then angered, broke out of confinement and turned to slaying those around him—the dead included poor Victor's wife. "It" then fled. Much of this is told in flashback form. The entire affair destroyed Victor's life. In Mary Shelley's original, Victor tries to track his creation down and dies from exhaustion and presumably grief. "It" discovers him and, filled with anguish, vows to destroy "itself." In the movie version, about which we'll say more below, the creature turns on Victor and kills him. Needless to say, Mary Shelley won the contest. It wasn't even close.

Frankenstein (orig. 1818, interestingly subtitled *The New Prometheus*) became the first entrant in a new fiction subgenre. It was eventually recognized as, in its own way, one of the most prophetic novels ever written. Lurking under the surface of its plot was a plethora of philosophical issues about the nature of life, consciousness, and what it means to be human, especially in light of how the prevailing worldview was changing when it was written.

Technology Gone Awry.

Frankenstein: The New Prometheus could be seen as an inadvertent warning. *Technology Gone Awry* is my phrase for this subgenre of horrific science fiction, giving rise to dystopias when the technological creation threatens a society or to wreak unwanted changes on humanity as a whole. Here's how it works: a human creation or invention, perhaps intended to advance science or be beneficial but really a product of hubris and self-deification, gets loose. It runs amuck, and faces its creators with the choice of destroying it or being destroyed by it—assuming it is not already too late! The idea challenges Third Stage faith in scientific and technological progress in the hands of those who make the Grandiose Assumption, that as science gets more comprehensive and technology gets better, they pave the way to Utopia.

Technology Gone Awry themes have proven more effective in film than in print—probably because the Secular Mass will see a movie before they read a book (and Mary Shelley's book is *not* light reading). When the original film version of *Frankenstein* debuted in 1931, playing against the backdrop of shocking current events (e.g., the bottom falling out of the stock market two years before and an economy pinwheeling over the cliff), it achieved a level of audience terror never before seen in the history of cinema.

Just so there would be no mistaking what the film was about, it opened with one of the lead characters/actors stepping from behind a curtain and saying:

> *How do you do? [Producer] Mr. Carl Laemmle feels it would be a little unkind to present this picture without just a word of friendly warning: We are about to unfold the story of Frankenstein, a man*

of science who sought to create a man after his own image without reckoning upon God. It is one of the strangest tales ever told. It deals with the two great mysteries of creation: life and death. I think it will thrill you. It may shock you. It might even horrify you. So, if any of you feel that you do not care to subject your nerves to such a strain, now's your chance to— Uh, well, we warned you.

Many popular science fiction films—*The Fly* (both versions), *Colossus: the Forbin Project*, the *Terminator* movies, *Jurassic Park*, *The Matrix*, and numerous less-visible releases—do not feature warnings such as this, as by then, the worldview implied in *Frankenstein* the film's opening statement had dropped from sight in popular culture. They nevertheless exemplify the various possibilities of Technology Gone Awry: a new and still-*very*-experimental technique (or a product of such) is developed. Something goes wrong. The entity gets loose, or a process goes out of control. It turns on its creator(s), or on the world at large. Such films should remind us of our moral fragility, invoking subconsciously the dangers of acting "without reckoning upon God."

In *Terminator II: Judgment Day* (1991), the Terminator cyborg (played by Arnold Schwarzenegger) relates in a wooden voice the world's near future (unless the film's protagonists can change it):

In a few months [computer engineer Myles Dyson of Cyberdyne Systems] creates a revolutionary type of microprocessor. . . . In three years, Cyberdyne will become the largest supplier of military computer systems. All stealth bombers are upgraded with Cyberdyne computers, becoming fully unmanned. Afterwards, they fly with a perfect operational record. . . . The Skynet Funding Bill is passed. The system goes online August 4, 1997. Human decisions are removed from strategic defense. Skynet begins to learn at a geometric rate. It becomes self-aware at 2:14 am, Eastern Time, August 29th. In a panic, they try to pull the plug.

Skynet! An artificial intelligence (AI) Frankenstein creation that also comes to conscious self-awareness! Its terrified creators try to shut it down but fail; "Skynet fights back" is the movie's next line. The stage is set for war between humans and the "intelligent machines" Skynet learns to create: Terminators which look and act increasingly human and can move among humans unnoticed—until they strike!

Jurassic Park envisions genetically reconstituted and engineered dinosaurs in a planned amusement park. It falls to the eccentric Dr. Ian Malcolm (played by Jeff Goldblum, who would played Seth Brundel in the ghastly David Cronenberg remake of *The Fly*) to warn:

"Your scientists were so preoccupied with whether or not they could, *they didn't stop to think if they* should!*"*

The scientists had set about to create dinosaur populations that were exclusively female and thus unable to breed. But as Dr. Malcolm also says, *"life finds a way."*

Naturally, the dinosaurs not only breed but get loose and wreak havoc.

Too few people today ask, of new technologies, whether or not we *should*. AI-based themes (which the Matrix films' computer-simulated reality also illustrates) as well as transhumanism, efforts to enhance human capabilities or connect us directly to the digital world through chemicals, microchip implants, etc., exemplify living issues becoming increasingly relevant. They highlight the application of Third Stage premises (even while subverting them in Fourth Stage fashion!), mired as each of these storylines is in materialism as a worldview (the Grandiose Assumption is not subverted!).

Recall the Turing Test, the thought experiment devised by mathematician Alan Turing back in 1950 for his landmark article "Computing Machinery and Intelligence." The argument: a properly programmed computing device can be deemed *intelligent* in any reasonable sense of that term if it responds to an extended series of ordinary questions or statements in such a way that neutral observers in a controlled experiment with a human respondent and a machine cannot distinguish which is which.[1]

In Turing's day this was impossible, but AI has come a long way! *Weak* AI, as it began to be called during the 1980s—expert systems—were soon able to replace human experts in a variety of occupations, the number of which grew rapidly. It is AI (far more than immigration!) that threatens the livelihoods of tens of thousands of workers in such guises as fully automated manufacturing facilities and driverless vehicles.

Weak AI programs were viewed as *simulating* specific formal (and therefore programmable) aspects of human intelligence. *Strong* AI is the view that a properly programmed computer *really would have a mind* in a relevant sense of this term. This idea may still be elusive, but since miniaturization made it possible for computers to appear in workplaces the idea has captivated a large and widening audience of computer engineers and programmers, cognitive scientists, entrepreneurs, and philosophers. Strong AI would consist of highly adaptive learning programs which, given the Turing test, *we would have no rational reason to refuse to say they had minds which were genuinely intelligent*. The idea that this could happen has now triggered a huge literature, some of it speculating on how strong

---

1. Turing, "Computing Machinery and Intelligence," 433–60.

AI was "strong" because there is a sense in which it could "reach inside itself" and adjust its own programming.²

This is the Grandiose Assumption at work. Materialism underwrites science and science requires materialism, applied to technology which is able to replace humans since it is faster, not vulnerable to the distractions that plague human workers, and is therefore less error-prone. And above all, because AI machines (as opposed to human ones) don't demand paychecks!

But even purveyors of the Grandiose Assumption should concede that Strong AI programs would not have *human* minds. They might not empathize with humans in "normal" ways beyond programmed responses. They could identify and solve problems, learn ("at a geometric rate"?) by acquiring new information about their surroundings. They could adapt, and adjust their own programming as needed. They could be given mobility and manual dexterity with artificial limbs and hands with fingers and an opposable thumb: robots. They could even be given human-sounding voices programmed to *sound* emotive, responding in ways appropriate to *our* emoting. What, *in principle*, would distinguish their data processing based on input and verbal behavior (output) from whatever it is *we* do?

As they came to look more and more like us, they would have become an artificial species: akin to a race of Frankenstein-like creations even if lacking the same physical-organic embodiments and the horrific appearance. Perhaps, organic components will have been built into them, as with the cyborgs in the Terminator films, or cybernetic components built into *us* to help us better communicate digitally with this new species, as with The Borg on *Star Trek*: cyborg is just a contraction for *cybernetic organism*, after all.

The programmers/designers trying to create Strong AI systems *could* attempt to build into their basic programming a version of Asimov's Laws of Robotics (developed by science fiction and science writer Isaac Asimov in his stories about robots): e.g., "No AI may harm, or through inaction allow harm to come, to a human being."

But if Strong AI *by design* can "reach inside itself" and adjust its own programming, there is no reason to think the code in which such injunctions are embedded couldn't be tampered with or summarily deleted if it became an impediment once the Strong AIs got tired of being ordered about by the human vermin that may have created them but are obviously inferior to them in every interesting respect!

---

2. Cf. Haugeland, *Artificial Intelligence*, for a discussion, although the book is extremely dated now. For up-to-date worries see Parsa and AI Organization, *Artificial Intelligence*.

According to futurist Ray Kurzweil, Strong AIs will not only soon surpass human intelligence but learn to design their own vastly superior AIs that will exceed not just human ability but human comprehension! A "singularity" is coming, Kurzweil states matter-of-factly, when the capacity of Strong AI to increase its abilities exponentially becomes effectively infinite. This will occur, he thinks, around 2045.[3]

Stephen Hawking once warned that Strong AI could render the human race expendable, as did Skynet in the *Terminator* films. Kurzweil and others resolve this by envisioning humans and AI blending together into a new, artificial species, "transhuman" entities, eventually existing more digitally than physically, and hence able to fulfill (I presume) not only the original highest ideals of Third Stage thinking (elimination of war, etc.) but transcending death and achieving immortality!

We would be as gods!

Not just replacing but *becoming* God, of course, was the apotheosis of the Third Stage mind!

But in most of these visions, humanity *qua* humanity is eliminated instead.

Did the majority of us sign off on this project? Or consider whether or not we *should*?

It is often difficult to tell where, in these visions, sensible scientific/technological projections end and pure science fiction (or fantasy) begins. Yesterday's science fiction, their authors say, is today's science fact; and there is every reason to think this will continue. At present, we still don't know how to program actual "self-aware" systems into a computer. The question for philosophers: is this only because of present-day technological limits? The Grandiose Assumption answers Yes. Those who are not materialists will say No, that Strong AI, a computer program that *really will have a mind*, is impossible in principle, a fantasy that will remain such. Can we console ourselves and breathe sighs of relief that there will never be a Colossus or a Skynet or a Matrix? Not so fast!

For CEOs of leviathan corporations chasing profits can use increasingly sophisticated Weak AI systems to eliminate jobs for humans: technological unemployment, which threatens the world with political-economic catastrophe in the near future. The sort of economic system in which even Weak AI is at home simply doesn't need as much human labor. Thus millions of people could find their jobs gone and end up as wards of the state, since even food delivery may one day be done by driverless vehicles with AI-based operating systems.[4]

3. Kurtzweil, *Singularity Is Near*.
4. Cf. Brain, *Manna: Two Visions*.

Third Stage technological advancement lifted not mere millions but hundreds of millions of people out of poverty—*if*, that is, we understand *poverty* as premised on a money-based political economy whose *impoverished* are such because they lack money. Its current direction threatens to send many of them back there, as wealth, power, and privilege concentrate in the hands of the transnational elite that controls financial systems, currencies, technological platforms, mass and social media, and the communications grid overall. We seem to be approaching not Utopia but Dystopia, in which we peons are at the mercy of technocrats who might, if we are obedient, administer Universal Basic Income and other policies of the presumed benign elite at the helm of a control grid able to make yesterday's "iron cage" look like the freedom of birds in the air by comparison. (Blockchain, contrary to a recent narrative spun by many Libertarians and tech pioneers, is not an exception.)

This brings us philosophers to one of the Big Questions of our time: *what kind of morality can persons invoke against those who would wield controlling power, political or financial or technological, directly or inadvertently, in the Future Secular City?*

Do we even have such a morality, appropriate for the prevailing worldview? Is there anything to give it teeth? Are there any enforcement mechanisms for it, that is, so that violators see punishment? In particular, is there anything to restrain those whose primary (or sole) motivation is power over global finance, over technology, and over the control grid generally, and hence over humanity as a whole?

Another way of posing the question: has the Grandiose Assumption left us with a Secular City whose Secular Mass is about to be rendered expendable, even obsolete, as nothing stops its power elites from doing essentially as they please, answering only to each other?[5]

And lastly, to what extent has the "retreat" of philosophy we considered above hobbled all efforts to advance a discussion of the fundamentals of morality in civilization?

Modern (i.e., Secular) Moral Philosophy.

Back in 1970, W. D. Hudson's illuminating *Modern Moral Philosophy* distinguished *moralism* from *moral philosophy*. His distinction accords well with the "retreat" of philosophy, as analytic moral philosophers do not *prescribe* (tell anyone what they *should* do) *qua* philosophers. That would

---

5. Sociologist C. Wright Mills appears to have coined this phrase *the power elite* in the 1950s. See Mills, *Power Elite*.

be moral*ism*. Rather, they *describe* what we are doing when we *talk about* what we should do. This, Hudson argues lucidly, is the job of the moral philosopher—the analytic philosopher is concerned not with ethics but the *language* of ethics: whether ethical terms refer to anything in the world such as properties of actions, whether ethical statements can be true or false, ethical arguments rationally justified, and so on.

There is, obviously, room for such discussion, and nothing here is intended to detract from that. But it isn't my primary concern, which is that much analytic treatment of the language of ethics only masks the fact, for fact it is, that secular ethical theory—secular moralism, if you will—has all but collapsed, if the efficacy of a *rationally justified* (in some sense of that term) moral point of view in the Secular City's power centers matters. While discussed by so-called applied philosophers, the closer one gets to centers of wealth and power, the weaker are the moral controls, even if this is never said openly. One visible result has been Gekkoism: the *greed is good* mindset, largely ignored or downplayed by those who profess great concern about, e.g., inequality, or racism, or climate change.

How did we get here?

That question again, as it is always useful to revisit the history of how a particular mess arose as a key to insights into what to do about it.

Let's take another foray into the philosophy of two hundred fifty years ago. Hume's empiricism and utility-mindedness had led him to conclude that morality came down to sentiment—especially sentiments we can observe benefiting civil society. For Hume, sentiment was what motivated action, not the arid conclusions of rational arguments. Even though Hume himself was mostly Second Stage in his building from a foundation ("impressions and ideas") and in his systematicity, his conclusions aligned him with the then-incipient Third Stage focus on the affairs of the world, especially the creation of wealth and prosperity through growing commerce. Hume and Adam Smith (author of *The Theory of Moral Sentiment* and *The Wealth of Nations*) corresponded and became intellectual allies as well as good friends.

Hume looked to Newtonian *natural* philosophy and its applications for what an adequate *moral* philosophy ought to look like, its foundation not in the natural world but in our humanness and what makes us happy and useful to others. The idea that many, many humans lived dreary, *un*-happy lives of endless toil, whether in fields or increasingly in factories as England industrialized, cannot have been lost on him. But as with Adam Smith, and even more so later, the philosophy-independent wheels of commerce as part of the growing Third Stage system in the slowly developing Secular City increasingly took precedence over the interests of persons. Even this is to the extent our prevalent images of Hume and Smith reflect what they actually believed about incipient capitalism and where it should go. There are reasons, based on their private correspondence, for thinking this doubtful.[6]

Kant's project differed from Hume's in fundamental ways. He wanted not to *align* ethics within the world Newtonian science, as had Hume, but *rescue* it from what he saw as the *determinism* of Newtonian science. He foresaw that science would be trained on human beings. He also sought to rescue the Second Stage idea of epistemically grounded logical certainty (a continuing legacy of Cartesianism) from the wrecking ball of Humean skeptical arguments (a different legacy of Cartesianism).

What resulted was the transcendental turn, which transformed philosophy as much as had the Cartesian turn. For Kant, morality is transcendentally-grounded duty, hermetically sealed logically from experientially-grounded inclination. We must act not merely in accordance with duty but for the sake of duty. Actions that merely accord with duty could be done from inclination and thus have no moral worth. If, from duty alone, we tell the truth and honor our contracts when our inclination might be to do the opposite, our actions have moral worth.

Kant thus argues deductively against the acceptability of ever lying, ever breaking one's promises, ever taking one's own life, and so on as a consequence of his categorical imperative. One cannot make exceptions for oneself; a duty for one a duty for all, as all are rational agents with transcendental rational wills. Exceptions sabotage the very ideas of truth-telling, promise keeping, and the immeasurable value of a rational agent able to grasp moral truth with transcendental reason. Why was Kant so intent on completely divorcing morality from inclination? Because to follow inclination, even should it accord with duty, would be to allow one's actions to fall prey to the determination of empirical *external causation* instead of transcendental *internal reason*. Kant's deontology stands as one of the achievements of Second Stage thought, according to which actions are to be judged independently of their consequences, also a matter of external causation.

Utilitarians (whom Hume anticipated in a number of ways) beg to differ. Jeremy Bentham, James Mill, and the latter's genius son John Stuart Mill, all British empiricists, take us back to consequentialism, the idea that morality depends on visible consequences, not formal duties—and to the idea that *morality* is the greatest amount of happiness or pleasure for the greatest number of people: the *principle of utility* or *greatest happiness principle*, operative in the empirical world and not the curious transcendental realm of German philosophy. *Always act in such a way as to maximize*

---

6. Cf. Perelman, *Invention of Capitalism*.

overall happiness and minimize overall unhappiness was what made sense to the Anglo mind, whatever variations existed between Bentham's and Mill's versions ("pushpin is as good as poetry" as opposed to "better Socrates dissatisfied than a pig satisfied"). Arguably, this became the leading ethic of the Secular University as the Anglo-American world assumed the lead in taking the Secular City to its twentieth-century heights, and its supremacy continued until around the 1980s. At that point, it began to be replaced by the Gekkoism of the neoliberals.

For there is that third secular abstract theory of morality: that of the rational egoism defended most visibly by nonacademic writers such as Ayn Rand and academic Libertarians such as Tibor R. Machan.[7] (It should be noted that not all who allied with Libertarianism in some form were egoists; Austrian economists such as Ludwig von Mises were essentially utilitarians).

What does rational ethical egoism hold? That you are *should* act in ways that serve your interests provided you do not forcibly interfere with others doing the same. Serve yourself; and never coerce others or support anyone who does. Trade with others voluntarily, so that each partner to the trade benefits (or believes he does). Above all, never invoke the state as an instrument of coercion. The ideal society is one of coordinated productive efforts of all sorts and peaceful trade of the fruits of our labors, i.e., voluntary, value-for-value exchanges. Egoism allows that your actions will benefit others secondarily via Adam Smith's "invisible hand," but benefit to others is the primary means to your own ends: your actions, especially in business, on behalf of others are intended to bring wealth and prosperity to yourself through voluntary trade. The key to a free society, all these writers agree, is responsible freedom of action and transaction. The primary agency of force is the state (government). *Ergo*, the state should be kept on as short a leash as possible (minarchism) or, if we are to be *fully consistent*, eliminated altogether as illegitimate as it can only exist at the expense of citizens while usually inflicting harm on them (anarchism).

How did neoliberalism enter this picture, and how does it differ?

First, it should be clear by this point that stances taken by intellectuals have real-world consequences, whether of the Marxian left or the individualist right. An implicit egoism (not necessarily rational) arguably became the leading ethic of the Secular City's commercial and financial centers (e.g., large corporations, especially when the latter became "legal persons"!) during the 1980s. Utility-type means served egoistic ends. Greed was *made* "good," because it "works"; the "invisible hand" ensures that focused and intelligently-directed greed brought benefits to those who

---

7. See Rand, *Virtue of Selfishness*; Machan, *Individuals and Their Rights*.

played its game, as the Secular Mass consumed what was placed before them. What the major players accrued was *capital*. Hence capit*alism*, which Miss Rand called "the unknown ideal."[8] This system was not *laissez-faire*, however. It made use of government when convenient, protecting specific markets. *Protectionism* was the word economists used for efforts to prevent manufacturing jobs from being outsourced to third-world countries for cheap labor (as opposed to *free trade*). This term was not used for maneuverings by corporations to secure and maintain marketplace advantages with the help of government encirclements.

Neoliberalism is steeped in the materialist worldview. First, nowhere in Miss Rand's ethical egoism was there room for a deity, Provincial or otherwise. Its metaphysics she describes as "objective reality" which also delegates to science what this reality consists of "ultimately," and where it came from (if such inquiries aren't profitable they aren't of much interest). Miss Rand was a materialist who speaks of "volitional consciousness" as somehow arising from a specific configuration of material substance: the human brain. She never claimed to have any idea how this takes place, only that it does.

Neoliberals, having little interest in such details, never raised the question. Neoliberalism's most visible founding father, Milton Friedman, was an economist all the way down, not a philosopher, when he took the view that the sole purpose of a business corporation is to earn profits for itself and its shareholders, and that any other designated purpose was "socialism." Friedman's discussions never reach the depth needed for comparative worldview discussion.[9]

Worth noting is that there is no logical connection between a free market outlook and materialism. Some classical liberals were explicitly Christian. Fredric Bastiat is an example. He saw human nature as flawed, in that we inevitably attempt to obtain as much as we can through the least possible effort, leaving us ever vulnerable to perverse incentives and bad moral and economic philosophies if they serve such incentives via short-term political purposes.[10] In this view, our having been created in God's image is still the ultimate source and grounding of our rationality, our capacity to grasp the essential natures of created things, and to act morally with regard to others ... although with sin in the world, we can never fully realize our potential. This last will only happen in the world to come, the world in which Jesus Christ has returned to establish his kingdom . . . .

8. See Rand, *Capitalism: The Unknown Ideal*.
9. Friedman, "Social Responsibility of Business," 17.
10. See Bastiat, *Law*.

With the rise of Third Stage thinking, this changed—even among free marketers whose apriorist methods tied them more to Second Stage thought. Miss Rand as we've seen was an atheist. Other free-marketers are also either explicit atheists or don't consider the matter of interest. This aligns them with materialism by default. Ludwig von Mises openly criticizes Christianity as inclining its practitioners towards socialism if they carry out Christian-based morality consistently (he assumes they will eventually be compelled to invoke state action to thwart the "free" decisions of *homo economicus*).[11]

Mises does have an explicit argument against the existence of the Christian God, moreover, arguing from the nature of *action* as he defines it. *Action* is always motivated by a sense of unease as well as the belief that the action will relieve the unease. A perfectly self-sufficient, omniscient, and omnipotent being would by nature experience no unease and hence have no motivation to act, not even to create the world. Mises ignores the fact that a such a being would not be spatiotemporal, much less human, and not be motivated by any of the things that motivate human beings.[12] Materialists are unlikely to grasp this, or recognize its force.

Arguably none of these positions would have been of much interest had they not fueled the rise of neoliberalism via what some historians of ideas came to call the *neoliberal thought collective*.[13] While Mises and his associates rejected central planning, neoliberals had no problem if corporations instead of the state did it. Hence it won support from corporations. Neoliberalism rationalized corporations maximizing their profits and shareholder profits, so it became dominant in the Secular City (and the Secular University, where it started to serve up the adjunct-zoning of all those new PhDs). In many respects, it became the path of least resistance into the brave new world of financialization and technological change starting in the 1980s and proceeding through the 1990s and into the 2000s—until things began to fall apart in 2008 and some scholars started to question where capitalism had taken us.[14]

Thus the range of ideas and positions associated in one way or another with egoism (rational and otherwise), classical liberalism, Libertarianism, and neoliberalism.

We would be remiss if we did not discuss the contractarian social-justice theory of morality put forth by John Rawls, to whom Libertarians such as

11. Mises, *Socialism*.
12. Mises, *Human Action*
13. See, e.g., Mirowski and Plehwe, *Road From Mont Pélerin*.
14. E.g., Piketty, *Capital in the Twenty-first Century*.

Robert Nozick were responding. Rawls's ideas and methods are closer to Kant's, since he argues deductively in Kantian fashion from an original thought experiment and arrives at a new kind of social contract. There is therefore, again, a whiff of the Second Stage about Rawls despite his broader appeal to liberals in the twentieth century sense of that term.

Rawls proposed that we place ourselves behind a *veil of ignorance*, arriving at our *original position*. In our original position, we've no inkling of our race, our class, our gender, etc.; nor do we know what talents or skills or personal psychological makeup we bring to the world.[15]

You're a Cartesian "thinking thing" once again, that is, following the Rawlsian methodological set-asides! But with Rawls you retain self-interest, the critical reasoning skills worthy of a "thinking thing," and a general knowledge of the workings of society, especially a crucial first premise: a moral point of view is more desirable than amoralism.

Rawls proceeds to argue that in our original position we will *all* be more likely to favor principles fair to all, and *not* try to rationalize anything that favors some at the expense of others, whether intentionally or inadvertently (systemically). As a Rawlsian "thinking thing," that is, you deduce not the epistemic certainty of a *cogito ergo sum* but equivalent principles of social justice: *cogito ergo sum omnibus aequa erit*, perhaps. From your self-interested but enlightened standpoint, knowing that your chances of being among the many nearer the bottom of society are far greater than being among the privileged few, even if your chances of being white are greater than your chances of being in a minority group (your chances of being male or female being roughly equal), you ask yourself, what principles of social order should you rationally accede to, as in *your* best interests? Your most enlightened and rational answer is your key to the just society.

Rawls deduced two principles. The first is his *liberty* principle (or *greatest liberty* principle). All persons ought to have as much basic liberty as is compatible with the same basic liberties of all other persons. The second pragmatically accepts inequality and tries to work with it, resulting in two separate components, a *difference* principle and an *equal opportunity* principle. The difference principle states that economic and social inequalities are to be arranged so that they bring the greatest possible benefit to the least advantaged. The equal opportunity principle then proposes that positions within society are to be open to all who are qualified for them. What inequalities the social contract permits cannot, that is, bar those less well off from seeking and obtaining specific jobs or public office.

---

15. Rawls, *Theory of Justice*.

It was a formidable theory, arguably the most significant contribution to academic moral and social philosophy of the second half of the twentieth century. It was Second Stage like Kant's but drew on Third Stage analysis, *and* was very much in tune with the times, which were ambitious and optimistic regarding civil rights activism in changing the priorities of the Secular City. Rawls wanted to incorporate what he saw as best in utilitarian and libertarian positions. He enhanced his position in a follow-up essay "Justice as Fairness" later expanded into a second book.[16]

The Failure of Secular Moralities I: Kant and Utilitarians

Thus the prevailing secular moralities, or moral theories—not necessarily committed to *materialism* when secular moralism originated, mind you, but committed to *the Enlightenment view* (rooted in the Cartesian turn) that *all had been razed to the ground, and that we could start over*. This view opened the door to materialism, which (its critics would argue later) left us vulnerable to human moral failings that would start to undermine everything that was *good* in what science, technology, commerce, and education would accomplish.

We would be unable to avoid political-economic Frankenstein's monsters, that is, whether of the left (e.g., Communism) or of the right (neoliberalism) or less ideologically specific (technocracy). Instead of just Technology Gone Awry, we would see Economics Gone Awry (or: Political Economy Gone Awry). Everyone would be objectified and turned into a *homo economicus*.

For *none* of these theories are adequate. None even *approximate* adequacy. In some cases, their failure is logical and internal. In others, they offer appallingly bad advice, or allow practices most ordinary people see as abhorrent when they learn of them. Ultimately, they get one or another aspect of human nature wrong, and so prove useless in controlling the passions unleashed in the largely anonymous Secular City, whether in its highest political offices, its brightly-lit boardrooms, its lowest and darkest alleyways, and everywhere in between. They provide no guidance, therefore, for easing into the Future Secular City.

Potential or actual conflicts between abstract duties were always a problem for Kant and his successors. Remember that moral duties no more admit of exceptions than can laws of logic or physics. They should not fall into conflict, but sometimes they do. The textbook counterexample is of the well-intentioned and empathetic German citizen trying to survive under the

---

16. Rawls, *Justice as Fairness*.

Nazis, recognizing that his Jewish neighbors are human beings like himself and are in grave danger. He is confronted by *Gestapo* stormtroopers, asked if he is harboring them. He is, in fact; he promised them protection (made a promise). His inclination because of his care for them is to lie, but we are not to lie out of inclination; we have an absolute duty to be truthful (even, presumably, to Nazis!). For if we are *ever* untruthful, we are saying that anyone, in any circumstance, may be untruthful, and this destroys the very meaningfulness of truth-telling. So our hapless German citizen tells the truth. He just broke his promise—violating and negating the meaningfulness of that duty—thus destroying the very meaningfulness of promise-keeping.

Kant's ethics, reduced to basics: our German citizen with a real world dilemma is damned if he does, and damned if he doesn't!

Later Kantians such as W. D. Ross tried to salvage the position by prioritizing duties. Surely saving a life has a higher moral priority than telling the truth (especially to a Nazi!), but it is unclear that the transcendental deductive machinery Kant's moral philosophy supplies justifies such *ad hoc* maneuvers. Kantians will disagree, of course. We need not belabor Kant's ethics and whatever problems it faces and whatever machinations later Kantians attempted, if only because Kant's ethics has not fared especially well in the Secular City. It is too abstract and obscure. It is, in a word: too *academic*. Rawls's contractarian version fared somewhat better when it first appeared, but as we'll see presently it has since splintered on the rocks of identity politics, for which the idea of an "original position" makes no sense.

With utilitarianism the matter has been very different.

At first glance, utilitarianism faces the problem in that happiness (and/or pleasure) is different for different people: what makes *me* happy may be quite different from what makes *you* happy. All and well, say commercial men and women (when they address such topics at all): the fact that we value different things makes trade possible and desirable, as both of us increase our levels of satisfaction, each of us walking away from any exchange with what we want. We increase the overall level of happiness in society, serving the greatest happiness principle. But even leaving aside the question of whether it is short-term or long-term happiness that is being served, the problems with utilitarianism run deeper than this.

Utilitarianism, in practice, runs ashore on the possibility—likelihood, in fact—that some will be sacrificed to bring about a greater good, or a greater amount of happiness, for others or (supposedly) for everyone else. Rawls noted this. To him, it was a decisive objection to the position. If utilitarianism has been a major influence in the Secular City, then we should be able to find instances of this sort of thing. Do we? Again we find a textbook illustration of the problem, and in this case, we have no doubt whatsoever that it actually happened because we know the gory details.

From 1932 until 1972, the US Public Health Service (PHS) conducted its infamous Tuskegee Experiment in Macon County, Alabama. Macon County was home to the Tuskegee Institute, the historically black college founded by Booker T. Washington in the late 1800s that gave the experiment its name. What happened: three hundred ninety-nine black men with untreated syphilis, all of them dirt-poor sharecroppers, were not informed of their condition. They knew *something* was wrong, and were given very weak medications for syphilis in some cases, or just placebos in others. They were told, when they were told anything, that they were being treated for "bad blood."

Even though these men were incentivized to cooperate with free medical care, not only was there no effort or intent to cure them, the PHS obstructed any efforts by blocking access to ongoing national efforts to cure venereal diseases. Doctors involved in the Tuskegee Experiment wanted to observe the effects of the disease as it progressed to its end and then study autopsy reports. By the end of the experiment, twenty-eight of the men had died directly from syphilis, one hundred were dead from complications related to syphilis, forty of their wives had been infected, and nineteen black children were born with congenital syphilis. The PHS clearly oversaw what amounted to a *sacrificing* of members of an uninformed and vulnerable population. None of the latter had signed consent forms or anything else agreeing to becoming laboratory specimens to be observed, like viruses under a microscope.

The Tuskegee Experiment was finally exposed by a whistleblower. Under the light of publicity, it was shamefully ended. To their discredit, PHS officials used the excuse, familiar from the Nuremberg Trials, that they were "just following orders." Trust in the American public health community fell among African-Americans, to the point where a 1990 survey yielded the result that 10 percent believed the US government had created the HIV virus that causes AIDS as part of a plot to exterminate blacks. Twenty percent more refused to rule out the idea. A "crazy conspiracy theory"? The same could be said of the Tuskegee Experiment itself during its time of operation. It had been conducted largely in secret, and support for it went all the way up to the Surgeon General's office.

On May 16, 1997, and in the presence of eight survivors of the Tuskegee Experiment, President Bill Clinton finally issued a formal apology to the black community for what was done to them during those years in Macon County, Alabama.

It is easy to blame old-fashioned racism for an experiment like this. But that wouldn't explain the support of a major black institute such as Tuskegee. Its affiliated hospital lent PHS doctors its facilities. Other black institutions and black doctors were involved. A nurse named Eunice Rivers, involved with the experiment for most of its forty years, was black. She stated, "we were taught that we never diagnosed, we never prescribed; we followed the doctor's instructions."[17]

Nor was the primary motivation behind the Tuskegee Experiment money. No one got rich from it. The primary motive was *knowledge*. Those conducting it hoped that this knowledge would be put to good use (some sacrificed for the greater good of the rest). As it turned out, little useful information was learned because some of the men had indeed been given syphilis medication however low the doses. Slipshod experimental protocols thus compromised an experiment on *untreated* syphilis from the start.

The bottom line here: the interests and finally the lives of real, flesh-and-blood human beings and their family members were sacrificed on the altar of "progress" in medical knowledge. Their health and lives were treated as expendable.

Experiments such as Tuskegee are rationalized, at least in part, by utilitarianism in the Secular City—and Secular University—even if at its most extreme (perhaps). We encounter problems with utilitarianism in practice if we look at other "applied" ethical issues like abortion, euthanasia, and capital punishment. Our question could be framed: does a utilitarian ethic make it possible to write entire categories of human being out of the moral community, the community of all those whom make moral claims on us if they are able, and to whom we ascribe moral properties that justify those claims? What, after all, is a human being? Who is a person, a member of the moral community?

The Failure of Secular Moralities II: How "Abortion Rights" Redrew the Boundaries of the Moral Community

Consider abortion, as it was our example earlier.

Feminists portray the "right" to an abortion euphemistically as a "woman's reproductive choice" or "freedom." It has been heresy for some time now to question this in the Secular University. But even if human life and personhood are understood as biology-based (something "third wave" feminists scorn), then what a "right" to an abortion does is *exemplify* writing a population out of the moral community—arguably *its most*

17. Jones, *Bad Blood*.

vulnerable members: totally helpless, completely unknowing, utterly unable to speak for themselves!

Abortion illustrates the corruption of a once-healthy movement which, in its "first wave," rightly demanded and won for women the right to vote, and then, in its "second wave," rightly demanded workplace equity (provided we understand *equity* as equal pay for equal work for equal experience). But then, feminists began to pull into their sphere of concern the worst fruits of the sexual revolution. It is a biological fact, after all, that unprotected sex leads to unplanned pregnancies, of which there was an upsurge during that era.

The literature on abortion illustrates the declining quality of philosophical argumentation since the period that culminated in *Roe v. Wade* (1973). Reasoning used to defend the practice is tortured; concepts are surprisingly unclear for analytically trained academic philosophers; and crucial issues are dodged—especially what happens to concepts of *humanity* and *personhood* once the materialist worldview is embraced (unidentified as such).

Let us consider these in turn.

The "pro-choice" argument, i.e., the argument that it is morally acceptable and should be legally acceptable to kill an unborn baby, tried to sever the conceptual ties between biological *humanity* and moral *personhood*, or membership in the moral community. The former is a matter of having human DNA. But what is the latter? Are there necessary and sufficient conditions other than biological ones for deeming an entity a *person* with moral properties held by all members of the moral community?

According to the Christian worldview, *persons* are created in God's image. This is the source of their moral properties, and of moral-communitarianism (the idea that we may speak of "the moral community" or community of all moral agents and all entities with moral properties). There is no severing of ties between the biological *kind*, humanity, and *personhood*. But if you are immersed in the materialist worldview, how do you specify necessary and sufficient conditions for who is a member of the moral community, i.e., *who* is a person versus *what* isn't?

Feminists began trying in the early 1970s. Their "reasoning" wasn't Kantian, nor was it utilitarian. It wasn't Rawlsian, as there was no sense of an original position in which *they* could be one of the unborn. Consider instead the "criteria for personhood" offered in Mary Anne Warren's widely anthologized defense of abortion.[18] Warren specifically resisted identifying *humans* with *persons*, in order to challenge the idea that *personhood* and *moral standing*

---

18. Warren, "On the Moral and Legal Status."

begin with *conception* (as they do in the Christian worldview). She offered a thought experiment: she asked how a space explorer might recognize alien beings on another world as having moral standing. Such beings would not be *human*. But would they be *people* (i.e., moral agents, members of the *universal* moral community)? Suppose they did not have science or technology as we do, because their culture developed in a completely different direction. What would a space explorer look for, to determine moral standing? Warren suggested adopting these criteria (I am paraphrasing):

1. Consciousness (of objects and events external and/or internal to the being), and in particular the capacity to feel pain;
2. Reasoning (the *developed* capacity to solve new and relatively complex problems);
3. Self-motivated activity (activity which is relatively independent of either genetic or direct external control);
4. The capacity to communicate, by whatever means, messages of an indefinite variety of types, that is, not just with an indefinite number of possible contents, but on indefinitely many possible topics;
5. The presence of self-concepts, and self-awareness, either individual or racial, or both.[19]

Warren acknowledged "there are apt to be a great many problems involved in formulating precise definitions of these criteria . . . [b]ut I will assume that both we and our explorer know approximately what (1)–(5) mean, and that he is also able to determine whether or not they apply."[20]

One can grant that a reasonably intelligent space explorer, having an extended encounter with an alien intelligence, might be able to satisfy himself that all of (1)–(5) apply given *some* understanding of what they mean. If the aliens have any kind of structured social order, then clearly (1)–(5) would be manifested straightforwardly. How does that help us here on Earth, though?

Warren's confusion deepens as she adds,

> We needn't suppose that an entity must have all of these attributes to be properly considered a person; (1) and (2) alone may well be sufficient for personhood, and quite possibly (1)–(3) are sufficient. Neither do we need to insist that any one of these criteria is necessary for personhood, although once again (1) and

19. See Warren, "On the Moral and Legal Status."
20. Warren, "On the Moral and Legal Status," 16.

(2) look like fairly good candidates for necessary conditions, as does (3), if activity is construed so as to include the activity of reasoning.[21]

Analytic philosophers should have been scratching their heads by this point! What on Earth is she even saying? Warren's (1) may be sufficient for considering many higher animals persons (as Peter Singer might well point out). Research has shown clearly, moreover, that fetuses can also feel pain in early stages of development. So in fact (1) clearly is sufficient for describing the unborn as persons.

Neither satisfies her condition (2). But neither would infants and very young children (and, sadly, probably many older ones, these days!). There is, at best, the potential to develop one's reasoning capabilities. For the purposes of discussing abortion, one wonders why it is on her list at all. What of her condition (3)? Fetuses again have been shown to satisfy (3). They will move away from a foreign object inserted into the woman's uterus. So (3), in addition to (1), is sufficient for personhood. Neither (1) nor (3) establish her point.

There are probably adults who would not be persons according to (4), although some do, and I will again presume that some adult space aliens with their own culture will satisfy (4). So condition (4) confuses more than it clarifies. And again, small children probably do not satisfy Warren's condition (5).

Warren follows up:

> All we need to claim, to demonstrate that a fetus is not a person, is that any being which satisfies none of (1) – (5) is certainly not a person. I consider this claim to be so obvious that I think anyone who denied it, and claimed that a being which satisfied none of (1) – (5) was a person all the same, would thereby demonstrate that he had no notion at all of what a person is—perhaps because he had confused the concept of a person with that of genetic humanity.[22]

But since by this analysis (1) and (3) is sufficient for personhood, this is irrelevant. Note that by Warren's "obvious" criteria, late-stage Alzheimer's patients might not be persons; nor those suffering from severe brain damage and in comas. This does not appear to bother her, for she continues without missing a beat:

---

21. Warren, "On the Moral and Legal Status," 16.
22. Warren, "On the Moral and Legal Status," 16.

Now if (1)–(5) are indeed the primary criteria for personhood, then it is clear that genetic humanity is neither necessary nor sufficient for establishing that an entity is a person. Some human beings are not people, and there may well be people who are not human beings. A man or woman whose consciousness has been permanently obliterated but who remains alive is a human being which is no longer a person; defective human beings, with no appreciable mental capacity, are not and presumably never will be people and a fetus is a human being which is not yet a person, and which therefore cannot coherently be said to have full moral rights.[23]

This is how Fourth Stage, post-Enlightenment thinkers began to write segments of humanity out of the moral community: by erecting an "obvious" set of criteria for membership in that community and then contending that the group deemed expendable falls outside it. While one hates to have to go there, Warren's effort is far more self-conscious than, say, that of the Nazis or the followers of Stalin or of Mao. If used to justify abortion, Warren's claim could *in principle* also be used to justify euthanizing late-stage Alzheimer's patients.

Philosophical defenses of abortion offer other examples of breathtakingly tortured reasoning. Judith Jarvis Thomson compared a pregnant woman wanting an abortion with a woman kidnapped and awakened to find herself attached to an unconscious famous violinist. The violinist had a severe kidney ailment, shared her bloodstream, and was thus dependent on her for survival for nine months.[24] Now surely an unconscious violinist is a person. Thomson's point, which hints at egoism, is that *granting* to a fetus a moral status of personhood is *no guarantee of having a right to live at someone else's expense* without that other person's express permission.

Her argument collapses at what should be an embarrassingly obvious juncture: the suggestion of an *analogy* between a kidnapping and a pregnancy. Kidnappings *by definition* are involuntary acts of force. Except in cases of rape—cases which are statistically very rare—and even if the woman may have felt pressured into sex, surely her pregnancy can't be rationally compared to a kidnapping!

(As an aside, among my most interesting experiences during my time in academia were teaching this material to undergraduates in introduction to ethics classes. My better students would tear these claims to pieces with almost no prompting on my part. Even female students thought they were

---

23. Warren, "On the Moral and Legal Status," 17.
24. Thomson, "Defense of Abortion," 47–66.

ridiculous. One class after another responded this way. In response to a query I once raised in class, long ago, whether a fetus is a person, one student—a woman, incidentally—quipped sarcastically, "Well, it isn't a fish.")

Sometimes arguments from women's health risks are used to justify ending a pregnancy. Again, statistics show such cases to be extremely rare. Well over 99 percent of abortions are abortions of convenience, not actions taken to safeguard a woman's life, or because she was raped. (Thomson herself casts doubt on whether someone pregnant due to rape ought to have an abortion: "Surely the question of whether you have a right to life at all, or how much of it you have, shouldn't turn on the question of whether or not you are the product of a rape."[25])

But at the conclusion of her article Thomson makes this astounding concession, "At this place, however, it should be remembered that we have only been pretending throughout that the fetus is a human being from the moment of conception. A very early abortion is surely not the killing of a person, and so is not dealt with by anything I have said here."[26]

In other words, she has been toying with us the whole time! At least Warren tried to supply criteria for personhood. Thomson has not done this much. She merely presumed, in tune with the times, that biological humanity—the possession of complete human DNA—is not an adequate criterion. She leaves us in the dark as to what such criteria might be, beyond, perhaps, the woman's desire to have a child. Can anyone in his right mind think this is adequate?

What we know is that as of this writing well over sixty million abortions have been performed in the United States alone since *Roe v. Wade*. They continue, despite the activities of well-funded anti-abortion (pro-life) groups. The fact that a great deal of money has been going into the anti-abortion cause from the get-go suggests that there is more to even this than meets the eye, as these groups would lose their *raison d'être* if the practice was ended. Hence while such groups may well save some lives, they do not end the practice of abortion, or fully address those factors that make abortion a tempting option for millions of teenage girls and women: the prevalence of casual sex, the relative absence of visible female role models with sound sexual values, an overall societal and media environment filled with sexual innuendo of every sort, and finally rising populations of singles alongside declining standards of living. The latter might tempt even women of sound sexual values to have an abortion instead of give birth to a baby she cannot afford to take care of. These

---

25. Thomson, "Defense of Abortion," 29.
26. Thomson, "Defense of Abortion," 37.

are all staples of the present-day Secular City and, of course, even more so in the Secular University where hormones rage out of control.

An abortion industry is likely to thrive where materialism prevails, because the latter will ratchet up the importance of money and the experience of ephemeral pleasure while ratcheting down the idea of intrinsic values, including the intrinsic value of human life. Does this idea even make sense if materialism is true?

What appears clear from subsequent philosophical conversation is that defenses of abortion that do not simultaneously offer unintended defenses of infanticide and involuntary euthanasia are extremely difficult if not impossible to come by. Biology alone suggests the utter arbitrariness of birth as a criterion for moral personhood. A few philosophers—Singer is again conspicuous—have seen fit to bite the bullet on this. As we have already noted, Singer believes that euthanizing severely mentally or physically handicapped infants is morally justified.

Rational Ethical Egoism, Libertarianism, Neoliberalism

Does an unborn child acquire moral standing because he/she is an *individual human being*, with the *potential* for reason? And can we not postulate, or stipulate, the Aristotelian man-the-rational-animal regulative ideal as our primary criterion for personhood? This would give us a powerful secular defense of "pro-life" if it could be defended.

Moreover from the standpoint of economic science, haven't societies and civilizations that recognized the value of individual initiative and freedom to transact as ends in themselves, with as few limitations as possible, been the most successful at creating prosperity and raising the standard of living for everyone in them (whatever perversions of this we can attribute to neoliberalism)?

To ask the pertinent question directly, hasn't some form of ethical egoism been the most viable secular theory of morality all along? And what we will call "actually existing" capitalism (neoliberal or otherwise) as the most viable political economy? Let us revisit the matter and find out.

Rational ethical egoism, as the phrase implies, has its roots in Aristotle. Being rooted in an *early* Second Stage philosophy has worked against the idea all along. Because later Second Stage philosophers began to cast doubt on it, especially Hobbes and Hume. Both in different ways cast doubt on the efficacy of this *reason* we rational animals are supposed to possess as essential to our nature. Hobbes presumed what came to be called *psychological* egoism, which makes *ethical* egoism redundant even as it removes the rational. Psychological egoism is the idea that we are "wired" to pursue our own interests and cannot truly act altruistically or even in accordance with a universalized morality such as Kant's (or even Mill's). If this is true, then all *ethical* theories of a universal *morality* are futile even if they may have *cultural* efficacy. That would be due to social approval versus social sanction working: one serves his/her interests by taking what the crowd thinks is moral seriously and acting accordingly. But recall what we learned above about the responsibility of crowds. Specifically, moral language applied to actions approved by the crowd gives them the equivalent of a pat on the back. Hume, as we noted, believed reason could infer conclusions from premises but could not motivate *action*. Hence his embrace of an ethical theory of sentiment which served societal utility—ideas he shared with Adam Smith to whom we will return in a minute.

As psychology developed, more evidence emerged for thinking human nature to be far less rational than its philosophical images portrayed. Some were more empiricist than others. Wilhelm Wundt's experimental psychology, for example, drew on an essentially mechanical view of human beings as responding to their environment. Wundt became the first to hit on the idea that *behavior* could be shaped by reshaping its surroundings, because what we had been calling human *nature* was a fluid product of its surroundings. Wundt, that is, was more Newtonian about human behavior than Hume had been.

The idea of morality as cultural artifact, either in part or in whole, was catching on. Freud looked to "deep structures" of the subconscious and invoked the cultural superego as the source of our strongest ethical imperatives: to this extent morality was a cultural artifact. Such structures would be far more difficult to condition, but they would not be rational. Other schools derived other deconstructions of our supposedly rational nature, sometimes deriving their impetus from the catastrophes of the last century casting cold water on Third Stage ideals: world wars, genocides, "softer" brutalisms that have emerged since.

Analytic philosophers, meanwhile, largely deconstructed the "free will" that had been invoked as a condition of rational ethical choice (although there have been a few holdouts such as Peter van Inwagen and the trio of Boyle, Grisez and Tollafsen[27]). What, precisely, was it that was "free," and what did it mean to be "free" in the requisite sense? Were free will's defenders saying that ethically-significant choices occurred outside the causal structure of physical reality? Indeed, Kant was saying exactly that as a condition for the moral worth of any action. But if there is nothing

---

27. Van Inwagen, *Essay on Free Will*; Boyle et al., *Free Choice*.

outside the physical or material, and if as seemed to be the case, the physical or material was bound by laws of efficient causality, then what sense did it make to say we were metaphysically "free" or make "free choices"? The paradox did not escape Christian authors such as C. S. Lewis who argued at length that any kind of moral view of the universe not only presupposes actions outside the structures of a "material world" but that any judgments at all about *better* or *worse* epistemically require the same presumption; this applies to materialist naturalism and its offshoots such as "determinism" as well, meaning that they are destroyed by their own self-referential logic. We will consider this argument at length below.[28]

In short, the weight of evidence we've amassed from the literature suggests that the *rational* in rational ethical egoism failed well before we get to someone such as Miss Rand, who never familiarized herself with any of it. Small wonder she saw herself as operating completely outside the edifice of modern and contemporary philosophy. Can ethical egoism work *without* its rational element? It seems unlikely, and what head-on analyses we have of ethical egoism are hardly encouraging.

James Rachels observes, for example, that if ethical egoism means that I am to be morally praised for acting in my own interests while allowing all others to do the same, new problems immediately arise. If another's interests conflict with mine, I know this, and I allow him to act anyway, then I am *not* acting in my own interests. If both of us are pursuing the same job opening, for example, and my attitude is one of, *Let the best man, woman, or child win* (i.e., taking a *laissez faire* attitude toward the whole thing), then I am consciously leaving the door open to not obtaining the job when it might be within my reach to close that door. My non-interference policy is hurting my chances, which I could enhance through creative positioning or manipulation or even sabotage of others if I could get away with it. Rachels (and others) conclude that in a world of scarcity I *cannot* serve my own interests consistently without interfering with others' supposed "right" to serve theirs. By leaving others alone, we are in effect *not* pursuing our needs and interests but allowing the actions of others to thwart them.[29]

Rational egoists' ideal world seems to be one in which all acting persons' interests are ultimately compatible despite their pursuit of scarce resources, and who are able to resolve all conflicts by acting responsibly, i.e., rationally, eschewing force. Their ideal Secular City is a stateless, borderless, global marketplace where everyone peacefully pursues their needs and wants through exchanges Their needs are, at base, economic, and once these

---

28. See Lewis, *Miracles*.
29. Rachels, *Elements of Moral Philosophy*.

are satisfied, other interests (wants) may be pursued. Supply and demand, the primary laws of the market, set the course for what gets produced, in what quantities, how much it is sold for, what laborers in divisions of labor can be paid in wages, and so on.

Even Adam Smith found this ideal dubious. He believed, and discussed in detail in *The Wealth of Nations* how, in the real world, businessmen try to circumvent the market process. They are motivated to pursue advantage, not open competition. They collude to fix prices and keep wages down if they can. They form alliances with those in government. In other words, they pursue courses of action Frederic Bastiat noted (see above): setting conditions for the greatest gain for the least effort. To prevent this, Smith wanted the marketplace circumscribed by regulatory laws. The majority of defenders of "actually existing" capitalism have *not* thought it self-regulating. Only Randians, members of the Austrian School of economics, and anarchist-leaning Libertarians have thought so, claiming that the state leviathan is invariably a worse and more violent master than the interlocking networks of corporate leviathans the real world presently confronts us with.[30]

In other words, the basic objections to ethical egoism comes from attending to human nature as it actually manifests itself in society, as opposed to in philosophical theory, especially where economic gain is concerned. How does it manifest itself? The answer to this lies in the rise of "actually existing capitalism" (which, it should be clear by now, is just neoliberalism), as opposed to the abstractions of Libertarian and anarchist academics and those within think-tank cubicles who are more observers than participants in the system.

As the Secular City's industrial base advanced into Third Stage maturity and its institutions (private or public) grew in size, the formation of hierarchies was inevitable. Anonymous capital was able to dictate terms to anonymous labor—especially if (as was always the case) there were more workers than jobs. Capital has an incentive to keep wages down, because profits go up. Marx understood that capital and labor are necessarily at odds for structural reasons: their systemic needs are incompatible (hence the "contradiction"). Capital must make a profit or it goes out of business. Capital*ism* must grow or stagnate—as Schumpeter would observe a century after Marx—due to its own internal "creative-destructive" tendencies, it cannot stand still.[31] Engines of profit enable it to grow, producing new items for consumption. At this point, what Marx considered one of the most basic irrationalities of capitalism began to emerge. It is not that labor

---

30. See Higgs, *Against Leviathan*.
31. Schumpeter, *Capitalism, Socialism and Democracy*.

merely *wants* higher wages: to eat, pay for housing, etc. Labor *must* have wages sufficient to consume what capital produces. If the Secular Mass cannot consume, the Secular City falls into recession or worse. Money must make its way to the Secular Mass, therefore. In "actually existing capitalism" this was accomplished through credit. Financialization, however, funneled the bulk of credit to the top, paving the ways for many of present-day inequities and instabilities.

We need not dwell on these specifics (having already taken one foray into them). All we need is a good overview. We should point out how abstract secular theories like ethical egoism greatly underestimate the way money can be, and therefore, has been, used as a means of control. For once "actually existing capitalism" is underwritten by the materialist worldview, your "value" in (or to) the Secular City is a function of essentially two things, your purchasing power and your capacity to put "value" into the system, where *value* is defined either by what an employer is willing to pay you or by the masses' ability and willingness to consume.

You must have purchasing power to survive and advance your interests in the Secular City. Your purchasing power can be controlled by those with far more of it than you. The way to control employees is with a constant threat of termination implied in their status as employees (tenure for academics was, for a time, an exception to this kind of arrangement—an exception being dismantled as we watch). What of the 'sovereign consumer' making choices in the marketplace? Other than in a very limited sense, there simply is no such person. Consumers, too, are controlled with incentives of various sorts, many operating without their knowledge. Some "choices" become almost inevitable (an example being putting mildly addictive flavor enhancers in foods to keep buyers coming back). In our twenty-first-century whirlwind of technological change, Big Tech leviathans have honed their algorithms to a fine science based on user behavior on their platforms. Other algorithms (beginning shortly after Trump was elected) are designed to de-emphasize the ready availability of unwanted narratives.

Few if any tech billionaires actually earned their billions through productive work. They took their companies public and sold stock to those also hoping for enrichment without working. Financialization enables systems of "money making money." Some are bound to become far better working those systems than others. This is something not different in kind from some being better writers than others, some being better artists than others, some being better auto mechanics than others. Divisions of labor within the Secular City were possible because members of the Secular Mass had different natural abilities.

The result has been a billionaire class that continues to enrich itself during crises in which millions of Secular Mass men and women are thrown out of work, as with the ongoing pandemic. At present, the prevailing solution is for the government just to print the money consumers need to keep spending. Our present financialized system is, however, destabilizing due to so many of its own systems being based entirely on the creation of debt-based money out of nothing, and the massive and rapidly worsening levels of inequality this has generated. The creation of fiat money literally out of nothing through the close cooperation of the Federal Reserve and the U.S. Treasury Department long predates the pandemic, obviously. President Richard M. Nixon opened this door when he "closed the gold window" in 1971, and the process has been accelerating ever since. The official response to the pandemic has sent it into overdrive!

Again, we need not pursue all these specifics. Our topic, after all, is the viability of rational ethical egoism as a viable secular morality. If that was its purpose, it fails, if only because human nature is too easily incentivized by the nonrational (or irrational) even if we do not invoke Christian concepts such as sin which I've purposefully avoided in this section. It fails because it cannot realistically be universalized. My pursuit of my interests precludes always allowing you to pursue yours since yours might prevent my pursuit of mine. And on the large, societal scale, since money and global finance became instruments for one's pursuit of interests, and because some inevitably are able to wield these instruments as formidable systems of control including the way information is presented to the rest of us, egoism (by this point neither rational nor ethical) collapses into a system in which a tiny elite is able to pursue its interests effectively at the expense of everyone else. This elite's collective purchasing power exceeds that of governments, obviously, and this becomes, via egoist definitions, *good*. In a global civilization, this occurs on a global level, ensuring elite domination of the world's resources and the impoverishing of its masses—actually delivering Marx's vision of the fate of capitalism. As neoliberalism became capitalism's dominant manifestation, we saw the kinds of events Marx could have predicted playing out on the world stage. Nation after nation, from the United States and United Kingdom, to India, to Chile, came under the dominance of corporate elites ultimately accountable only to each other. This continued until exposures of corruption and the worsening situations of their common people provoked mass unrest. Chile, to take a prominent example, has moved noticeably to the left. Neoliberalism as a secular system *has had the effect of pushing populations leftward*.

Can a position such as Rawls's bail us out? The answer is no.

The Disappearance of Rawls's "Original Position"

In the case of Rawls's "original position," academic developments themselves intervened. It is almost sad that so-discussed a position as Rawls's turns out to further confirm the essential irrelevance of Secular University academic philosophy. Today's identity-political culture of "woke" can't abide it even if they studied it and understood it (I am surmising here that few "social justice warriors" have read or are even capable of reading a tome such as *A Theory of Justice*).

For what is, or was, the "original position"? Recall that step behind a "veil of ignorance" about our race/ethnicity, sex/gender identity, class standing, the "intersectionality" of any of these, or other characteristics that allegedly advantage some and disadvantage others. We remain ignorant of personal talents or inclinations, but knowledgeable of the workings of our society and committed to the ideals of the just society. Given this and given our inherent self-interest, what principles of social and distributive justice would it be in our rational self-interest to support?

Now clearly, Rawls's "original position" is hard for anyone—even critics of identity politics!—to imagine. And with identity politics, once you remove group characteristics (identities), you have, effectively, *nothing*. Because it's group identity(-ies) all the way down!

I once was asked by an English professor at an event where I had challenged the premises of identity politics—this was back in the 1990s (today I'd be risking my employability even broaching the subject!)—what, once I'd subtracted my various group identities as a white heterosexual male with a (mostly) middle-class background, was left? This gentleman looked at my challenge through the lenses of his categories, looked at me as a *person*, and saw, literally, *nothing*.

Even the Cartesian "thinking thing" was gone!

And indeed, just as Descartes recovered all his former beliefs intact and unchanged, Rawls recovers all of his as well, in tune with his times: the aftermath of the 1960s civil rights struggles, the left-liberal leanings of the Secular University, and the start of the difficulties in implementing political favoritism in the real world. These policies were already coming under withering criticism, some from professional philosophers.[32] All prior to the disasters that have befallen academia in the new millennium.

No one supported preferential policies because they had gone behind a "veil of ignorance." Nor did these policies fail because of the "racism" and "sexism" of their critics. They failed, in large part, because key terms (including

---

32. See Gross, *Reverse Discrimination*; Gross, *Discrimination in Reverse*; Capaldi, *Out of Order*; Yates, *Civil Wrongs*; Eastland, *Ending Affirmative Action*.

affirmative action itself) were never defined, it was never made clear to what they were intended to accomplish, and because they introduced perverse incentives. US Supreme Court decisions changed with the Court's composition over time, further muddying rather than clarifying the issues.

What we know is that in the 1960s, the percentage of African-American philosophy professors stood at between 1 and 2 percent. In the 2000s, the percentage of African American philosophy professors remains at between 1 and 2 percent. Evidence of discrimination by academic philosophers against African-Americans would have required a large number of accomplished and highly qualified black men and women trying to enter the field but finding their career paths blocked by systemic racism. The truth is, when such people appeared as they did a few times, they tended to be hired almost on the spot!

Many spoke darkly that the systemic racism occurs at a still more basic level, that the Secular University structurally discouraged black men and women from even trying to enter, because of the prevalence of white men among the historically important figures. Little can be done about this although today's "cancel culture" is certainly trying! We had no realistic strategy for overcoming any psychological discouragement minorities might have felt, disincentivizing them from pursuing academic careers. What were academic recruiters supposed to do, pull them off the street? As numerous writers have shown, it was not possible to overcome the real disadvantages they faced through top-down policy that often left us "losing ground."[33]

This was the state of affairs *prior* to the full emergence of identity politics and the fragmentation of scholarship along the lines of group interests, as well as the adoption of a hypersensitivity that was bound eventually to turn on some of its own if they got too adventurous. The latter include highly visible (and embarrassing!) episodes such as the witch hunt which ensured when young and doubtless well-intentioned feminist author Rebecca Tuvel penned an article on "trans-racialism" modeled on "transgenderism," got it accepted for publication in the radical feminist journal *Hypatia*, and it came under blistering attack from "transgender scholars" resulting in calls for retraction, editorial resignations from the journal's editorial board, and further recriminations, due to its author's "cultural expropriations."[34]

Bottom-line here: there is *no* evidence of the workability of the kind of social justice secular ethics that began with Rawls, either in theory or practice. In today's environment, Rawls's position is barely even intelligible!

---

33. Murray, *Losing Ground*; Sowell, *Civil Rights*; Sowell, *Preferential Policies*=.

34. McKenzie et al., "Journal Article Provoked a Schism"; see also Schuessler, "Defense of 'Transracial' Identity"; or Singal, "Modern Day Witch Hunt."

In the last analysis, *none* of the major candidates for a secular morality have proven helpful or insightful or useful. On the contrary, like the "contributions" of Marcuse, the Straussians, etc., they have probably done more harm than good. They leave the *honest* secular moralist with, essentially, *nothing*.

Small wonder one of the more significant recent figures in moral philosophy, Alasdair MacIntyre, began his signature work *After Virtue* by revisiting Nietzsche, as part of an upsurge of interest in Nietzsche and Hegel in recent philosophy. Bernard Williams, meanwhile, pondered *Ethics and the Limits of Philosophy*.[35] These were Fourth Stage contributions in a broad sense. MacIntyre went on to explore, and encouraged others to explore, what we would call a Second Stage morality, an Aristotelian-based character or virtue ethic that takes us back to teleology—to a teleological view of reality. *That* isn't necessarily a problem, but in the universe as it is imagined to exist by the materialist naturalist, teleology makes no sense as a form of causation or as a guide to conduct except, perhaps, as a metaphor. As more than this, it implies that a projected future state existing only in one's imagination can have causal efficacy in the present. Whatever metaphysics this enjoins upon us, it isn't materialist!

Is the Secular City Then Nihilist?

A specter thus haunts *all* ethical theorizing and application in the Secular University and therefore in the Secular City: the specter of nihilism: the nihilism Nietzsche warned us about well over a century ago. He called for a "revaluation of all values" he saw as necessary with the "death of God" at the hands of the Enlightenment and modern science, replaced by Matter. This was the replacement of the Christian worldview by materialism, within the broader naturalism. This called for the replacement of any morality steeped in Christian commitments, however well concealed by rhetoric. Imperatives favoring equality derived their moral force from the idea that we are all equal in the eyes of the Christian God.

But with the Christian God gone, in what sense are we equal?

In no sense at all!

We have different intellectual as well as physical capabilities, different talents. We have different levels of motivation and come from different backgrounds, some rich, some poor. We have no idea what kind of social policy would change this wholesale, even assuming such change desirable. What we have is the "actually existing capitalism" of neoliberalism: wealth

---

35. MacIntyre, *After Virtue*; Williams, *Ethics and the Limits of Philosophy*.

accumulation for the few, their policies leading to the rapid disappearance of middle classes everywhere, into a Secular Mass of increasingly "precarious" laborers who are floundering helplessly, often in oceans of debt. In this environment, especially since 2000, we have seen escalating rates of depression and other forms of mental illness and suicide, especially among the young. Violent crime had fallen all through the twentieth century. Now, very recently, in the cities it has begun to rise again.

Current calls for change have an aura of confrontation and potential violence about them that vastly exceeds that of the 1960s. All one need do is read Martin Luther King Jr.'s many statements. His leadership was gradually abandoned after his tragic assassination in 1968. Today, instead of calls for colorblindness, we see open attacks on white males, and those who defend themselves from public attacks by blacks (and white leftists) find themselves jailed and prosecuted for felonies.

In accordance with Fourth Stage decomposition, truth has literally disappeared. It is not to be found on either "left" or "right." Corporate media outlets pontificate for hours about the melee in Charlottesville back in 2017, for example, without once mentioning the role of the leftist group Antifa in instigating the violence that later that day cost one woman her life. They are more likely to assert that Heather Heyer was killed protesting at a white nationalist rally. The truth is, there was no rally. One had been scheduled that did not take place, as the city canceled it at the last minute and ordered attendees to disperse. Miss Heyer was killed over four hours later.

I could cite numerous other examples of blatant disregard for truth in mass media. The utter disregard for what is true seems to be a characteristic peculiar to our times. It bespeaks of nihilism. So then is today's Secular City nihilist?

No one I know of is openly promoting nihilism, of course. No one would. Secular City nihilism is structural. It emerges from Secular City systems themselves—verbal as well as institutional.

What we can say for starters is that what has passed for secular moralism (e.g., "social justice" via preferential policies) has required force of law, often via Supreme Court decisions. Preferential policies have received a lot of pushback, suggesting that whatever moral element they were supposed to presuppose failed to take hold over more than a fraction of the Secular Mass.

In terms of political economy, we've seen a slow shift from the utilitarianism of the pre-1970s Secular City to the quasi-egoist neoliberalism that has come about since. This shift has been far from universal, and there are influential philosophers (Peter Singer is an example) who continue to promote their own brand of utilitarianism. But a quasi-egoism has proven to be the "ethic" most compatible with the "actually existing capitalism" of today. This "ethic" exalts extracting resources from communities through "privatization"; structurally encourages private wealth to concentrate while imposing "austerity" on the public; ignores culture even as culture disintegrates; disregards any commons or common public goods except to sell them off; sees human beings exclusively as commodities to be monetized or discarded.

Small wonder we have seen what could be called a "global populist revolt"!

Neoliberalism gravitates toward a "morality" in which those with money and power have the "right" to do essentially as they please because, after all, they have "succeeded" in the "free market." It is as if they read Strauss alongside Friedman and absorbed the former's ideas as well. Neoliberalism perverts the language of political economy at the top, e.g., by ignoring the help afforded an Amazon.com or a Facebook by US intelligence agencies and other elements of what some call (though the term is not a popular one with the mainstream because Trump so often used it) the "American deep state"[36]

When one considers the full range of cultural as well as political-economic effects, including the way the relevant subjects are presented to students at all levels, one can only think of the dystopian science fiction film *The Matrix* (1999): returning us to the Technology Gone Awry themes that began this chapter. This film portrays the world at the end of the twentieth century as a computer-generated artificial reality programmed to keep the masses under control while AI draw sustenance from their life energies. Heroic figures Morpheus and Neo learn the truth and organize a rebellion.

Fourth Stage civilization has supported a *Real Matrix*, if you will. This *Real Matrix* employs education at all levels, government, and ever-present mass media to assure the masses that they live in a functional if imperfect democracy because they can vote every two and four years. It is designed to assure them that public education is really about learning; that capitalism as it really exists is about "free markets" and that if you don't get rich it is exclusively "your fault"; that globalization is (or will be) good for the world. And that in this world you should be prepared to "reinvent yourself" every few years to keep up with changing technology in a "changing economy" even though neither you nor anyone you know voted for these changes. That you should trust your betters, the political "adults in the room" or "experts" in all the relevant areas: money and financialization, politics, the economy, science, and medicine (think: vaccines).

This *Real Matrix* offers you generous doses of Huxleyan "soma" to be consumed as entertainment: sports, celebrities, social media, even the violent protests. Some of these are aimed at the educated, sometimes to incentivize them to watch other groups or defenders of the ideology

---

36. Cf. Scott, *American Deep State*.

across the aisle with suspicion and not watching their presumed betters, the transnational elites in organizations such as the World Economic Forum who have enriched themselves from financialization and its global redistribution of wealth upwards.

The actual system—in the "Desert of the Real," if you will—is where you'll find the nihilism: the reduction of all "value" to exchange value, where differences between "public" and "private" and between political party have become illusory especially at the top, where the actual ruling power is a kind of global corporatocracy (to use John Perkins's term[37]). Where *might is right* (based on financial power) and *there is no alternative*. Where persuasion fails, brutal force will be applied. For *nothing* transcends money and power. Thus neoliberal-directed capital has no qualms about destroying local economies and ruining indigenous cultures, although it might allow members of those cultures to make and sell trinkets. What does not generate revenue is of no value to it.

As we can see, Fourth Stage civilization is broader than academic postmodernism(-ity). Arguably the earliest prophet of Fourth Stage thinking was who told Socrates that *justice is the will of the stronger party*, and whose argument boils down to the idea that *the stronger party gets to define what the term means*. What Fourth Stage power personalities and their propagandists do is define justice and other morally and politically pregnant terms in such a way that the interests of the stronger are served by them.

Is this not how neoliberals see markets?

Or how the apostles of "woke" see "social justice"?

The Stephen Hawkings of the world thus conclude that philosophy is dead. The world's Richard Dawkinses also promote science alone as providing us with truth, if indeed there is any truth to be had. The "transhumanists" promise techniques currently on the horizon able eventually to merge AI into our organic bodies and make us immortal!

Actually, the "Desert of the Real" is an amalgamation of Third and Fourth Stage thought, incentives, and hence civilization—with all the unease and tensions you're likely to find when such different modes of thought try to exist in the same civilization despite their being at cross-purposes. In terms of basic convictions, the most politically-economically powerful and culturally influential elements align with the idea of a universe emptied of any binding morality. *Binding* here means: there are existential rewards for those who obey its rules and punishments for those who violate its rules. The result is the ultimately absurd lives of its elites as well as its masses: all are Last Men of whom Nietzsche spoke. Life's bottom-line absurdity can be bemoaned. Or it can be celebrated as an instrument of personal and cultural

---

37. Perkins, *Confessions of an Economic Hit Man*; see also Perkins, *New Confessions of an Economic Hit Man*.

liberation. Or it can be ignored by those who bury themselves in busywork or in some personal passion. Sartre and Camus took the first route. Some (not all) of Beat Generation writers and artists pursued the second. Contemporary celebrity and entrepreneurial cultures exemplify the third. A few "younger" authors, younger in the sense that they emerged after the 1970s—Bret Easton Ellis being an example—accepted and portrayed nihilism. They literally shoved it in our faces as with novels like *Less Than Zero* (1985) and *American Psycho* (1991), edgy tales that received mixed reviews when they were made into controversial films.

There have been a few philosophers—Paul Feyerabend is the best example—who kicked doors open to alternatives to the Secular University's God-surrogates Science and Reason. No professional philosopher I know of has argued that Money is the larger Secular City's actual god (or its brutalist and controlling demon, if you don't possess any).

Feyerabend was a Fourth Stage thinker through and through, however, and as a system smasher had no real prescription other than unrestrained plurality. He advanced "epistemological anarchy" as a "medicine" for the scientism of Third Stage thought. There is to be no permanent and enduring consensus or Settled Science, only the philosophical equivalent of anchors, as with large boats, which create temporary oases of stability but can be pulled up at the captain's command. All, that is, can be criticized and replaced. Not even Feyerabend could see what was going on beneath the deck of the ship, however.

For as uncomfortable and outside our comfort zones as it sounds, the legacy of the Secular City may just be the adage that do as thou wilt shall be the whole of the law. If God does not exist, then everything is permitted (Dostoevsky). But as Raskolnikov learned—also Leopold and Loeb—it is best not to get caught!

Summation of This Chapter: The Need for *Worldview* Studies

Academia—the Secular University—has been overwhelmed with studies of various sorts over the past forty years: first it was *women's studies*, then *African-American studies*. Soon we saw *cultural studies*; *women's studies* was replaced by *gender studies*. Later came *queer theory*, and sometimes we now see *transgender studies* or other variations on the gender-bending identity politics has encouraged.

What is really needed, it should be clear by now, especially among academic philosophers but hardly limited to them, is what I would call *worldview studies*. Its subject matter: *worldviews*, obviously. What they are, with examples; how they originated historically; and what they accomplish in civilization or do for us as persons. Clearly the subject has been neglected.

Few have asked what worldviews are, or if a given worldview is helpful or harmful, to whom, and in what ways? Few are in a position, therefore, to answer whether it is reasonable and justifiable for philosophers to recommend that a given worldview be supported or scrapped.

Thus far, the prognosis for the materialist worldview, to the extent it underwrites the amalgamation of Third and Fourth Stage thinking and civilization, is not good. This worldview developed within the intellectual environment of Enlightenment calls for mental or intellectual liberation (such as those found in Kant), traceable to the autonomous intellect of Descartes's "thinking thing." It has ended with the Secular City's encirclements and subordinations of various sorts. "Humanist" efforts at a secular moralism have ended disastrously. Those with money and power do essentially as they please, often while pretending to be doing something quite different (as benevolent Platonist philosopher-kings); the rest of the world is getting stuck with a very steep bill!

There is something we need to keep in mind, however. So far, our evaluation of materialism and broader naturalism as a worldview has been limited to claims that it has this or that set of consequences, that these consequences are manifestly undesirable, and that therefore philosophers have reasonable grounds for reconsidering their commitment to materialism and urging others to do so: not allowing themselves or others to fall into the paralysis of the Grandiose Assumption.

That a worldview has negative consequences is *not decisive*, however. For where is it written that truth must have desirable or pleasant consequences? Many truths *aren't* pleasant, after all. Think of a cancer diagnosis, for example; or an economic meltdown; or the realization that one's country has enemies who will attack from without and perhaps from within when they are able.

Maybe, for all we have demonstrated at this point, the universe just *is* as the materialist describes it—that there is no such thing as a supervening morality outside of human decisions (personal or communal), and that we really *are* on our own with how we interpret the fact and what we choose to do about it. Nothing we have said so far lays this possibility to rest.

We thus turn from consequences to a direct assessment on materialism as a worldview. Our argument in the next chapter is that materialism sets up specific scientific and intellectual problems, or challenges, for itself. These are logically independent of any implications it might have or not have for morality, and need not have anything to do with anyone's religious convictions. If materialism fails to solve these problems it sets for itself, this destroys its credibility even if every argument in this chapter about its consequences for morality for some reason fails.

5

Worldview Evaluation and Philosophy II: Materialism and Science

Thus far, we have discussed the materialist worldview emphasizing its having this or that negative consequence, especially for morality, whether as theorized in the Secular University or practiced in the Secular City implicit in public and corporate policy. We reached the view that Secular City "morality" has no teeth in it, beyond what secular authorities and social sanction can muster. It often sanctions malevolent practices (e.g., the Tuskegee Experiment), offers bad advice, can be tailored to justify brutalist political-economic arrangements, and is impossible to sustain once the right (often forbidden) questions of it are asked.

There are, that is, simply no compelling reasons for someone whose mind operates independently of the crowd to take Secular City "morality" seriously if he is resourceful enough to get away with not doing so, and some are: e.g., those with power, whose power comes from their ability to command tremendous monetary resources accumulated opportunistically. One can, perhaps, simply define his/her own "morality" based on some principle such as non-aggression. This proves impotent against those who refuse to recognize it. The materialism at the core of secular moralism does not create but certainly permits, and even aggravates, a certain cultural and/or political-economic ethos in which all sorts of mischief can flourish unimpeded, given that social sanction is easily circumvented by slick talkers and clever wordsmiths.

Secular City "morality," that is, is at root nihilist. It is compelled to hide its nihilism from itself, although it comes out in artistic products and in a predilection towards brutalism and violence, including the violence of neglect. These may be violent domestic policies sanctioned by their legality and by political correctness (e.g., abortion), corporate overseas activities that are equally destructive, say, of indigenous cultures, out-and-out criminal conspiratorial activity, or wars of choice to control the extraction of resources capitalism needs, papering over these latter in pseudo-humanitarian propaganda (e.g., "*Saddam was a monster!*").

Since in this world truth need not always have pleasant consequences, such arguments, however compelling, *are not decisive*. Given the above and nothing else, materialism could still offer a true account of "the way things are," could it not? The Grandiose Assumption indeed says so, and invokes Settled Science for support. It asks for reasons why anyone should believe there is a God.

We need, therefore, additional lines of evaluation that show how materialism falls well short of what it should be able to do, Grandiose Assumption or no, as a viable underpinning for the explanations underlying Settled Science. Such lines of evaluation include the curious position of human consciousness or conscious, self-valuing self-awareness, I will call it. They include the contrast between what a materialist must conclude about the origin of life on Earth (or anywhere), versus the utter absence of actual empirical evidence and the statistical basis for denying that life could have originated that way. Finally, there is the issue over whether materialism and its defense as a rational philosophy is destroyed by its own internal logic—if it renders rational cognition epistemically impotent and thus conclusions about itself useless on their own terms.

In this chapter, we consider these in turn.

The Mystery of "Consciousness In a Material World"

The Grandiose Assumption has compelled philosophers to assume there must be a materialist basis for this curious phenomenon we call consciousness, or conscious self-awareness, or which we might also call conscious *self-valuing* self-awareness.

Why the *self-valuing* element here? Because not only does each of us see the world from his/her own very specific and unique perspective, he/she *values this perspective as integral to himself/herself*. We are each *special to ourselves*. Other persons and a wide variety of entities in our surroundings may be special as well, but this is because they are in a sense extensions of ourselves, essential parts of our world that provide us with meaning, even if they are not *us*. There might be principles we would lay down our lives to defend, but this is because these, too, have become *part of how we self-identify* and so are part of the special relationship each of us has with ourselves.

Recognizing this specialness of the relationship each person has with himself/herself is a potential starting point for understanding axiological agency: *each of us is a center or sphere of valuation*. Philosophy then inquires into what *grounds* this self-aware valuation that seems both a given and completely natural to us. Is it a cosmic accident of evolution, existing because it had/has survival value? Or is there a transcendent Agency behind it? Or is it just a strange *illusion* of some sort?

Philosophy of mind is that area of modern and contemporary philosophy that considers the so-called problem of consciousness, or conscious self-awareness. Its commitment to the Grandiose Assumption has been wide and sweeping. Most philosophers of mind have felt the need to be "scientifically correct," one might say (with a touch of irony), even when looking straight at something that has always appeared, and when considered honestly on its own terms, continues to appear fundamentally alien and inexplicable in materialist terms.

This is unfortunate because even with this conspicuous Achilles heel, *much of the best philosophical work of the past seventy years, has been done in this area.* The resulting literature fills many bookshelves. In just this section we cannot begin to do justice to all the efforts philosophers of mind have made to grapple with their subject matter. Under Wittgenstein's enormous influence, many philosophers went linguistic and tried to explain our sense of conscious self-awareness as a product of the great influence of certain ways of speaking. These culminated in Rorty's attempted dissolution of the problem which we'll examine next. In recent years much effort has focused less on this and more on cognition as a brain process (or brain, senses, and central nervous system process), in tune with the Grandiose Assumption, leaving linguistic arguments aside. But let's look at these first.

Richard Rorty, in his key tract *Philosophy and the Mirror of Nature*, summarized the state of affairs as it existed in the late 1970s. It all began—again!—with Descartes and Locke (ultimately Plato) and ended with the so-called "mind-body problem" of our era.[1] Rorty walks us through various attempts to identify "marks of the mental" converging on the idea that the "mind-body problem" rides piggyback, as it were, on the "problem of universals." He then urges us to "be nominalists": not to reify predicates as if they referred to Platonist entities. If this argument worked, it would get rid of the "mind-body problem"!

Descartes, Rorty continues, "invented the mind" as an "inner stage" of private contemplation inaccessible to science/others, and thus vulnerable to Wittgenstein's well-known argument against the intelligibility of a "private language." Rorty pursued the consequences: inveighing against epistemology itself as it has understood itself since Descartes, in one or another sense, representational: the idea that "we," i.e., minds, use

---

1. Rorty, *Philosophy and the Mirror of Nature*.

language, conceptual schemes, theories, etc., to "represent" the (material, external) world to "ourselves"—to the "glassy essences" of that private inner stage. He believed his analysis showed that ultimately this makes no sense. It was not that "the material" had triumphed. "What did it triumph over?" he asks rhetorically, affecting head-scratching bewilderment. "The mental? What was that?"[2]

Rorty may well supply solid reasons for not being a Cartesian dualist. Defending Cartesian dualism is hardly my purpose here. What *specific stance* regarding the nature of consciousness we should be defending from materialism is a good question, but goes beyond the scope of this effort. It should be sufficient if we have pointed out that contrary to Rorty (another Fourth Stage system smasher in my sense although more modest than Feyerabend) and other materialists there are indeed features of consciousness that cannot be compressed into that kind of worldview, or gotten rid of by going linguistic ("be[ing] nominalists"). On the contrary, close attention to what goes on when we use language only highlights and enhances these features.

So my discussion will focus on what seem to me the four most significant contributions to recent philosophy of mind of the years since Rorty's attempted deconstruction of the "mind-body problem": John Searle's infamous "Chinese room" thought experiment, David J. Chalmers's invocation of the "hard problem" of consciousness, Thomas Nagel's focused if brief call for an abandonment of materialism based on its failures to account for the unique "quality space" a conscious entity has that, in human beings, manifests as conscious self-valuing self-awareness, and Colin McGinn's "New Mysterianism" which in desperation clings to the Grandiose Assumption but abandons hope of explanation with the idea that our brains are material objects simply not structured in ways enabling them to understand themselves.

Nagel's discussion goes the furthest, and will take us into the next section: despite their belligerent assertions (and arrogant rejections of theistic alternatives), not only have materialists been unable to explain conscious self-awareness, but neither have they produced a credible explanation for the origin of life from nonliving "matter" despite over a century of efforts. Even Nagel's views, it seems worth noting, are delivered from within a broader naturalism—in his case, interestingly (as Alasdair MacIntyre ended up here as well from a different direction), a broader teleological naturalism he leaves to others to work out more fully and justify.

---

2. Rorty, *Philosophy and the Mirror of Nature*, p. 122.

Starting with Searle, the "Chinese room" came with his magnificent short essay "Minds, Brains, and Programs." Given the mixed reception this article received—philosophers (joined by a few others in cognate areas) loved or hated it, with very little in-between—it was clear that something of significance had just happened. Searle quickly expanded his discussion into the slim book *Minds, Brains, and Science*. We must be clear: Searle's aim was considerably more modest than ours. Under no circumstances would he or most of his colleagues endorse *this* essay! Searle was critical of the then-popular academic fashion that what we call *the mind is* akin to a *computer program*, this being the basis for the Strong AI we noted earlier: if it passed the Turing test, there would be no rational basis for denying that a properly programmed computer "has a mind." This, and not materialism, was Searle's target. My contention is that in squarely hitting his target, Searle unintentionally provides more ammunition against materialism than he thought.

Computer programs, Searle observed, consist of signs and sets of instructions how to combine them according to formal rules. They receive input, deduce further signs in further combinations as output, with no capacity of their own for interpretation. They are, that is, *syntactic engines*. Minds clearly do have this curious interpretative capacity Searle calls *intentionality*. Minds are—one might say—*semantic engines*. Intentionality is the capacity of mental states to be *about* nonmental/nonlinguistic entities. For Searle, philosophy of language was a branch of the philosophy of mind because language by its very nature in "ordinary" (i.e., natural) usages is also *about* nonlinguistic entities. It points beyond itself. For us as language *users*, we give signs meanings, so that they refer to nonlinguistic entities, be they individuals, classes, events, or states of affairs. Language is used in a complex and constantly changing environment, not always predictable, and not written or designed the way computer programs are written (with a few exceptions like Esperanto). Natural language is more "organic," in other words. Instructions for combining its signs include grammar, obviously, but are not exclusively formal, and our derivations are not mechanical. They involve pragmatics, which introduces the relations between signs and sign-users as agents acting in proximate environments and with purposes "in mind."

Hence there is a vast *disanalogy* between minds and programs if we take mental states on their own terms and what we actually use language to *do*. It seems clear that this disanalogy persists despite any and all insistence on seeing "the mental" as a complex array of brain and central nervous system processes, organic instead of formal. The obvious question is: how can organic brain processes or events be *about* anything?

Searle's thought experiment is well-known, so I will only sketch it here. He, John Searle, is locked in a room and given "a large batch of Chinese writing." He knows no Chinese, written or spoken. He is then given a second batch of Chinese pictograms—and a set of instructions, a *manual* that is, for correlating the first set of symbols with the second, so that were a Chinese speaker to present him with a symbol from the first batch, he could consult the manual, locate the proper response, and supply it. The manual is, of course, written in English. It explains in great detail which symbols in the first batch if encountered ought to prompt which responses in the second as output.

Now he receives a third batch of symbols, with another manual in English for how to use these as responses to Chinese symbols from the other two. He can combine still more Chinese pictograms in the right way, possibly eventually without even consulting the manual—having recognized *patterns* among the symbols and creating *habits*. Suppose that after a great deal of practice he gets so good at providing the correct Chinese symbols in the third batch in response to prompts from the first or second, or correlating symbols from the first two batches, that from the point of view of an observer outside the room, his responses are indistinguishable from those of a native Chinese speaker. "Nobody just looking at my answers," said Searle, "can tell that I don't speak a word of Chinese."

He is behaving the way a computer program would behave (much more slowly, of course): when given Chinese symbols, he goes to the manual, looks up the appropriate response, and mechanically supplies it—or, having learned it from repetition, supplies it. The manual is sufficiently complete that he can do this for a wide range of Chinese pictographs. He can *simulate*, from within his "Chinese room," an understanding of Chinese. In other words, *the system of which he is a part could pass the Turing test.*

But surely we wouldn't say he has learned Chinese! He is combining symbols, and that's all! He recognizes that symbol A, when he sees it, calls forth symbol B.

Is there more to "understanding Chinese writing" than being able to combine pictographs in the right way, in ways Chinese speakers will recognize and assent to? At first blush, it would seem so. The deeper philosophical question is *what it means to say we understand a word, or sign, or language.* Surely *understanding* is more than an ability to receive stimuli and deliver a conditioned response. Machines operate that way; persons do not. Searle compares his actions in the "Chinese room" to those of a computer program, which combines signs given input but doesn't "understand" them, and then to other, simpler, mechanical devices such as a door that opens automatically based on a photovoltaic cell that registers motion. The claim that the automatic door opener at the airport functions as it does because it "sees" and "understands" that a person with luggage is approaching seems very odd, if not absurd.

Again, it is important that Searle is not criticizing the idea that mental phenomena including conscious self-awareness are in some sense *material* in nature, or have a material basis, only that they are *programmable*, reducible to a formal system. "I see no reason," he says later in a key passage in his essay,

> why we couldn't give a machine the capacity to understand English or Chinese, since in an important sense our bodies with our brains are precisely such machines. But I do see very strong arguments for saying that we could not give such a thing to a machine where the operation of the machine is defined solely in terms of computational processes over formally defined elements.... It is not because I am the instantiation of a computer program that I am able to understand English and have other forms of intentionality ... but ... because I am a certain sort of organism with a certain biological (i e., chemical and physical) structure, and this structure, under certain conditions, is causally capable of producing perception, action, understanding, learning and other intentional phenomena.[3]

In *Minds, Brains and Science* Searle outlines his position. (1) *Brains cause minds.* What he means to say is that brains set the conditions for all that we call "the mental." Brain processes alone are sufficient for mental processes. That is a materialist stance. (2) *Syntax is not sufficient for semantics.* Syntax is the relation signs hold to each other. Semantics is the relation between signs and something in the world; hence the need for interpretation, and hence understanding. Here is where things get interesting, and puzzling. How does a material entity, the brain, do this? (3) *Computer programs are entirely defined by their formal, or syntactical, structure.* This seems self-evident. (4) *Minds have semantic content.* This, too, seems self-evident.

From these Searle concludes: *No computer program is sufficient by itself to give a system a mind.* This follows from (2), (3), and (4). He then concludes: *The way that brains function to cause minds cannot be solely in virtue of running a computer program.* This follows from all of the above, and (1).

But Searle has not supported (1). He has presupposed (1). (1) is just a specification of the Grandiose Assumption. He concludes, finally, that *Anything else that caused minds would have to have causal powers at least*

---

3. Searle, "Minds, Brains, and Programs," 422.

equivalent to those of the brain. Perhaps. Can conscious, *self-valuing self-awareness* be shown to result from brain processes?

Searle may have shown decisively that the conscious, interpreting mind is not akin to a computer program. But for him this does not go against materialism. For him, mind is something the brain generates, in a way analogous to digestion being what the stomach does. But we are left in the dark about how a material entity, the brain, does this. How does it create sufficient conditions for the *interpretation* that sets apart the semantic (and pragmatic) from the syntactic? Interpretation calls forth conscious *awareness* of what is interpreted. We will return to this point below.

Let's turn to the "hard problem" of consciousness. This phrase originated in a lecture given by Australian philosopher David J. Chalmers in the early 1990s (he appears to have ignored Rorty's claim to have "dissolved" the problem). He distinguished "easy problems" such as reports of sensations from the "hard problem" of *why we, and apparently all other higher forms of life, have conscious awareness at all.* Why, in a material world, do we have specific experiences qualitatively different from the putative scientific descriptions of what must be going on simultaneously, physiologically, in our senses, nervous systems, and brains? What does self-aware consciousness *add* to the "furniture of the world"? Why couldn't the biological problems of survival be solved by nonconscious zombies (as lower forms of life such as bacteria have solved their survival problem presumably without consciousness)?

In his excellent "Facing Up to the Problem of Consciousness" (1995) Chalmers wrote,

"The really hard problem of consciousness is the problem of experience. When we think and perceive there is a whir of information processing, but there is also a subjective aspect."[4] This subjective aspect is our own private experience, the sense all persons have of being at the center of "their" world: their actions, based on their concerns, and viewing the passing show like a continuous three-dimensional movie within which we act as "our" movie's central and supremely important character—its protagonist—and source of the self-valuing element. This is also the source of that Cartesian sense of our "private inner-stage" on which our beliefs, thoughts, etc., interact and relate to the "external world" in which we act and live.

The question is not just *how*, but *why*, putatively physical processes give rise to this state of affairs? That's the "hard problem" of consciousness.

The query is not new—an indication of philosophers' failure to "face up to" it. Thomas Nagel raised essentially this same issue long ago in his famous

---

4. Chalmers, "Facing Up To the Problem," 200–219. Cf. Chalmers, *Conscious Mind*.

(or infamous) article "What Is It Like to Be a Bat?" This article begins, "Consciousness is what makes the mind-body problem really intractable. Perhaps this is why current discussions of the problem give it little attention or get it obviously wrong."[5] Just from observing bats in their natural environment and reasoning by analogy, we have every reason to believe that there is *something* it is like to be a bat—a subjective, experienced quality space unique to bat sensory physiology, but so radically unlike human experienced quality space that we cannot really imagine it "from the inside." The question is not, after all, What would it be like for a *human* to *imagine himself* being a bat? but rather, *What is it like for the bat*? What is the bat experiencing "from the inside"? With bats relying on "bat sonar" to navigate around walls and past stalactites in dark caves, the incommensurability of human quality space and bat quality space is palpable.

Just so we are clear: the question is not just *how* brain and central nervous system physiology "cause" or "create sufficient conditions for" this subjective quality space that differs from living species to living species, but: *why does it exist at all?*

To some philosophers, it *doesn't!* Daniel Dennett, a hardline defender of the Grandiose Assumption, has responded by denying there really is a "hard problem" of consciousness. He insists that this subjective aspect of conscious experience, or quality space, about which we can be self-aware if we, uh, put our minds to it, is fundamentally an *illusion*.[6] This, as Chalmers wryly observed in response, is counterintuitive, to say the least. Even illusions, he points out, are *subjective experiences*. Our consciousness is immediately "present" to us. It seems an intractable, ineliminable *given*. Denying its existence isn't even coherent, as the affirming or denying of anything logically presupposes the denier's *conscious awareness of what is affirmed or denied*. The problem for authors like Dennett: conscious awareness has proven impossible to integrate smoothly into the "scientific" (i.e., materialist) view of human beings and of reality more broadly. Take it on its own terms, and it is one of the great *mysteries* of existence. Given the Grandiose Assumption that has underwritten all research deemed *scientific*, it is an *anomaly!*

In an interesting, colorful, and useful TED talk, Chalmers describes himself as having *wanted* to be a good "scientific materialist" looking at how the brain and senses somehow generate this "wide screen movie" we

---

5. Nagel, "What Is It Like To Be a Bat?" 435-50.

6. Dennett, "Facing Backwards on the Problem of Consciousness," , 4-6; Chalmers, "Moving Forward on the Problem of Consciousness," 3-46. See Dennett, *Intuition Pumps and Other Tools For Thinking*, 310f.

all find ourselves in, every waking moment.[7] In other words, he started out sympathetic to the Grandiose Assumption. He goes on to describe the main conclusion of his research, which is that we may need "radical thinking" if we are to integrate consciousness into any scientific understanding of the world and of ourselves. Dennett's view, that consciousness is an illusion, he includes as one of the radical thoughts to be entertained, before dismissing it as untenable. Other kinds of radical thinking include adding consciousness to our list of the fundamental constituents of reality, like space and time. Instead of trying to "explain it" by reducing it to something it manifestly *isn't*, or trying to eliminate it, we should take it on its own terms and try to work out the laws that govern it, as we have with other scientific basics. The second radical suggestion he makes follows from that: we should at least entertain *panpsychism*, the idea that consciousness is a natural property of systems, i.e., all systems have some degree of consciousness of their proximate surroundings, in proportion to their configuration and degree of complexity. This would accommodate animal consciousness (e.g., that of Nagel's bat), and suggest even that microorganisms have a very small degree of consciousness manifested in their capacity to respond to their environment.[8]

Panpsychism generates its own counterintuitive results, however, as it compels us to see systems of all kinds as "aware" of their surroundings even as they respond mechanically in the ways they are designed or programmed. That is, it compels us to say that *the automatic door really is aware* in some sense of the approaching person in its mechanical way, even as it mechanically opens to allow him or her to pass through? "Awareness" in such cases seems superfluous. It adds nothing to our account of what we see happening, which is of a mechanism responding as it was programmed.

So again, what does *our* consciousness add?

According to the materialist, we're all "programmed"; the difference really is just configuration and complexity, not kind. But once we are toying with the idea that consciousness is a property of all systems, we have abandoned materialism, confessing to have found it inadequate. Chalmers is clearly groping for *something* that will accommodate consciousness while remaining inside the boundaries of "scientific respectability," i.e., the Grandiose Assumption in a broad sense. That *something* has remained frustratingly elusive, however. Hence Chalmers's reach for "radical suggestions."

Thomas Nagel recently made a radical suggestion.

7. Chalmers, "How Do You Explain Consciousness?" March, 2014 < https://www.ted.com/talks/david_chalmers_how_do_you_explain_consciousness >.

8. For a recent articulate defense of a brand of panpsychism see Goff, *Consciousness and Fundamental Reality*; Goff, *Galileo's Error*.

In his boldly subtitled short tract *Mind and Cosmos: Why the Materialist Neo-Darwinian Conception of Nature Is Almost Certainly False*, Nagel takes the plunge and argues that the apparent inexplicability of both consciousness and life itself on their own terms should be seen as reasons to abandon materialism.[9] Regarding such scientific heresies as intelligent design theory, Nagel writes:

> In thinking about these questions I have been stimulated by criticisms of the prevailing scientific world picture from a very different direction: the attack on Darwinism mounted in recent years from a religious perspective by the defenders of intelligent design. Even though writers like Michael Behe and Stephen Meyer are motivated at least in part by their religious beliefs, the empirical arguments they offer against the likelihood that the origin of life and its evolutionary history can be fully explained by physics and chemistry are of great interest in themselves. Another skeptic, David Berlinski, has brought out these problems vividly without reference to the design inference. Even if one is not drawn to the alternative of an explanation by the actions of a designer, the problems that these iconoclasts pose for the orthodox scientific consensus should be taken seriously. They do not deserve the scorn with which they are commonly met. It is manifestly unfair.[10]

Scorn tends to be the weapon of choice wielded across worldview divides. Those committed to the Grandiose Assumption do not see those not so committed as intellectually legitimate. Nagel argues convincingly that while the writings of intelligent design theorists do not necessarily point to the Christian God, neither do their critics respond effectively to the problems they raise, such as the extremely high statistical improbability of *abiogenesis*, sometimes called the "chemical evolution" of life from nonlife, through natural processes alone,[11] or the issues raised by what Michael Behe, a biochemist, calls irreducible complexity.[12] Scorn is hardly an appropriate response to mathematics! The substance of the responses we see come down to the following: once, eons ago, we had a oceanic prebiotic soup. Then we

---

9. Nagel, *Mind and Cosmos*.

10. Nagel, *Mind and Cosmos*, 10. See Behe, *Darwin's Black Box*; Meyer, *Darwin's Doubt*; Berlinski, *Devil's Delusion*.

11. Bradley and Thaxton, "Information and the Origin of Life," 190. For a comprehensive discussion of the problem, which is not new but has proven persistent, see Thaxton, Bradley and Olsen, *The Mystery of Life's Origin*. See finally Shapiro, *Origins*.

12. Behe, *Darwin's Black Box*.

had oceans of time. Together these change the odds of a self-replicating entity from highly improbable to virtually inevitable.

This is circular reasoning. We do not know, from observation and experiment, that there even *was* a "pre-biotic soup." There is no independent physical evidence for such. The materialist worldview just *requires* that it existed. The matter is surely therefore open, regarding both the capacity of materialist theories to explain either the immediate presence of consciousness, especially the conscious self-awareness that appears unique to humanity, or the origin of life from nonlife. One is tempted to return the scorn by asking materialists, with a nod to late-1980s sensibilities, *Where's the beef?*

Summarizing at this point: were the entire panorama of contemporary science seen as a single discipline guided by the metaphysical equivalent of its Kuhnian paradigm, that being materialist naturalism, the Grandiose Assumption, *intellectually* that paradigm would have to be seen as in crisis or as rapidly approaching one. *Institutionally* the matter may be different, of course, just in case materialism is being administratively protected (and shielded by the scorn noted above). But look what we have. Materialists' efforts to make room for moral agency *on its own terms* failed miserably. When dealing with practical problems of power and propaganda, or even life and death, Third Stage secular moralism leaves us at sea. Materialists' efforts to "face up to the problem of consciousness" are equally awkward and unconvincing.

Since Rorty (and many other philosophers) believed they were able to get rid of the "mind-body problem" by sorting out linguistic confusions, let's take a closer look at what is going on with language, and why the phenomenon of understanding a language should be seen as a further reason for rejecting materialism.

First, a brief autobiographical digression. I write as a native English-speaking philosopher living in a foreign country where the official language is *not* English, and so I have actually performed variations on the following not once but *many* times. Consider this situation: a friend and I, native English speakers, are listening to two other people standing nearby converse in (let us say) Russian. The two Russian speakers are discussing something they are reading; this seems likely from one of them pointing to something in his smartphone. What they are seeing in his phone is in Russian, of course, and they are using Russian to talk about it. My friend and I don't speak or understand a word of Russian, and since we cannot read the Cyrillic alphabet, even supposing we could see into the phone we'd have little idea how even to pronounce what we saw, much less how the words are put together into coherent sentences and paragraphs.

Yet it is manifestly clear from direct observation: the Russian speakers understand each other perfectly, and they understand perfectly what they are reading.

What, specifically, is it that they are able to do that we, English speakers and readers who do not understand or read Russian, are thereby not able to do?

Note also: were my friend and I to begin speaking in the Russian speakers' presence in English, and assuming the latter don't speak or understand a word of English, our situations would be exactly reversed. We would be speaking words and phrases and communicating ideas familiar to *us*.

Each pair of speakers understands each other perfectly, that is. But when listening to the other pair, each hears only structured sound made by human vocal cords. We each hear, that is, streams of consonants and vowels, unintelligible. Nor, most likely, would the Russians be able to read anything on my smartphone, any more than I could read anything in theirs.

What is it *each of us is doing* that the other pair is *unable to do*?

Communicate in our own language, of course. Individuating its words as meaningful units, combined into sentences, combined further into paragraphs, all from mere physical sound made with our vocal cords and mouths. And the equivalent in writing. What each of us is unable to do is understand the linguistic product of the other pair, spoken or written.

Even though the physical or material output is the same for each of us!

Both we and the Russian speakers recognize that what we are hearing is language. We came to the situation knowing what human languages sound and look like, even if we can't read or understand a word of a specific foreign language. What each of us hears is *sound*; what we see on the others' smartphones are *inscriptions*.

This is the materialist's predicament: for him (her), all that exists are those streams of sound coming from vocal cords and mouths, or inscriptions on some medium such as paper or a phone. *Physically and physiologically, that's all language is!* The sound may well be accompanied by electrochemical brain events, as would be both the act of speaking and the act of hearing, or of reading. But when we understand sentences in a language, *we do not perceive and understand electrochemical brain events*. When one fails to understand a foreign language, either reading it or speaking it, *that language's physics and the speakers' physiology is all that is apprehended, and this would include any added knowledge, if it miraculously became available, of whatever is going on in their brains and nervous systems when they speak or read.*

There is manifestly more to language than the physics of sound, the physiology of one's vocal cords, and whatever brain events are also occurring when one reads, hears, speaks. The sentences of a language are irreducibly human instruments, the instruments of beings with conscious awareness living and interacting in friendships, partnerships, relationships, families, worksites, churches, communities generally. There is understanding between them in natural conversational exchange, accomplished through continuous conscious awareness given the speakers' backgrounds of learning: their "movies" playing out as they have their whole lives which include vague recollections of acquiring words of their native language as children.

Understanding is far from perfect. Sometimes there are *mis*understandings. Sometimes language (like technology) goes awry, because motives are not transparent and some will purposefully try to deceive. We noted this at the outset, as one of the things philosophers can diagnose. *None* of these events of language or many others which occur all the time are captured in any description of its physics or speakers' vocal physiology or even necessarily their facial expressions or other observable behaviors, much less in brain events alone.

All of which may be one reason Orwell probably has more to teach us about the misuse and abuse of language than even Wittgenstein!

Suffice it to say, materialism looks to be a dead end when it comes to, er, *understanding* what is going on when two or more persons use language to communicate—given that what is communicated is not vocalized sound or written inscriptions or brain events but ideas, comments on the weather or what went on that day, memories of what occurred yesterday or last week, wishes for tomorrow, requests for information or for action, plans and hopes for the future, fears of what could go wrong, etc., all those things making up the warp and woof of our lives. A natural language with millions of native speakers is simply (and embarrassingly) not a "material process" in any sense that *makes* sense. Sir Karl Popper's "World 3" may come closer to capturing the complex ontology necessary for natural language.[13]

Colin McGinn has thus argued the pessimistic stance (for materialists, that is) that the problem of consciousness is not solvable on its own terms.[14] His position has been called the New Mysterianism (the old Mysterians, it turns out, were a 1960s rock band). This kind of thinking accords with the gradual move within academic philosophy from Third Stage optimism to Fourth Stage despair, giving it an epistemological twist.

Within the boundaries of materialism, that is, *consciousness* is a *mystery* we may never solve. McGinn, like Chalmers, wants to stay within the bounds of the Third Stage scientific respectability provided by the

---

13. See Popper, *Objective Knowledge*.

14. McGinn, "Can We Solve the Mind-Body Problem?" 349–66; McGinn, *Problem of Consciousness*; see also McGinn, *Mysterious Flame*; McGinn, "All Machine and No Ghost?"

Grandiose Assumption. He goes on to make the startling confession that nothing we've learned about the brain over the past century suggests that it is an instrument able to generate Chalmers's "3D movie" of conscious awareness. As Chalmers observed, biological "programming" could lead to complex forms of life solving the problems of their survival without it, just as mechanisms accomplish goals in accordance with their programming absent consciousness (I assume here for the sake of argument here that universal panpsychism is wrong).

McGinn develops his argument in *The Mysterious Flame* where he correctly observes that existing explanations of consciousness all fail. He concludes that consciousness is destined to remain "a mystery that human intelligence will never unravel." In the more recent informal piece entitled "All Machine and No Ghost" (2012) McGinn tries to cut his own position down to size, along with the pretenses of philosophers of mind generally:

> The "mysterianism" I advocate is really nothing more than the acknowledgement that human intelligence is a local, contingent, temporal, practical and expendable feature of life on earth—an incremental adaptation based on earlier forms of intelligence that no one would regard as faintly omniscient. The current state of the philosophy of mind, from my point of view, is just a reflection of one evolutionary time-slice of a particular bipedal species on a particular humid planet at this fleeting moment in cosmic history—as is everything else about the human animal. There is more ignorance in it than there is knowledge.[15]

How Fourth Stage in its pessimism! This is an interesting remark for what it presupposes, however. We assume Darwinism as if it were able to serve as an epistemological foundation. But given these very results—given these limitations on our knowledge—what legitimates Darwinian evolution as a foundation for knowledge over, say, the pronouncement of the preacher that "God made us this way"? What, besides the Third Stage Grandiose Assumption, the administrative protections behind it (which ensure, especially these days, that no one who openly says "God made us this way" will ever obtain tenure in any philosophy department in the Anglo-European world outside a tiny handful of Christian colleges), and finally the scorn Nagel mentioned is reserved for other worldviews? (Similar remarks can be made for those who speak of "pseudoscience" and "fundies.")

Philosophers who are intellectually honest should no longer permit themselves to play or fall for such gambits as if they led stealthily back to the equivalent of a Cartesian bedrock of epistemic certainty, in the face of

---

15. McGinn, "All Machine and No Ghost?"

the enormous difficulties we've seen so far. "Evolutionary epistemology" is hardly viable if the materialism underwriting it is not viable. It involves blatantly circular reasoning. In logic it is a mainstay that no chain of reasoning is stronger than its weakest link, especially if that link stands at its foundation.

Materialist Naturalism and the Origin of Life

We come to what will doubtless be one of the most controversial sections in this book. We did an overview above. So we reiterate: *materialism created this problem for itself*. If it cannot solve the problem on the problem's own terms after an extended period of time and an abundance of resources thrown its way, then this militates even more strongly against the materialist worldview.

As everybody presumably knows, early modern science rejected as untenable the idea of the spontaneous generation of life from nonlife (*heterogenesis*, the idea that living things can come from accumulations of dead organic matter, e.g., maggots from decaying meat). Louis Pasteur's pioneering work decisively refuted the notion. But then, very gradually, subsequent generations came to a disturbing realization: there are only *two options* regarding the origin of life on Earth. Either there was an Intelligent Designer, with the most prevalent (but not the only) theory of intelligent design being the Christian view that all living things, including humanity, were created supernaturally by a Supreme Being as *kinds*, even if scholars differ on how to read Genesis. The materialist alternative is *abiogenesis*, which proposes in a far more sophisticated fashion the idea that self-replicating entities came from nonliving matter through a complex but entirely natural chemical process. Such ideas (minus the chemistry, of course) had been around since the ancient Greeks. Heraclitus, the pre-Socratic philosopher of *limitless change*, posited one such notion. When Christianity became the dominant worldview in rising Western civilization, all such ideas were shelved. But as materialism became the prevailing worldview of science, scientists found themselves compelled to revisit them and figure out how to make them work.

They found themselves embracing abiogenesis, sometimes called the theory of the chemical evolution of life from nonlife. They set about trying to develop speculative but hopefully plausible scenarios on how life could originate from lifeless chemicals over eons of time in a "primordial" or "prebiotic soup" bombarded by electrical discharges and ultraviolet radiation from the young sun. They postulated the existence of a highly reactive environment vastly different from today's world. In accordance with broader naturalism, this all came about without design by an intelligent agency.

Let's expand on the idea as it developed. Initially, the sun and all its satellites cooled from an initial state as globes of accumulated gases and cosmic debris: largely hydrogen and helium but with substantial amounts of carbon, nitrogen, oxygen, and a few somewhat heavier elements (silicon, iron, etc.) believed to have originated in now-exploded stars (supernovae). This mixture congealed first into liquid and then the heavier elements combined into rocky surfaces underneath thick atmospheres of methane, ammonia, nitrogen, and water vapor. At some point (we don't need to worry over the specifics), the Earth acquired its large satellite which exercised substantial gravitational tidal forces on the young world. Eventually torrential rains fell, forming the oceans, above which violent electrical storms raged, producing simple organic molecules such as amino acids which rained down into the oceans.

Developing in the oceans was a brew of hydrocarbons and other potential building blocks of life. These, under continuing bombardment by furious electrical discharges from above over a sufficiently long period of time, gave rise to the first complex organic molecules such as proteins and finally led to the first organisms. Millions more years went by. Ocean life grew more complex and diverse. Geophysical activity pushed up land masses, forming the first massive continents (possibly it was the single vast continent dubbed Pangaea). Eventually both plant and animal species made their way onto land and formed the earliest ecosystems.

The rest, as they say, is evolutionary history. But how plausible is that initial step, the genesis of life from nonlife in a "prebiotic soup"?

Life as we know it involves four families of chemicals: lipids (fatty cell walls), carbohydrates (cellulose and sugars), amino acids (protein metabolism), and nucleic acids (RNA and DNA, which encode, at the molecular level, a highly complex array of information determining an individual organism's physical properties down to the finest details). Materialists saw hope in the realization that given the right conditions, the formation of progressively more complex combinations of carbon molecules from simple ones was possible. This is due to carbon's being able to form long and stable molecular chains with other chemical elements: hydrogen, oxygen, and sometimes nitrogen, including rings and combinations thereof. Some of these combinations eventually had atomic weights in the thousands and then in the tens of thousands.

Hence according to the abiogenetic theory, laws of physics and chemistry alone produced complexity from simplicity within the oceanic "soup." At a crucial juncture, a molecule formed that was able—no one claims to know the exact process, or whether it happened just once or millions of times—to interact with its immediate environment in such a way as to make a copy of itself: the very first act of reproduction, and the production of the "common ancestor" of all subsequent life according to Darwinians, some 3.5 billion years or so ago. The term *protocell* was coined for this entity, standing as a hypothetical bridge between large but nonliving molecules and the first self-replicating organisms. The protocell was able to make more copies of itself, eventually undergoing natural deviations from the original pattern that remained chemically and physiologically stable. Protocells mutated, that is. Thus they would not just reproduce but propagate differences and give rise to the earliest biodiversity.

These protocells—again, no one claims to know the specifics—began to accumulate in clusters, perhaps as films on the ocean surface or along rocky shorelines where there was light and other radiation from the sun and exposure to continued bursts of energy from lightning. Further deviations from original patterns led to increased specialization to the extent this enhanced the odds of survival in this hostile environment: natural selection beginning to do its work now that it had something to work with. Some protocell types, embedded for generations within clusters, lost the ability to survive on their own, even as their specialized work helped the cluster survive.

Thus the coming to be of single-celled organisms from clusters, and eventually a new form of reproduction: division. Over tens of millions of years of time, some single-celled organisms would naturally clump into larger colonies, in which higher-order specialization would begin to emerge: some of the colonies directing themselves toward gathering energy from above, some catching loose organisms or loose organic matter, some towards breaking those organisms or chemicals down (digesting them), some serving other purposes. Eventually many single-celled entities would lose the ability to survive outside larger systems: further biological specialization and the beginning of distinct internal systems such as ingestion and digestion, elimination of waste, division into *male* and *female* and an eventual capacity for *sexual* reproduction, and a central coordinating hub or nucleus: the stepping-stone towards a primitive brain.

The impetus behind the abiogenetic narrative should be clear. It was the same as the impetus behind Darwinian theory as a whole. Every so often, an authoritative text lets the cat out of the bag, so to speak. In this case, it was paleontologist J. Marvin Waller, in his *The Course of Evolution* (1969) which opened with a lucid summation of mainstream opinion as it then existed and how it had developed, serving as the foundation for all that followed. Waller revealed:

The idea of some kind of evolution, or progressive change, in organisms is very old. Some of the ancient Greeks visualized nebulous transitions from the inorganic to the organic and from plants to animals in a series attaining more and more perfection and leading up to man. Later in the Western world, complete faith in the scriptural story of creation effectively inhibited thinking about evolution. New and unorthodox views did not begin to form importantly until about the middle of the eighteenth century. . . .

The first completely integrated theory of biologic evolution was presented half a century later by the French zoologist Lamarck. This theory postulated that new characters were acquired by individual animals as the result of their needs or wants and that these characters, modified by use or disuse, were passed on by inheritance to their descendants. Lamarck visualized all animals as having diversified from a simple common beginning into very numerous increasingly more complex and highly organized lineages. His theory did not win much acceptance among contemporary naturalists, and it was ridiculed by some of the most prominent men of science at that time. . . .

The announcement of Darwin's theory of evolution in the mid-nineteenth century marked the beginning of a new era in biologic science. Actually this theory embodied no fundamentally new idea, but it did combine older concepts in a fresh and convincing way and carried them to their logical conclusion. Darwin was particularly fortunate in his timing *because the intellectual atmosphere in England was favorable for the consideration of a new materialistic theory of evolution, and he promptly gained the active support of several able and aggressive young biologists.*[16]

Among the "aggressive young biologists" was Thomas Henry Huxley, grandfather of Aldous and Julian Huxley, who became known as "Darwin's bulldog." Darwinism's other early promoters included botanist Joseph Dalton Hooker, and another botanist, Asa Gray, who wrote a rave review of *The Origin of Species*. Huxley founded a periodical in 1861 entitled *Natural History Review* to further the new paradigm, develop its main ideas, and look for supporting evidence while drawing younger biologists into the fold. Where Darwin differed from Lamarck was his view that genetic variation alone, not characteristics acquired after the organism's birth, was the source of variety and driver of speciation. Some of these genetic variants would be better adapted to their environment, increasing

---

16. Weller, *Course of Evolution*, 1–2. Emphasis mine.

the likelihood that those possessing them would survive, breed, and pass the variants on to their descendants.

Darwin had a competitor, Alfred Russell Wallace who also had a theory of the evolution of life. Where the two differed was that in the end, Wallace exempted humanity from his account, holding out for the action of a divine agency in our arrival on the scene. Darwinists rejected this on principle. It seemed to violate Occam's Razor by multiplying hypotheses beyond necessity. In other words, Darwin had no need of that hypothesis. He introduced the view that humanity differs from other species in complexity, not in kind, and introduced a mechanism intended to explain how this was biologically possible. The mechanism was natural selection. Nothing else was needed, except a changing environment to which species would adapt or die out.

Darwin drew on two previous thinkers. One was geologist Charles Lyell, for his *principle of uniformitarianism*, which held that "the present is the key to the past." In explaining geologic formations, that is, we should appeal only to processes we can observe occurring today instead of postulating "a great flood" or series of "global catastrophes" as his predecessors such as Georges Cuvier had done. The other was Thomas Malthus, the population biologist who held that populations increased in size geometrically while their ability to command resources only increased arithmetically. This meant that survival within a population as well as between populations would invariably be a struggle which the less adapted would lose. From such notions the philosopher Herbert Spencer would coin the phrase *survival of the fittest*.

In *The Descent of Man* (1871) Darwin articulated the "dangerous idea" (Dennett's phrase[17]) that humanity is the product of the same long-term natural forces that produced every other species of animal and plant on the planet—a topic he'd all but shunned in *Origin*. In this, he seemed to be doing good Newtonian science: applying the idea of explaining as much of one's subject matter as possible on the basis of the fewest basic postulates and tying his explanation to observations he'd made, e.g., of finches and other flora and fauna while traveling with the *Beagle* crew. Newton's method had used universal gravitation to provide a unified explanation of both terrestrial and celestial realms as Aristotelians had understood them. Darwin saw natural selection as the only postulate needed to explain the development and diversification of species from their most primitive their most complex. An idea that, as Dennett observes, "has inspired intense reactions ranging from ferocious condemnation to ecstatic allegiance, sometimes tantamount

---

17. Dennett, *Darwin's Dangerous Idea*.

to religious zeal."[18] Major statements that articulate the foundational narrative underwriting a worldview rising to dominance are bound to have this character: both structurally and in terms of purpose (motivating support) they are almost indistinguishable from religious doctrines and political-economic ideologies.

The problem of origins, though not a part of the Darwinian theory *per se*, remained, however. For half a century, scientists were stymied. It was a glaring gap in materialist biology, even if we assumed that Darwinist research could close all the other gaps. Eventually this larger gap would have to be closed with a plausible, *evidence-based* account of how life had emerged from nonlife, something akin to the above narrative, consistent with the Darwinian picture of the natural order.

The first scientist to take up the challenge was Russian biochemist Aleksandr I. Oparin. In 1924 Oparin became the first to work out the idea that functional biological systems evolved from simpler molecules. Organic molecules he called "coacervates" or colloid aggregates could have formed, and these were able to continue to absorb organic chemicals in a manner akin to primitive metabolism. In accordance with the materialist worldview, Oparin denied that there was any *fundamental* difference in kind between living and nonliving matter beyond the former's ability to make imperfect but functional copies of itself. He drew a parallel between what astronomers were learning about the atmospheres of gas giant planets like Jupiter and Saturn and developed the idea that the early Earth's atmosphere was also strongly reducing, with the kind of composition noted above, giving rise to conditions that could have generated the very first self-replicating entities.

Later that same decade and independently of Oparin whose work had not yet been translated into English, British biologist J. B. S. Haldane outlined essentially the same set of ideas. Haldane suggested that ultraviolet solar radiation had led to the production of sugars and amino acids, using for the first time this phrase *prebiotic soup*. This vast chemical laboratory under an oxygen-free atmosphere soon contained a host of monomers and polymers. These acquired lipid membranes in aggregates on their way to forming the first truly living organisms.

Neither Oparin nor Haldane had any effective means of testing their ideas, which therefore remained tantalizing but speculative. And thus matters stood for two more decades: speculations consistent with Darwinism and the requirements of materialism as a worldview but outside the parameters of empirical, evidence-based laboratory science.

---

18. Dennett, *Darwin's Dangerous Idea*, Ch. 1.

The empirical untestability of abiogenesis was the proverbial elephant in the front room.

In 1947, J. D. Bernal proposed some mechanisms by which biomonomers might concentrate sufficiently in the "prebiotic soup" to produce the more complex biomolecular building blocks that would lead to life. Harold Urey speculated that the hydrogen-rich environment from which the planets had formed would have created a reducing environment. Urey suggested that as Earth's atmosphere cooled and changed, it became oxidizing, providing more favorable conditions for the formation of stable organic compounds. At the time, though, there was no explanation for where free oxygen could come from. Obviously there was no photosynthesis, for there were no plants.

In the 1950s it became possible to begin devising experimental arrangements to test these ideas. The first was performed in 1953 by Stanley Miller, then a graduate student studying under Urey. Miller and Urey, working in a basement laboratory in the chemistry department at the University of Chicago, believed they had replicated the prebiotic soup and an atmosphere characterized by continuous electrical discharges. Their tabletop experiment obtained a number of amino acids. Subsequent experiments conducted elsewhere replicated the Miller-Urey results. The idea of abiogenesis had received a major boost in the scientific community. That same year, Francis Crick and James Watson published their landmark study laying out the structure of DNA, providing the first full account of the molecular basis for life—but also a sense of life's enormous complexity.

Later efforts tried to build on these and close the huge gap between relatively simple organic molecules and that first self-replicating entity, and tried to exhibit the origin of life as the product of a step-by-step process rather than some kind of quantum leap. An extended conversation began that continues to this day. One of its questions was which came first: proteins, RNA or DNA. The conversants found themselves in a chicken-or-egg situation. Proteins catalyze chemical reactions while RNA and DNA store information. None of these alone is sufficient to yield a living organism, however. DNA and proteins must already be present.

What experimental results we have are sometimes cited as "proof of concept." This is too easy. It is just as easy to get so caught up in the specifics of the chemistry that we lose sight of the far more interesting question: *what drew us into chemistry to begin with?* The answer is that scientists committed to the Grandiose Assumption had no alternative. This time a group of scientific authors let the cat out of the bag, in this abstract:

> The origin of life is a historical event that has left no relevant fossils; therefore, it is unrealistic to reconstruct the chronology of its occurrence. Instead, by performing laboratory experiments under conditions that resemble the prebiotic world, one might validate feasible reaction pathways and reconstruct model systems of artificial life. Creating such life in a test tube should go a long way toward removing the shroud of mystery over how it began naturally.[19]

In other words, again: *there is no empirical evidence*. And what no one appeared to realize was how questionable it was to infer from artificial circumstances, based on pure speculation, what is supposed to have occurred spontaneously in the natural world all those epochs ago. Miller and Urey had hardly produced substances capable of combining further into protocells, much less organisms. Moreover, for their experimental conditions to duplicate what might have prevailed on a primitive Earth, they would have needed an experiment arrangement able to last for millions of years, an obvious impossibility.

The plain fact remained and remains still: *there is no hard geological or geophysical evidence that this reactive broth, or prebiotic soup, or whatever one wants to call it, ever existed*. It is what philosophers of science call an *auxiliary hypothesis*. It is a construction of those committed to the Grandiose Assumption. The idea has remained on the table, elaborated to greater lengths than space limits will allow here, because as good materialists, scientists forbade themselves from considering the most prevalent alternative: intelligent design, which would include the laws of physics and chemistry as parts of the design as well as many of the seemingly unique properties of Earth. Relying only on the Grandiose Assumption and the consensus of Settled Science for support, scientists eliminated intelligent design *a priori* and ostracized anyone who broached the topic. Thus the scorn Nagel noted: especially if they explicitly identify the designer as the Christian God for Whom there is also no proof or evidence. But the absence of any hard physical evidence for a prebiotic soup as a medium in which life could have emerged from nonlife continues to loom as a solid riposte to naturalistic materialists however much they have continued to work in that paradigm.

Biochemists have criticized the above scenario on a variety of grounds. They have debated what kind of atmosphere the early Earth had; only an oxidizing atmosphere would have been suitable for the formation of complex organic molecules leading to living systems, but in that case, again, where did the free oxygen come from? Others have observed that

19. Weissbuch et al., "β-Sheets as Templates of Relevance," 1128–40.

the radiation coming from the early sun and from space would have been more destructive of organic molecules than likely to enhance their creation. Still others have contended that the prebiotic soup would have been too dilute for complex molecules to form in sufficient quantity. Finally, this soup, assuming it existed, should have given rise to thousands upon thousands of biochemical dead ends, in addition to whatever sequences are presumed to have led to the first entities able to replicate themselves. How much time are we to allow for the latter? Are we to postulate a limit, or assume that it must have happened within the limit imposed by what Settled Science says about the age of Earth?

If one surveys hypotheses that have appeared more recently, one might sense desperation. We need not even consider authors who question the Grandiose Assumption. A few scientists have surveyed what materialistic theories of the origin of life require, mathematically or statistically, absent some kind of design either inherent in them or directed from outside. Their argument is based not on a theistic worldview but the nature of genetically encoded information. Leaving aside technicalities that would require additional lengthy pages of discussion, the conclusion: the odds of the universe itself, or the Earth as it exists, or the panorama of living things we see, having resulted from nothing beyond the blind operations of the laws of physics and chemistry, given the time frame we have, are trillions to one: *against*.

This conclusion has been endorsed, however reluctantly, by nontheists as well as by theists. Astronomer Fred Hoyle, who was not a theist, wryly observed, "A common sense interpretation of the facts suggests that a super intellect has monkeyed with physics, as well as with chemistry and biology, and that there are no blind forces in nature worth speaking about."[20] William Dembski and Jonathan Witt elaborate:

> Scientists have learned that within the known physical universe there are about 10^{80} elementary particles. . . . Scientists also have learned that a change from one state of matter to another can't happen faster than what physicists call the Planck time. . . . The Planck time is 1 second divided by 10^{45} (1 followed by forty five zeroes). . . . Finally, scientists estimate that the universe is about fourteen billion years old, meaning the universe is itself millions of times younger than 10^{25} seconds. If we now assume that any physical event in the universe requires the transition of at least one elementary particle (most events require far more, of course), then these limits on the universe suggest that the total number of events throughout cosmic history could not have exceeded $10^{80} \times 10^{45} \times 10^{25} = 10^{150}$.

20. Hoyle, "Universe," 36.

This means that any specified event whose probability is less than 1 chance in 10^{150} will remain improbable even if we let every corner and every moment of the universe roll the proverbial dice. The universe isn't big enough, fast enough or old enough to roll the dice enough times to have a realistic chance of randomly generating specified events that are this improbable.[21]

In other words, *even if our present-day model of the age of the physical universe is correct, it does not supply sufficient time for biogenesis to take place.* This comes in addition to arguments from irreducible complexity. What, exactly, are these arguments? They start with a realization no one should find objectionable: most mutations are unhelpful if not actually destructive of an organism's viability. A select few will confer an advantage. The question then is whether these few will be sufficient to drive speciation, as opposed to a minor modification within a single species. The argument from irreducible complexity is then the claim that a great number of beneficial mutations must occur all at once, otherwise we end up either with a minor modification or an unviable entity. Materialist critics of intelligent design theorists claim the latter don't really do any scientific research. This is simply wrong. The latter have shown that there are many biological structures that would require multiple beneficial mutations to happen at once.[22] Molecular biologist Douglas Axe argued compellingly that six simultaneous beneficial mutations occurring at the same time would be so improbable as to be unlikely to happen in the entire history of our planet even if it is four and one half billion years old.[23] Axe had been studying bacteria, which are (relatively speaking!) simple organisms. Imagine the requirements on the natural production of beings such as ourselves!

Long ago, a few philosophers thought there might be a "principle of organization" inherent in material substance itself, a sort of "biochemical predestination" through which complex molecules formed and gave rise to the earliest forms of life. Alfred North Whitehead speculated on such a principle in his slim volume *The Function of Reason* (1929). Whitehead's speculation followed from the philosophy of organism he was developing, a Second Stage perspective in our sense. Again, there is no visible evidence for the operations of any such principle in any scientific-empirical account of "blind matter," i.e., material substance obeying just the laws of physics and chemistry, which Aristotle would have called efficient causation, the

---

21. Dembski and Witt, *Intelligent Design Uncensored*, 68–69.
22. Behe and Snoke, "Simulating Evolution by Gene Duplication," 2651–64.
23. Axe, "Limits of Complex Adaptation," 1–10.

only one of his "four causes" to survive the transition from Second Stage philosophy to Third Stage science.

Over time, speculations about the origin of life on Earth have grown more extravagant. *Panspermia*, an old idea suggested numerous times by early scientists, was developed after Darwin by chemist Svante Arrhenius and revisited more recently by Hoyle and fellow astronomer Chandra Wickramasinghe. This is the idea that life did not originate on Earth at all, but arrived from elsewhere, as spores on meteors or comets, perhaps, or some equivalent. Alternatively, the dust and gasses to be found in stellar or interstellar space contain organic matter which found its way to Earth where there existed an environment conducive for survival and propagation in the early oceans.[24]

This theory not only offers no explanation of how and where the spores or organic matter originated, *it renders scientific testability impossible*. How are scientists supposed to test the idea that organic matter originated in space, or on some other planet perhaps light years distant and for all we know, destroyed long ago? Surely this is no more *empirical* than proposals about creative actions by an intelligent designer! All that has been adduced in support of the idea is the presence of organic molecules found in a few meteorites, with nothing found that even remotely approximates the complexity of RNA, DNA, or self-replicating living systems.

This has not stopped purveyors of the Grandiose Assumption.

The most radical form of panspermia is *directed* panspermia, seriously proposed first by Carl Sagan and I. S. Shklovskii in the 1960s and again by Francis Crick and Leslie Orgel in the 1970s.[25] Science fiction writers (e.g., Olaf Stapleton) introduced the idea as far back as the 1930s. Directed panspermia invokes a science fiction scenario by conjuring, out of nowhere, a spacecraft piloted by advanced extraterrestrials who visited Earth during its early geologic history. The ETs either purposefully seeded the planet with self-replicating organisms or did so accidentally (maybe they flushed their sewage in high orbit before going into warp drive).

The immense complexity of RNA and DNA surely gives *honest* materialists sleepless nights. Surely they contemplate *what they are up against*, seeking naturalistic explanations for the complex and intricate structures we actually observe, structures which biochemically encode the equivalent of *thousands* of libraries of information, each individual organism on this planet slightly different from each of its fellows and therefore unique.

24. Arrhenius, *Worlds in the Making*. Cf. Hoyle and Wickramasinghe, *Evolution from Space*.

25. Sagan and Shklovskii, *Intelligent Life in the Universe*; Crick and Orgel, "Directed Panspermia," 341–46.

As we can affirm, from personal observation, that every single *person* in this world is unique.

"Where Is Everybody?"

Directed panspermia invokes another presumption of contemporary science that (1) lacks any specific empirical evidence in its favor, and (2) smacks of the desperation we've mentioned. This is the idea that in a universe as big as ours appears to be, assumed to have originated without intelligent design, there must be life elsewhere, with some of that life having evolved into intelligent species like ourselves able to build advanced Third Stage civilizations like ours. The Drake Equation proposed in 1961 posits that other things being equal, there should be millions of advanced civilizations in our galaxy alone. The idea works like this:

> The formula is as follows: $N = R* * fp * ne * fl * fi * fc * L$
>
> N is the total number of civilizations within the galaxy with which we could theoretically communicate.
>
> $R*$ is the average rate at which stars in our galaxy form.
>
> fp is the fraction of those stars that have planets.
>
> ne is the number of planets that can potentially support life per solar system.
>
> fl is the fraction of those planets that actually do develop life at some point.
>
> fi is the even smaller fraction of life-supporting planets that actually give rise to intelligent life.
>
> Of those civilized planets, fc is the fraction that acquire technology that releases detectable signs of their existence into space such as radio signals.
>
> Finally, L measures the lifespan of those advanced civilizations in years. In humanity's case L is roughly 100, as that's how many years we've had telecommunications technology.[26]

The Drake Equation has been modified a few times, including by those who see it as overly optimistic. One conclusion is that extraterrestrial civilizations are going to be quite rare. But given the vastness of outer space, again *extremely rare* translates into *inevitable*.

---

26. See Drake and Sobel, *Is Anyone Out There?*

Inevitability ran up against the well-known Fermi Paradox, named for physicist Enrico Fermi and dating to a 1950 conversation with a number of other leading physicists in which he was a lead participant. The Fermi Paradox is more of a contradiction than a paradox in the logical sense. To cut to the chase and again keep technical considerations to a minimum, predictions rooted in the Grandiose Assumption suggest that we should be able to find physical evidence of extraterrestrial civilizations. We have been probing the skies with increasingly powerful telescopes. We have not only found nothing decisive, but very little that is even suggestive of extraterrestrial intelligence. The Fermi Paradox thus invites the question, *where is everybody?*[27] The specifics:

- There appear to be billions of stars in the Milky Way similar to our Sun.

- There is a high probability that some of these stars have Earthlike planets.

- According to the prevailing theories in contemporary cosmology, many of these stars, and hence their planets, are considerably older than the sun. Intelligent life may have developed on some of these worlds long ago and built advanced civilizations.

- Some of these civilizations should have become spacefaring, building megastructures in space and undertaking interstellar travel, presumably having discovered the secret to faster-than-light travel. Perhaps they would have had sufficient time to solve the problems of Third Stage civilizations discussed in this book and not succumbed to those of the Fourth Stage.

- A few such civilizations could have traversed and perhaps colonized the galaxy, perhaps in a few million years of civilizational development.

- It follows that Earth should have already been visited by extraterrestrial civilizations. Or at least, there should be physical or astronomical evidence of their existence.

- However, there is no convincing evidence that such civilizations exist.

(I am leaving aside issues related to UFOs as while there is not space to discuss the matter here, there are, shall we say, good reasons for thinking that if they exist they are of terrestrial origin.)

27. See Jones, *Where Is Everybody?*

Making the Fermi Paradox even more acute has been the discovery, over the past three decades, of over four thousand exoplanets, a handful of them seemingly almost earthlike (although often larger and heavier) and in what astronomers call the "Goldilocks zone" where water can exist in liquid form under earthlike atmospheric pressures. With the advances of our own technology and the recognition of the effects of industrial civilization on the Earth's environment, e.g., the presence of atmospheric contaminants sometimes associated with climate change considerations that would be detectable with very high-resolution equipment, our ideas about what to look for on exo-worlds have improved by leaps and bounds. Surely, again, given the lengths of time and the law of averages, at least some extraterrestrial civilizations should both exist and be far ahead of us technologically. Should they not have built mega-structures in space able to capture most if not all their sun's energy? Perhaps they've undertaken massive engineering projects such as Dyson spheres or similar structures greatly increasing their capacity for expanding their civilization.

Astronomers' eyes and telescopes have been peeled, employing the most advanced technology we have for such purposes.

Nothing.

Speculations about the anomalous behavior of a curious star designated KIC 8462852, or "Tabby's star" (named for astrophysicist Tabetha Boyajian who spent the most time studying it) were initially tantalizing, but ultimately those who originally thought they had evidence of ET have come up empty. What she and others observed or drew from earlier records of the star's behavior were two phenomena: irregular variations in brightness, sometimes up to 22 percent, and also long-term dimming. KIC 8462852 was considerably brighter when it was discovered over a hundred years ago. Neither is consistent with the idea of a single large planet moving across its face (the way most exoplanets have been detected). Some "citizen scientists" and a few academic astronomers observing the star suggested that a megastructure being built in stellar orbit by an advanced extraterrestrial civilization was consistent with all their observations.

This hypothesis appears to have failed, however. Efforts to detect signals bespeaking of communications by intelligent agencies amongst themselves came up empty, although this makes the questionable assumption that our technology would be able to detect communications by a vastly more advanced spacefaring race, to whom our listening devices might be akin to looking for smoke signals. The data now seems most consistent with either the idea that an object in orbit around the star—possibly a large planet—recently broke up, or that a vast field of interstellar dust has interposed itself over time between our instruments and the star. Either would explain the dimming as well as the star's irregularity in brightness. Astronomers continue to train instruments on KIC 8462852, which is fourteen hundred light-years away. There remains, as of this writing, no evidence of alien intelligences that would have begun to engineer their megastructure more than fourteen hundred of our years ago.[28]

One answer (of many!) to Fermi's Paradox has been to postulate a Great Filter: an existential challenge every developing civilization faces.[29] The pessimistic stance is that very few, if any, civilizations get past this Great Filter. Instead, they self-destruct and disappear. Perhaps all civilizations, everywhere, enter a Third Stage as they industrialize, it always transitions to a Fourth Stage as ours has, for mostly the same reasons, and self-destructs as we risk doing. An unavoidable speculation: they rely indefinitely on extractive systems that eventually destroy instead of harmonizing with surrounding ecosystems, cannot adjust when a crisis point is reached, and are in turn destroyed by the consequences.

Another answer to the perplexities of Fermi's Paradox is that some civilizations indeed get past the Great Filter (advancing to a Fifth Stage?), but once they are millions of years ahead of us technologically, even with our own exponential advances we might be visually surrounded by them and unable to recognize them as such. The situation is less analogous to Socrates looking at a smartphone and more to a column of ants encountering one on a sidewalk (or traversing the sidewalk itself!).

Indeed, according to this somewhat disturbing speculation, there could be megastructures constructed by some extremely advanced ET all around us, perhaps woven into the very fabric of space and time itself at a microphysical level! We primitive Third/Fourth Stagers, still dependent on extractive technologies and fighting stupid, destructive wars based on territorialism and greed, would never guess what we were looking at!

There is no scientific way to test any of these speculations, of course, which is why they must remain in the realm of science fiction—for all we know, forever.

My point is that biogenesis is not fundamentally different. We seem to have arrived at the unhappy result—unhappy for materialists, that is— that origins questions amount to little more than educated guessing games: games surely no less preposterous than the idea of an intelligent designer.

Bottom line: given vast improvements in our technological capability to peer out into the depths of space, when all is said and done, we've

---

28. Boyajian et al., "Planet Hunters IX"; Andersen, "Most Mysterious Star in Our Sky"; Wright et al., "Ĝ Search for Extraterrestrial Civilizations"; Tabor, "Scientific Quest"; Boyajian et al., "First Post-Kepler Brightness Dips."

29. Webb, *If the Universe Is Teeming With Aliens*.

detected *no hard* evidence of life elsewhere, much less civilizations elsewhere. We may well be alone. Some scientists now think so.[30] One may turn (if one dares) to a Christian astrophysicist such as Hugh Ross who notes over thirty physical constants and specifics about Earth which, if they were only microscopically different, would render life here impossible.[31]

Earth may well be unique in harboring intelligent life (dare we flatter ourselves?).

These results are consistent with the lack of empirical support that life resulted from nonliving matter by spontaneous processes: laws of physics, chemistry, and efficient causation.

We have to think about the philosophical implications. One of these is that if materialist premises suggest that we *should* be able to find both life and intelligence in abundance elsewhere, as they seem to, and when we look we see nothing, then perhaps it is time to check these premises at the door. Or at least allow alternatives a place at the table of serious discussion.

On grounds of fundamental logic and basic principles of scientific methodology alone including Occam's Razor, invoked by Darwinists against Wallace, isn't it time to question if materialism, or broader naturalism, offers any sounder a basis for science than it does for the study of our moral agency?

Isn't it time, that is, to question the Grandiose Assumption openly and publicly?

With this last, we come to the philosopher whose work has been waiting at the end of the road we've been traveling: Alvin Plantinga, an unabashed Christian theist who rejects naturalism in all forms as inadequate. Back in the 1990s, and more recently, Plantinga penned several works articulating, within the sphere of analytic philosophy, the case for a Christian philosophical perspective able to solve the problems naturalism cannot solve.

His important book *Where the Conflict Really Lies: Science, Religion, and Naturalism* (2011) raises the core question to be discussed next: does materialist naturalism have logical consequences *for itself* that effectively stultify our ability to say we know *anything*, or can justify *any* of our truth claims, once we presuppose it? This sort of argument has never been popular. I maintain that it is necessary.

---

30. See Ward and Brownlee, *Rare Earth*.

31. See Ross, *Creator and the Cosmos*; Ross, *Improbable Planet*; Ross, *Weathering Climate Change*. See also Gonzalez and Richards, *Privileged Planet*.

Materialist Naturalism and Our Capacity for Knowledge

Back in the 1990s Plantinga penned a trilogy providing a systematic critique of materialist naturalism, ending with an analytic-friendly defense of Christian belief.[32] These works exposed the self-stultifying weakness inherent in naturalism in whatever form. All were predecessors of *Where the Conflict Really Lies*, the culmination of a life's work.

One important upshot of Plantinga's dense and detailed arguments is that naturalism (his focus was always broader than just materialism) does not have the logical-conceptual machinery necessary to make sense of our epistemic capabilities. Consider *proper function*. This latter notion requires more than just an intuitive sense of better versus worse. It appeals implicitly to the ideal states or ranges of states or conditions that systems are in when they are serving their highest purpose, even if this purpose is survival. Is it possible to talk about "proper" function without invoking such concepts as design, which in turn suggest intelligence? This is just another way of saying that again, materialism and other forms of naturalism are at sea when it comes to making sense of the evaluative side even of nonhuman existence.

Plantinga's argument goes further than this. He argues that the naturalist account of cognition has unacceptable consequences for knowledge acquisition as a whole, and therefore for itself. In *Where the Conflict Really Lies*, he shows that if we assume materialist naturalism to be true, the reliability of our cognitive faculties is in doubt. To frame the discussion, Plantinga argues that there is no fundamental *deep conflict* between science—even evolutionary biological science—and a Christian worldview. There is actually a *deep concord* between the two if one knows what to look for (we suggested something similar in Chapter 3). The actual *deep conflict* is between science as an enterprise able to obtain epistemically decisive results, and the conditions in which materialist naturalism's description of our cognitive faculties places us. Again, and as always, one has to know what to look for.

First, Plantinga's argument is that contrary to what biologists such as Richard Dawkins and philosophers such as Daniel Dennett and Philip Kitcher claim, nothing in evolutionary biology *logically eliminates* the idea that God intended to create beings in his image even if by some freak chance out of the blue he used evolution by natural selection to do it.

Evolution by natural selection does not *logically compel* the conclusion that we inhabit a universe without design, that is. Arguments to the contrary lean not on specific empirical findings but, again, on the materialist premise. It is, as we've insisted throughout, a *premise* and not a *conclusive finding* of

---

32. Plantinga, *Warrant*; Plantinga, *Warrant and Proper Function*; Plantinga, *Warranted Christian Belief*.

any empirical science. Materialism, as we've discovered, comes into conflict with our sense of ourselves as moral agents, and leaves us unable to offer a credible explanation of conscious self-awareness or how life originated. This is why I've referred to it as the Grandiose Assumption, to be found in the commitment to a worldview, not empirical results. How, though, can there be a *deep conflict* between the capacity of empirical science able to achieve decisive results if there be such, and materialism?

As Plantinga asks this, "suppose you are a naturalist: you think there is no such person as God, and that we and our cognitive faculties have been cobbled together by natural selection. Can you then sensibly think that our cognitive faculties are for the most part reliable?"[33] His answer, as we'll see momentarily, is *No*. The problem is that materialism leaves us with a *defeater* for belief in our cognitive faculties' reliability, and therefore a defeater for our belief that materialism is justified, empirically or otherwise.

A defeater, he'd explained earlier in the tract,[34] is a proposition based on an observed state of affairs that undermines a belief I might hold. It may directly contradict the belief, or present relevant information that undercuts one or more of its key premises. This is easily illustrated. If I believe I see a sheep standing in a field some distance away, and you tell me you own the field and you know it's a sheepdog you have there because you own several sheepdogs and put one out there early this morning (perhaps going on to advise me to have my eyeglasses checked), this defeats my belief that it is a sheep I see from this distance. New information corrects old.

Another example: an archeologist is investigating a previously unknown culture he had "learned" did not possess writing. His dig uncovers new artifacts which appear to feature unknown inscriptions. This could constitute a defeater for the consensus that this civilization did not have a written language, unless it could also be shown through further investigation that these artifacts were bought in from elsewhere, or that the inscriptions served some purpose other than writing. Let's suppose, from a detailed examination of the artifacts' physical attributes including specifics of design and composition, comparing them to artifacts from previous digs, everything about them is consistent with the claim that they originated within this culture. And that we can discern within them patterns, unintelligible to us perhaps, but clearly indicative of the idea that these were intended to record and communicate information. The consensus is defeated, assuming we are being reasonable and not piling on additional auxiliary hypotheses

---

33. Plantinga, *Where the Conflict Really Lies*, 313.
34. Plantinga, *Where the Conflict Really Lies*, 163–68.

to save it. The culture possessed writing, although it may have been limited to certain groups, e.g., an upper caste or class.

Now consider this third example, more pertinent to the matter at hand. Cultural relativism about truth (often just called epistemological relativism) is the idea that truth, not just in morality but about the world itself, is dependent on the culture in which speakers' claims are made. This idea is not to be confused with the structurally similar one that different cultures have held different *beliefs* about what is true. No one would quarrel with that. We are interested in the more radical notion that *truth itself* differs from place to place, or from one people to another. This idea defeats itself from within. We have to inquire, whenever someone asserts it, within which culture, or within what kind of culture, has this claim itself been made? By its own logic, the relativist claim is just as dependent for whatever truth it can be said to possess on that culture (probably an academic one) in which it is asserted. Assuming this argument from self-referential incoherence is not enough, do we not also defeat the relativist claim *absolutely* just by stepping outside that culture and into one holding that truth is *absolute*—however difficult it may be to determine?[35]

I submit that this is materialism's predicament. How does it defeat the credibility of our cognitive claims, and therefore defeat itself? By supporting the wrong capabilities, from an epistemic standpoint. Natural selection selects those characteristics members of a population have that ensure their greatest *adaptation* to their immediate environment. These, in the human animal no less than other animals and plants, aim at survival and enhancing opportunities for reproduction, not adopting true beliefs about their surroundings (much less the world as a whole). They could, in fact, have beliefs that were false through and through, e.g., the belief, common to most primitive peoples, that their familiar location is the physical center of the cosmos. Having such beliefs would not inhibit their survival.

Plantinga calls this "Darwin's doubt," since Darwin himself appears to have been conscious of it. He quotes Darwin:

> With me the horrid doubt always arises whether the convictions of man's mind, which has been developed from the mind of the lower animals, are of any value or at all trustworthy. Would any one trust in the convictions of a monkey's mind, if there are any convictions in such a mind?[36]

---

35. Cf. Siegel, *Relativism Refuted*.

36. Plantinga, *Where the Conflict Really Lies*, 316, quoting Darwin's letter to William Godwin, July 3, 1881.

How Plantinga explains the problem (having cited naturalist philosophers including Thomas Nagel and Patricia Smith Churchland): if the materialist variant of naturalism is true, than *all* our convictions or *beliefs*, scientific or otherwise—all they can ever be—are neural patterns somehow stored in our brains and expressed as language. All my conscious thought can ever be is a sequence of neurological events, a firing of neurons undergoing electro-chemical and neuro-physiological processes. These somehow have *content properties*: Plantinga's term for what Searle called intentionality. My belief that the Earth is round and not flat is a belief about the shape and nature of the Earth, and if the content of my belief reflects physical reality, then my belief is true. Other content properties might not be true, e.g., my belief that an ancient civilization did not have writing when in fact it did. A Chinese scientist, incidentally and obviously, will use different words to express the same content, and his belief will be true (or not) for the same reasons mine is true (or not). Can materialism convincingly handle the content property or intentionality of language? We encountered this above, and saw grounds for doubt. How can electrochemical interactions in firing neurons be *about* anything? But even were there no grounds for doubting that materialism could make sense of the intentionality of language and understanding, this new question of Plantinga's would then arise:

> what is the likelihood, given *evolution and naturalism* (construed as including materialism about human beings) that the content thus arising is in fact *true*? In particular, what is the likelihood . . . that the content associated with *our* neural structures is true? What is the likelihood . . . that our cognitive faculties are reliable, thereby producing mostly true beliefs?[37]

His answer is that this likelihood is low, and that those who accept materialist naturalism are obligated logically to give up our commonsense assumption (commonsense to everyone except many academic philosophers, that is) that most of the time our cognitive faculties are reliable.

Does it even make sense to give up this assumption?

As I write this during my morning work hours I have a clear and veridical perception of the room in which I am working: laptop computer on my desk, pictures on the wall, books on the bookshelf; closed door to the outer hallway; etc. I have clear memories (veridical when the remembered events occurred) of feeding my cats earlier this morning, of the eastern sky brightening as dawn approached; and now of the residual taste in my mouth of the coffee I drank earlier. Am I *certain* that these reflect real events and states of affairs? Plantinga is not going to argue, like a Cartesian (or like

37. Plantinga, *Where the Conflict Really Lies*, 325.

the many philosophical stepchildren of Cartesianism), that we should, in some sense, "bracket" our commonsense assumptions about the general reliability of our senses, memories, etc., until we have a deductive proof of them from first premises. That is Second Stage thinking again. Plantinga is going to turn the Third Stage obviousness of their reliability against the presumption of materialist naturalism: "like everyone else, I believe that our cognitive faculties *are*, in fact, mostly reliable. What I do mean to argue is that the *naturalist*—at any rate a naturalist who accepts evolution—is rationally obligated to give up this assumption."[38] In our terms, he is arguing for a rupture between Third Stage thinking and materialist naturalism. The latter defeats the former.

The problem is that natural selection is about solving immediate problems that lead to adaptation. This may enhance the chance of survival, but does not guarantee truth. Beliefs about my surroundings are one thing. I affirm my conviction that (with rare exceptions) they are accurate and reliable, and that the burden should be on the skeptic to show me grounds for questioning any of them. This includes beliefs about states of affairs outside my immediate surroundings such as the shape of the Earth, etc. The point is, many more general beliefs held by peoples in the past—and conceivably in the present—have *not* been true. Yet these beliefs were adapted well enough to their immediate environment and needs that the cultures relying on them survived for centuries. For example, the idea that the Earth may be round but is at the center of the universe, a mainstay of Aristotelian cosmology, was used successfully by navigators on the oceans for centuries. Despite its falsity it solved problems and was perfectly suited to their needs. (Earlier seafaring cultures probably figured out navigation systems for a flat Earth, for that matter.)

The point: *there is no logically or epistemically necessary connection between having solved a problem and having arrived at a truth.* Darwinian evolution itself is in this predicament. Social scientists as well as biologists use the idea to provide explanations, e.g., about our "reptilian brain" and fight-or-flight responses to danger. Darwinism was formulated to solve intellectual problems, and explain how living things have solved the problems of survival. In that case, we humans evolved in such a way as to begin concerning ourselves with matters of truth and falsity, not mere survival. Survival does not appear to require truth, however. It requires only adaptation. We may be faced with the choice of giving up the idea that our cognitive faculties are able to do the work we give them credit for, i.e., finding *general* truths (and possibly even *specific* ones), if we continue to embrace

---

38. Plantinga, *Where the Conflict Really Lies*, 326.

materialism and its Darwinist offspring. For if we're logically consistent, this argument applies to Darwinism itself. Darwinism puts forth general truths (also specific ones, about this or that species). We are, or should be, compelled to admit that we are not as sure of the truth of the Darwinian theory as we thought we were.

The situation is worse than even this. Materialist theories of evolution contend that *the human brain itself* came about exclusively through natural processes. Leaving aside the *extreme* improbability of an entity the complexity of which vastly exceeds all the computer systems in the world put together occurring unplanned as a result of natural processes, a problem magnitudes worse than that of blind matter somehow combining to form a self-replicating entity in a prebiotic soup, if materialism is true then all our perceptions and all our knowledge result from, and must be explained by, material processes. For the latter exhausts all of what exists. And this is extremely bad news!

For in that case, *our experience is never of our actual surroundings, our proximate environment and all its particulars. It is of those electro-chemical/neuro-physiological impulses in our brains*, which our brains have learned to interpret for themselves using the signs, grammar, and semantics of natural language. In other words, I had no *real* experiences early this morning *of* feeding my two cats, looking out my home office window at the approaching dawn, or savoring my morning coffee. Intentionality, or the having of content properties, is an illusion. It is in the same predicament Dennett believed conscious self-awareness itself was in. We never have *direct* experience of events in or interactions with an external world, that is, a world outside our skins and senses, only of the brain's *representations* which are invariably local and particular: *"reality," i.e., the world outside our skins and senses, is an impenetrable black box in reverse.* "Experience" is a *brain construction* of neurochemical data. "Knowledge" is stored information that the brain has interpreted as solved problems via successful, adaptive actions by the organism based on discerned patterns in its brain constructions: patterns which can shift or change at any time. Only through interpretations of signs can we infer "contact" with "other minds" which, again, are never more than the interpreted visible or audible actions of other bodies (speaking, bodily motion, etc.). Part of that interpretation is of a congruence of whatever is stored in "other brains" with what is stored in our own (my own). All we have is an equation of signs, and this is itself a representation. And an inference by way of analogy

We've arrived at epistemological solipsism. We are absolutely isolated, trapped within the meditations of that Cartesian "thinking thing" which is actually our brains, senses, and nervous systems, constructing that irreducibly private inner stage of self-awareness, itself a product of the electrochemical firings of neurons in our brains. We never experience anything but what our brains represent to themselves (Rorty's attacks on "representationalism" notwithstanding).

This is rightly rejected as absurd.

But if solipsism indeed follows from materialism, naturalism applied to the human person in the manner of Plantinga, then materialist naturalism as a worldview must also be rejected as absurd. It fails the most basic test of logic. It cannot only not establish itself, for that would be circular reasoning, it actually *undermines* itself. To use a familiar metaphor, it saws off the tree limb it is sitting on.

Should Philosophers Continue to Swear Fealty to Materialism?

Few of the arguments assembled here are original with me; all that is new is their packaging. This is telling in and of itself. Their conclusion is that taken as a whole, the materialist worldview is worse than inadequate. Look at it under a sufficiently powerful philosophical microscope, and one sees an incoherent morass of unsolved problems. These are made worse by self-deception about the worldview's potential, and positively harmful if looked to as offering any kind of basis for our lives as moral agents. In terms of our moral lives, materialism leaves us at sea, especially given the human nature we actually confront in the real world (as opposed to the constructions of idealistic intellectuals whether or the left or a few on the right).

Science, technology, commerce, and public education have given us myriad creature comforts and conveniences, but have manifestly *not* made us *better persons* in any sense this phrase conveys. Third Stage thinking pursued a set of ideals, including an ideal unique to the West, of universal human rights applicable to all, an idea borrowed from the Christian worldview in which God created all persons in his image, including their moral agency. When God "died," first among intellectuals and then in the broader culture, what cultural (as opposed to technological) progress we were making slowed and then gradually reversed, and now we are hurling at warp speed in the opposite direction, towards retribalization, e.g., identity politics and "woke" cancel culture. In this Fourth Stage environment, truth is null and void. It literally does not factor into any equation.

We are told that "black lives matter" even though African-American men kill each other in south Chicago neighborhoods with efficiency and enthusiasm! Not even their own leaders seem to care, and one has to wonder if such movements don't also illustrate the nihilism Nietzsche warned us about. It is not just black lives failing to "matter" in any substantive way. In foreign wars of choice, white lives are no less expendable, because human life itself is expendable. Lives are wantonly cast aside in multiple arenas (abortion, war, black men killing other black men, rising suicide rates). As we've noted, elite technocrats work out plans to cure us of our ills through various controls-driven schemes. For them, money and a capacity to implement (i.e., power) get the last word. This invokes, in most people who learn of it, the Technology-Gone-Awry feelings of science-fiction horror we examined at the start of Chapter 4.[39] What should be clear: authors such as Steven Pinker notwithstanding, Enlightenment-derived hopes for universal progress based on *universal human rights* are fading before our eyes!

This is the world materialism has left us. Returning to its grip on science, when all is said and done, materialist premises used in science leave us with no explanation of the origin of life from nonlife that is scientifically testable at a crucial juncture: the production, by exclusively natural means, of a fully functional entity that can replicate itself in such a way that the copies can repeat the process and eventually generate variations that can also replicate themselves. Absent this, Darwinian natural selection has nothing on which to operate, and there is little point in even talking about whether it really generated the relatively sudden proliferation of new species geologists tell us mark the beginning of the Cambrian era, whether there are transitional forms to species that purportedly evolved later including ourselves, whether the appeal to "index fossils" to date layers of rock in the geologic column also involves circular reasoning, or any other staples raised by those who have doubts about Darwinism.

What we have is an intense effort by scientists and other scholars to hide such failures, not just from the world at large but from themselves. The Grandiose Assumption has, in fact, created and perpetuated a mass delusion of the adequacy of the materialist worldview. Laboratory-based efforts to understand how life could come from nonlife via laws of physics and chemistry alone continue, but much of the wild speculation (e.g., life having originated on another planet and been transported here in comets, or by ETs) has such a ring of desperation about it as to be a *dead giveaway* that something is wrong.

There is a sense of desperation about scientists' search for evidence of life elsewhere in the cosmos—and for intelligent life. Thus far our highest resolution telescopes have disclosed no evidence at all of any ecosystems besides our own. Much of the universe is resolutely *hostile* to life as we

---

39. See again Wood, *Technocracy Rising*.

know it. It is either too hot or too cold, filled with exoplanets, perhaps, but even those we know about that are not too close to their suns appear to have violent and poisonous atmospheres, or are subjected to life-destroying radiation. There is abundant evidence of past stellar events of unimaginable violence, e.g., supernovae and stellar collisions. There appear to be black holes with gravity wells capable of destroying solar systems. One such object, millions of times more massive than our sun, appears to dominate space at the center of our galaxy. Our own best theories compel us to infer the presence of immense radiation that would make complex living systems impossible.

Again, yes, we have found primitive organic molecules in a few meteorites, and scientists have gleefully held onto this as evidence that complex ecosystems "probably" exist *somewhere* out there. Perhaps they do. Not having found positive evidence of p is not proof that p does not exist. But the bottom line is, if we are looking for *factual evidence* elsewhere in the universe of something approximating the complexity of human DNA/RNA, *science has found nothing*. And as skeptics of things transcendent love to point out, the burden of argument is on the claimant, not on the critic. What such (pseudo) skeptics don't care to have pointed out is that this applies to their premises and speculations as well.

Maybe, again, we're not looking at the right things or in the right places; or maybe we're making geocentric assumptions—that life is everywhere the same or at least similar (based on liquid water, carbon-based, oxygen-breathing, etc.). Maybe we've assumed that ETs would be as interested in building a technological civilization as we have been. I grant all this. But then I have to ask: what contrary assumptions are we supposed to make? Can they be supported by either empirical science or any reasonable philosophical speculation, or are they just *ad hoc* efforts to salvage something materialist naturalism desperately needs?

If science has found *nothing*, surely it is just as reasonable to hypothesize that *this is because there is nothing to find*. As depressing as this might seem. (And I confess to having been on the other side of this fence on this issue!)

What we have found—when we troubled to look for such things—are more than three dozen physical constants and other features of our world and its immediate surroundings which, if they were only slightly different, *Earth* would be uninhabitable.[40]

Isn't *that* interesting?

---

40. See again Ross, *Creator and the Cosmos*.

This, of course, is much bigger than the question of whether materialism has a viable explanation of consciousness or conscious self-awareness: why, in a material universe, there even *is* such a thing. Here we found philosophical proposals that ring of that same desperation, such as Colin McGinn's "new mysterianism." I understand the need to try to hang onto the Grandiose Assumption to remain "academically respectable," but the intellectual costs seem, well, astronomically high. For if Plantinga is right, then not merely is the human brain unable in principle to explain itself and how its strange abilities fit into the "material world," it cannot explain how its cognitions can yield reliable judgments of *any* kind.

The situation is still worse. A fully consistent materialist account that integrates perception and cognition appears to imply not just that our cognitive faculties are less reliable than we ever thought—our brains do not seek truth but whatever will provide advantages in one's environment—but *never do we even truly experience an environment!* What we "experience" are just the products our brains receive as neural impulses from our sensory organs, interpreted symbolically with a system of signs (language): representations. This is just what the neurophysiological process of perception is. Surely this is not acceptable. It renders our capacity for rationality itself as utterly mysterious: it permits descriptions but not prescriptions, not just in morality but in rationality itself! There is no foothold, or even a toehold, for normativity outside whatever it is that helps the organism survive and propagate. This is if we are honest about these matters in allowing the premises and full consequences of the materialist worldview to work themselves out. Few philosophers or scientists are willing to do this.

Materialism and Human Emotions

Let me end this chapter with something of an aside. Over the years as the thoughts leading to this manuscript developed, I've grown accustomed to materialists trying to "explain religion" (i.e , theistic worldviews) as "meeting emotional needs" or some such rubric. Or that "religion" has an evolutionary origin (Dennett) [41] This is supposed to discredit all "religious" ideas and hypotheses, including such notions as an intelligent designer.

The first question that comes to mind by way of reply is to invite critics to point to those passages in the above sections which actually mention anyone's religion—aside from Plantinga who is up front about his beliefs, but this hardly constitutes an objection to his detailed analysis. Indeed, the case against materialism can be made simply by holding materialists, who tend

---

41. Dennett, *Breaking the Spell*.

to be empiricists (or say they are), to their own rules and showing that they break these rules all the time. And by demonstrating the overall incoherence of their position. Returning to the emotional-needs argument, though (to the extent it is that), even assuming such needs exist, is materialism not *also* constructed to meet emotional needs?

One example, whatever its origins as we look at our explorations of what may be an empty cosmos, is the apparent collective need *not to be utterly alone*. Hence the frantic-seeming attempts to use, e.g., the Drake equation to estimate the number of potential alien civilizations like our own out there, even if there are no means of empirically testing the results of what come down to pure mathematics, and to eagerly record discoveries of the latest exoplanets and gauge their similarity to Earth and hence presumed likelihood of being able to sustain life as we know it—perhaps intelligent life.

This does not go to the heart of the matter, though. Perhaps materialists' most basic emotional need is for freedom from the idea of one day having to answer to a Power outside and higher than themselves, a Power outside their community of respected peers and their consensus or society, who commanded obligations they did not sign off on. Materialists do not *want* to answer to a transcendent morality not having their stamp of approval. Having granted the implicit Cartesian philosophical move razing all the old traditions to the ground and starting over as "thinking things" that turn out to be made of matter—where God is superfluous—they do not want to answer to anyone besides themselves and perhaps a few ungrounded abstract principles (e.g., never initiate physical force against another). Thus their feeling of total freedom to recreate themselves from scratch and put themselves on a path toward the God-surrogate of Self, via (for example) Maslov's "self-actualization" in which Self replaces God.

These are as much emotional and non-empirical as the needs Christian theists stand accused of having. You do not have to be a materialist to play this sort of game.

I do not object to the idea that there are emotional needs at the core of worldview commitments. I do not even object to the idea that our biology might impact on our thinking and its development, and definitely not to the idea that traditions and culture do so. What is objectionable is the idea that materialists have somehow gotten *outside* such needs and states of affairs. This seems dishonest to me. Materialism is as emotional at its core as any form of Christianity (or Islam or Hinduism or any other faith).

What philosophers or any scientists happening upon this book should *do* with this information is the question I end with. And I emphasize, this is a *should* question. What *should* they do? I am under no illusions that most *will* do *anything* with it. The need to be "scientific" (i.e., retaining the

Grandiose Assumption) or "academically respectable" is too strong, too deeply engrained in higher education, i.e., in the sociology of the Secular University, despite the latter's (rapidly worsening) problems. It is a habit of thought as deep as anything Hume uncovered. Hence, again, the scorn reserved for theorists of, say, intelligent design, extended to those who speak of anything "transcendent" or "supernatural" or "paranormal," rejected *a priori* as superstition, unreason, "pseudoscience," or at the very best, *outside* what is empirically testable. Never mind what we have shown, how the proposition that in the natural world (as opposed to the artificial world of the laboratory), *life came from nonlife*, is no more empirically testable than the statement that God created life *ex nihilo* on the fifth day!

Those professing philosophy (i.e., professional philosophers) *should* consider these arguments, even though they range across disciplines (do not conform to the specialism that has long hobbled academia). I can strongly *recommend* that they do. I can reach out to younger scholars and students who find philosophy both interesting and important. But neither I nor anyone else can *compel* anyone to do anything. Some may argue the paranoid thesis that arguments such as these are steeped in a wish or psychological need (yet another one!) to *suppress* scientific truth—confused with the Grandiose Assumption *still*.

Some even speak darkly of a conspiracy of "dominionists" who want to set up a theocracy. Those who champion life over "choice," for example, are scolded and told to read a book called *The Handmaid's Tale* by Margaret Atwood, which presents a dystopian future in which "fundamentalists" have taken over the United States and reinstituted "repression" of women's "choices." I can't guarantee that *no one* wants theocracy, of course. I can only say that no such motives exist *here*, nor do they seem to exist in anyone I've consulted. Christian authors have no power to "repress" anyone. No one in the Secular City is positioned to set up a theocracy even if they wanted to, even if a few paranoid secularists are saying so. Their fervently *saying* so doesn't make it so.

Those who read these two chapters eviscerating materialism ought to see this. Let's recall the *context* of this whole discussion. *My primary interest here hasn't been to attack materialism, or to defend a Christian worldview. It has been to articulate a specific vision for what philosophy should do, if it is to avoid becoming even more moribund and culturally irrelevant than it is now, and providing an example*. The past two chapters provide that example, by way of a concrete illustration of what that vision should inspire philosophers to do, *by doing it boldly here*. What motivates the vision, as I said at the outset, is just this conviction: *philosophy has a job to do in society, in the Secular City and in the Secular University*. It cannot do this job if it uncritically retains the Grandiose Assumption and remains, essentially, a handmaiden to science—or, for that matter, a discipline confining itself to teaching service courses in a tiny corner of the Secular University and otherwise keeping out from underfoot.

The reality, however, is that because of the grip the Grandiose Assumption holds over the academic imagination, and further, because of the rising culture of "wokeness," the reactions to the arguments presented here are likely to be hostile. Indeed, the program for philosophy advocated here might not even be possible in academia as it currently exists for reasons coming down to the political economy of academia quite apart from materialism and "wokeness." What then? Pondering the available vehicles for how philosophers can further articulate and pursue this vision shall be the job of this essay's sixth and final chapter.

6

Philosophy's Present and Civilization's Future: Two Proposals

As we move into our home stretch, here is the problem we face: *Philosophy may have a job to do in civilization*, that of unearthing often unstated worldview assumptions, bringing them to light, assessing them critically, and proposing they be rejected when necessary, especially if an alternative is available.

Present institutional arrangements and political-economic realities, however, as well as prevailing ideological commitments, stand solidly in the way of academic philosophy doing anything of this sort. Philosophy, whatever influences specific philosophers have had in the present world, is expected to know its place. Now, in an academic environment not merely favoring materialism overall but having grown increasingly hostile to such values as freedom of speech and inquiry, can worldview analysis and criticism be done in the Secular University at all? Can it even be conceived?

The job of philosophy envisioned here would take professional academics into waters no less treacherous than what Socrates faced. No one will be forced to drink hemlock, of course (or some equivalent). But they might find their careers in ruins, and that threat is usually sufficient to deter the adventurous. Worldview studies as a topic is sure to seem utterly alien, moreover, to the new order of "woke" that has spread from the Secular University through Secular City media culture like a tsunami.

So in addition to, *What should philosophy do?* we also need to ask, *Can philosophers survive doing it?*

This chapter will put forth two proposals, therefore.

(1) Those philosophers who recognize the merits of this kind of approach *need to take matters into their own hands, and not wait for, or expect, approval from others.* It won't be easy. They will need to step outside their comfort zones. They must get over whatever distaste they might harbor for marketing and becoming sellers of their ideas. Prior to that they must

write clearly and concisely, reaching for a potential nonacademic audience clamoring for philosophical guidance. This audience might be small, but it is there. It might not be conscious of worldviews at the start, but can be brought around if the right leadership is offered. Philosophers must write about that audience's problems as seen by them and present solutions, while keeping their eye on the ball, so to speak. If they want to be visible in the present environment of distraction, disinformation, and general chaos, *there is no alternative*. They must become *thought leaders* on the path to a better and more humane world, if such a world is still possible.

(2) Having critically (and negatively) evaluated the materialism at the core of our increasingly volatile and unstable amalgamation of Third and Fourth Stage thinking and institutions, *philosophers must offer a way forward. They must provide a compelling vision of a Fifth Stage of civilization, I will call it. They must make it compelling, by whatever means are necessary, including perchance outlining or telling stories of what menaces us if we continue on our present path, contrasting this with what is possible if we care about the future and starting assuming responsibility for it, for our futures.*

This will mean walking a tightrope.

We cannot propose some new and comprehensive Utopia, another Platonistic *Republic* or Rousseau-like *Social Contract* or another *Looking Backwards* in the sense of Bellamy. There can be no more social engineering exercises imposed top-down on unwilling populations.

That would just repeat the mistakes we have been seeing all along, all over again.

What I have in mind can only be done piecemeal, acting horizontally, working with those willing, given many factors known and unknown which we cannot control. We will not know in advance what the final product will look like, any more than Francis Bacon or Voltaire could have visualized Third Stage civilization in the mid-twentieth century. Nor should we. We should seek marginal improvements, not comprehensive systems to be delivered all at once. This is the mistake of every technocrat. What I am talking about will take time, even if time seems to be the one thing we don't have in abundance. We must hurry, but not be hurried. Our actions will be imperfect, and course corrections will doubtless be necessary. But given our present situation, we have little choice but to begin taking baby steps now.

The Background: Philosophy's Present Revisited

What should philosophy do? morphs at once into *What should philosophers do?* Should philosophers rest content teaching service courses in institutions whose values allow only the barest room for sustained philosophical inquiry, much less what we're advocating here? Especially places hijacked by the "woke" inquisition?

Even this much assumes those with both the motivation and advanced philosophy degrees to carry a program such as this forward can *find* viable teaching positions. Those who find themselves adjunct-zoned are looking at economic deprivation, whatever their sympathies. This is the direction the Secular University has gone, towards hiring ever cheaper academic labor. The pandemic of 2020 has made matters magnitudes worse, at least as of this writing.

Yet the questions must be asked: *Is Western civilization as a whole, as well as Western inquiry, philosophical and otherwise, in the grip of a prevailing worldview?*

What is this worldview? How do we identify it?

Is its prevalence the result of actual evidential findings and intellectual superiority, or has it resulted from its advocates' skill at using rhetoric, academic politics, financial resources, and sometimes outright bullying, to push alternatives off the table?

Is this worldview delivering the goods, or is it doing more harm than good? To whom, in either case?

Has it solved the intellectual problems it sets for itself?

Are its advocates being honest with us, or with themselves, about its failures?

Are there viable alternatives? What can be done to bring them back to the table?

The challenge is to create this conversation. But how? And where?

Obviously, philosophers' accepting the Grandiose Assumption without much question is *very helpful* to their careers, especially if they are doing philosophy of mind. Visibly having the wrong worldview, the wrong politics, or no "people skills," can be deadly! Any of these can prevent a young scholar from being *interviewed* for a job in academia, much less *hired*, much less *tenured* at a place where such questions can be asked. One *might* have a future at a vocational-technical school where almost no one will care about one's ideas on, say, biogenesis, or whether or not one is committed to identity politics. In such institutions your superiors will care about one thing and one thing only: *can you teach?* Can you handle five classes per semester? Six, perchance?

Such places (as I can testify from personal experience) make poor home bases for any sort of cutting-edge philosophical conversation.

There are, of course, philosophers, doctorates in hand, some conceivably with great potential, who for whatever reason (PhD from outside the Ivies, poor networking skills, being too white and too male, or some combination of these) fall through the cracks altogether and must support themselves with nonacademic work. Some, finally, voluntarily exit a Secular University they come to realize cannot be fixed from the inside.

This last is my story in one sentence.

Assuming they are not compelled by the demands of earning a living to give up philosophical aspirations, what options do exiled (or self-exiled) philosophers have for making a difference in the Secular City? Here is where matters are already starting to get interesting, if we know where to look and what to look for!

Philosophy in the Secular City Today.

Overall, of course, the Secular City is indifferent to philosophy, for reasons we've canvassed. Its authorities, or others with specific programs they are pursuing or agendas they are pushing, aren't comfortable with philosophy. They never have been.

Analytic philosophy was able to thrive in the Secular University because it produced enormous quantities of publications that made its authors' home institutions look good, but analytic philosophy by its nature never challenged the overriding values or authority structures of the Secular City. It wasn't political and mostly accepted Settled Science. Thus arguably, analytic philosophy enjoyed a "golden age" that began during the post-war years, especially with logical empiricism's ambitious attempts at formalizing inductive inference and logic of justification in science, Wittgenstein's return to the field and the rise of British-derived linguistic and conceptual analysis, and Quine's "naturalizing" of epistemology.

Then came the broadening challenges from Toulmin, Hanson, Kuhn, Lakatos, Feyerabend, and others. These went off various combinations of Wittgenstein's "later" philosophy, Sir Karl Popper's critical rationalism, and the rising interest in the history of science which offered a barometer for assessing theories of the rationality of science—and opportunities to examine actual science's nonempirical aspects. Eventually we saw some convergence between the analytic and the continental schools, uniting considerations to be found in, say, Kuhn, or Feyerabend, with those of, say, Foucault.[1] Moral philosophers, meanwhile, could compare and contrast the ideas of Stevenson, Hare, Rawls, Nozick, Dworkin, and others. The period from the late 1940s until around 1975 was a fantastic time to be an academic philosopher!

---

1. For an account see Gutting, *Paradigms and Revolutions*; Gutting, *Continental Philosophy of Science*.

The collapse of the academic job market in the 1970s ended the "golden age." While later "stars" (e.g., Rorty) had yet to produce their most compelling works, nothing like that era has existed since, and while there has been important and high quality philosophical work done during subsequent years, the ambience of that earlier era is gone and isn't coming back (a promised "turnaround" in the academic job market never materialized, for one thing). Even if both Third Stage and Fourth Stage thought emphasized philosophy's *limits*, major works of philosophy after around 1975 more and more exhibited the pessimistic spirit of Fourth Stage postmodernity rather than the relative cheer of Third Stage logical positivism.

So where are we now?

At first glance, in the position described at the start of the Introduction. We've come full circle. Significant scientists and science's media popularizers—entertainers, to some extent perhaps, but influential given today's culture—hold that philosophy is dead except perhaps as an ethical scold. As Fourth Stage postmodernist *philosophy* is all but unintelligible to the Third Stage *scientific* mind, the latter would like nothing better than to go back to a kind of native positivism. Be it physics, or studies of the brain and consciousness, science can do it unaided by philosophy. If anything, the Stephen Hawkings of the world of contemporary cosmology became their own philosophers.

The Secular University has thus reached the point of curtailing its philosophy offerings, if anything out of a sense that philosophy has little to offer—and we do not know yet how much damage will be done by budgetary collapses growing out of the 2020 pandemic. We cannot single out the pandemic, though, since some universities were already eliminating philosophy programs and "terminating" even tenured faculty before *coronavirus* and *COVID-19* entered our vocabularies.

In the present environment, there is no reason for thinking that the academic job market for philosophers will return. It is more likely to get worse.

Add to all this the general mayhem in Western civilization today, and the realization that many people who otherwise might find philosophy interesting and worthwhile have far more immediate problems, including survival. It is easy to conclude that philosophy as a "leisure class" activity is over.

Can a community of philosophers survive outside the Secular University in this environment?

The answer: they must!

A few intrepid souls are doing it! Not all self-identify as *philosophers*, but that's neither here nor there at this point.

Let's not misunderstand. Some may note that there is an abundance of things those with philosophical training can do in the workplace—for example, training in formal logic is directly applicable to coding and computer programming. Articles, sometimes in business publications, tout the utility of a philosophy degree because of the unique analytic skills philosophy can confer.[2] There are other answers to those who declare philosophy dead.[3]

I do not refer to those with some philosophical training (e.g., a BA or MA) who went on to become software developers or managers and found their philosophical training useful. *Learn to code!* may sound like a good adage but I am neutral on the subject. Philosophers must decide for themselves whether they want to go that route to earn a living, but what I am advocating here is not a hobby.

Nor do I refer to philosophy professors who decided to present the subject to a general audience, or start up a blog (there are a gazillion philosophy blogs and informal articles on sites like Medium), or post lectures to their YouTube channels, or begin doing podcasts. While there is certainly a place for all of these, and they've helped keep philosophy alive in cyberspace, they are not what I have in mind, either.

I refer to philosophers clearly independent of academia and *nevertheless doing philosophy*: raising issues that are fundamentally philosophical and drawing their consequences, sometimes being "gadflies" as was Socrates.

Are there any such people?

Yes. And they might help answer, *What should a philosopher do to survive outside the Secular University? How does he or she gain and keep attention, given cyberspace clutter, reduced attention spans, and the general mayhem of our present moment?*

Doing Philosophy Outside Academia:
From *The Black Swan* to Stoicism

Consider again Nassim Taleb. Taleb's *black swan* meme has crept into public discourse, where it refers to any unanticipated event with a massively disruptive impact. Coming out when it did, Taleb's book had an instant audience, which grew with the financial meltdown of 2008–9. Whether that was a true black swan event is questionable, as there were observers predicting that such an event was the inevitable outcome of rampant speculation,

---

2. See Satell, "How Philosophy Can Make You a Better Manager"; Pace, "Can Philosophy Influence Business."

3. See Hughes, "Four Reasons Why Philosophy Is as Relevant as Ever"; or Siegel, "No, Science Will Never Make Philosophy or Religion Obsolete."

the instruments then in use (e.g., derivatives), and the transformation of markets into gambling casinos. *The Black Swan* itself contained a rich and complex tapestry of observations on the vagaries of probability and how to navigate our way through the unexpected.

The Black Swan's follow-up, *Anti-Fragile: The Things That Gain From Disorder*, turned to the problem of establishing personal and institutional resiliency in, and even drawing benefits from, the flexibility and versatility necessary for life in a disrupted environment.

Such as the one we are in as this work nears completion and publication!

Philosophy needs to become anti-fragile! It needs to draw impetus from our present disrupted environment. What kind of philosophy can help? I am, for the moment, purposefully avoiding Christian authors. We will return to them in due course. Who else is out there?

Stoicism is an ancient philosophy garnering attention these days. A rich library of recent books and articles has emerged drawing on insights from Epictetus, Marcus Aurelius, and Seneca, the three most influential Stoics, going beyond them to identify and apply Stoic principles today. The most significant authors working with Stoicism today are not professional philosophers. It apparently never occurred to them to pursue academic careers.

First, let us consider the Stoics themselves. The early Stoics, especially those of the school founded in Athens by Zeno who lectured from a painted porch (*stoa*), were teachers in a broad sense, such as nonacademic philosophers today can be teachers in a broad sense. Early Stoics distinguished physics, logic, and ethics. Physics was the study of the world and how it works. Today we would speak of causes and effects. Logic was the study of our thought about the world, not distinct in their minds from psychology. Ethics picks up at this point as the counsel on how to live a good life in a world of causes and effects, many of them outside our control, amidst other people with lives and priorities of their own also outside our control. Stoics counsel their listeners on how to have more inner peace and harmony with the world as it is, however oppressive it can seem in the sense of its being run according to rules we never voted on or gave our stamp of approval. Fraught with suffering or at least disappointment, often handing us setbacks or losses, leaving us potentially angry or sad, the world poses immense challenges for the thoughtful.

Epictetus, who began life in slavery, drew an important distinction between that small portion of the world we can control and that much larger portion we cannot control. He counseled focusing our efforts on the former and leaving the latter aside. This is key to understanding Stoicism. The concept is easy; implementing it is harder than we think.

What one can learn to control, says the Stoic, are one's emotions, especially reactions to events outside one's control. Though there are obvious exceptions, typically it is not *events* that disturb us but our emotional *reactions* to them. For this reason it is silly to complain about the weather, or traffic. Nor can we control the attitudes of others, nor the vagaries of the economy, the outcomes of elections, nor "acts of God" (interesting phrase, that!).

The most we can do is embrace an outlook which counsels focus on how to live with each of these while minimizing their worst effects. Because we can learn how the systems around us work, the *wise* can increase, in increments, the range of things within their control, and act accordingly. The Stoic will focus on diagnosing a problem rather than on his/her having been inconvenienced by it. He or she will remember that the objects in our world always operate according to species of the general rule of causes and effects. Things go awry because of causes; we observe the effects. In any such situation we may ask, What caused this? What might fix it?

If the seeming problem is with another person—or people generally—we are talking about a much greater need for mindfulness and care, which the Stoics also counseled. None of us is going to change human nature or the fact that people respond to incentives (cause and effect in the human world). What we might discover, if only through trial and error, is that *benevolence* is helpful. Those who are benevolent, sincerely wishing to make life better for those around them, or in general, must determine what rules are in play in the situation, what the incentives are, and if they can be altered. What, again, is within our control?

This is especially important where public policy is concerned. Public policy often fails because of unknowns—things *no one* can know as they are private, because a given policy can affect millions of people, all of them different. Very often things go awry because of circumstances we did not know about until they began to thwart our goals. Sometimes the problem is that we are within the range of influence by someone who is anything but benevolent. Seneca, one of the greatest of the Roman Stoics, served as counsel to the borderline-insane Nero. He doubtless understood, more than any of us ever will, the silent heartache of having his counsel ignored. Persistence in his standards eventually cost him his life!

Marcus Aurelius, a Roman Emperor who was a Stoic and more than aware of how much he could control because of his position, spent his life seeking to be a better person. The collection of meditations he penned to clarify his own thoughts are filled with advice useful to us today. Ascertain what is beneficial. Be mindful of purpose. Don't act out of frivolous, whim-of-the-moment impulses. Have a goal or end in mind, and tailor your actions and their immediate objectives around this goal.

Is Stoicism a worldview in our sense? That's a very good question. Not all worldviews can be shoehorned into our streamlined model in Chapter 3. Some will be half-articulated, because those immersed in them are not intellectuals writing treatises but followers of established paths organically integrated into their communities and their institutions, ultimately into the warp and woof of people's lives. The kind of precision analytic philosophers prefer may be sacrificed if our primary concern is *living*, not *intellectualizing*. Philosophers should be concerned with *both*, and how they integrate.

Surely philosophy should be concerned with what is *true*, and whether claims to truth can be *validated*. This isn't always immediately possible, in a world where the Internet brings to our attention conflicting claims about events well outside our immediate surroundings. We need to learn to live with that, especially where conflicting political ideologies are producing quite different accounts of some event or state of affairs. Much more extreme is validating in any *final* way how life might have originated, unless someone invents a time machine. From the standpoint of living, *we don't need those specifics*. What we need most is a sense that *our lives matter*, that we are each important—special—this being integrated seamlessly into communities, so our institutions and technologies serve us instead of us serving them.

From this it should be clear why Stoicism is of interest today. It is conscious of our sometimes-acute pain points or sources of anxiety, and it suggests strategies of relief. It offers ideas for helping us take charge of our lives to the extent this is possible. It may well have a sound approach to living in a disrupted world filled with uncertainties. It reminds us of how little personal control we have in the kinds of civilizations we have collectively built, and offers advice on how to navigate and perhaps even learn how to thrive and be happy in this environment.

Practiced Stoics know they are not the center of the world. None of us has any special claim on the attention of others, wherever and whoever we are—unless, perhaps, we are delivering, e.g., a philosophy lecture in some official capacity such as a classroom, of course. Even there, none of us can influence others' beliefs, attitudes, or even prejudices, against their will. One can legitimately attempt to change opinions with arguments or stories with illustrations or even rhetoric, but at the end of the day, if the other person refuses to be moved, there is nothing one can do except bid the person farewell and wish them well. Anger tends to be counterproductive and invites retaliatory responses. Some must learn this the hard way. One wishes every so-called social justice warrior would realize it—and also every alt-rightist.

The Stoics stressed self-control for disciplined living, to be at peace with oneself as well as with others and with the world generally. Within the world there may seem to be little we can control, but conceivably within that *little* may actually be *a great deal* if we choose to be mindful of it. We are talking here about a potentially good path to personal resilience and anti-fragility in Taleb's sense.

What is interesting is that Marcus Aurelius wrote his best known work for an audience of one. It probably never occurred to him that the private notes that became *Meditations* would one day be recognized as a philosophical classic. He held the most powerful position in the world at the time, but underwriting his efforts was an awareness that is exceedingly rare in the powerful: with enormous power comes enormous responsibility, including seeing things and people as they are, as opposed to how we wish they were. Marcus was all-too-aware, moreover, of his own temptations and frailties.

Thus his efforts to improve himself and his dealings with others. He understood the value of writing things down. What you write down clearly, you understand (or at least understand better). Can you then implement, put into practice, what you're written down? Marcus had learned the importance of *gratitude*. His tract begins accordingly, by thanking those who influenced him, whether by example or as warnings of what *not* to do. None of us begin our lives and educations in a vacuum. Most of us had a parent or parents, teachers, role models, mentors, whose thoughts and actions shape us—whether for better or for worse. We should be grateful for the successful habits both large and small of our elders and mentors; for institutions whatever their failings (because the majority of those in them—even in public education!—mean well), for customs and traditions that did not become what they are for no reason at all. The Cartesian illusion is that we are free to tear everything down at will, start over from scratch, and expect to have a functional society in the future.

Stoicism opens doors into the lives of many nonphilosophers who demonstrate the value of philosophy in the troubled Secular City, and in the world generally. US Navy Vice Admiral James Stockdale, prisoner-of-war in Vietnam for over seven years, who was tortured by the Viet Cong, and had no idea if he would ever live to see his native soil again, drew comfort from his having studied the writings of Epictetus in particular.[4]

Stoicism is clearly a good potential vehicle for finding a wider audience for philosophy *prior to* carrying out worldview analyses and criticisms. The latter may be our highest priority in the long run. But we have to get people in the door; otherwise anything we say about materialism will fall not so much

---

4. Stockdale, *Courage Under Fire*.

on deaf ears but walls of empty rooms (or their online equivalent). If no one is there to hear it, does philosophy make a sound?

Are there advocates/practitioners of Stoicism today? Yes. A large and growing literature, both popular and scholarly, has recently emerged. Author and one-time media strategist Ryan Holiday has written books like *The Obstacle Is the Way*, which gathers thoughts on taking action, living life, and doing well in this world; and collected the thoughts of famous Stoic writers and compiled *The Daily Stoic*.[5] One of Holiday's heroes is—surprise, surprise—Marcus Aurelius. Holiday correctly pinpoints Marcus's preoccupations with questions like, How can I be a better leader? Marcus invites us to ask: how can I deal with the obstacles I face? How can I find in them opportunities? How can I find greater peace in my life? And so on. These are not academic questions, obviously. They call on mental self-discipline to work effectively with others and achieve goals. The Stoics have many things to teach us today, as Holiday realized. He has an organized group of latter-day Stoics around his and other websites offering courses on Stoicism for self-improvement purposes.

Others have investigated and become nonacademic promoters of Stoicism. Donald Robertson recently published *How To Think Like a Roman Emperor: the Stoic Philosophy of Marcus Aurelius* (2019) which draws on his experiences as a cognitive psychotherapist applying Stoic principles in his psychological and psychiatric practice.[6] His online organization, Modern Stoicism, is devoted to bringing together practitioners from this and related professions to increase life satisfaction.

Such authors, and others besides, offer evidence of the willingness of at least some in the Secular City to engage with an important philosophy.[7] The world that gave Stoicism birth over two thousand years ago was tumultuous and dangerous. Ours is tumultuous and has its dangers even if the dangers are different. All ages probably seem tumultuous and dangerous to those living in them. Whether ours is truly an exception remains to be seen—but as I've tried to argue, our civilization appears to be at a crossroad, and what we do over the next decade or so could well determine our fate as a species.

Stoicism would have us focus on ourselves and contend, with reason, that building a better civilization begins at home, by using the tools we have at our disposal to work to improve ourselves. None of us can change the

---

5. Holiday, *Obstacle Is the Way*; Holiday and Hanselman, *Daily Stoic*; Holiday *Stillness Is the Key*.

6. Robertson, *How To Think Like a Roman Emperor*.

7. See also Van Natta, *Beginner's Guide to Stoicism*; for a treatment from a professional philosopher see Pigliucci, *How To Be a Stoic*.

past, or our personal pasts, not the circumstances in which we were born, whatever abuse we suffered, nor the opportunities we missed—or privileges we did or did not have. All we can do is redirect our *present* thoughts. Only *these*, the Stoic urges, can be controlled. We can assume ownership of where we are, consider where we want to be in x number of years (or months), and work out a conversation with others about what we can and should change in the present to get there. This conversation should be open to all who are well-intentioned and wish to participate. We can then develop a rational strategy, i.e., a strategy that recognizes cause and effect, that human beings respond to incentives, and so on.

The difference between what we can and cannot change is not an absolute dichotomy, but a fluid and shifting continuum. This is because our knowledge is always changing, growing, allowing us to increase the range of what we can influence. In Third and Fourth Stage civilizations, the more money you have, the more things and people you can influence—which frustrates most intellectuals, because (with very rare exceptions) they tend not to have much money. But again this falls into the range of things none of us can change—at least not immediately. Our best option is to use what tools we have to advocate what I characterize as civilization's Fifth Stage, to be envisioned out of the failures of the Third and Fourth.

What we cannot do is allow ourselves to sink into abject pessimism. There is no time for that. The influence of Stoicism is small—the equivalent of drops of water in a big ocean. In that larger ocean, the vacuum of philosophically grounded ideas persists because of what has been forgotten. There is no Marcus Aurelius in today's Secular City, or even in its Secular University. The intellectual leadership vacuum in the latter opened the door to destructive movements like identity politics. In the former, it permitted neoliberal hypercapitalism and its dangerous financial instruments to get out of control. It enabled Donald Trump to be elected president of the United States, as much from the frustration of his supporters as anything else, because he was perceived by them as an outsider in an environment where the insiders were seen as a corrupt "swamp" needing "drained." Trump's election might have seemed the ultimate political "black swan" event, but leadership in both mainstream politics and culture had collapsed. Trump, a disruptor, won the White House because absent any credible vision or viable and constructive plan for the future from the insiders in his own party, we had reached the point where immense media savvy and the ability to sway increasingly angered crowds is sufficient to win a critical mass of support.

But political-economic considerations aside, many are clamoring for something to fill the philosophical, psychological, and spiritual vacuums in their lives, even if they have trouble articulating what they seek.

Philosophers, Stoic or otherwise, with a sense of perspective can and should step up! We have the training! The technology has never been better! We can justify stepping up by announcing that *we are just doing our job!* Hopefully this section has illuminated what may have previously been overlooked: much good can be done just in activities aimed at "getting people in the door" such as highlighting what Stoicism brings to the table.

Beginning the Philosophy of the Future: Deep Stages-of-Civilization Analysis

Having taken matters into their own hands and gone in search of their audience, philosophers need to be motivated by, and motivate that audience toward, a compelling vision for the future—not just for their personal futures or the future of their discipline, but for the future of civilization itself. They must then outline a path towards civilization's next Stage, even if any vision of such is bound to be incomplete.

This *second* proposal in this Chapter therefore begins with what I will call *deep Stages-of-civilization analysis*. We have done this, by identifying, with Comte, the Stages civilization has gone through over the past three centuries, each characterized by fairly specific political economies, cultures, and worldviews—some theistic, some not. Comte simply did not specify enough Stages. In the mid-1800s, he was in no position to do so. We are.

We've concentrated the bulk of our effort on what past and present Stages got *wrong*. Maybe we should spend a little time on what they got *right*. Can we mine past Stages for valuable insights? I think we can. For reasons that should become clear shortly, we will walk back through them in reverse order.

Purveyors of *Fourth* Stage postmodernism were sometimes *right*, for example, to look at *claims* to truth and see institutional domination driven by authority structures (or dominant personalities) relying on propagandistic language and what Marxists called false consciousness. This is because absent philosophically (logically) grounded clarity, narratives spun by authorities and supported by authoritarian gestures based on a few choice words or phrases can easily be made to pass for truth. Critics can be denounced as deluded or evil instead of engaged with. They can be censored or "canceled." Institutions trusted to dispense truth instead of questionable narratives or "fake news" can protect official narratives. I am sure we can all think of examples. When this happens, institutions become *de facto barriers* to the discovery and dissemination of truth. Authoritarians of whatever stripe surround their narratives with invective, censorship, and "cancelation" because open discussion, especially of first premises, exposes them, as well as helps us see what the truth really is or might be. Had postmodernists figured this out, they might not have felt the need to "cancel" truth itself as a useless concept.

For left to itself, the postmodernist component of Fourth Stage thinking which includes identity politics, engenders only cynicism, despair, and division. When it cannot deliver on its promises, whatever they are, its rank and file grow angry. Their writings testify to this abundantly, as do their actions on the streets of cities. Witness the explosive anger of "woke" culture into which identity politics has evolved, paving the way for its own Orwellian Ministry of Truth as it tears down statues and monuments to the past, anything its rank and file has been trained to find "offensive" whether they know anything about it or not.

In other words, while the Fourth Stage drew attention to a few things worth noting, it is no guide for the future.

A Fifth Stage of civilization will recognize the value of truth—and perhaps how hard it is to come by outside of immediacy. It will accept the need for epistemic humility.

What of the *Third* Stage, about which we have also said a great deal, much of it negative? Third Stage thinkers from the Enlightenment forward were by and large *right* to put aside their predecessors' obsession with epistemic certainty. Science, of course, never developed from *a priori*, apodictically certain first premises (although as we've seen, it has been unable to avoid dogma completely). It was, as in their different ways the historicists (Kuhn, Feyerabend) pointed out, far "messier" as any largely organic development is bound to be when contrasted with the streamlined demands of Cartesian perfectionism. The sciences often found themselves needing to revisit their paradigmatic, *working* first premises and find new ones when existing ones proved inadequate. They did this *successfully*, working *piecemeal*, in ways that varied from case to case, and their successes surely indicated a serious defect in modern philosophy still caught up in Second Stage thought (also those aspects of Third Stage thought that covertly call for epistemic perfection through logical closure).

The *successes* science, technology, and commerce have enjoyed doubtless reflect *real discoveries* about how the world's systems work, both natural and manmade. Third Stage thinkers, including philosophers, think this lends unique support to the Grandiose Assumption, however, and not to the Feyerabendian realization that multiple methodologies (and even metaphysical systems) may be necessary for addressing diverse problem sets. Commitment to a single worldview might be holding scientific (or other) communities *back*. Third Stage thinkers now refuse to countenance comprehensive criticisms of materialism, or proposals of comprehensive alternatives to it, as legitimate. This proves to be their undoing. But realism about *the concrete discoveries themselves* survives this objection as much as it survives postmodernist denials of truth and objectivity.

A Fifth Stage of civilization will recognize that worldviews, tacit and explicit, are ways human communities have always striven to bring order into their surroundings and lives, that these vary from place to place and time to time—and that a given worldview that is effective in one situation might fail in another, because circumstances change. What seems utterly alien in one community might be treasured in another, moreover. So a Fifth Stage of civilization will embrace and encourage plurality when we look at civilization from a global perspective. Again: none of us is at the center of the universe!

What survives from Second Stage thought? *Systematicity*, to which we have been appealing all along, as it is capable of supplying a bridge across the best of Second, Third, and (possibly) Fourth Stage thinking via systems theory *"the first principle of all things is system."* The clichéd version of this notion is that the whole is always more than the sum of its parts. Relationships between parts emerge that are not properties of any of the parts either singularly or together, and could not have been predicted in advance. What we see when we look deeply into systems are both hierarchical and multilateral arrangements of component subsystems working together both horizontally and vertically as an integrated package to achieve a common goal or outcome, or to solve a problem. It is the job of systems theory to study how this happens, and come up with ways of applying systems thinking in the world.

What we know is that systems exist in an *environment* which always presents them with challenges (problems), some potentially disruptive. They both affect and are affected by their surroundings (or *proximate* environment) which include surrounding systems which are potentially collaborative. Systems must parry or absorb and neutralize potential sources of disruption, and may collaborate with other systems in doing so. Some of these collaborations turn into supersystems. Governments, businesses, and other human organizations are all supersystems formed by human persons or smaller systemic groups.

Healthy systems are healthy because they have learned to resist or neutralize a wide range of possible disruptions through absorbing or parrying the source or possibly modifying themselves (adapting) to embrace it. They learn from experience, including the experiences of other systems. They can strengthen themselves and learn to anticipate, or how to prevent, an ever-widening range of pressures and challenges from their proximate and eventually their remote environment. They become less and less fragile—more and more "anti-fragile." Their goal has sometimes been described with the term *wellness*, in which there is not just freedom from sickness but the strength of *resilience*, a spirit desirous of *constant improvement*, and in the improvement of the system's *environment*, maybe as a means to the system's own improvement or perhaps as a benevolent end in itself for all the surrounding systems willing and able to be influenced. Systems theory/thinking represents the best that remains of the Second Stage mind.[8]

Systems theory is Second Stage because it begins with a foundational postulate—the ubiquity of *systematicity*—and deduces a comprehensive way of looking at the world that matches a great deal of reality, both as experienced and beyond our experience: organic; mechanical; molecular, atomic, and subatomic; organizational; theoretical and conceptual; theological (perhaps); artistic; and perhaps more. It suggests a different and healthier road into science, technology, and commerce than came about through the Cartesian-derived substance metaphysics that led to a mysterious, nonempirical *material substance* and from there to materialism. This road will preserve what is best in the existing sciences while avoiding drawbacks that resulted from trying to reduce all systems to something they are not: "material" entities undergoing "material" processes. We now see this to be superfluous and unnecessary, no more helpful than saying "God did it." Systems thinking urges us to take systems on their own terms metaphysically, epistemologically, methodologically, and ethically. *System* and *environment* are metaphysical givens; the former and the latter are symbiotic. Hence for a thinking system (e.g., a person) to doubt the existence of something outside its borders is absurd. Instead of generalized (Cartesian) methodical skepticism that can lead, at best, to a consensus about what "works" and at worst to complete mental paralysis, systems theory (like Peircean pragmatism) recommends doubt when we have a positive reason for it: because we have observed an inexplicable and ineliminable anomaly relative to our favored theory, encountered an unexpected source of disruption which might include doubts about the motivations operating in an institution, or hit some other deep roadblock that compels us to rethink our premises or reasoning.

A Fifth Stage of civilization will not eschew the idea of having an epistemically solid and stable starting point for its inquiries, and will see this starting point as able to integrate philosophy, science, technology, health, and life.

---

8. For further development of the ideas in this and the preceding paragraph see Ureda and Yates, "Systems View of Health Promotion," 5–38. Cf. again Taleb, *Anti-Fragile*.

Christian versus Materialist Worldviews—Revisiting the Conflict, Drawing Out the Main Implication: Plurality

Such are the contributions of the Fourth, Third, and Second Stages to the outlook in the making. What of the First Stage? By contrast it seems (by most present-day "standards" anyway) the most primitive. It is easy to dismiss the First Stage as a repository of mindless dogma, backwardness, and a haven for potential theocrats. Does it have anything at its core we ought to preserve because we've learned from it? I think so. It has something we can draw on today and tomorrow: given the realization that at the core of any worldview is a metaphysics, a theory of the way the world is at its most fundamental level, and that this by its nature goes beyond what can be tested empirically or proven by logic alone, conscious commitment to a worldview is invariably an *act of faith: committed belief in the absence of decisive evidence or logical proof.* For most people, the commitment may be habitual, of course. For the thoughtful among them, it may be seen as a reflective act of *trust* in where one stands and what one sees as functional in one's place, time, and culture. One makes a commitment that is more than merely provisional and is not to be changed on a whim.

The Christian worldview is based on faith in this sense. The Christian implicitly trusts in God's existence, perfect goodness, and ultimate benevolence, that he created the world and is sovereign over his creation, and has revealed himself to humanity. The Christian need not be bothered over disagreements of detail and specifics, since these exist in every worldview, materialism included. And even if numerous Christian philosophers and theologians have formulated "proofs" of God's existence that failed, the Christian need not be alarmed by this. Such (Second Stage) proofs, she might reply, are misguided since they place more trust in human reasoning based on an abstract *Logos* than they do in God's revelation to humanity. God is ontologically and epistemologically prior to *Logos* which, at best, is part of his essence. "In the beginning God created the heaven and the earth" (Gen 1:1) is presented as a statement to be accepted, not as the conclusion of an argument proven via formal rules of a *Logos* seen as standing apart from God. This is truer of, "In the beginning was the Word, and the Word was with God, and the Word was God" (John 1:1). The word translated from the original Greek as *Word* is *Logos*. Does this answer every question one might ask? Of course not! The Christian worldview does not set out to do that. It does not promise a world free of evil and suffering because—referring to our outline in Chapter 3—mankind fell into sin, to which Christians are as prone as non-Christians. The answer to the traditional "problem of evil and suffering" is that God has a reason for every instance of evil and suffering he permits; and his reasons are based on a comprehensive "God's eye point of view" that our finite nature, even absent sin, is in no position to see. One hears God asking Job, "Where were you when I laid the foundations of the Earth? Tell Me if you have understanding" (Job 38:4).

All this leaves materialists shaking their heads. They've accepted a mostly different set of first premises. But their worldview is also based on faith, denials notwithstanding. The materialist trusts fully that nature is orderly and not chaotic or subject to abrupt, inexplicable discontinuities, and that human reasoning based on speculation and supportive analogies from laboratory findings is therefore sufficient. It can make credible the *prior* proposition that life came from nonlife through natural processes, that conscious self-awareness is in the last analysis a brain (material) process, and that no transcendent reality or sense of such is necessary for a moral view of the world. No one has ever "seen God," the materialist will insist (with a gesture, perhaps, to indicate the statement's presumed obviousness); or to put the matter more clinically, the "God hypothesis" suggests no testable consequences. The materialist thus has no need of that hypothesis.

There have been many gods, moreover, worshipped by many peoples in many different places. Whose god is real, and why should we "privilege" the god of a single ancient tribe (the Hebrews) on the word of a single holy book? Granted: the God of the Old and New Testaments was/is unseen, and seems a bit exclusive for today's "woke" mindset of "inclusivity" (which includes all except for white male Christians—almost as if women could not be authentically Christian, or other ethnicities could not authentically embrace a Christian worldview).

The development of life from nonlife was also unseen. There are no empirical tests for its most basic claims. The materialist contends that his laboratory results offer supporting evidence for abiogenesis by that "proof of concept" analogy. Critics of abiogenesis "just don't understand the science!" says the materialist (often with visible irritation). The bottom line just *is*, however, that no scientist has ever *observed* life to originate from nonlife, or produced hard evidence that it can happen, even in a laboratory.

And even if he observed it happen in a laboratory of sufficient advance and sophistication under controlled conditions, the most this would prove is that *life can be intelligently designed if all the necessary and sufficient controlling conditions are there.*

We also do not see, hear, touch, taste, or smell, a mysterious substance, *matter* (as Hume observed almost three hundred years ago; he used the term *body*). What do we see, hear, touch, taste, and smell? Objects, other persons, animals, plants, spoken and written language, pictures, musical performances and recordings, other events: *systems* of various sorts, often interacting, *instances* of things we can categorize *mentally* however we understand this (and neither need we postulate a *mental substance* as Hume also argued). Where, in any of this, is *matter*, or the material *substance* implied in materialism, to which all phenomena including those of consciousness are ultimately reducible or explicable?

Why have we any need of *that* hypothesis?

Bishop Berkeley asked a similar question before Hume, and the supposed refutation by Samuel Johnson was to kick a stone and declare, "I refute [him] thus." I sincerely hope no one who has read this far thinks such a refutation of "immaterialism" (or antimaterialism) is intellectually serious!

The point is, the fundamental postulates of both worldviews are in the last analysis based on *faith* as we defined it above: epistemic confidence or trust in the absence of empirical evidence or proof. Advocates of both worldviews can point to their favorite's presumed strengths and ignore or downplay its weaknesses. Critics of one or the other can emphasize the latter in the worldview they reject. Neither worldview can be made compelling or even credible to those who refuse to grant the first premises or "step into the circle" that leads to confidence and trust. But each is deeply meaningful to those immersed in them.

Materialists will reply that they can point to *observations* of, e.g., an extensive fossil record, an undeniable discovery of the past three hundred or so years of geology, revealing worlds before our own in which the dominant forms of biological life were very different from those of today. They can (not unreasonably, from within their "circle") claim that this supports the idea of a long and unbroken (hundreds of millions of years!) process of evolution unguided by anything other than natural selection working within the constantly changing ecosystems. They can map out the Milky Way Galaxy, point to our sun, and deny that it—and, therefore, Earth—occupy any special or significant place, especially as there appear to be billions of galaxies of all shapes and sizes, each with millions of stars, and of our having discovered, so far, over four thousand exoplanets, a few with oceans, oxygen-rich atmospheres, and temperature ranges capable of sustaining life as we know it. Again there is the extrapolation: planets are rather common phenomena, and there are probably trillions of them in the universe. The improbable (life coming into be from nonlife) becomes the inevitable, not just here but elsewhere in the universe: probably countless times!

This is still interpretative and extrapolatory. We have, in the last analysis, no means of determining what is going on with, e.g., star KIC 8462852, which at fourteen hundred light years away is in our galactic neighborhood relatively speaking. The further away we get from Earth, the greater the extrapolation and the greater the chance that our projections will be wrong.

Yes, there could be vast civilizations out there. But the bottom line is, we have no *observations* that such civilizations exist, even with our greatly improved sense of what we are looking for in examining stars and exoplanets.

The Apostles who began the first Christian congregations claimed to have *directly observed* the resurrected Jesus Christ (seeing and even touching the holes still in his hands or possibly wrists from the crucifixion). The Book of Acts records how He spoke to them and gave them their mission, which was to spread the gospel (from two Greek words meaning *good news*) to the world. This transformed their lives. They were literally not the same people. Instead of living for themselves and for the world, they lived for their Lord and Savior, to spread His unique message of salvation and hope.

Miraculous transforming events continued. Acts also records how the ascended Jesus supernaturally appeared to the man named Saul, on the road to Damascus. Saul had built a reputation persecuting Christians without mercy. At that encounter, during which he was asked, "Why do you persecute Me?!" Saul became Paul, a Christian called by Christ himself, who founded Christian congregations all across Greece and in Rome during the first century AD, going on to pen a substantial fraction of the documents that comprise our New Testament.

None of this makes sense to the materialist. It simply *can't* be true. The materialist must explain away what early Christians claim to have seen. Maybe they had ingested mind-altering chemicals. Or maybe the documents themselves are fakes. Maybe Jesus never existed, and later church figures made up all these stories (Jesus surely didn't have that exact name!). The records are spotty (although manuscripts of the four biblical Gospels have been found dating to within the lifetimes of the first Christians, something which cannot be said for the oldest known manuscripts of the writings of, say, Plato or Aristotle).

The materialist might follow Hume, for whom miracles are by their nature unique events that violate observed regularities of nature which form the basis for the habits of thought we confidently rely on. Materialists who came later were able to dismiss accounts of miraculous transformations as superstitions or hallucinations.

But how *does* the materialist explain the *power* of the narratives of the early Christians? How does he explain the thousands that were tortured and then went willingly to brutal deaths for their faith, eventually including the apostle Paul? *Crucifixion*, by the way—the tying or nailing of a person to a wooden cross and leaving him exposed to the elements for a lingering death that could take days—was one of the most brutal forms of execution ever devised by the hands of those Christians call sinful men.

The Christian worldview's historical power continued nevertheless, as the new faith survived just short of three centuries of persecution at the hands of sometimes sadistic Roman emperors. Then Constantine converted, and the Christianizing of Rome began with the convening of the Council of Nicaea and other events. So was Christian doctrine established. Did it reflect the actual teachings of the historical Jesus? Some, invariably operating from naturalist premises, doubt that it possibly could. Christians contend that it is the living Jesus operating through the Holy Spirit (the third Person of the Trinity), the same Jesus who supernaturally saved them, and who lives and supernaturally saves people today, who maintained and furthered the Christian worldview through the Council of Nicaea and beyond, sustaining the Christendom that came down to us as core postulates of the Western outlook. These built the greatest civilization ever achieved, whatever mistakes were made by Christian institutions and the political systems the West brought about.

Millions of Christians claim to feel the presence and power of God in their lives. Millions, worldwide, continue to suffer and sometimes go to torturous deaths, a trend that continued down to the Third Stage era's confrontations between Christians and Communists in the officially atheistic Soviet Union, and those between Christians and radical Muslim groups such as ISIS today. Christians have successfully sustained a real and living faith in regimes such as Communist China, despite the brutality of Chinese prisons. Christians continue to trust in God's Providence as their ultimate Protector, and therefore that their sufferings in this world are ultimately ephemeral however brutal, and will one day be recompensed. We inhabit a fallen world turned hostile to everything the Christian worldview stands for. Because of original sin, moreover, we cannot save ourselves. Christianity is the *only* faith that denies the existence of any path to salvation of human origin. Jesus Christ provides the one path to salvation, and to an eternity with God. We should not be overly attached to this world, therefore, or the things in it, or the surrogates for God the world worships (*Logos*, Science, Power, Mammon). The Christian's hope is not in this world but in the world to come.

To materialists, again this is just nonsense. What do they hope for? Restoring unending progress, whatever stumbles and falls we've endured as a species. Accepting that although life ends in physical death, the extinction of one's personal consciousness, one can leave a legacy in a world that will go on. Is this convincing even to them, however? Again, the literature we've reviewed suggests doubts going back at least to Dostoevsky. Suppose the surrogate for God is Mammon, criticized specifically in the Gospels. When one has amassed more wealth than can be spent in one lifetime, then what?

The pleasure of living better than the royalty of past eras? That seems not to have sufficed. Power to redesign the faults and foibles out of a civilization based on freely acting persons?! There remain those, whom I have referred to obliquely throughout this work, who believe themselves most fit to rule: plutocratic superelites, whose existence others dismiss as "conspiracy theories" although their own writings testify abundantly to their existence, as well as a belief in their ability to institute technocratic controls in the name of "social justice," "sustainability," "the planet," and so on. Are they, as some suspect, presently exercising their collective will not militarily, as did governments in the past, but through health scares such as the present pandemic, and through whatever forms of systemic coercion this makes possible? Will their efforts succeed, or will they result only in destruction and misery. If accompanied by the apostles of "woke," will they operate in the wake of the "canceling" of all that made genuine wealth and prosperity in Third Stage civilization possible?

To the Christian, surrogates for God are seen not to work. All they accomplish is elevating one group into power at the expense of others. They sacrifice lives wantonly, often by expediently writing them out of the moral community, because they have no sense of persons' intrinsic value. This may have been the Jews under Hitler, those who resisted collective farming under Stalin, or the unborn in our abortion-friendly culture. Will it soon include the infirm, or dementia patients, perhaps, who can be euthanized? Today's rhetorical questions may become tomorrow's realities, as the logic of a world absent persons' intrinsic value plays out.

More than one person, immersed in a materialist outlook and only partly realizing it, moreover, will decide that life contains more pain than pleasure, more suffering than joy, more tragedy than treasure, more hate or indifference than love and caring, and their desire to escape takes over. There may be more immediate catalyzing factors involved, such as a crippling financial calamity, or the death of a spouse or child, or perhaps some other loss that deprives the person of all sense of identity or source of happiness. The person takes his/her own life. Suicide rates have increased among aging rural white populations, as everyone knows, along with drug overdoses, some of which may well be deliberate. Sensitive teenagers suffering severe bullying in our often brutalist social media culture, moreover, have occasionally seen suicide as the only way out. In the absence of any moral center or grounding anchor outside their own sometimes horrid lives they answer Camus's question in the negative.

Today Christianity is the most persecuted faith in the world. Think especially of the Middle East and Africa, as well as Communist China and North Korea where families disappear into labor camps because one member was overheard to say something favorable about God or Jesus Christ. In all these places, Christians have been imprisoned and tortured. They triumph nevertheless, and Christianity remains the fastest growing faith in Communist China. It is the fastest growing faith in the world outside the Third Stage/Fourth Stage West, where hostility (or indifference) to the Christian worldview has grown. Christians' hope makes them survivors with a sense of joy in their lives despite brutal treatment which is, after all, what the apostle Paul and his immediate disciples sometimes suffered, recorded in places like Acts 16 and his letter to the Philippians.[9]

Be all this as it may, an important bottom line here is that neither is going to convince the other with arguments and evidence. I'm under no illusions that materialists are going to give up their materialism because of my demonstrations that they've failed to make their case that life came from nonlife. Nor will Christians give up Christianity because of the Richard Dawkins's of the world, for whom evolution is at the center of their particular faith. There are, of course, other worldviews just in the West. Muslims are a growing population whom, perhaps, we should refrain from judging as a whole because of radical groups such as ISIS. There are around 1.8 billion Muslims in the world. Most are peaceful, and want the same things the rest of us want: loving relationships that bring joy, meaningful and creative work or activity, and something to hope for. Christians and materialists both want these same things, of course.

Given that none of these will vanquish the others by legitimate means (I am assuming that everyone will agree that war and extermination are not legitimate ways of accomplishing anything.), the answer is *peaceful plurality* which acknowledges others' right to their worldview and to organize their communities in ways that advance and achieve the above goals, providing they are not interfering with those who believe differently. This follows from recognizing the intrinsic value of the persons in these communities, even if some of them don't initially (or ever) see this.

The Christian worldview may be marginal in Secular City culture, and even more so in the Secular University, but under conditions of plurality in both academic and nonacademic forms of life, I have little trouble envisioning it making a comeback. This could happen as Fifth Stage communities organize and reject materialism in the wake of its manifest failures in a world growing less and less free, less and less compassionate, more and more controlled, less and less healthy, and less and less stable.

---

9. For an astounding example of someone who had no doubt whatsoever of the truth of the Christian worldview see Yun and Hattaway, *Heavenly Man*. I am grateful to Rev. Samuel A. Mateer for bringing Brother Yun's story to my attention.

Materialists may cry foul about Christians' "pseudoscience" as they lose ground, as is their right (including to weaponize the language). This is not the problem. Their insistence on monopolizing the intellectual conversation is the problem. Philosophers can take this conversation in a new direction, towards the intrinsic value of persons and plurality of communities. We have the skills. Technology supplies us with an abundance of platforms and possibilities. If readers, viewers, listeners, are persuaded of benefits to be had, that real problems are being addressed on their own terms, and a vision for the future is being furthered, they will read and hear.

Now what is this vision of which we speak? To this we now turn.

A Fifth Stage of Civilization?

And so we find ourselves, as actual free thinking, independence-minded philosophers, nearing the end of this adventure in ideas. We should be ready to envision the next Stage of Western civilization. We've called it the Fifth Stage of civilization, spoken of Fifth Stage thinking, and begun working toward Fifth Stage political economy, culture, and society.

Time for some specifics.

First, Fifth Stage thinking will draw on the realization that for the first time ever we are positioned to advance consciously to a new Stage of civilization, using what we've learned from the past. We can draw on the strengths of past Stages while avoiding their weaknesses. It will not be possible to imagine this Fifth Stage fully—any more than Voltaire or Hume or Comte could have properly imagined the Third Stage, or Kierkegaard or Dostoevsky or Nietzsche could have fully envisioned the Fourth Stage despite powerfully prophetic suggestions. We should avoid thinking in Utopian terms, for reasons that should be clear. But we can make some hopefully useful projections about what a Fifth Stage thinker might value, and how he or she might proceed to try and build a future that is better than the recent past and present.

A Fifth Stage thinker will value truth and want to recover it—while acknowledging that many truths are very hard if not impossible to come by, given our present state of knowledge and technology, and human limitations themselves. Truths we *can* come by and may have to confront do not necessarily flatter our preconceptions, especially about ourselves. A Fifth Stage thinker will not be paralyzed by this if he sees *ethical* truths as more significant than *epistemic* ones.

The core ethical truth is one we've referred to several times already: *human lives—persons—have intrinsic value. Intrinsic* here means innate or inherent, not culturally-derived or pulled out of thin air by intellectuals' incantations. For Christians, intrinsic value will be seen as derived from having had a Creator, so they can say definitively, yes, *all lives matter*, and it is up to us to make it so, through actions and not mere words.

What are persons? They are unanalyzable (in the philosopher's sense) givens. *Persons* are *who we are*, in all our differences but also similarities, in all our richness as a combination of know-how and talents, all somewhat different, and *who we see and interact with daily*. We are not Cartesian "thinking things," the ancestral abstraction, "the individuals" in the Libertarian sense and the *homo economicus* of classical liberals and neoliberals. *Persons* cannot be compressed and siloed by inadvisable policy decisions into groups or collectives of "victims" which calls forth visions of "oppressor" groups (or one oppressor group). Fifth Stage thinking sweeps Hegel aside along with his identitarian stepchildren no less than it does Descartes and his stepchildren, hopefully for good reasons.

However much some attacked Trump's calls to "build a wall," can they truly justify their condemnation if they've spent four decades (not just four years) building political-cultural walls of their own?

So as we look to the future, *let us offer to build bridges instead of walls!* Let us build them on this idea that we *all* have intrinsic worth, that we *all* matter. This includes identifying and rejecting those things that only serve to divide us, even if they claim to be doing something else. It means escaping the mental cages of the distant and recent past, instead of continuing to dwell on them, and then fall prey to academic and media fabrications or be tempted by bad policy proposals (e.g., reparations for slavery, an institution that has not existed in the United States for 155 years as of this writing). Academic and media fabrications can turn out to be very marketable for their authors, but accomplish little otherwise except to worsen existing divides, leaving their ostensible targets alienated, frustrated, and unable to express their alienation and frustration without being condemned as racists![10]

From this intrinsic value of persons, *plurality* as described near the closing of the previous section follows. A Fifth Stage thinker might conclude that persons should be free to organize their lives within communities as they see fit. *First*, we are social beings. This is so obvious as to need little if anything in the way of further discussion. We thrive best in the company of others; even introverts who are energized by working in isolation bring their results to the community table. The hermit exists, but is a rare creature. *Second*, different groups do have different worldviews, and as we've seen,

10. For one recent example of this sort of thing see DiAngelo, *White Fragility*. DiAngelo has enriched herself selling her "anti-racist" programs and conducting "anti-racist" workshops in corporations, spreading the gospel of "woke" through the Secular City.

their starting points are postulates that are givens in philosophers' sense, not resulting from proofs or empirical tests. What do we do about differences? Historically, sadly, we've often seen them as threats and tried to wipe them out! In a global civilization there is no room for that any longer. The answer is to accept differences and learn from them where possible. Those unable to do so or who find differences threatening should be free to wall themselves off in their communities and suffer the resulting losses. For cross-cultural exchanges start from the premise that cultural differences exist and can be interesting, fruitful, and worth celebrating!

The vision of the world that results is that of a highly decentralized, loosely networked through technology, and hopefully mostly tolerant place where an abundance of forms of life can flourish without unwanted interference from outside. What of communities who seek to exclude members of certain ethnic or religious groups? The answer to this lies with asking ourselves to consider objectively, if we can do that, how much grief has been caused by forcing peoples to associate against their will. The freedom of association includes the freedom to not associate, and to have to deal with whatever losses ensue, be these economic or in terms of reputation.

What of those communities where the presumed (by us!) intrinsic value of their members is not recognized, because bullying will still occur? The desire for power on the part of a few will not have gone anywhere. There is a great danger of lapsing back into what brought down previous orders of society. Given technology, communicating our displeasure to the leaders of such communities will be straightforward. Then comes the hard part: responding not with *threats* but with *good examples*. With illustrations of the *benefits* of an intrinsic-value rooted ethic. With love and with service, where possible. And where possible, allowing the exit of those who wish to leave—since our universal provision, a check on the irresponsible wielding of power—is the assumed right of persons to leave a community that fails to suit them. This *right of personal or communal separation or secession* also follows from the intrinsic value of persons.

We've frequently mentioned technology and its effects throughout this work. As Fifth Stage thinkers we should note that science and technology are, themselves, ethically neutral tools that can be used to do good or harm. They can liberate or enslave. They can free us from "iron cages," or build more insidious ones as they advance in the hands of those who find technocracy tempting.

So let us advocate using science and technology to *create systems that yield abundance instead of maintaining systems based on a presumption of universal scarcity*, as has been the case for all of modern and recent history. This, I confess, is probably a radical suggestion. It may be the most radical idea in this book. It is intended to address the likely reality that technology will continue to render many jobs presently done by persons obsolete, and conceivably at an accelerating rate. This Fifth Stage thought, however, goes beyond such bromides as Universal Basic Income, suggested as a cure-all for technological unemployment. For among the consequences of a civilization based on the creation of abundance instead of maintaining systems based on scarcity is that the price of basic goods, produced by robots (clean water, food, housing, clothing, energy), *drops to zero or near-zero, rendering a money political economy obsolete.* Conversations about Universal Basic Income are also, therefore, rendered obsolete—especially as Universal Basic Income is probably not a workable solution to technological unemployment. Its continuous creation will devalue and destroy the value of currency dispensed (so-called Modern Monetary Theory notwithstanding), and if conditions are placed on its receipt, this will afford great power to those handing it out and place its recipients at a great disadvantage. The point is, advancing technology is a grave threat to many persons and communities. The Fifth Stage thinker asks if it is possible to turn advancing technology from a threat to an advantage. How? By proposing a means of liberating persons from the need to involuntarily "reinvent themselves" at an ever accelerating rate to fit a constantly changing and unpredictable job market. Need a population be compelled to seek a (dwindling) number of good-paying jobs, always with the threat of *human* obsolescence, indigence, and a fear of starvation hanging over their heads?

Will the Fifth Stage of civilization therefore not require people to work? What they will be freed from is the necessity of working for money to service basic needs (though obviously they can *choose* to do so). They will be free to pursue creative endeavors that could not be pursued as adjunct instructors or Geiko salespersons. Or to draw on the tremendous educational resources that exist online now (and contribute more). Persons should be encouraged to develop their personal superpowers and use them creatively. If they do not—or for those who do not—the Fifth Stage will seem to fail them. Undoubtedly there will be people who spend their days playing video games, and it may seem wrong, somehow, that such people can have clean water, fresh food, and a roof over their heads (the result, perhaps, of 3D printing) for nearly free. A workable Fifth Stage of civilization will require these kinds of compromises and a willingness to leave others alone even if we do not approve of their lifestyles or choices of activity. A wasted life according to our judgment may be a shame, but it is still the person's free choice we are obligated to respect.

Money and wealth will still be around, because many items (collectable art, for example) will still be scarce. I imagine yachts and mansions will continue to be expensive. Let us use money and wealth to do good where we can, being mindful of their limitations. What they will not be is objects of worship, or lifelong nooses around the necks of the have-nots. What we will have done is remove the incentive of profit as the center of political economy. Having given what Libertarians and other individualists much of what they say they want, with the intrinsic value of persons and community autonomy, this should give progressives what they say they want, which is to end neoliberal hyper-capitalism. This can happen only with energy that no longer results from extraction. We have been seeking a means of generating energy from renewable resources, and this needs to continue, drawing on and riding systems without disrupting them. Technologists have a great deal of work to do in this area; the pursuit of "green energy" is only a start in finding out how we can power a technological advanced civilization with natural systems that are perpetual instead of extractive. Do we wish to find sources of energy that are unlimited, or continue using one (oil) that will one day run out, whether we have passed Peak Oil or not?

Thinking about and then working toward a Fifth Stage of civilization is admittedly a tall and ambitious call, but we have no choice, I hold, except to think about how to make the attempt. For the alternative is to continue in our present direction. We will see the continued disappearance of all that most of us hold dear. Ongoing technological change, empowered by the profit motive and the Secular Mass wanting ever-faster bandwidth speeds for ever-faster downloads, the instant-gratification mindset, will further the development of a techno-neofeudal order. Already, most technology platforms are controlled by a tiny elite whose members have encouraged the attention economy. They are interested primarily in what they have, and how they can obtain more. Absent sustained thought about where we go from here, we can expect these trends to accelerate. Keep in mind that the primary beneficiaries of the pandemic of 2020 have been billionaires, and that the world has grown more dependent on technology that this elite owns and controls.

The Dangers of Technocracy and the Projected Great Reset

Let us consider this last in a bit more detail. Technology continues to advance by leaps and bounds, driven by incentives of greater convenience for the masses and profitability for those atop corporations. But culturally and educationally, recent decades have been downhill (denials notwithstanding). This slide has driven the paths consumerism has taken. Surely fewer and fewer people would reject observing that market-driven changes have taken us away from the kinds of ideals that sent men to the moon and returned them safely (late 1960s, early 1970s), through the increasing narcissism of the late 1970s and then the 1980s, and towards more recent decades that yielded "selfies" and the shrinking attention spans of the Twitterati.[11] Media saturation of our lives is now almost total. Distractions from that which is serious are ubiquitous. I mentioned the *attention economy* in which our ability to focus is challenged. This is very bad news if it prevents us from paying attention to things we had better *start* paying attention to.

It is hard not to return to one of the upshots of our critique: *with materialism money and power surely appear to get the last word.* This may not be the intent. I am not asserting, or implying, that billionaires are somehow evil by definition. But this is what happens in a Secular City immersed in the materialist worldview that is also committed to untethered profits, employs incentives, and uses ubiquitous images in the name of mass consumption. The twin lures of money and power have become wrecking balls not just against viable philosophy but against a viable common culture, needed to reach across differences and boundaries, and build respect for healthy plurality. I trust it is clear that materialism threatens far more than Christian premises, or the idea that "the mind" isn't just the brain. What materialism really works against in the Secular City, away from Secular University philosophy departments and their dusty debates over mind and body, is *anyone and anything that cannot be commodified.* Bad news sells! So media outlets are dominated by bad news! Horrific events sell! Hence we see horrific events twenty-four-seven! Differences and conflicts and crises are incited and exaggerated for public consumption and private profit. They are transformed into mass spectacles because they bring in advertising dollars.

This despite real people getting hurt or destroyed!

Truth is often unattractive (or simply unspectacular), and so does not sell. It thus becomes expendable, as the attention marketplace caters to fears, exaggerations, falsehoods, illusions, delusions, and short attention spans. This was part of how Third Stage thinking, which at least valued objectively knowable truth, began to be replaced by Fourth Stage thinking in which "objectively-knowable truth" is lost. Our amalgam of the two invariably "bewitches our intelligence" through media language and images of various sorts. It is owned and operated by a global plutocracy devoted to increasing its wealth and power, now wielding them against those it labels "populists," "anti-democracy" politicians, and "conspiracy theorists." This, I hold, is the

---

11. See, e.g., Lasch, *Culture of Narcissism*; Postman, *Amusing Ourselves To Death*; Hedges, *Empire of Illusion*.

real danger we face, that something far different and dystopian faces us in the near future if we do not think consciously and publicly about civilization's Fifth Stage without wasting time!

I refer to what some call the *Great Reset*, which may well be in motion by the time this reaches print!

First, can anyone object that we have entered a cultural environment that is resolutely hostile to the free and open expression of ideas? These are not the 1960s. This is the era of "woke," of "cancel culture." "Cancel culture" is Fourth Stage through and through, in that it does not care about truth. It cannot create anything, however. It can only tear down. Its denizens think in terms of power, seeing it in what they've torn down. They have no idea where the real power will come from, and that it won't come from them!

This is also the era of Big Tech censorship, as YouTube (owned by Google), Facebook, Twitter, etc., deplatform those they label "conspiracy theorists" and remove (or cover over) posts with tags like "False Information (independently fact-checked)." Those with the ability to do it because they command the resources to do it are more interested than ever before in controlling information. Election 2020 offered countless examples.

The danger is from top-down power coming from those presently hard at work designing their own "next stage of civilization," which they call the *Fourth Industrial Revolution*, a state of affairs in which, courtesy of technology, there will be no privacy as such, no property as such, and no freedoms in any traditional sense, including of basic mobility. Technology will definitely *not* be our servant if we are outside the point-zero-zero-one percent.

This is not a "conspiracy theory." It should hardly need saying that a projected plan is not a "conspiracy theory" when the planners *tell you openly and up front* what they are planning.[12] The primary architects of the projected Great Reset have done this. Their plans for the world are to be carried forth in the name of laudable-sounding goals such as sustainable development and addressing climate change, reducing poverty, promoting ethnic and gender diversity, and so on. What are the specifics? One of their key leaders tells us:

> Sooner than most anticipate, the work of professions as different as lawyers, financial analysts, doctors, journalists, accountants, insurance underwriters or librarians may be partly or completely automated.... The technology is progressing so fast that

---

12. Schwab, *Fourth Industrial Revolution*; Schwab et al., *Shaping the Fourth Industrial Revolution*; see also Schwab and Malleret, *Covid-19: The Great Reset*. See again Khanna, *Technocracy in America*.

> Kristian Hammond, cofounder of Narrative Science, a company specializing in automated narrative generation, forecasts that by the mid-2020s, 90% of news could be generated by an algorithm, most of it without any kind of human intervention (apart from the design of the algorithm, of course).[13]

This expresses the coming technological obsolescence of many persons which we've discussed. But there is far more going on here than just that. Consider, further,

> the unlimited possibilities of having billions of people connected by mobile devices, giving rise to unprecedented processing power, storage capabilities and knowledge access. Or think about the staggering confluence of emerging technology breakthroughs, covering wide-ranging fields such as artificial intelligence (AI), robotics, the internet of things (IoT), autonomous vehicles, 3D printing, nanotechnology, biotechnology, materials science, energy storage and quantum computing, to name a few. Many of these innovations are in their infancy, but they are already reaching an inflection point in their development as they build on and amplify each other in a fusion of technologies across the physical, digital and *biological* worlds.[14]

Note the final reference to the *biological* world. That's us. Klaus Schwab states openly that personal privacy will be sacrificed: "Establishing trust in the data and algorithms used to make decisions will be vital. Citizen concerns over privacy and establishing accountability in business and legal structures will require adjustments in thinking."[15] Readers should be wondering, accountability to *whom*? The answer: not so much to the controllers but to the top-down system itself. We will have to "adjust our thinking" about who we are, about what it means to be human, and it will soon be clear: there is no commitment to the intrinsic value of persons or to plurality in our sense to be found anywhere here. For "the tools of the Fourth Industrial Revolution enable new forms of surveillance and other means of control that run counter to healthy, open societies."[16]

This idea is not new. It predates the pandemic by years. Readers may infer from this what they will. The point is, important discussions about our future have been taking place behind closed doors. But every so often, the

---

13. Schwab, *Fourth Industrial Revolution*, p. 39.
14. Schwab, *Fourth Industrial Revolution*, italics mine, p. 7.
15. Schwab, *Fourth Industrial Revolution*, p. 133.
16. Schwab, *Fourth Industrial Revolution*, p. 90.

doors are opened and we peasants are afforded a glimpse of what has been going on behind them. For example (this dates from November, 2016):

> Welcome to the year 2030. Welcome to my city—or should I say, "our city." I don't own anything. I don't own a car. I don't own a house. . . . It made no sense for us to own cars anymore, because we could call a driverless vehicle . . . within minutes. . . . In our city we don't pay any rent, because someone else is using our free space whenever we do not need it. My living room is used for business meetings when I am not there. . . . Shopping? For most of us, it has been turned into choosing things to use. Sometimes I find this fun, and sometimes I just want the algorithm to do it for me. It knows my taste better than I do by now. . . . Once in a while I get annoyed about the fact that I have no real privacy. Nowhere can I go and not be registered. I know that, somewhere, everything I do, think and dream of is recorded. I just hope that nobody will use it against me. All in all, it is a good life. Much better than the path we were on. . . .[17]

There isn't space here to explore all the ramifications, which include predictions of brain scans at border crossings and "pre-crime" style detentions recalling the science fiction film *Minority Report* as technology reaches ever deeper into the human brain itself—note the materialist assumption there. Finally:

> Fourth Industrial Revolution technologies will not stop at becoming part of the physical world around us—they will become part of us. Indeed, some of us already feel that our smartphones have become an extension of ourselves. Today's external devices—from wearable computers to virtual reality headsets—will almost certainly become implantable in our bodies and brains. Exoskeletons and prosthetics will increase our physical power, while advances in neurotechnology enhance our cognitive abilities.
>
> We will become better able to manipulate our own genes, and those of our children. These developments raise profound questions: Where do we draw the line between human and machine? What does it mean to be human?[18]

---

17. Auken, *Forbes*, https://www.forbes.com/sites/worldeconomicforum/2016/11/10/shopping-i-cant-really-remember-what-that-is-or-how-differently-well-live-in-2030/?sh=2d80b39f1735.

18. Schwab and Davis, *Shaping the Future of the Fourth Industrial Revolution*, p. 41.

I imagine most readers believed that the idea of genetically engineered children and implants into the human brain or body was either the stuff of science fiction, or "conspiracy theory" paranoia. I hope this material dispels that notion, because here is someone with a great deal of influence seriously thinking about and promoting such ideas, sometimes labeled with the term *transhumanism*. Transhumanism begins with the idea that what it means to be human is fluid and subject to fundamental alteration, beyond, e.g., a prosthetic limb which is not "smart," i.e., connected to a computer. I recommend revisiting the opening section of Chapter 4 which preceded our excursions into the failures of secular ethical theories. While no one I know of is contemplating the creation of a human being from body parts somehow infused with life, we are clearly looking at a great potential of a real life Technology Gone Awry scenario if the World Economic Forum and that portion of the globe's billionaire class that supports such endeavors is able to further them unimpeded.

This is the future technocrats want.[19] This represents the top-down, technocratic approach to civilizational problem solving, the *opposite* of what is being proposed here. Perhaps the present pandemic will be used as the triggering crisis to impose technocracy on a reluctant world.[20] Perhaps it will be something we haven't seen yet. What will result is not "capitalism reimagined" but a form of technology-based feudalism in which persons are numbered like cattle and their every move, their every transaction, is monitored and recorded. Compliance may become a condition of living a normal life, including buying food.

Whatever label we pin on it, I hope it is clear: technocracy is not a path toward freedom based on persons' intrinsic value or communities organized according to the worldview and institutions of their choosing, It is not a *Fifth* Stage of civilization, but the potential culmination of the amalgamation of the *Third* and *Fourth* we are living in now, in which persons are, at best, chess pieces to be moved around on the global chessboard, and at worst, no different morally speaking from cattle.

What Philosophers Can Do for the Near Future?

Between the pandemic, the most fractious election in the U.S. since 1860, and abundant evidence of continued divisions that are actually global in scope, we are entering what will likely be an *über*-turbulent decade. Worldwide impoverishment due to draconian reactions to the pandemic;

19. Wood, *Technocracy Rising*.
20. Schwab and Malleret, *COVID-19: The Great Reset*.

inequality born of what are now two different "economies" (that of Wall Street and financial elites generally, versus that of the rest of the world's populations); fires and weather disturbances attributed to climate change; disruptive technologies often created for the benefit of said elites; will likely lead to still more political and economic instability around the world.

Add to this the corruption that is inevitable when power is not held accountable. The result, potentially, is a civilization living on borrowed time!

We cannot turn back the clock to a supposedly more tranquil age (that probably never existed). We can only go forward. If *progress* means anything at all in the wake of the Fourth Stage—if there is any sense to be made of the idea of *making things better*—the Fifth beckons those able and willing to articulate philosophical values, answer the call, and rise to the occasion.

Philosophy can play a major role in building a better future, if we are to have one. It can urge rejection of the Grandiose Assumption, that a scientific/rational outlook on the universe requires materialism, or a naturalist methodology. Philosophers can encourage respect for the importance of ideas, open discussion, and a tolerant appreciation for the fact that we will continue to differ over many fundamentals. Because of our genuine differences in background, experiences, etc., this is part of being human. Sometimes we are our own barriers to finding out what is true; and sometimes the world itself presents an insurmountable (for now) barrier. That, too, is part of the human condition.

Philosophers can then propose plurality as the proper course to keep us in tolerant conversation with one another, absent proof of our first premises, whatever our differences, respecting a right to *be* different as part of our recognition of persons' intrinsic value.

Obviously, not all who might be attracted to such ideas as these will be Christian. We can live with that. One may look to interfaith dialogue, no less than ecumenicism within Christianity. Such will be the keys to viable Fifth Stage conversation, partnerships, and alliances.

What is important to reject—and here we may be taking cues from what was healthiest in Libertarian and cognate philosophies—is thinking anything *good* can result from *forcing* people to believe, act, or live against their will. This includes the *de facto* force involved in disrupting their lives with, e.g., trade accords that benefit primarily those same elites. Philosophers should urge respect for persons' right to live, organize, and preserve their communities and institutions in ways reflective of what provides their lives with meaning and joy. This, too, follows from the intrinsic value of persons.

What sets this work apart will be this: from implementing the two proposals discussed here—taking their destiny into their own hands and then creating a compelling vision of the future—sustainability, inclusion, diversity, and so on, will be more than just words masking ideologies and virtue signaling. They will not be weapons concealing agendas of domination of which we have also had enough, thank you very much. We should seek unity where we can find it, but not on the terms currently available (agree with us or else!). If a global civilization is coming, or possibly already here, then the choice before us is whether it will be highly centralized with its wealth concentrated, its methods technocratic and based on controls; or whether we will choose decentralization, networking, and pluralism, with built-in checks on controls such as the right to *leave*. In other words, will persons be free or *de facto* slaves? Will the technology of the near future liberate us and make our lives genuinely *better*, or will it chain us further inside digital "iron cages"? Will peoples be pulled in against their will, or will they have usable opt-out provisions?

Or to ask this another way, will a Fifth Stage retaining the ambitious option of global civilization be global without being *globalist* as we presently understand that term? *Globalism* designates high centralization, concentrations of wealth and power, hierarchy, technocracy, and control, with the bulk of the benefits redistributed *upwards*: socialism for the rich and powerful, one might say; capitalism for the masses. Our goal, in this case, is global civilization based on peace, conversation, and cooperation, but not global*ism* based on systems of domination.

Are the proposals here workable, or absurdly ambitious?

There are no guarantees of anything.

We have little choice except to try, however.

A few final cautions are in order.

For reasons already noted, it is impossible to produce more than an outline of a Fifth Stage of civilization—something emerging as a kind of "afterlife" following the Fourth Stage descent into infirmity, decrepitude, and inevitable death. This might strike many as strange. Should the Christian worldview as we sketched it above make a comeback, consistency demands recognizing that whatever future we try to build, by its very premises we cannot free ourselves from our fundamental fallenness. We cannot use science, reason, technology, or markets, to save ourselves and make a perfect world, following those secular visions going back ultimately to Plato's *Republic*. The two greatest counterpoints to Utopian endeavors are still Dystopias such as Aldous Huxley's *Brave New World* and George Orwell's *1984*. Neither author was Christian. But their warnings remain valid, because the dangers they warned against are still very much around.

In "community-making," meanwhile, one should meditate upon the words of the great German theologian Dietrich Bonhoeffer: "The person who's in love with their vision of community will destroy community.

But the person who loves the people around them will create community wherever they go."[21]

My takeaway from this: *the project of building a better future begins at home, sometimes by looking in the mirror.*

We can work to improve ourselves, and constantly review our motivations. Can we learn to love those around us, as Bonhoeffer wisely counsels, even those who think and believe (and, yes, look and act) different from us, even if we do not personally approve of all that they do? (This, of course, is what Jesus counseled.) Can we learn to be unconditionally *kind* to them? Can we see them as at the center of their journeys through life, the protagonists of their "3D movies" Chalmers spoke of, just as we are each at the center of ours? Can we begin with the premise that their journeys matter *to them*, and that therefore they matter *period*? For all others are struggling with issues we cannot see. Recognizing that what gives meaning and brings joy to others may be quite different from what gives meaning and brings joy to us should make it easier to embrace plurality as our way of being.

Then we can act horizontally, talking to those willing to listen. This may mean eschewing a singular vision that can lead only to a new Secular City. If we can stop the "cancelers" of history, we can still learn from it.

Once the discussion of worldviews is on the table, these are the kinds of ideas philosophers should assume responsibility for producing. Indeed, this is the responsibility philosophers must assume, as we move ever more deeply into an increasingly unstable, uncertain, and possibly dangerous decade!

How to pay for philosophical endeavors while the money political-economy continues to function? By serving others in whatever capacity one is able to do that meets their needs. That may be teaching; it may be counseling; or it may be something else.

If we can set aside the materialism that has partially hobbled our world as not meriting its present dominance in intellectual centers and other institutions, it should be easier to embrace the idea of the intrinsic value of life—of *lives*—and of the *planet itself* (because for many of us, the Creation will be seen to have its own intrinsic value). Perhaps if this inspires new discoveries in the production of energy that put an end to the need for extraction and lead to abundance instead of scarcity, then how to *fund* philosophical endeavors will cease to be a problem. For philosophy will manifestly have contributed something of the first importance to the world to come. Philosophers will have done their part to bring about a better future for humanity and for the planet.

---

21. Bonhoeffer, *Life Together*,

Conclusion

This book has covered a lot of territory—far more than your average philosophical tome these days! This, I submit, is a good thing! We have articulated bold and potentially disruptive conclusions! That, too, I submit, is a good thing!

Disruption *can* be good for us!

What have we accomplished?

What Philosophy Should Do: Recapitulation

Lest the idea need one final recapitulation: *philosophy should identify, clarify, and evaluate worldviews as it finds them in civilization, whether in the Secular University or in the broader Secular City.* Although nonphilosophers are capable of it, trained philosophers are uniquely qualified to become thought leaders undertaking the task. And then go beyond this by conceiving the possibilities of a Fifth Stage of civilization, in which persons' intrinsic value is restored (or perhaps acknowledged for the first time), technology becomes servant and not master, and a decentralized global plurality of cultures and communities is the regulative ideal.

We've illustrated worldview criticism with an example: with materialism, or materialist naturalism, and its method of avoiding as explanatory anything outside the spatiotemporal world. This worldview, we argued, guided Third Stage civilization into a cul-de-sac. This cul-de-sac became manifest in a variety of ways. Secular moralities all fail, as we saw, and often resulted in massive harm done to innocent persons. While rightly holding onto truth as a value, Third Stage civilization served up a stream of nihilist and alienated artistic, literary, and other products. These began its transforming into the present amalgamation of Third and Fourth Stage cultures in which commitment to truth is tenuous at the very best and the idea of narratives "all the way down" becomes an almost-irresistible temptation.

The amalgamation is unstable, as we have seen. It is epistemologically and anthropologically schizophrenic. According to Third Stage thinking, we humans are capable of standing on our own morally, and reaching for the stars technologically. And finally, even redesigning ourselves! Fourth Stage thinking is a product of the manifest failure of this vision, which began with this view of ourselves as autonomous (Cartesian) agents able to base our entire lives, our institutions, and world as a whole, first on Pure Reason and then on Settled Science. This left us ethically at sea, despairingly cynical, increasingly retribalized, and finally at the mercy of those for whom money and power get the last word. The actual political economy, whatever its expressed ideals, gravitates toward corruption and brutalism.

Philosophy is the discipline best suited to diagnose the causes of our present cultural malaise and political-economic quagmire, eventually helping us climb out of it. It can draw attention to our first premises as key to what has gone wrong, and then urge us to think about about a future Fifth Stage of civilization that learns from the first four and sets about to make things better. Along the way philosophers can offer people critical thinking, self-improvement, and perhaps other skills, to the extent these are needed to get people in the front door of whatever novel home base(s) philosophers can assemble. Having immersed themselves in the ways language is used to mislead and bully, philosophers can expose and diagnose these in dramatic fashion. They can undertake that "battle against the bewitchment of our intelligence" in ways that did not occur to Wittgenstein, who lived in somewhat saner times.

What comes next? What are the first, best action steps philosophers can take, if they wish their discipline to avoid following its present trajectory from academic decoration to endangered species?

Philosophers: What Happens Next Is Up To You!

This depends on what philosophers choose to do with these ideas. I stated above that they should be motivated to do something with them. They might not find my recommendations new or interesting or compelling, of course. This is assuming they even notice, as the ideas come from someone they probably never heard of, operating not just outside their familiar networks but outside a Secular University he abandoned.

Moreover: can any of us—even conscientious philosophers still aboard the Secular University ship—really do much to affect the trajectory of Western civilization? For example, is the Great Reset, or Fourth Industrial Revolution if one prefers, even stoppable at this point?

I don't know. The challenges before us are very, very big. A work such as this can, at best, scratch the surface.

I believe we are obligated to try.

Margaret Meade, the anthropologist, is sometimes quoted as having said, "Never doubt that a small group of thoughtful, committed citizens can change the world; indeed, it is the only thing that ever has." Whether she actually said this is unknown. Maybe she didn't. It still stands as one of the more powerful, inspirational quotes from the past century.[1]

What we know is that the present system is not working! It is, in fact, failing disastrously in slow motion!

If I may be allowed a final pair of examples, the last I will inflict on my readers. We're told incessantly these days that Black Lives Matter, and if human lives all have intrinsic value, then of course they do. But the murder rate of black men by other black men in big cities (Chicago comes to mind) continues unabated, as do shootings even of small children and abortions of unborn black babies.

What philosophers can do is refuse to write these persons off!

For yes, their lives matter! But we can't just say that. We have to do something about it.

What can fix this?

Only affirming, loudly, the intrinsic value of those lives, broadcasting it as loudly as possible.

If the kind of intrinsic value that leads to genuine improvement begins at home, of course, then members of the black community must value black lives and act accordingly. Black lives mattering cannot be a mere political slogan. It must lead to personal action, building self-worth, skills, resilience, community support, educational institutions, etc., or it goes nowhere. History shall judge us all by our results.

Our challenges are far larger than those of living in a multi-ethnic world. In an earlier draft of this work I wrote: *The next economic meltdown might have arrived by the time this reaches print. It will likely be more horrendous than the one in 2008–9 was. More livelihoods will likely be wiped out, for those who trusted in the wrong instruments or institutions or practices, or if they simply had no options they could discern as realistic.*

Given the pandemic of 2020, was I right or am I right?

There may not be any economic "recovery" this time, moreover. The one from 2009–19 was the weakest on record. Wall Street soared; Main Street suffered. Those on the left blamed capitalism, which was just the neoliberal hyper-capitalism we have.

---

1. For a standard attribution of this remark to Meade cf. Keys, *Earth At Omega*, 79.

Many of those on the right, including neoliberals, hold Main Street (i.e., rural and predominantly white Americans) responsible for its own failures. Its people did not accept the encirclements and "reinvent themselves," keep up with changing technology, etc. *Average is over*, scolds neoliberal economist Tyler Cowen.[2] Progressives also blame Main Street for its own failings, but for different reasons. Not only did those in the mostly white, former middle class not change with the times, they did not embrace the diversity and inclusion of the Secular City.

Thus the fate of "deplorables" who only deserve "cancelation," right?

Do *their* lives matter? These are human beings. They are our neighbors. Their suffering is real, and could worsen in future decades.

Philosophers with a moral view of the world cannot write these people off, either!

Because again, if all lives have intrinsic value, indeed all lives matter. Even if that is now a "systemic racist" heresy according to the ideological screeds of "woke," their ancestry going back through the dichotomies in Marcuse ultimately to Hegel.

But will anyone act on this realization, even if they agree with it?

People are scared!

That means we philosophers have our work cut out for us!

Philosophy has "reinvented itself" before. It can do so again. It must. Philosophers must adapt to present conditions of disruption and uncertainty, and either make use of the tools and platforms available, or create new ones. Philosophers must grow more assertive, ask the right questions, and propose answers that will be actionable and impactful.

But to achieve any of this, they must get noticed. If this means sometimes uttering frightening, apocryphal pronouncements, then so be it!

The COVID-19 panic of 2020 made one thing abundantly clear: *if people respond to incentives, then human mass behavior responds extremely well to invocations of fear, of immediate and present danger, especially when repeated hysterically by mass media twenty-four-seven!*

The unstable amalgamation of Third and Fourth Stage civilization is the clear and present danger, which will still be around when the pandemic ends, as all pandemics do. The clear and present danger is of the highly centralized, technocratic, global inverted totalitarianism (Sheldon Wolin's genius concept) sketched above. It will not matter what label we put on it, once the control systems descend.

---

2. Cowen, *Average Is Over*.

Fifth Stage thinking offers to work out an alternative to technology-based (and Mammon-dependent) inverted totalitarianism, and to base it on ideas other than the Grandiose Assumption.

Philosophers should step forward with such warnings, and also with constructive ideas and the spirit of thought leadership intent on bringing people to the table. They can make use of conversations already happening, such as those of Peak Oil and man-made climate change, and argue for the development of technologies that do not rely on extractive methods. True, philosophers are not engineers. But neither are most climate change activists professional climatologists.

The future is coming, ready or not. Will philosophers play a part in having built it? If they do not accept such challenges as this, then the pronouncement we opened our Introduction with, by Stephen Hawking, will be true, if not for the reason he gave.

Philosophy will be intellectually dead, and institutionally on life support.

Philosophers should be motivated to avoid that sort of future, whatever the cost! That will mean stepping out into the Secular City, as Socrates did into Athens, and challenging what needs challenging. It won't necessarily be easy. Nothing worthwhile ever is.

We can partner with others already thinking constructively about the near (and distant) future. The San Francisco-based Long Now Foundation comes to mind.[3] Another, quite different group, is Local Futures, based on the assumption that top-down-styled political-economic globalization is obsolete, and that "the future is local."[4] There are doubtless others unknown to me. There is abundant information to draw on, much of it challenging disciplinary dogmas, crossing interdisciplinary boundaries, and breaking out of existing conceptual and ideological straightjackets. Such activity has already begun to move the needle towards a Fifth Stage mindset. What we must do is take the quantum leap of becoming conscious of our need to build a Fifth Stage of civilization so that we can take charge and direct it.

Final Reflection

Here we stand, in our present moment, in a Secular City in great trouble, its Secular University in confusion and disarray, its Secular Mass divided, confused, frightened, and desperate for new and credible leadership. Philosophical leadership perhaps, able to fill the moral vacuum that has

   3. Cf. Brand, *Clock of the Long Now*.
   4. Cf. Norberg-Hodge, *Local Is Our Future*.

swamped our civilization like a tsunami and threatens to drown all that we have achieved.

I rest my case. Except to reiterate, one last time, that we have little to lose, and much to gain, by making the effort I urge here. We may find ourselves positioned to find out what philosophers can still make of philosophy, even in times such as these, and what we can accomplish, if we choose to assume responsibility for the future.

END

Bibliography

Adovasio, J. N., and Jake Page. "Searching for the First Americans: A 500-Year Quest." *Western Pennsylvania History* (Summer 2002) 15–29.

Andersen, Kurt. *Fantasyland: How America Went Haywire: A 500-Year History*. New York: RandomHouse, 2017.

Andersen, Ross. "The Most Mysterious Star in Our Galaxy." *The Atlantic Monthly*, October 2015. https://www.theatlantic.com/science/archive/2015/10/the-most-interesting-star-in-our-galaxy/410023/.

Arrhenius, Svante. *Worlds in the Making: The Evolution of the Universe*. New York: Harper & Row, 1908.

Arum, Richard, and Josipa Roksa. *Academically Adrift: Limited Learning on College Campuses*. Chicago: University of Chicago Press, 2011.

Auken, Ida. "Welcome to 2030: I Own Nothing, Have No Privacy and Life Has Never Been Better." *Forbes*, November 10, 2016. https://www.forbes.com/sites/worldeconomicforum/2016/11/10/shopping-i-cant-really-remember-what-that-is-or-how-differently-well-live-in-2030/?sh=2d80b39f1735.

Axe, Douglas. "The Limits of Complex Adaptation: An Analysis Based on a Simple Model of Structured Bacterial Populations." *BIO-Complexity* 4 (2010) 1–10.

Axelrod, Robert. *The Evolution of Cooperation*. New York: Basic Books, 1984.

Ayer, Alfred Jules. *Language, Truth, and Logic*. London: Gollancz, 1936.

Bastiat, Frederic. *The Law*. Irvington-on-Hudson, NY: Foundation for Economic Education, 1994.

Bauman, Valerie. "Is America Becoming Godless? The Number of People Who Have No Religion Has Risen 266 Per Cent—One Third of the Population—In Three Decades." *The Daily Mail*, April 4, 2019. https://www.dailymail.co.uk/news/article-6886705/Is-America-Godless-number-people-no-religion-rose-266-three-decades.html.

Beauvoir, Simone de. *The Second Sex*. New York: Penguin, 1972.

Behe, Michael. *Darwin's Black Box: The Biochemical Challenge to the Theory of Evolution*. New York: Free Press, 1996.

Behe, Michael, and David Snoke. "Simulating Evolution by Gene Duplication of Protein Features That Require Multiple Amino Acid Residues." *Protein Science* 13 (2004) 2651–64.

Benedict, Ruth. *Patterns of Culture*. London: Routledge & Kegan Paul, 1934.

Berlinski, Claire. *Menace in Europe: Why Europe's Crisis Is America's*. New York: Three Rivers, 2006.

Berlinski, David. *The Devil's Delusion: Atheism and Its Scientific Pretensions.* New York: Basic Books, 2008.

Berman, Paul, ed. *Debating P.C.: The Controversy Over Political Correctness on College Campuses.* New York: Random House, 1992.

Bernays, Edward Louis. *Propaganda.* New York: Ig Publishing, 2005.

Bernstein, Richard. "The Rising Hegemony of the Politically Correct." *The New York Times,* October 28, 1990.

Bonhoeffer, Dietrich. *Life Together: The Classic Exploration of Christian Community.* New York: Harper, 1954.

Booker, Christopher, and Richard North. *The Great Deception: Can the European Union Survive?* New York: Continuum, 2003.

Boyajian, Tabetha S., et al. "The First Post-Kepler Brightness Dips of KIC 8462852." *The Astrophysical Journal* 853 (January 2018).

———. "Planet Hunters IX. KIC 8462852 – Where's the Flux?" *Monthly Notices of the Royal Astronomical Society* 457 (April 2016).

Boyle, Joseph M, et al. *Free Choice: A Self-Referential Argument.* Notre Dame, IN: University of Notre Dame Press, 1976.

Bradley, Walter L., and Charles B. Thaxton. "Information and the Origin of Life." In *The Creation Hypothesis,* edited by J. P. Moreland, 173–210. Grand Rapids: InterVarsity, 1994.

Brain, Marshall. *Manna: Two Visions of Humanity's Future.* Cary, NC: BYG Publishing, 2012.

Brand, Stewart. *The Clock of the Long Now: Time and Responsibility.* New York: Basic Books, 2000.

Brown, Harold I. *Perception, Theory, and Commitment.* Chicago: University of Chicago Press, 1977.

Brush, Stephen. "Should the History of Science Be Rated X?" *Science* 183.4130 (1974) 1164–72.

Burke, Edmund. *Reflections on the Revolution in France.* New York: Penguin Classics, 1986.

Butler, Judith. *Gender Trouble: Feminism and the Subversion of Identity.* New York: Routledge, 1990.

Carnap, Rudolph. "Testability and Meaning." *Philosophy of Science* 3 (1936) 420–68; *Philosophy of Science* 4 (1937) 1–40.

Capaldi, Nicholas. *Out of Order: Affirmative Action and the Crisis of Doctrinaire Liberalism.* Buffalo, NY: Prometheus, 1985.

Carse, James B. *Finite and Infinite Games: A Vision of Life as Play and Possibility.* New York: Free Press, 1986.

Chalmers, David J. *The Conscious Mind: In Search of a Fundamental Theory.* Oxford: Oxford University Press, 1996.

———. "Facing Up To the Problem of Consciousness," *Journal of Consciousness Studies* 2 (1995) 200–219.

———. "How Do You Explain Consciousness?" *TED Talk,* March 2014. https://www.ted.com/talks/david_chalmers_how_do_you_explain_consciousness.

———. "Moving Forward on the Problem of Consciousness." *Journal of Consciousness Studies* 4 (1996) 3–46.

Churchland, Patricia Smith. *Neurophilosophy: Toward a Unified Science of Mind-Brain.* Cambridge: MIT Press, 1984.

Churchland, Paul. *Scientific Realism and the Plasticity of Mind.* Cambridge: Cambridge University Press, 1979.

Clugston, Christopher O. *BLIP: Humanity's 300-Year-Old Self-Terminating Experiment With Industrialism.* St. Petersburg, FL: BookLocker.com, 2019.

Cobin, John M. *Christian Theology and Public Policy: Highlighting the American Experience.* Greenville, SC: Alertness Books, 2006.

Cowen, Tyler. *Average Is Over: Powering America Beyond the Great Stagnation.* New York: Plume, 2013.

Cox, Harvey. *The Secular City.* 2nd ed. New York: Macmillan, 1966.

Crick, Francis, and Leslie E. Orgel. "Directed Panspermia." *Icarus* 19 (1973) 341–46.

Damore, James. "Google's Ideological Echo Chamber." http://www.dhillonlaw.com/wp-content/uploads/2018/01/Damore-Google-Manifesto.pdf.

Dass, Ram. *Be Here Now.* San Cristobal, NM: Lama Foundation, 1971.

Dawkins, Richard. *The God Delusion.* New York: Houghton-Mifflin, 2006.

DeHaven-Smith, Lance. *Conspiracy Theory in America.* Austin, TX: University of Texas Press, 2013.

Dembski, William, and Jonathan Witt. *Intelligent Design Uncensored.* Grand Rapids, MI: InterVarsity, 2010.

Dennett, Daniel. *Breaking the Spell: Religion as a Natural Phenomenon.* New York: Penguin, 2007.

———. *Darwin's Dangerous Idea: Evolution and the Meanings of Life.* New York: Simon & Schuster, 1995.

———. "Facing Backwards on the Problem of Consciousness." *Journal of Consciousness Studies* 3 (1996) 4–6.

———. *Intuition Pumps and Other Tools For Thinking.* New York: Norton, 2013.

Dewey, John, et al. *The Humanist Manifesto.* New York: The New Humanist, 1933.

DiAngelo, Robin. *White Fragility: Why It's So Hard for White People to Talk About Racism.* Boston: Beacon, 2018.

Drake, Frank, and Dava Sobel. *Is Anyone Out There? The Scientific Search for Extraterrestrial Intelligence.* New York: Pocket, 1994.

Drury, Shadia B. *Leo Strauss and the American Right.* New York: Palgrave-Macmillan, 1997.

D'Souza, Dinesh. *Illiberal Education: The Politics of Race and Sex on Campus.* New York: Free Press, 1991.

Eastland, Terry. *Ending Affirmative Action: The Case for Colorblind Justice.* New York: Basic Books, 1996.

Eidelson, Josh. "Google's Firing of Engineer James Damore Did Not Break Labor Law, NLRB Lawyer Concludes." *Los Angeles Times,* February 16, 2018. https://www.latimes.com/business/la-fi-tn-google-james-damore-20180216-story.html.

Fetzer, James, ed. *The 9/11 Conspiracy: The Scamming of America.* LaSalle, IL: Open Court, 2008.

Feuer, Lewis. "American Philosophy Is Dead." *New York Times Magazine,* April 24, 1966.

Feyerabend, Paul K. *Against Method: Outline of an Anarchistic Theory of Knowledge.* London: New Left Books, 1975.

———. *Farewell to Reason.* London: Verso, 1987.

———. *Science in a Free Society.* London: New Left Books, 1978.

Fitzgerald, Randall. *The One-Hundred Year Lie: How Food and Medicine Are Destroying Your Health*. New York: Dutton, 2006.
Flesch, Rudolf. *Why John Can't Read*. New York: Harper, 1955.
Foucault, Michel. *The Archeology of Knowledge*. New York: Harper & Row, 1972.
———. *The Order of Things*. New York: Pantheon, 1970.
Frankfurt, Harry. *On Bullshit*. Princeton, NJ: Princeton University Press, 2005.
———. *On Inequality*. Princeton, NJ: Princeton University Press, 2015.
Frankl, Victor. *Man's Search for Meaning: An Introduction to Logotherapy*. New York: Simon & Schuster, 1959.
Fraser, Nancy. *Fortunes of Feminism: From State-Managed Capitalism to Neoliberal Crisis*. Brooklyn: Verso, 2013.
Friedman, Milton. *Capitalism and Freedom*. Chicago: University of Chicago Press, 1962.
———. "Neoliberalism and Its Prospects." *Farmand*, February 17, 1951.
———. "The Social Responsibility of Business Is To Increase Its Profits." *The New York Times Magazine*, September 13, 1970.
Friedman, Milton, and Rose D. Friedman. *Free to Choose: A Personal Statement*. New York: Harcourt, 1980.
Fukuyama, Francis. *The End of History and the Last Man*. New York: Free Press, 1991.
Gardner, Martin. *Fads and Fallacies in the Name of Science*. New York: Dover, 1957.
Gatto, John Taylor. *The Underground History of American Education*. New York: Oxford Village Press, 2001.
Gilens, Martin, and Benjamin Page. "Testing Theories of American Politics: Elites, Interest Groups, and Average Citizens." *Perspectives in Politics* 12 (2014) 564–81.
Goff, Philip. *Consciousness and Fundamental Reality*. Oxford: Oxford University Press, 2017.
———. *Galileo's Error: Foundations For a New Science of Consciousness*. Oxford: Oxford University Press, 2019.
Gonzalez, Guillermo, and Jay Richards. *The Privileged Planet: How Our Place in the Cosmos Is Designed for Discovery*. Washington, DC: Regnary, 2004.
Goodman, Nelson. *Fact, Fiction, and Forecast*. Cambridge: Harvard University Press, 1955.
Graeber, David. *Bullshit Jobs: A Theory*. New York: Simon & Schuster, 2018.
Griffin, David Ray. *The New Pearl Harbor: Disturbing Questions About the Bush Administration and 9/11*. Northhampton, MA: Olive Branch, 2004.
Gross, Barry R. *Discrimination In Reverse: Is Turnabout Fair Play?* New York: New York University Press, 1978.
Gross, Barry R., ed. *Reverse Discrimination*. Buffalo, NY: Prometheus, 1977.
Gutting, Gary. *Paradigms and Revolutions*. Notre Dame, IN: University of Notre Dame Press, 1980.
Gutting, Gary, ed. *Continental Philosophy of Science*. New York: Wiley-Blackwell, 2005.
Gutting, Gary, and Nancy Fraser. "A Feminism Where 'Leaning In' Means Leaning on Others." *New York Opinionator Blog*, October 15, 2015. https://opinionator.blogs.nytimes.com/author/nancy-fraser/?_r=0.
Haack, Susan. "Epistemological Reflections of an Old Feminist." *Reason Papers* 18 (1993) 31–43.
———. "Science 'from a Feminist Perspective.'" *Philosophy* 67 (1992) 5-18.

Hanson, Norwood Russell. *Patterns of Discovery*. Cambridge, U.K.: Cambridge University Press, 1958.
Hapgood, Charles H. *Earth's Shifting Crust*. New York: Pantheon, 1958.
Harding, Sandra. *The Science Question in Feminism*. Ithaca, NY: Cornell University Press, 1986.
Harris, Sam. *The End of Faith: Religion, Terror, and the Future of Reason*. New York: W.W. Norton, 2005.
Haugeland, John. *Artificial Intelligence: The Very Idea*. Cambridge: MIT Press, 1985.
Hawking, Stephen. *The Grand Design: New Answers to the Ultimate Questions of Life*. New York: Bantam, 2010
Hayek, Friedrich A. *The Road to Serfdom*. Chicago: University of Chicago Press, 1948.
Hedges, Chris. *Empire of Illusion: The Death of Literacy and the Triumph of Spectacle*. New York: Nation, 2009.
Hempel, Carl G. *Aspects of Scientific Explanation*. New York: The Free Press, 1965.
———. "Studies in the Logic of Confirmation." *Mind* 54 (1945) 1-20.
———. "Studies in the Logic of Confirmation II." *Mind*, 54 (1945) 97-121.
Hermon, Edward, and Noam Chomsky. *Manufacturing Consent: The Political Economy of the Mass Media*. New York: Pantheon, 1988.
Higgs, Robert. *Against Leviathan: Government Power and a Free Society*. Oakland, CA: Independent Institute, 2004.
Hitchens, Christopher. *God Is Not Great: How Religion Poisons Everything*. New York: Hachette Book Group, 2007.
Holiday, Ryan. *The Obstacle Is the Way*. New York: Penguin, 2014.
———. *Stillness Is the Key*. New York: Portfolio, 2019.
Holiday, Ryan, and Stephen Hanselman. *The Daily Stoic: 366 Meditations on Wisdom, Perseverance, and the Art of Living*. New York: Portfolio, 2016.
Hopkins, Claude C. *Scientific Advertising*. New York: Bell, 1960.
Hoppe, Hans Herman. *Democracy: The God That Failed*. New Brunswick, NJ: Transaction, 2000.
Hoyle, Fred. "The Universe: Past and Present Reflections." *Annual Review of Astronomy and Astrophysics* 20 (1982) 1-36.
Hoyle, Fred, and Chandra Wickramasinghe. *Evolution from Space*. New York: Simon & Schuster, 1981.
Hubbert, M. King, et al. *Introduction to Technocracy*. New York: The John Day Co., 1933.
Hudson, W.D. *Modern Moral Philosophy*. London: U.K.: Macmillan, 1970.
Hughes, Joanna. "Four Reasons Why Philosophy Is as Relevant as Ever." *Bachelor Studies*, November 16, 2018. https://www.bachelorstudies.com/article/four-reasons-why-philosophy-is-as-relevant-as-ever/.
Hume, David. *An Enquiry Concerning Human Understanding*. Indianapolis, IN: Bobbs-Merrill, 1955.
Johnstone, Caitlin. "Society Is Made Of Narrative. Realizing This Is Awakening From the Matrix." *Medium*, https://medium.com/@caityjohnstone/society-is-made-of-narrative-realizing-this-is-awakening-from-the-matrix-787c7e2535ae, August 21, 2018.
Jones, Eric M. *Where Is Everybody? An Account of Fermi's Question*, Technical Report LA-10311-MS. Los Alamos, NM: Los Alamos National Laboratory, March 1985.

Jones, James H. *Bad Blood: The Tuskegee Syphilis Experiment, expanded edition.* New York: The Free Press, 1993.
Kant, Immanuel. "What Is Enlightenment?" In *The Portable Enlightenment Reader*, edited by Isaac Kramnick, 1-7. New York: Penguin, 1995.
Kekes, John. *The Nature of Philosophy*. Totowa, NJ: Rowman & Littlefield, 1980.
Keys, Donald. *Earth At Omega: Passage to Planetization*. Boston, MA: Brandon, 1982.
Khanna, Parag. *Technocracy in America: Rise of the Info-State*. New York: Parag Khanna, 2017.
Kimball, Roger. *Tenured Radicals: How Politics Has Corrupted Our Higher Education.* New York: Harper-Perennial, 1990.
Kinsey, Alfred C., et al. *Sexual Behavior in the Human Female*. Philadelphia: W.B. Saunders, 1952.
———. *Sexual Behavior in the Human Male*. Philadelphia: W.B. Saunders, 1948.
Kitcher, Philip. *Living with Darwin: Evolution, Design, and the Future of Faith*. Oxford, U.K. Oxford University Press, 2007.
Klein, Naomi. *The Shock Doctrine: The Rise of Disaster Capitalism*. New York: Picador, 2008.
Kluckhohn, Clyde. "Culture and Behavior." In *The Collected Essays of Clyde Kluckhohn*, edited by R. Kluckhohn, 297–98. New York: The Free Press, 1962.
Kramnick, Isaac, ed. *The Portable Enlightenment Reader*. New York: Penguin, 1995.
Kripke, Saul. *Naming and Necessity*. Cambridge: Harvard University Press, 1980.
Kuhn, Thomas S. *The Structure of Scientific Revolutions*. 2nd ed. Chicago: University of Chicago Press, 1970.
Kurtzweil, Ray. *The Singularity Is Near: When Humans Transcend Biology*. New York: Viking, 2005.
Lakatos, Imre. "Falsification and the Methodology of Scientific Research Programs." In *Criticism and the Growth of Knowledge*, edited by Imre Lakatos and Alan Musgrave, 91–196. Cambridge: Cambridge University Press, 1970.
Lakatos, Imre, and Alan Musgrave. *Criticism and the Growth of Knowledge*. Cambridge: Cambridge University Press, 1970.
Lasch, Christopher. *The Culture of Narcissism: American Life In an Age of Diminishing Expectations*. New York: W. W. Norton.
Laszlo, Ervin. *The Systems View of the World*. New York: Brazilier, 1972.
Le Bon, Gustave. *The Crowd: A Study of the Popular Mind*. London: Unwin, 1895.
Lenzer, Gertrud, ed. *Auguste Comte and Positivism: The Essential Writings*. New York: Harper & Row, 1975.
Lewis, C. S. *Miracles*. New York: Touchstone, 1960.
Lippman, Walter. *Public Opinion*. New York: Harcourt, Brace, 1922.
Lyotard, Jean-François. *The Postmodern Condition: A Report on Knowledge*. Minneapolis: University of Minnesota Press, 1984.
MacCormack, Patricia. *The A-Human Manifesto: Activism for the End of the Anthropocene*. New York: Bloomsbury Academic, 2020.
Machan, Tibor R. *Individuals and Their Rights*. LaSalle, IL: Open Court, 1989.
Machen, J. Gresham. *Christianity and Liberalism*. New York: Macmillan, 1923.
MacIntyre, Alasdair. *After Virtue: A Study in Moral Theory*. Notre Dame, IN: University of Notre Dame Press, 1981.
Mackay, Charles. *Extraordinary Popular Delusions and the Madness of Crowds*. London: Bentley, 1841.

MacKinnon, Catharine. "Feminism, Marxism, Method, and the State: Toward Feminist Jurisprudence." *Signs: Journal of Women in Culture and Society* 8 (1983) 635–58.

———. *Feminism Unmodified: Discourses on Life and Law*. Cambridge: Harvard University Press, 1988.

Malcolm, Norman. *Ludwig Wittgenstein: A Memoir (New Edition With Wittgenstein's Letters to Malcolm)*. Oxford: Oxford University Press, 1984.

Marcuse, Herbert. *Eros and Civilization*. 2nd ed. Boston: Beacon, 1966.

———. *One-Dimensional Man*. Boston: Beacon, 1964.

———. "Repressive Tolerance." In *A Critique of Pure Tolerance*, edited by R. P. Wolff et al., 81–123. Boston: Beacon, 1965.

Martinich, A. P., and David Sosa, eds. *Analytic Philosophy: An Anthology*. Oxford: Basil Blackwell, 2001.

Marx, Karl, and Friedrich Engels. *Karl Marx Friedrich Engels: Collected Works*. 50 vols. New York: International Publishers, 1976.

Maxwell, Nicholas. *From Knowledge to Wisdom: A Revolution in the Aims and Methods of Science*. London: Basil-Blackwell, 1984.

———. *How Universities Can Help Create a Wiser World: The Urgent Need For an Academic Revolution*. Exeter, UK: Imprint Academic, 2014.

———. "Induction, Simplicity, and Scientific Progress." *Scientia* 114 (1979) 629–53.

———. "The Rationality of Scientific Discovery, Parts I and II." *Philosophy of Science* 41 (1974) 123–53, 247–95

———. "Science, Reason, Knowledge, and Wisdom: A Critique of Specialism." *Inquiry* 23 (1980) 19–81.

McCoy, Alfred. *In the Shadows of the American Century: The Rise and Decline of U.S. Global Power*. Chicago: Haymarket, 2017.

McGinn, Colin. "All Machine and No Ghost?" *New Statesman*, February 20, 2012.

———. "Can We Solve the Mind-Body Problem?" *Mind* 98 (1989) 349–66.

———. *The Mysterious Flame: Conscious Minds in a Material World*. New York: Basic Books, 1999.

———. *The Problem of Consciousness*. London: Basil Blackwell, 1991.

McKenzie, Lindsay, et al. "A Journal Article Provoked a Schism in Philosophy. Now the Rifts Are Deepening." *The Chronicle of Higher Education*, May 6, 2017.

Meyer, Stephen. *Darwin's Doubt: The Explosive Origin of Animal Life and the Case for Intelligent Design*. New York: HarperCollins, 2013.

Mills, C. Wright. *The Power Elite*. Oxford: Oxford University Press, 1956.

Mirowski, Philip, and Dieter Plehwe, eds. *The Road From Mont Pélerin: The Rise of the Neoliberal Thought Collective*. Cambridge: Harvard University Press, 2009.

Mises, Ludwig von. *Human Action: A Treatise on Economics*. New Haven, CT: Yale University Press, 1949.

———. *Socialism: An Economic and Sociological Analysis*. Indianapolis, IN: Liberty Press Liberty Classics, 1981.

Murray, Charles. *Losing Ground: American Social Policy 1950–1980*. New York: Basic Books, 1980.

Nagel, Thomas. *Mind and Cosmos: Why the Materialist Neo-Darwinian Conception of Nature Is Almost Certainly False*. Oxford: Oxford University Press, 2012.

———. "What Is It Like To Be a Bat?" *Philosophical Review* 83 (1974) 435–50.

Nichols, Tom. *The Death of Expertise: The Campaign Against Established Knowledge and Why It Matters*. Cambridge: Cambridge University Press, 2017.

Norberg-Hodge, Helena. *Ancient Futures: Lessons from Ladakh for a Globalizing World.* 2nd ed. San Francisco: Sierra Club, 2009.

———. *Local Is Our Future: Steps to an Economics of Happiness.* East Hardwick, VT: Local Futures, 2019

Nozick, Robert. *Anarchy, State, and Utopia.* New York: Basic Books, 1974.

Nute, Donald. *Essential Formal Semantics.* Totowa, NJ: Rowman & Littlefield, 1981.

O'Neill, William. *With Charity Toward None: An Analysis of Ayn Rand's Philosophy.* Totowa, NJ: Littlefield & Adam, 1972.

Orlov, Dmitry. *The Five Stages of Collapse: Survivors Toolkit.* Gabriola Island, BC: New Society, 2013.

———. *Shrinking the Technosphere: Getting a Grip on Technologies That Limit Our Autonomy, Self-Sufficiency, and Freedom.* Gabriola Island, BC: New Society, 2016.

Pace, Eugenio. "Can Philosophy Influence Business: Here's What the Stoics Have Taught Me." *Forbes Magazine*, December 26, 2018.

Parsa, Cyrus A., and the AI Organization. *Artificial Intelligence: Dangers to Humanity.* La Jolla, CA: The AI Organization, 2019.

Paul, Ron. *End the Fed.* New York: Grand Central, 2009.

———. *A Foreign Policy of Freedom, Peace, Honest Commerce, and Friendship.* Lake Jackson, TX: Foundation for Rational Economics and Education, 2007.

Perelman, Michael. *The Invention of Capitalism: Classical Political Economy and the Secret History of Primitive Accumulation.* Durham, NC: Duke University Press, 2000.

Perkins, John. *Confessions of an Economic Hit Man.* Oakland, CA: Berrett-Koehler, 2004.

———. *The New Confessions of an Economic Hit Man.* Oakland, CA: Berrett-Koehler, 2016.

Pigliucci, Massimo. *How To Be a Stoic: Using Ancient Philosophy To Live a Modern Life.* New York: Basic Books, 2017.

Piketty, Thomas. *Capital in the Twenty-first Century.* Cambridge: Belknap, 2014.

Pinker, Steven. *Enlightenment Now: The Case for Science, Reason, Humanism, and Progress.* New York: Viking, 2018.

Plantinga, Alvin. *Warrant and Proper Function.* Oxford: Oxford University Press, 1993.

———. *Warrant: The Current Debate.* Oxford: Oxford University Press, 1993.

———. *Warranted Christian Belief.* Oxford: Oxford University Press, 2000.

———. *Where the Conflict Really Lies: Science, Religion, and Naturalism.* Oxford: Oxford University Press, 2011.

"The Poetry of Science: Richard Dawkins and Neil deGrasse Tyson." https://www.richarddawkins.net/2010/10/the-poetry-of-science-richard-dawkins-and-neil-degrasse-tyson-2/.

Polanyi, Michael. *Personal Knowledge: Towards a Post-Critical Philosophy.* New York: Harper Torchbooks, 1964

———. *The Tacit Dimension.* New York: Doubleday, 1966

Popper, Karl. *Conjectures and Refutations: The Growth of Scientific Knowledge.* 2nd ed. New York: Basic, 1965.

———. *The Logic of Scientific Discovery.* London: Hutchinson, 1959.

———. *Objective Knowledge: An Evolutionary Approach.* Oxford: Clarendon, 1979.

Postman, Neil. *Amusing Ourselves To Death: Public Discourse in the Age of Show Business.* New York: Viking Penguin, 1985.

Putnam, Robert D. *Bowling Alone: The Collapse and Revival of American Community*. New York: Simon & Schuster, 2000.
Putney, Snell, and Gail Putney. *The Adjusted American: Normal Neuroses in the Individual and Society*. New York: Harper & Row, 1966.
Quine, Willard Van Orman. "Two Dogmas of Empiricism." In *From a Logical Point of View*, 20–46. Cambridge: Harvard University Press, 1953.
Rachels, James. *The Elements of Moral Philosophy*. 4th ed. New York: McGraw-Hill, 2002.
Rand, Ayn. *Atlas Shrugged*. New York: Random House, 1957.
———. *Capitalism: The Unknown Ideal*. New York: New American Library, 1967.
———. *Introduction to Objectivist Epistemology*. 2nd ed. New York: Meridian, 1990.
———. *The Virtue of Selfishness*. New York: New American Library, 1964.
———. "What Is Capitalism?" In *Capitalism: The Unknown Ideal*, by Ayn Rand, 11–34. New York: New American Library, 1967.
Rawls, John. *Justice as Fairness: A Restatement*. Cambridge: Belknap, 2001.
———. *A Theory of Justice*. Cambridge: Belknap, 1972.
Reitz, Matthew. "Is Philosophy Dead?" *Times Higher Education*, February 22, 2015. https://www.timeshighereducation.com/news/is-philosophy-dead/2018686.article.
Ridley, Matt. *The Rational Optimist: How Prosperity Evolves*. New York: HarperCollins, 2010.
Robertson, Donald. *How to Think Like a Roman Emperor: The Stoic Philosophy of Marcus Aurelius*. New York: St. Martin's, 2019.
Rockwell, Llewellyn H. *Against the State: An Anarcho-Capitalist Manifesto*. Auburn, AL: Rockwell Communications, 2014.
Rorty, Richard. *Philosophy and the Mirror of Nature*. Princeton, NJ: Princeton University Press, 1979.
Ross, Hugh. *The Creator and the Cosmos: How the Greatest Scientific Discoveries of the Century Reveal God*. Carol Stream, IL: NavPress, 1993.
———. *Improbable Planet: How Earth Became Humanity's Home*. Grand Rapids, MI: Baker, 2017.
———. *Weathering Climate Change: A Fresh Approach*. Covina, CA: RTB Press, 2020.
Rothbard, Murray N. *For a New Liberty: A Libertarian Manifesto*. New York: Collier, 1973.
———. *Man, Economy, and State*. New York: Von Nostrand, 1962.
Russell, Bertrand. "A Free Man's Worship." In *Mysticism and Logic and Other Essays*, by Bertrand Russell, 46–57. London: Allen & Unwin, 1917.
———. *The Impact of Science on Society*. London: Allen & Unwin, 1952.
———. *The Scientific Outlook*. London: Allen & Unwin, 1931.
Sagan, Carl, and S. I. Shklovskii. *Intelligent Life in the Universe*. New York: Dell, 1966.
Sanoff, Alvin P. "Bringing Philosophy Back To Life." *U.S. News and World Report*, April 25, 1988.
Satell, Greg. "How Philosophy Can Make You a Better Manager." *Forbes*, July 31, 2015.
Schaeffer, Francis A. *The God Who Is There*. Downers Grove, IL: InterVarsity, 1968.
———. *How Should We Then Live? The Rise and Decline of Western Thought and Culture*. Old Tappen, NJ: Revel, 1976.
Schuessler, Jennifer. "A Defense of 'Transracial' Identity Roils Philosophy World." *New York Times*, May 19, 2017.

Schumpeter, Joseph A. *Capitalism, Socialism and Democracy.* New York: Harper, 1942.
Schwab, Klaus. *The Fourth Industrial Revolution.* New York: Currency, 2018.
Schwab, Klaus, and Nicholas Davis. *Shaping the Future of the Fourth Industrial Revolution: A Guide to Building a Better World.* Geneva: World Economic Forum, 2018.
Schwab, Klaus, and Thierry Malleret. *COVID-19: The Great Reset.* Geneva: World Economic Forum, 2020.
Scott, Peter Dale. *The American Deep State: Wall Street, Big Oil, and the Attack on U.S. Democracy.* Totowa, NJ: Rowman & Littlefield, 2014.
Searle, John. *Intentionality: An Essay in the Philosophy of Mind.* Cambridge: Cambridge University Press, 1983.
———. "Minds, Brains, and Programs." *The Behavioral and Brain Sciences* 3 (1981) 417–57.
———. *Minds, Brains, and Science.* Cambridge: Harvard University Press, 1986.
Shapiro, Robert. *Origins: A Skeptic's Guide To the Creation of Life On Earth.* New York: Summit, 1985.
Sheppard, David. *On Some Faraway Beach: The Life and Times of Brian Eno.* London: Orion, 2008.
Siegel, Ethan. "No, Science Will Never Make Philosophy or Religion Obsolete." *Forbes Magazine*, July 30, 2020.
Siegel, Harvey. *Relativism Refuted: A Critique of Contemporary Epistemological Relativism.* Dordrecht, the Netherlands: Reidel, 1987.
Singal, Jesse. "This Is What a Modern Day Witch Hunt Looks Like." *New York Magazine*, May 2, 2017.
Singer, Peter. *Animal Liberation: A New Ethics for Our Treatment of Animals.* New York: HarperCollins, 1973.
———. "Famine, Affluence, and Morality." *Philosophy and Public Affairs* 1 (1972) 229–43.
———. *Practical Ethics.* 2nd ed. Cambridge: Cambridge University Press, 1993.
Sommers, Christina Hoff. *Who Stole Feminism? How Women Have Betrayed Women.* New York: Simon & Schuster, 1994.
Sowell, Thomas. *Civil Rights: Rhetoric or Reality?* New York: Morrow, 1985.
———. *Preferential Policies: An International Perspective.* New York: Morrow, 1990.
Stace, Walter T. *Man Against Darkness and Other Essays.* Pittsburgh: University of Pittsburgh Press, 1967.
Standing, Guy. *The Precariat: The Dangerous New Class.* New York: Bloomsbury USA, 2011.
Stark, Rodney. *The Victory of Reason: How Christianity Led to Freedom, Capitalism, and Western Success.* New York: Random House, 2005.
Stich, Stephen. *From Folk Psychology to Cognitive Science: The Case Against Belief.* Cambridge: MIT Press, 1985.
Stockdale, James Bond. *Courage Under Fire: Testing Epictetus's Doctrines in a Laboratory of Human Behavior.* Stanford: Hoover Institution, 1993.
Strauss, Leo. *Natural Right and History.* Chicago: University of Chicago Press, 1953.
Tabor, Abby. "The Scientific Quest to Explain Kepler's Most Enigmatic Find." https://www.nasa.gov/feature/ames/the-scientific-quest-to-explain-kepler-s-most-enigmatic-find.

Taleb, Nassim Nicholas. *Anti-Fragile: The Things That Gain From Disorder.* New York: Random House, 2012.
———. *The Black Swan: The Impact of the Highly Improbable.* New York: Random House, 2007.
Thaxton, Charles B., et al. *The Mystery of Life's Origins: Reassessing Current Theories.* New York: Philosophical Library, 1984.
Thomson, Judith Jarvis. "A Defense of Abortion." In *Social Ethics: Morality and Social Policy*, edited by Thomas A. Mappes and Jane S. Zembady, 27–38. 7th ed. New York: McGraw-Hill, 2007.
Tonelson, Alan. *The Race to the Bottom: Why a Worldwide Worker Surplus and Uncontrolled Free Trade Are Sinking American Living Standards.* New York: Basic Books, 2005.
Toulmin, Stephen. *Foresight and Understanding.* New York: Harper Torchbooks, 1961.
———. *The Philosophy of Science: An Introduction.* London: Hutchinson University Library, 1953.
Turing, Alan. "Computing Machinery and Intelligence." *Mind* 59 (1950) 433–60.
Ureda, John, and Steven Yates. "A Systems View of Health Promotion." *Journal of Health and Human Services Administration* 28 (2005) 5–38.
Van Inwagen, Peter. *An Essay on Free Will.* Oxford: Oxford University Press, 1983.
Van Natta, Matthew J. *The Beginner's Guide to Stoicism: Tools for Emotional Resilience and Positivity.* Emeryville, CA: Althea, 2019.
Ward, Peter, and Donald Brownlee. *Rare Earth: Why Complex Life Is Uncommon In the Universe.* New York: Copernicus, 2000.
Warren, Mary Ann. "On the Moral and Legal Status of Abortion." In *Social Ethics: Morality and Social Policy*, edited by Thomas A. Mappes and Jane S. Zembady, 13–21. 7th ed. New York: McGraw-Hill, 2007.
Warren, Rick. *The Purpose-Driven Life.* Grand Rapids, MI: Zondervan, 2002.
Webb, Stephen. *If the Universe Is Teeming With Aliens . . . WHERE IS EVERYBODY? Seventy-Five Solutions To the Fermi Paradox and the Problem of Extraterrestrial Life.* Dordrecht, The Netherlands: Springer, 2015.
Weber, Max. *The Protestant Ethic and the Spirit of Capitalism.* Translated by Talcott Parsons. New York: Scribner, 1930.
Weissbuch, I., et al. "β-Sheets as Templates of Relevance to the Origin of Homochirality of Peptides: Lessons from Crystal Chemistry." *Accounts of Chemical Research* 42 (2009) 1128–40.
Weller, J. Marvin. *The Course of Evolution.* New York: McGraw-Hill, 1969.
Wells, G. A. *Did Jesus Exist?* Rev. ed. Amherst, NY: Prometheus, 1986.
Whitehead, Alfred North. *The Function of Reason.* Princeton: Princeton University Press, 1929.
Williams, Bernard. *Ethics and the Limits of Philosophy.* Cambridge: Harvard University Press, 1986.
Wilmsen, E. N. "An Outline of Early Man Studies in the United States." *American Antiquity* 31 (1965) 175–95.
Wilson, John. *The Myth of Political Correctness: The Conservative Attack on Higher Education.* Durham, NC: Duke University Press, 1995.
Wittgenstein, Ludwig. *Philosophical Investigations.* 3rd ed. Translated by G. E. M. Anscombe. New York: Macmillan, 1958.

———. *Tractatus Logico-Philosophicus*. Translated by D. F. Pears and B. F. McGuinness. London: Routledge & Kegan Paul, 1961.

Wolin, Sheldon. *Democracy, Inc.: Managed Democracy and the Specter of Inverted Totalitarianism*. Princeton, NJ: Princeton University Press, 2008.

Wood, Patrick M. *Technocracy Rising: The Trojan Horse of Global Transformation*. Mesa, AZ: Coherent Publishing, 2014.

Wormser, René A. *Foundations: Their Power and Influence*. San Pedro, CA: Covenant House, 1993.

Wright, Jason, et al. "The Ĝ Search for Extraterrestrial Civilizations With Large Energy Supplies, IV, The Signatures and Information Content of Transiting Megastructures," *The Astrophysical Journal* 816.17 (2016). https://iopscience.iop.org/article/10.3847/0004-637X/816/1/17.

Yates, Steven. *Civil Wrongs: What Went Wrong With Affirmative Action*. San Francisco: ICS Press, 1994.

———. *Four Cardinal Errors: Reasons for the Decline of America*. Drayton, SC: Brush Fire Press International, 2011.

Yun, Brother, and Paul Hattaway. *The Heavenly Man: The Remarkable True Story of Christian Brother Yun*. Grand Rapids, MI: Kregel, 2002.

www.ingramcontent.com/pod-product-compliance
Lightning Source LLC
Chambersburg PA
CBHW071231230426
43668CB00011B/1394